OECD
Economic Surveys

India

2007

OECD

ORGANISATION FOR ECONOMIC CO-OPERATION AND DEVELOPMENT

ORGANISATION FOR ECONOMIC CO-OPERATION AND DEVELOPMENT

The OECD is a unique forum where the governments of 30 democracies work together to address the economic, social and environmental challenges of globalisation. The OECD is also at the forefront of efforts to understand and to help governments respond to new developments and concerns, such as corporate governance, the information economy and the challenges of an ageing population. The Organisation provides a setting where governments can compare policy experiences, seek answers to common problems, identify good practice and work to co-ordinate domestic and international policies.

The OECD member countries are: Australia, Austria, Belgium, Canada, the Czech Republic, Denmark, Finland, France, Germany, Greece, Hungary, Iceland, Ireland, Italy, Japan, Korea, Luxembourg, Mexico, the Netherlands, New Zealand, Norway, Poland, Portugal, the Slovak Republic, Spain, Sweden, Switzerland, Turkey, the United Kingdom and the United States. The Commission of the European Communities takes part in the work of the OECD.

OECD Publishing disseminates widely the results of the Organisation's statistics gathering and research on economic, social and environmental issues, as well as the conventions, guidelines and standards agreed by its members.

This work is published on the responsibility of the Secretary-General of the OECD.

Also available in French

Table of contents

Executive summary 9

Assessment and recommendations 11

Chapter 1. **India's key challenges to sustaining high growth** 21
    Economic reforms have transformed the Indian economy 22
    The economy has responded positively to the reforms 26
    Looking into the future 41
    Easing regulation in goods and service markets 44
    Removing barriers to employment in the formal sector 46
    Improving the efficiency of the financial system 49
    Orienting public finances to achieve more rapid growth 50
    Improving infrastructure 56
    Improving education 63
    Conclusions 66

    Notes 66
    Bibliography 66

Chapter 2. **India's growth pattern and obstacles to higher growth** 69
    Productivity gains from shifting labour out of agriculture have been modest 70
    Manufacturing's contribution to growth could be much greater 73
    Evidence suggests that weaknesses in framework conditions are at fault 83

    Notes 84
    Bibliography 85

Chapter 3. **Reforming India's product and service markets** 89
    Despite extensive liberalisation in some areas regulations are on average
    rather restrictive 90
    Policies to improve product market regulations 94

    Notes 114
    Bibliography 115

    Annex 3.A1. OECD PMR indicators by state 117

Chapter 4. **Improving the performance of the labour market** 119
    Employment has expanded in the economy as a whole,
    but not in the organised sector 120
    State-level labour reforms 130
    What can feasibly be done to improve India's labour markets? 134

    Notes 138
    Bibliography 140

    Annex 4.A1. State labour reform questionnaire summary responses 143

Chapter 5. **Reforming the financial system** · 145
    The banking system 146
    Other financial markets 152
    Foreign ownership 157
    Financial inclusion 158
    Conclusions 159

    Notes 161
    Bibliography 161

Chapter 6. **Improving the fiscal system** · 163
    Improving the quality of government spending 164
    India's tax system has been fundamentally reformed 168
    Improving fiscal federalism to limit borrowing and increase responsiveness
    to local needs 179

    Notes 191
    Bibliography 191

Chapter 7. **Removing infrastructure bottlenecks** · 193
    Infrastructure is a major constraint on growth 194
    The private sector has a crucial role to play in narrowing infrastructure gaps 195
    Private sector involvement is transforming certain sectors 199
    A more limited start has been made in other sectors 200
    In other sectors, the framework is not conducive to competition 213

    Notes 218
    Bibliography 219

Chapter 8. **Improving human capital formation** · 221
    Human capital needs to be improved 222
    Deeper institutional changes are the best hope 230
    Conclusion 238

    Notes 239
    Bibliography 239

Boxes

  1.1.   Special Economic Zones 37
  1.2.   Measuring poverty 39
  3.1.   Corporate governance of state-owned enterprises in OECD countries 100
  3.2.   Policy recommendations for reforming India's product and service markets 113
  4.1.   Measuring job flows in India 123
  4.2.   Policy recommendations for labour market reform 138
  5.1.   Policy recommendations for reforming India's financial markets 160
  6.1.   A multi-level VAT system designed to avoid cross-border fraud 177
  6.2.   Policy recommendations for reforming the fiscal system 190
  7.1.   Policy recommendations for improving infrastucture 217
  8.1.   The *Progresa* programme in Mexico 229
  8.2.   The returns to education in India and financing of higher education 235
  8.3.   Policy recommendations for improving human capital formation 238

Tables

  1.1.   The evolution of the ten largest economies over 30 years 28
  1.2.   The evolution of shares in world exports of commercial services
       and manufactures by country 29

1.3.   Factors behind Indian growth   31
1.4.   Growth of value added by sector   34
1.5.   Alternative measures of well-being   39
1.6.   Evolution of employment by type of job and employer   47
1.7.   Government budget balances   51
1.8.   Subsidies in the electricity industry   58
1.9.   An international comparison of road infrastructure   59
1.10. Selected indicators of efficiency in the water supply industry in Asia   61
1.11. Illiteracy rates by age group   64
2.1.   Labour productivity and employment shares by industry and institutional sector   72
2.2.   Growth in the value of merchandise exports   75
2.3.   International comparison of industry concentration in 2002   82
3.1.   Product market regulations: an international comparison   91
3.2.   Performance of state-level public sector enterprises   97
3.3.   Foreign direct investment: ceiling on investment in a given company by sector .   111
3.A1.1. The PMR indicator values by State   118
4.1.   Gross job flows in the Indian manufacturing sector   124
4.2.   Job creation and destruction by size of plant workforce and type of worker . .   126
4.3.   Capital intensity of plants   126
4.4.   Job flow rates for publicly and privately owned plants   127
4.A1.1. State labour reform index questionnaire   143
5.1.   Interest spreads for Indian commercial banks   151
5.2.   Transaction costs in India's equity market   153
5.3.   Funds raised in the Indian equity market   154
5.4.   Gross issuance in bond markets   155
6.1.   Structure and amounts of taxation, FY 2005   170
6.2.   Implicit tax rates on main macroeconomic aggregates   171
6.3.   Tariff revenue foregone as the result of concessions and exemptions   174
6.4.   The current VAT system and cross-border trade   178
6.5.   Illustrating the operating of VAT: Reform options with a dual VAT   178
6.6.   Tax and revenue structure of state governments in selected federal countries . . .   181
6.7.   Central transfers to states by type of programme   182
6.8.   Rules governing borrowing by lower level governments
       in selected federal systems   185
6.9.   Tax and grant revenue of local level government in selected federal countries . .   188
7.1.   Electricity generating capacity: India and selected Asian countries   203
7.2.   Status of power sector reforms in selected states   207
7.3.   Efficiency comparison of India and China Rail   215
8.1.   Provision of schools by level of education   222
8.2.   Expenditure on education (2002)   223
8.3.   State educational indicators 2004   226
8.4.   Participation in higher education by type of study, institution and age   233
8.5.   Private rates of return to education   235

Figures

1.1.   Evolution of tariff revenue relative to import value   24
1.2.   Evolution of taxation since 1980   25
1.3.   GDP per capita in India and elsewhere relative to the United States   27
1.4.   Exports relative to GDP: India compared to China   29
1.5.   Factors contributing to the catch-up process in the period 1990 to 2005   30

1.6. Estimated potential output growth, output gap and impact of rainfall fluctuations 33

1.7. Reasons for investment in country of origin by US-based Indian and Chinese entrepreneurs 35

1.8. Exports of software and related services by physical location of exporter and state... 36

1.9. State-wide poverty reduction and average per capita consumption growth, 1993-2004 40

1.10. Growth tends to be more rapid in richer states 41

1.11. Projected growth of the working age population and the dependency ratio ... 42

1.12. Growth of potential GDP per capita over the longer term.................. 43

1.13. Product market regulations: An international comparison 45

1.14. Product market regulations and average labour productivity 46

1.15. An international comparison of employment protection legislation 48

1.16. The share of public sector banks in the assets of all banks 49

1.17. India's national net savings rate and its components...................... 51

1.18. Government debt 53

1.19. General government budgetary subsidies............................... 54

1.20. Growth of capital stock by institutional sector......................... 56

1.21. Urbanisation and GDP per capita 60

1.22. Youth literacy rates and primary school spending in selected countries 64

1.23. Number of research articles: An international comparison.................. 65

2.1. Share of manufacturing by per capita income 70

2.2. Relative employee compensation, productivity and unit labour costs........ 73

2.3. Relative unit labour costs across countries............................ 74

2.4. International comparison of the distribution of firm size in manufacturing 76

2.5. Gains in productivity from larger plant size in India....................... 77

2.6. Distribution of the level of total factor productivity of industrial plants 78

2.7. Measures of regional specialisation 80

3.1. Indicators of product market regulation by state......................... 92

3.2. Product market regulation and foreign direct investment by state 93

3.3. Administrative regulation and average organised employment share by state ... 93

3.4. The PMR indicators of state control by state............................ 95

3.5. Assets of state-level public sector enterprises by state..................... 95

3.6. Involvement of government enterprises in the economy.................... 96

3.7. Rate of return of public enterprises before interest, tax and subsidies 96

3.8. Distribution of rates of return of central public sector enterprises........... 97

3.9. The PMR indicators of barriers to entrepreneurship by state................ 102

3.10. Tariff revenue relative to import value in selected countries 110

3.11. A cross-country comparison of simple-average tariffs..................... 110

3.12. Inflows of Foreign Direct Investment................................. 112

4.1. Organised and unorganised sector employment in industry................. 121

4.2. International comparison of employment protection legislation in 2006 123

4.3. Plant size distribution in the organised manufacturing sector by size of employment 128

4.4. Areas of state-level labour law reform................................ 131

4.5. State labour reforms and gross job flows, 2001-04........................ 133

4.6. The change in labour turnover and the change in the labour share of value added 134

4.7. Change in job creation rates and the share of unorganised employment, by state 134

5.1. Development of gross and net non-performing loans for public and new private banks 148

5.2. Gross non-performing loans in the priority and non-priority sectors by ownership of banks 149

5.3. Institutional investors: An international comparison of funds under management 157

5.4. Market share of informal lenders by asset class of households 158

6.1. Government spending by type and function relative to GDP, 2003 165

6.2. The relationship between the ratio of tax to GDP and per capita incomes: An international comparison 169

6.3. Statutory and effective standard tax rates across countries 173

6.4. Distribution of companies by average corporate tax rate 174

6.5. State tax and grant income before and after central transfers, 2005 183

6.6. Access of urban population to basic services and municipal revenue per capita, by state 189

7.1. Infrastructure and productivity by state 194

7.2. Total value of all PPP projects to date by sector 197

7.3. Product market regulation and infrastructure provision by state 197

7.4. Teledensity 201

7.5. Electricity prices in selected countries, 2004 205

7.6. Price of electricity for heavy industry by state 206

7.7. Electricity reforms and the change in distribution and commercial losses, 2000/01 to 2004/05 207

7.8. Highway development 209

7.9. Return on capital and operating ratio for Indian Rail 214

8.1. National literacy rates by age group in 2004 224

8.2. Literacy rates and the size of the organised sector 225

8.3. Participation rate in secondary education at ages 16 and 17 228

8.4. Participation in private grade schools 231

8.5. Private expenditure on tertiary education for selected countries 233

8.6. Growth rates of R&D expenditure and personnel 237

This Survey was prepared in the Economics Department by Richard Herd, Paul Conway and Sean Dougherty, under the supervision of Wilhem Leibfritz.

Technical assistance was provided by Thomas Chalaux; secretarial assistance by Nadine Dufour and Therese Walsh.

The Survey was discussed at a special seminar of the Economic and Development Review Committee on 28 May 2007 in which members of the Committee and representatives of the Indian government participated.

BASIC STATISTICS OF INDIA

THE LAND

Area (1 000 sq. km)	2 971
Agricultural area, 2005 (1 000 sq. km)	1 802
Forests, 2005 (1 000 sq. km)	677

THE PEOPLE

Population, 2006/07 (million)	1 122	Total employment, 2003/04 (million)	442
Annual rate of change of population, 2006/07	1.36	Distribution by sector, 2003/04 (%):	
Per sq. km, 2006/07	378	Agriculture, forestry, fishing	58
Major cities, 2001 (million):		Manufacturing, mining, utilities, and construction	18
Greater Mumbai	16.4	Services	24
Delhi	12.8	Unemployment rate, 2004/05 (%)	4.7
Chennais	6.4		
Bangalore	5.7		
Hyderabad	5.5		

PRODUCTION

GDP (2006/07, billion rupees)	41 257	Gross fixed capital formation (2006/07, billion rupees):	12 166
GDP per head (2006/07, USD)	812	Per cent of GDP	29.5
GDP per head (2005, USD PPP)	3 452	Per head (USD)	239
Origin of GDP, 2006/07 (per cent of total computed at factor cost):			
Agriculture, forestry, fishing	17.5		
Manufacturing, mining, utilities and construction	27.9		
Services	54.6		

THE GOVERNMENT

Government final consumption, (2006/07, per cent of GDP)	11.3
Government expenditure central state and local (2006/07, per cent of GDP)	30.2
Government revenue central state and local (2006/07, per cent of GDP)	30.1

FOREIGN TRADE

Exports of goods and services, (2006/07, per cent of GDP)	23.0	Imports of goods and services, (2006/07, per cent of GDP)	25.8
Main exports (per cent of total exports of goods, 2005/06):		Main imports (per cent of total imports of goods, 2005/06):	
Other manufactured goods	21.0	Petroleum and crude products	26.2
Engineering goods	20.9	Electronics goods	9.9
Petroleum and crude products	11.2	Gold and silver	8.4
Chemicals and related products	9.8	Non-electrical machinery	7.4

THE CURRENCY

Monetary unit: rupee	Currency unit per USD, average of daily figures:	
	2005/06	44.3
	2006/07	45.3

Executive summary

India has undergone a profound shift in economic management

Since the mid-1980s successive reforms have progressively moved the Indian economy towards a market-based system. State intervention and control over economic activity has been reduced significantly and the role of private-sector entrepreneurship increased. To varying degrees, liberalisation has touched on most aspects of economic policy including industrial policy, fiscal policy, financial market regulation, and trade and foreign investment.

Overall, reform has had a major beneficial impact on the economy

Annual growth in GDP per capita has accelerated from just 1¼ per cent in the three decades after Independence to 7½ per cent currently, a rate of growth that will double average income in a decade. Potential output growth is currently estimated to be 8½ per cent annually and India is now the third largest economy in the world. Increased economic growth has helped reduce poverty, which has begun to fall in absolute terms.

Areas that have been liberalised have responded well

In service sectors where government regulation has been eased significantly or is less burdensome – such as communications, insurance, asset management and information technology – output has grown rapidly, with exports of information technology enabled services particularly strong. In those infrastructure sectors which have been opened to competition, such as telecoms and civil aviation, the private sector has proven to be extremely effective and growth has been phenomenal. At the state level, economic performance is much better in states with a relatively liberal regulatory environment than in the relatively more restrictive states.

Significant problems remain and the next round of reforms needs to focus on a number of key areas

In labour markets, employment growth has been concentrated in firms that operate in sectors not covered by India's highly restrictive labour laws. In the formal sector, where these labour laws apply, employment has been falling and firms are becoming more capital intensive despite abundant low-cost labour. Labour market reform is essential to achieve a broader-based development and provide sufficient and higher productivity jobs for the growing labour force. In product markets, inefficient government procedures, particularly in some of the states, acts as a barrier to entrepreneurship and needs to be improved. Public companies are generally less productive than private firms and the privatisation programme should be revitalised. A number of barriers to competition in financial markets and some of the infrastructure sectors, which are other constraints on growth, also need to be addressed. The indirect tax system needs to be simplified to create a true national market, while for direct taxes, the taxable base should be broadened and rates lowered. Public expenditure should be reoriented towards infrastructure investment by reducing subsidies. Furthermore, social policies should be improved to better reach the poor and – given the importance of human capital – the education system also needs to be made more efficient.

Reform must continue if government is to achieve its growth targets

The government's target of reaching GDP growth of 10% in 2011 is achievable if reforms continue. In addition, if the relatively restrictive states improve their regulatory frameworks towards that of the better-run states, growth will be more inclusive and income gaps across states will narrow. The impressive response of the Indian economy to past reforms should give policy makers confidence that further liberalisation will deliver additional growth dividends and foster the process of pulling millions of people out of poverty.

OECD ECONOMIC SURVEYS: INDIA – ISBN 978-92-64-03351-1 – © OECD 2007

ISBN 978-92-64-03351-1
OECD Economic Surveys: India
© OECD 2007

Assessment and recommendations

The Indian economy has been transformed
by fundamental reforms

Over the past two decades, India has moved away from its former *dirigiste* model and has become a market-based economy. This process started in the mid-1980s and gathered substantial momentum at the beginning of the 1990s. Direct tax rates were significantly reduced, pervasive government licensing of industrial activity was almost eliminated, and restrictions on investment by large companies were eased. Furthermore, financial markets were reformed, with banks restored to health, entry barriers lowered, equity markets transformed and new supervisory bodies introduced. The process of reform has continued in this decade with a further opening of the economy to competition. The number of industries reserved for very small firms has been significantly reduced, and foreign suppliers have been encouraged to enter the market by a progressive lowering of tariffs to an average of 10% in 2007. The rules governing foreign direct investment have been markedly eased, notably in the manufacturing sector. Last but not least, fiscal discipline has been improved by the passage of fiscal responsibility laws for the central government and all but three of the 28 state governments.

Reforms have led to a spectacular improvement
in economic performance

These reforms have had a major beneficial impact on the economy. By 2006, the average share of imports and exports in GDP had risen to 24%, up from 6% in 1985. Inflows of foreign direct investment increased to 2% of GDP from less than 0.1% of GDP in 1990, with outflows of foreign direct investment picking up substantially at the end of 2006. The combined fiscal deficit of central and state governments has been reduced from 10% of GDP in 2002 to just over 6% of GDP by 2006, with the ratio of debt to GDP falling from 82% in 2004 to 75% by March 2007. There has been a massive increase in output, with the potential growth rate of the economy estimated to be around 8½ per cent per year in 2006. GDP per capita is now rising by 7½ per cent annually, a rate that leads to its doubling in a decade. This contrasts to annual growth of GDP per capita of just 1¼ per cent in the three decades from 1950 to 1980. Faster growth has resulted in India becoming the third largest economy in the world (after the United States and China and just ahead of Japan) in 2006, when measured at purchasing power parities, accounting for nearly 7% of world GDP. Moreover, with increased openness and rapid growth in exports of merchandise and IT-related services, its share in world trade in goods and services had risen to slightly over one per cent in 2005, when measured at market exchange rates.

Monetary policy is focusing on lowering inflation over the medium term

The current expansion, which started in 2003, has not led to an imbalance between supply and demand, despite annual GDP growth reaching 9% in 2006. The non-agricultural GDP deflator, a broad measure of prices, has shown little tendency to accelerate and increased by less than 5% year on year in 2006. Some measures of inflation have moved above the authorities' goal of keeping the annual inflation rate in the range of 5-5½ per cent, reflecting sharp increases for food in other commodity prices. However, the monetary authorities are acting to ensure that such increases do not become entrenched and announced, in April 2007, that monetary policy will aim at achieving an inflation rate of 4-4½ per cent per year over the medium term. In this respect, they are being helped by the appreciation of the currency. The current account balance has moved into a deficit, but only similar in relation to GDP to that of the second half of the 1990s and, moreover, is being financed by foreign direct investment. Such a benign outcome has been helped by increased domestic saving including the recent fiscal consolidation.

Whereas fiscal policy should aim to make more resources available for growth

The fiscal reforms enacted in 2004 have permitted a significant reduction in the extent to which the government pre-empts national savings to finance consumption. The fiscal deficit, which has been reduced substantially, is on track to meet the legislated target of a combined central and state government fiscal deficit of 6% of GDP by fiscal year 2008. Already, the reduction in government dissaving contributed almost half of the increase in the net national saving rate between 2001 and 2005, which has now reached almost 22% of GDP, with the gross saving rate being some ten percentage points higher at 32%. Faster economic growth will require that a greater share of output be devoted to investment for both business expansion and infrastructure. This implies the need to raise savings further by continuing the fiscal consolidation strategy. At the same time, it is necessary to improve the quality of spending.

The main challenge is to build on past success by continuing the reform process and making growth more inclusive

Increased growth since the mid-1980s has helped substantially reduce the national poverty rate to 22% of the population in 2004, with the speed of poverty reduction appearing to increase between 1999 and 2004. Moreover, in this period, the absolute number of people living below the poverty line fell for the first time since Independence. To meet one of its Millennium Development Goals, of halving poverty by 2015, the government is aiming to achieve an even higher medium-term economic annual growth rate of 10%. With additional structural reforms, this goal is achievable. In addition, growth needs to become more inclusive by increasing the prosperity of poorer states, whose economies have expanded at a slower pace than those of the richer states in the past decade, and so reducing their difficulties in lowering poverty. The analysis of this report suggests that differences in economic performance across states are associated with the extent to which states have introduced market-oriented reforms. Thus, further reforms on these lines, complemented with measures to improve infrastructure, education and basic services, would increase the potential for growth outside of agriculture and thus boost better-paid employment, which is a key to sharing the fruits of growth and lowering poverty.

A comprehensive reform package is needed to enhance growth potential and spread income growth more widely

The next round of reforms needs to focus on a number of key areas that have the potential to further boost economic growth, while ensuring that the expansion becomes more inclusive. Recent reforms have made a number of sectors of the economy more dynamic, especially in the service sector. However, there are still a number of barriers to growth in product, labour and financial markets, and the provision of infrastructure, where reform is needed both at the central and state levels. While the optimal policy would be to remove these bottlenecks across the country, the creation of Special Economic Zones that aim to reduce a number of these barriers locally might demonstrate the benefits of such reforms and so act as a catalyst for more generalised change, but care needs to be taken as to the extent of tax concessions that are granted. Furthermore, taxation policies need to be reformed in order to create a truly national market and improve incentives and release resources for reducing bottlenecks in infrastructure, which are a key constraint on growth. In addition, education needs to be delivered more efficiently so as to improve human capital formation. There are undoubtedly further challenges facing the economy, but this report focuses on these areas which are key to boosting growth further.

High-quality employment is the key to inclusive growth

Economic growth could be made more inclusive by achieving faster growth in regular employment, as opposed to casual and self-employment. Although regular employment has risen, it still represents only 15% of total employment and its growth has been almost exclusively in the smaller, least productive enterprises. Employment in firms with more than ten employees accounts for only around 3¾ per cent of total employment (one-quarter of regular employment) and has been falling. Indeed, India has a much smaller proportion of employment in enterprises with ten or more employees than any OECD country. The number of workers has also fallen in the manufacturing sector where the share of labour income in value added is low compared to other countries and the capital-intensity is relatively high. Such developments indicate that India is not fully exploiting its comparative advantage as a labour-abundant economy.

Labour market reform is essential

The level of employment protection needs to be reformed in order to increase employment, particularly in larger companies, which are the only ones covered by this legislation, and to remove barriers which hinder firms from exploiting economies of scale. New indicators presented in this *Survey* show that laws governing regular employment contracts in India are stricter than those in Brazil, Chile, China and all but two OECD countries. A major, but by no means the only, reason for this stringency is the requirement to obtain government permission to lay off just one worker from manufacturing plants with more than 100 workers (but not from establishments in the service sector). On the other hand, the extent of protection for people working on temporary or fixed-term contracts and for smaller firms, all areas where regular employment is increasing, is similar to the OECD average. Moreover, indicators of labour regulations at the state level suggest that states that have introduced reforms have more fluid labour markets. *Some reduction in the stringency of employment protection laws is needed and could be balanced by an increase in the extent of accrual-based severance payments. At the same time, a consolidation of the 46 central and around 200 state labour laws should be considered.* These reforms would remove an important barrier to the expansion of smaller companies and would increase employment, productivity, real wages and the number of social benefit recipients, as well as facilitating the movement of labour out of agriculture to more productive areas.

Reforms in product markets have gone a long way but should go further…

Improving the business environment is essential for boosting the growth potential of the economy. Excessive regulation of markets is a barrier to the diffusion of technology and lowers the speed with which labour productivity catches up to the level of the best performing economies. According to new indicators presented in this *Survey*, there are a number of areas where reforms have already lowered regulatory barriers to international best practice. Nonetheless, overall, regulation is more restrictive than in Brazil, Chile and all OECD countries. Moreover, there are wide differences in the extent of regulation across states, which affect their respective economic performance.

… by strengthening the enforcement of competition law and facilitating market exit of unproductive firms and entry of new firm…

There are a number of areas where barriers to competition need to be reduced. Innovation and responsiveness to changing market demands require the ability to create new firms quickly. *All levels of government should lower the barriers to entrepreneurship by re-engineering procedures to reduce administrative burdens on new and existing firms and reduce the extent of inspections, as well as the number of returns. A specific unit should be charged with undertaking regulatory impact analyses of existing and proposed laws.Reservation of specific product areas for small-scale enterprises should be ended in line with the government's timetable.* It is important to ensure that there is a competitive environment for existing firms to operate in, including in those manufacturing industries which are still highly concentrated. There is an urgent need for the new Competition Commission to become a fully functioning agency capable of enforcing the competition law introduced in 2003. Finally, it is also a difficult and lengthy process to restructure or close insolvent or bankrupt companies. *A modern bankruptcy law is needed which should also reduce the role of the courts.*

... and further opening the economy
to international trade and direct foreign
investment...

Competition can also be increased through a further opening to the world economy. *Recent tariff cuts need to be continued and go beyond the government's target of alignment with average ASEAN tariffs by 2010.* The dispersion of tariffs rates is also high in India, a relic of past activist industrial policies. *Reducing the dispersion of tariff rates (or, in the end, moving to one uniform tariff rate) would further increase efficiency.* Barriers to foreign direct investment (FDI) have been lowered in the manufacturing sector, which has led to a marked increase in investment inflows. *But restrictions still exist in a number of service areas and reducing these would benefit the Indian economy. For example, removing the cap on FDI in the insurance sector would allow a welcome expansion of the industries capital base. Lifting the ban on FDI in retail trading would help to improve productivity, supply chain management, reduce the exceptionally high rate of waste of agricultural produce and so lower retail prices and raise producer prices.*

... and privatising state-owned enterprises
while improving the governance system
for those remaining in government ownership

Public-sector ownership in industry is still extensive in India. In the so-called organised sector of the economy, state-owned enterprises produce 38% of business-sector value added. There is a large tail of loss-making public enterprises, particularly at the state level and, on average, the productivity and profitability of publicly owned firms have been lower than in the private sector. Privatisation would thus appear to offer considerable possibilities for improving productivity. However, the privatisation programme has stalled and, in any case, has involved mainly selling minority stakes, rather than transferring control. Government firms represent a small share of output in manufacturing, construction and non-financial services. *Given the potentially competitive nature of these industries, government ownership should be reduced. Privatising firms in sectors where the government share of output is larger (banking, insurance, coal and electricity) would also be desirable but may need to be phased in (see below). In the meantime, public companies should be controlled by a government investment agency, rather than by a sponsoring ministry, so as to separate the ownership and policy-making functions.*

The financial market is developing rapidly after
its opening but should be further deregulated

The financial sector has one of the highest shares of public ownership in the economy and needs to be liberalised further. Successful reforms have already restored the health of the public banks, most of which now have minority private shareholders, and have created new regulators. The functions of the Reserve Bank of India (RBI) as the owner of some public banks and manager of government debt are being reduced but, *consideration should be also given to whether the supervision of the banking sector should remain inside the RBI.* Despite progressive deregulation, banks can still allocate only 41% of their assets completely freely, notwithstanding long-standing recommendations by government committees that this ratio should be increased. Private-sector services (and new banks in particular) have been successful in India and so *progressive privatisation of the public banks would most likely improve the efficiency of the sector, especially if they were given greater freedom to allocate assets and restrictions on foreign direct investment in the sector were removed. As capital would be better allocated, the efficiency of the whole economy would be improved.* Equity markets have been transformed as the result of private-sector initiative and new regulatory agencies, and have become competitive with leading world markets. *However, a much broader range of exchange-traded derivative instruments needs to be allowed in order to improve the market for bonds. In this regard, opening markets to all participants would help. A more principle-based approach to capital market regulation might help speed up the introduction of new instruments and, as in product markets, supervisory bodies should be subject to periodic regulatory impact reviews.*

Successful reforms in some formerly state-owned infrastructure sectors should pave the way for speeding up reforms in others...

In some of the former fully government-owned infrastructure sectors, such as telecommunications and domestic civil aviation, the opening to the private sector has produced exemplary results. In both sectors, new private entrants now have market shares of over three-quarters. Since the easing of regulatory constraints in 2004, the telecommunications network has become the third largest in the world. In both sectors, choice has expanded and prices have fallen. *Even so, more needs to be done to promote competition in the fixed-line market, given the possibilities offered by broadband technology.*

... such as the electricity sector

Electricity is one sector where public enterprises are still dominant and demand consistently outstrips supply, representing a major constraint on growth, particularly in electricity-intensive sectors such as manufacturing. On the basis of current plans, electricity generating capacity will rise by 6% annually over the period 2007 to 2012, double the rate of the past five years and the second largest absolute increase in capacity in the world. However, this is still well below the likely growth rate of GDP. The underinvestment in this sector is caused by low profitability. In 2000, as much as 40% of electricity was not paid for due to poor management of distribution enterprises and a failure to eradicate theft. Revenues were further limited by a legacy of political constraints on pricing policy at the state level, such as extensive cross-subsidisation in favour of farmers and households at the cost of industrial and commercial firms. In 2003, the government introduced a new policy framework that addresses distribution problems, mandates a more competitive electricity market with more private-sector involvement and progressively lowers the extent of cross-subsidies. In addition, there is a programme that gives financial incentives to states that meet specific milestones in the reform process. In states where implementation of the new framework is more advanced, some progress has been made, but still only a few areas have an uninterrupted electricity supply. Overall, there has been only a modest increase in the proportion of electricity that is paid for since the programme started. *The government should encourage speedier implementation of reforms, consider reducing transfers to states that do not advance sufficiently rapidly and rewarding those that find ways to reduce losses, and increase private participation in the sector to a greater extent than in existing electricity reform programmes.* The development of the electricity sector is also influenced by the coal sector, which is controlled by two public enterprises whose output is allocated to users by an inter-ministerial committee, with prices set on cost-plus basis. *The government should auction coal mining concessions to the private sector and allow coal to be allocated by the market mechanism.*

Public-private partnerships are proving their worth in the transport sector

A significant start has been made in involving the private sector in the provision of transport infrastructure. By end-2006, the outstanding value of public-private partnerships (PPPs) had risen to an amount equivalent to 3½ per cent of GDP, with most contracts having been awarded in the previous two years. The government encourages private involvement in the construction and operation of ports and airports. *Here there is a need to change the tariff-setting process in a way that encourages productivity improvements, moving away from a cost-plus basis system of price determination.* Private involvement in the road sector is increasing, enabling a marked improvement in the quality of the national network; this will include an 18 000 kilometre-long national network of tolled dual-carriageway roads by end-2009. States are also improving their networks. The government has introduced model PPP concessions, which are awarded on the basis of competitive bids for subsidies, or payments if the concession is estimated to be commercially viable. *Early experience with private involvement in these areas is generally positive, but outcomes under contracts need careful monitoring.* A significant implementation problem has been the need to obtain cabinet approval for road contracts that are sufficiently large to attract private-sector interest. *Greater authority should be delegated to the Highways Authority to speed up the process.*

The quality of public spending needs to improve

Despite increased use of PPPs in infrastructure provision, greater government investment outlays are needed and could be funded by a reorganisation of public spending. At the same time, there is a need to reduce outlays on subsidies, which are much higher than in a number of emerging economies (such as Brazil and China). Moreover, electricity, food and petroleum subsidies do not reach the poorest groups in society because of poor administration and corruption. Indeed, the government estimates that to transfer one rupee to the poor by way of food and fuel subsidies it is necessary to spend almost four rupees. *The government should reduce outlays on subsidies by better targeting them to reach poor people, as well as lowering support to companies, including loss-making public enterprises. In this way more funds could be made available for much needed infrastructure investment.*

Direct taxes have been reformed, but more needs to be done

Reform of direct taxation also has the potential to further improve growth. Despite large cuts in direct tax rates, which have strengthened the economy, the share of direct tax revenues in GDP has risen. Nonetheless, the tax system still bears some traces of past interventionism, through extensive loopholes and exemptions which introduce distortions and complexity, facilitating tax evasion. These are most noticeable in the areas of saving, agriculture and corporate taxation. The treatment of some forms of savings is so favourable that they are often exempted from taxation at the time of initial savings, during the period when invested funds earn returns, and finally when investments are liquidated – a level of generosity that has rarely been found in the OECD area. Agricultural incomes are not subject to income tax and numerous exemptions exist in the corporate tax system. Indeed, these are so prevalent that corporate tax collections are only half of the theoretical yield. *The government should consider reducing exemptions and loopholes in all these areas, creating room for cuts in statutory rates, thereby moving towards equalisation of effective tax rates across sectors and activities.*

The planned nationwide VAT should be designed in a way that reduces barriers to internal trade and limits fraud

---

Significant reform of indirect taxation has also been undertaken, including the introduction of a destination-based, state-level VAT on goods in 2005. However, as taxes still represent a barrier to trade between states, further reform is needed to achieve a true internal market for goods and services. At present, there are a series of indirect taxes at the central and state levels that need to be integrated into a single tax that is neutral, both as to the sector and location of production, and minimises the possibilities for fraud. At present, the major barrier to interstate trade is the Central Sales Tax and this is being phased out. When this process is completed, controls could be abolished on nearly all state borders as they would not be needed for this purpose. The government is committed to the introduction of a nationwide goods and services tax by 2010 that would meet these objectives, but its final form has yet to be determined. Experience with VAT systems in Europe shows that careful design is necessary to simultaneously reduce trade barriers and contain fraud. *The government should consider two options: either, moving to a national VAT with central revenue collection and redistribution of the tax yield to the states through a formula, or, introducing a two-tier system that would allow both a central VAT and a state VAT. The first option would not exempt interstate exports while the second option would for the state VAT (as is currently the case) but not for the federal VAT. Such a system would maintain the audit chain in interstate trade (through the federal VAT), thereby facilitating tax enforcement. With this option states could retain a degree of fiscal sovereignty and could also set different tax rates. The second option would require close co-operation between state fiscal authorities to limit fraud. However, if this system were to also include a central rebatable VAT surcharge on cross-border trade, then fraud could be minimised.*

Fiscal transfers are playing a key role in income redistribution towards poorer states…

In a country as large and diverse as India, a good system of revenue sharing across the country is essential. Without it, differences in government spending across states would be extremely large. Amongst the 20 largest states, incomes in the three richest states are three and a half times higher than in the three poorest states, which have a combined population of over 300 million people. Although the system of tax-sharing and inter-governmental transfers markedly reduces spending inequalities, it has become very complex and involves a degree of central control over state investment outlays that may be excessive. *The government should simplify the transfer system, improve its administration and make it more transparent. It should further increase incentives towards fiscal discipline, in particular by replacing the obligation for states to borrow from the National Small Saving Fund, and thereby increasing their use of the capital market.*

... but local bodies should receive more resources and autonomy to provide high-quality public services

---

A major drawback of India's fiscal federalism is that the local level of government remains underdeveloped. This is a particularly important inefficiency in a country where three-quarters of the population lives in states with over 50 million inhabitants. Local authorities raise little tax revenue themselves and their autonomy to set rates is very limited. Key local activities have been retained in state-run boards and authorities, which have been generally inefficient in meeting the rising demand for local services. Such shortfalls hit the poorer parts of the population particularly hard and contribute to the relatively low rate of urbanisation in India, which restrains gains from agglomeration economies. *Improving local public service provision is essential and requires an increase in the revenue base of local bodies, increasing tax-sharing with state governments and raising their autonomy, accountability and administrative abilities.*

Improving human capital is essential and requires additional reforms in basic education...

There is an urgent need to improve education in India. Public expenditure on primary and secondary education is somewhat lower than in other emerging economies, but substantial private outlays result in overall spending being similar to that in developed OECD countries. Nonetheless, despite recent gains, the level of literacy is low and children receive on average only ten years of education, three years less than in many emerging countries. There are also marked differences in educational attainment across gender and social backgrounds. Here, it might be possible to *draw on the positive experiences in countries such as Mexico and Brazil of giving the poor cash grants that are linked to the continued education of their children, hence helping to reduce poverty through the accumulation of human capital.* Such a policy would, though, require a strong local administration to implement the programme. Poor educational performance also affects labour market outcomes, with illiterate people finding it difficult to obtain regular employment. The government is attempting to implement free and compulsory education for children between the ages of 6 and 14, and has banned the employment of children under the age of 14. However, higher enrolment is just a first step to better outcomes. *More needs to be done to raise the quality of education, including providing stronger incentives for teachers to work and improving both the attendance and completion rates of students and teachers' training. Education reforms at the state-level and in OECD countries suggest that decentralisation helps to raise efficiency and should be encouraged.* Private-sector schools are expanding and typically cost less than public schools as a result of more market-based teacher salaries and better attendance of teachers. *The government should experiment with vouchers which might allow further growth in private education.*

... and also in higher education

In contrast to spending on primary and secondary education, outlays on tertiary education are low even after accounting for private spending. Total outlays are 0.8% of GDP, almost half the level in a large number of other emerging and developed countries. Moreover, a smaller proportion of younger age groups graduates from higher education than in many emerging countries. This shortfall appears to occur because of low private expenditure – even if it is high relative to that in continental European countries. Given the limited room for increased public spending and the high private return to tertiary education, *one option would be to allow public universities to expand by charging higher fees and to permit more, appropriately regulated, private universities (including from abroad) to enter the market. One way to encourage higher private outlays would be to significantly expand the provision of loans with repayment contingent on income,* so that all students are able to finance their studies, independent of their family background. The current loan programme is too small, overly complex and reaches only 2-3% of students.

In sum

Market-oriented reforms – which started in the mid-1980s and were followed by more fundamental reforms since the early 1990s and renewed in the 2000s – have lifted the Indian economy on to a significantly higher growth path, helping to reduce poverty. This success should encourage policy makers to continue with this strategy by, in particular: further reducing restrictions in labour and product markets; improving infrastructure, human capital formation and general public services; and further reducing tax distortions. Speeding up such reforms would help the government to achieve its objective of further raising India's sustainable growth path and at the same time make growth more inclusive.

ISBN 978-92-64-03351-1
OECD Economic Surveys: India
© OECD 2007

Chapter 1

India's key challenges to sustaining high growth

The Indian economy has undergone a remarkable transformation over the past two decades. The growth rate of average incomes has increased from 1¼ per cent prior to 1980 to 7% by 2006. Between 1999 and 2004, the absolute number of people living under the national poverty line has fallen for the first time since Independence. Faster growth has been brought about by a paradigm shift in economic polices that has opened the economy to foreign trade and markedly reduced direct tax rates and government influence over most investment decisions. Despite this favourable performance, there is still much room for improving policy settings to further raise growth potential. This chapter first looks at India's past reforms and the main sources of its improved growth performance and then identifies a number of key challenges that could make growth faster, more sustainable and more even across the country: i) making goods and service markets more competitive; ii) enhancing employment in the formal sector through broad-ranging labour market reforms; iii) further liberalising the banking sector; iv) improving public finances to achieve more rapid growth through a more ambitious fiscal consolidation, reducing subsidies and further reducing tax distortions; v) improving infrastructure and facilitating urbanisation by involving private players more intensely; and vi) upgrading the quality of educational outcomes through institutional reforms.

Economic performance in India has improved appreciably over the past two decades, bringing a marked increase in real incomes and reductions in poverty levels. This constant improvement stands in stark contrast to the outcomes of the first four decades after Independence when growth was low. India's catching-up over the past two decades has more than exceeded the performance of nearly all other emerging economies. The abandonment of extremely interventionist economic policies that relegated market decisions to government officials and isolated the market from the constraints and opportunities of the global economy have been at the origin of this change. This re-orientation of policy started in the mid-1980s and was strengthened at the beginning of the 1990s, with reforms in the area of foreign trade, foreign direct investment and the financial sector. After an intervening period of relatively low key changes in policies, reform efforts were renewed this decade with further trade liberalisation, a marked effort to reduce budget deficits, improvements to the tax system and efforts to improve infrastructure. These reforms transformed the Indian economy into a more open and market-based economy and played a key role in enhancing growth. Nonetheless, a number of factors continue to restrain growth and prevent India from catching-up even faster. After a discussion of India's economic reforms, this chapter examines the main sources of India's improved growth performance. It then discusses key economic policy challenges that India currently faces to sustain and enhance its catch-up process.

Economic reforms have transformed the Indian economy

Poor economic performance in the first decades after Independence...

Since Independence in 1947, India's economic policies have followed a number of distinct paths. Initially, policies were based on socialist planning and a philosophy of self-sufficiency through large-scale state intervention in industrial production, price setting and foreign trade. Most imports were strictly controlled by government and purchases of most foreign capital goods were banned. Government also extended the scope of the commercial public sector well outside the area of transport and utilities and controlled the expansion of the remaining private sector domain. Certain areas of economic activity were reserved for small enterprises and credit flows were directed towards priority sectors. Larger firms were subjected to highly restrictive labour laws. These policies led to excessive bureaucracy (the so-called *license-Raj* system) and failed to achieve the desired outcome of raising growth. As a result, poverty remained high and government policies, from the mid-1960s onwards, were oriented towards redistributing income and providing food and energy subsidies to the poor.

... leading to a progressive improvement in policies in the 1980s...

The precise date when economic policy changed course is difficult to determine. From the late 1970s onwards, reforms were undertaken in a piecemeal fashion. In the late 1970s, there were only 79 products, all capital goods, which could be imported without a license. Following a major reform push in the mid-1980s, the number of items on the list increased enormously, rising almost twentyfold during the 1980s and outright bans on imports were replaced by a combination of import quotas and tariff rates. Furthermore, the extent of the state-trading import monopoly fell markedly (Panagariya, 2004). As a result of this liberalisation, importers' rents were reduced and revenue from tariffs rose by almost one percentage point of GDP in the second half of the decade, doubling the revenue from tariffs relative to the value of imports. While such a reform was a step forward, the import-weighted tariff was 87% and quantitative restrictions were rampant: 92% of internationally tradable domestic production was sheltered behind quantitative import restrictions in the late 1980s (Pursell, 2002). Moreover, for most products the permitted volume of imports was extremely low in most areas: 84% of possible five-digit SITC products accounted for only 10% of total imports (Mukerji, 2004). However, from the mid-1980s, governments began to reduce the extent to which domestic firms required permission to expand their activities or enter new product areas, freeing 31 industries of restrictions and raising the asset ceiling over which government permission for investment was required from USD 12 million to USD 600 million.

The 1980s can thus be seen as a period of transition and the beginning of the move away from a *dirigiste* economic model. Reforms during this period were essentially oriented towards improving the position of domestic producers rather than increasing competition through a generalised opening of the economy. The policy environment, though, moved away from distributional concerns towards improving productivity; but progress was limited. For example, as reductions in energy and food subsidies in the mid-1980s proved unpopular, the government sharply increased subsidies to agricultural inputs (power, fertiliser and irrigation), which quadrupled during the decade to reach 2.4% of GDP. Reforms to public sector enterprises were limited to raising performance through setting efficiency targets for management. In sum, reforms during the 1980s were hesitant and un-systematic and have often been characterised as reform "by stealth".

... and more fundamental reforms since the early 1990s

Rapid economic growth in the second half of the 1980s, driven in large part by expansionary fiscal policies, proved unsustainable. The resulting foreign exchange crisis in 1991, led to the introduction of a more far-reaching set of economic reforms, covering a broader number of areas. The industrial licensing system was changed from a system under which positive approval was required for any investment in all but a few selected industries, to a system where, by the end of the decade, approval was only required for certain items like alcohol, tobacco and defence-related industries. The sectors reserved for public sector enterprises were reduced to just railways, mining and petroleum refining, defence equipment and atomic energy. In contrast, little progress was made during the 1990s in reducing the number of industries reserved for small enterprises or "small-scale industries" (SSIs): only 17 industries were removed from the list leaving 821 areas still restricted to SSIs despite there being no import restrictions in these areas by the end of the 1990s. Hence, foreign large scale firms were allowed to compete in these areas but large domestic companies were forbidden. This anomaly was tackled only after 2002 when industry reservations for SSIs were progressively reduced.

Reducing trade barriers was the second plank of policy reform in the first half of the 1990s. After the reforms of the second half of the 1980s, quantitative import restrictions and licensing were abandoned for capital goods and intermediate products but retained for consumer products, until negotiations with major trading partners led to their eventual abolition at the end of the decade. More importantly, import tariffs were progressively reduced to 35.5% (simple average) and 29.8% (import weighted basis) by 1999, but were still the third highest amongst the seventy countries for which data is available (Government of India, 2001). Moreover, the pattern of tariffs was such that, in effective terms, intermediate products were more protected than final products. Despite the major fall in tariffs, the ratio of import duties to total imports was still 22% by the end of the decade (Figure 1.1).

Figure 1.1. **Evolution of tariff revenue relative to import value**

Including domestic taxes levied on imports for India

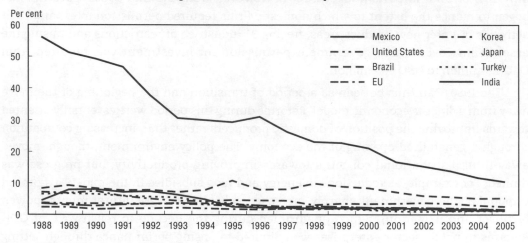

Source: OECD Revenue Statistics, Public Finance Statistics.

Tariff reductions were resumed in 2001 when the government committed to reducing tariffs to the level of ASEAN countries. The highest standard tariff rate was reduced from 35% in 2001 to 10% by 2007, bringing a commensurate fall in the ratio of tariff revenues to the total value of imports. Nonetheless, India continues to belong to the group of countries with relatively high level of Most Favored Nation (MFN) import tariffs. As with other countries, there are numerous derogations from the standard tariff. In other countries, for exemple Turkey and Mexico, these often take the form of regional tariff arrangements but in the case of India the exemptions are mainly domestic. Taking account of these derogations, the ratio of import duties to the value of imports was well below the standard tariff (at 10% and half that once domestic taxes on imports are removed from the total) but was nonetheless still well above the levels seen in ASEAN countries (see Chapter 3).

At the beginning of the 1990s, fundamental reforms were also undertaken in the area of taxation in a manner that enhanced the efficiency of the economy. Marginal tax rates for individuals and companies were reduced significantly, building on the cuts that had been introduced in the previous decade. Furthermore, during the 1990s economic distortions stemming from indirect taxes were reduced by converting excises on manufactured products into a form of value added tax while the tax base was gradually widened by the introduction of a service tax. In 2005, the cascading system of state sales tax on goods was also switched to a value added tax. The reforms of tariffs and excises considerably lowered tax revenues from these sources but was partially offset by an increase in direct tax revenues as the tax base increased, perhaps linked to the reduction in direct tax rates. Overall, these reforms reversed the temporary increase in revenues that had occurred in the second half of the 1980s due to tariffication (Figure 1.2). By the second half of the 1990s, the combined tax ratio of the centre and the states was, at around 14% of GDP, a similar rate to that in the first half of the 1980s prior to reform, but with much lower marginal tax rates. After 2002, with the upswing in the economy and the introduction of the service tax, the tax-GDP ratio increased again, exceeding the peaks reached in the late 1980s, even though all marginal tax rates remain appreciably lower than in the second half of the 1980s.

Figure 1.2. **Evolution of taxation since 1980**
Per cent of GDP at market prices

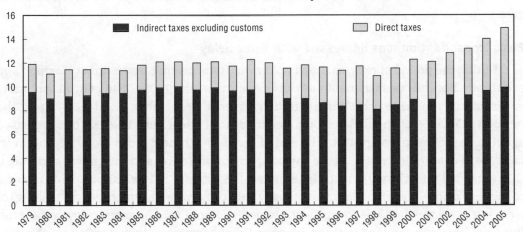

Source: Public Finance statistics.

Financial market liberalisation was another area of reform that started after 1991, although the pace of reform was slower than in product markets and taxes, in part because product market reforms had revealed significant problems in banks' asset portfolios. Financial market reform started from a position in which state-owned banks controlled 90% of bank deposits and channelled an extremely high proportion of funds to the government; interest rates were determined administratively; credit was allocated on the basis of government policy and approval from the Reserve Bank of India was required for individual loans above a certain threshold.

Bank interest rates were deregulated as part of the reform process and are only subject to control in four remaining areas: saving deposit accounts, small loans in priority areas, export credits and non-resident transferable rupee deposits. The deposit rate in the government small saving system remains administratively determined. The government bond market was also liberalised. Although some broad restrictions on the areas in which banks can lend remain in force, the share of bank deposits that must be lent to the government, through the mechanism of the Statutory Liquidity Ratio, has been reduced to 25% while the proportion of deposits that must be deposited with the Reserve Bank through the Cash Reserve Ratio is now 6½ per cent. Competition in the banking system was also increased by allowing new private banks, including foreign ones, to enter the market.

The financial regulatory system has been considerably strengthened. A Board of Financial Supervision was created within the Reserve Bank to focus on supervision, and the rules governing the recognition of bad loans have been substantially tightened. By the early 1990s, capital requirements were also strengthened by the establishment of a system under which banks are required to promptly undertake specified changes to their portfolios and management when various trigger points are reached. In addition, bank capital was considerably strengthened. Government funds were used to recapitalise banks – at a cost of rupee (or INR henceforth) 2 200 billion up to 2001 (nearly 10% of GDP in 2001) – although the recapitalisation of rural co-operative banks has still not taken place. By 2004, new laws and institutions were functioning that allowed banks to foreclose on secured loans that were in default, so removing one of the major hurdles to the development of credit.

Fiscal consolidation was addressed with some delay

During the period of reforms, fiscal policy was managed in a discretionary fashion and eventually became unsustainable at the beginning of the 2000s. The central and state governments ran large fiscal deficits initially, averaging together 8% of GDP during the period 1985 to 1991. The deficits then declined until fiscal year 1996-97, but increased again in the following years. Until the end of the 1990s, these deficits did not result in an increase in debt to GDP ratios, as the gap between interest rates and the growth of nominal GDP exceeded the primary deficit. Nonetheless, the increase in interest payments forced a reduction in non-interest outlays, particularly public investment, which led to a build-up of large infrastructure bottlenecks and was problematic from a development viewpoint. After financial liberalisation, and with an increased emphasis on reducing inflation, the debt position became unsustainable, as the gap between interest rates and nominal GDP growth narrowed substantially and the primary deficit increased. These two adverse developments resulted in a sharp increase of the consolidated debt of central and state governments, which reached 81% of GDP in March 2003 after rising by almost five percentage points of GDP per year in the previous four years.

The central government decided to move away from discretionary fiscal policy and limit its future fiscal freedom by passing the Fiscal Responsibility and Budget Management Act (FRBMA) in 2003. This Act set an upper deficit ceiling of 3% of GDP for the central government to be reached by fiscal year 2008. Under the influence of the Twelfth Finance Commission, which is the latest of the quinquennial constitutionally authorized body that determines fiscal relations between the central and state governments, and supported by financial incentives from the central government, nearly all state governments have introduced similar acts. As a result, the overall fiscal deficit was targeted to be reduced to 6% of GDP by 2008. Such a deficit, while still high, will be sufficient to ensure that debt starts falling relative to GDP. The benefits of this consolidation policy are beginning to be seen; interest payments are now falling as a share of national income, and total government capital spending (including the repayment of some forms of debt) is starting to rise once again, a process that is being helped by buoyant tax revenues.

The economy has responded positively to the reforms

India has achieved a higher growth path

Overall, the performance of the economy has improved markedly since the 1980s. Since 2000, the annual trend growth of GDP and GDP per capita has been 6½ per cent and

4¾ per cent respectively, almost three times the growth rate in the first three decades after Independence. Moreover, there is evidence more recently (see below) that the sustainable growth rate of the economy has reached 8½ per cent. If this growth path continues, then average income levels will double in a decade while, with the growth path experienced prior to 1980, it would have taken 55 years to double income levels. This pace of growth has brought a steady catch-up in Indian per capita incomes from 5½ per cent of the US level in 1985 to 8% in 2005, when income is valued at estimated purchasing power parity (PPP).

Compared to all non-OECD countries, India's recent growth performance has also been good, outperforming all but 10% of this group of economies. Some of the larger Indian states (with population sizes above 50 million) have outperformed many of the much smaller economies in this best performing non-OECD group. Given that India is a large and diverse country of subcontinental size with a population of 1.1 billion, it is more appropriate to compare its growth performance to four country groupings with a similar population size – China, countries that had incomes per head below $ 3 000 measured at international prices, countries with incomes between $ 3 000 and $ 8 000, and all other countries. The level of income in India has moved above that of the low-income group and is growing faster than the middle-income countries – though it has fallen behind both the level and growth of incomes in China (Figure 1.3). Although India's average income level is still low – India ranked 107 out of 186 countries and territories for which data was available in 2005 – the size of its population, and its rapid growth during the past 25 years, made it the fourth largest economy in the world in 2005 when measured at current prices and using purchasing power parities (Table 1.1), and continued rapid growth suggests that it was the third largest economy in 2006. Note that on these estimates, in 1980 the Indian economy was smaller than that of Germany, France, Italy, Japan, the United Kingdom and even Brazil; and had by 2006 overtaken all of these economies, even if it had, itself, been overtaken by China.

Figure 1.3. GDP per capita in India and elsewhere relative to the United States

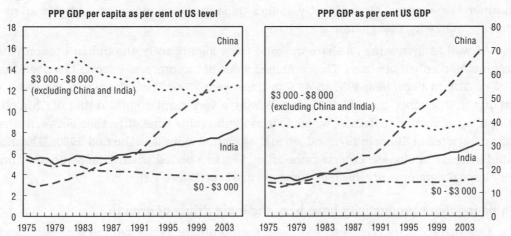

Source: World Bank, World Development Indicators Online database and OECD calculations.

Table 1.1. **The evolution of the ten largest economies over 30 years**

Share of world GDP valued at purchasing power parities

	1975	1980	1990	2000	2005
			%		
United States	21.8	21.5	21.4	21.2	20.3
China	2.8	3.1	5.5	11.0	14.1
Japan	8.2	8.3	8.8	7.4	6.5
India	3.6	3.4	4.4	5.4	6.3
Germany	5.8	5.6	5.0	4.6	4.0
United Kingdom	4.4	4.1	3.8	3.5	3.2
France	4.2	4.0	3.8	3.4	3.0
Italy	4.0	4.1	3.7	3.2	2.7
Brazil	3.0	3.5	2.9	2.8	2.7
Russian Federation	..	..	4.6	2.3	2.6
Memorandum item					
OECD Europe (1975 members)	28.0	26.8	24.9	22.8	20.5

Source: World Bank World Development Indicators.

The impact of the Indian economy on the rest of the world is importantly determined by its share in international trade, which is still much lower than its share in world GDP. The market share of India's exports of goods and services has almost doubled in the ten years to 2005, reaching 1.2% of world exports of goods and commercial services, which is only one-sixth of India's share in world GDP (measured in PPP, Table 1.2). The impact of India has been more pronounced in the service sector. The initial boost to Indian exports came from sales of computer programming services, software exports and other information technology related services (including call centres and outsourced business processes such as dealing with insurance claims), with their share in total Indian exports increasing from 2% to 27% in the ten years to 2005. More recently, exports of other business services have also been expanding rapidly. This growth has quadrupled India's share of world trade in services in the decade to 2005 and made India the 11th largest exporter of commercials services. More recently, India's trade in merchandise goods has started to increase markedly, though from a low base.

As well as increasing its share in world trade significantly, the Indian economy has become markedly more open. The combined value of imports and exports has risen from 13% of GDP in fiscal year 1985 to 49% in fiscal year 2006. The increase in the share of exports in GDP since the mid-1980s is following a very similar path to that of China but with a lag of about one decade, which is broadly the same time difference between when reforms started in China in 1978 and when they started in India in the mid-1980s. The most rapid increase in Chinese exports came after 1997, in a period when China embarked on a very large programme of reform of domestic markets (Figure 1.4).

Gains in labour productivity have been the main driver of growth

Labour productivity growth has been the dominant factor behind the catch-up in incomes between 1990 and 2005. Over this period, average labour productivity growth in India outstripped that of all OECD countries with the exception of Korea, but was lower than in China. Demographic change has also boosted India's GDP per capita growth, especially since 2000, as India is currently in a beneficial phase, with the working age population growing faster than the total population (Figure 1.5 and Table 1.3).

Table 1.2. **The evolution of shares in world exports of commercial services and manufactures by country**

	1980	1990	1995	2000	2005	1980	2005
	Share of world exports of commercial services					Rank	
United States	10.4	17.0	16.7	18.7	14.7	2	1
United Kingdom	9.4	6.9	6.5	7.9	7.8	3	2
Germany	7.6	6.5	6.2	5.3	6.2	4	3
France	11.5	8.5	7.0	5.4	4.8	1	4
Japan	5.1	5.3	5.8	4.9	4.5	6	5
Italy	5.2	6.2	5.2	3.8	3.9	5	6
Spain	3.1	3.5	3.4	3.5	3.8	9	7
Netherlands	4.6	3.6	3.8	3.2	3.2	7	8
China	0.6	0.7	1.6	2.0	3.1	30	9
Hong Kong, China	1.6	2.3	2.9	2.7	2.6	15	10
India	**0.8**	**0.6**	**0.6**	**1.1**	**2.3**	**24**	**11**
Ireland	0.4	0.4	0.4	1.2	2.2	37	12
Austria	2.4	2.9	2.7	2.1	2.2	10	13
Canada	1.9	2.4	2.1	2.6	2.2	11	14
Memorandum item							
OECD Europe (1975 definition)	57.3	52.2	47.1	45.4	47.9		
	Share of world exports of manufactures						
India	0.4	0.5	0.6	0.7	0.9		
	Share of world exports of goods and services						
India	0.5	0.5	0.6	0.7	1.2		

1. The three countries that were in the top 15 commercial service exporters in 1980 but not in 2005 were Switzerland, Sweden and Norway. They were ranked 17th, 19th and 22nd, respectively, in 2005.
Source: World Trade Organisation, Interactive Statistical database; World Bank, *World Development Indicators Online*.

Figure 1.4. **Exports relative to GDP: India compared to China**
Exports of goods and services as per cent of GDP at market prices and current exchange rate

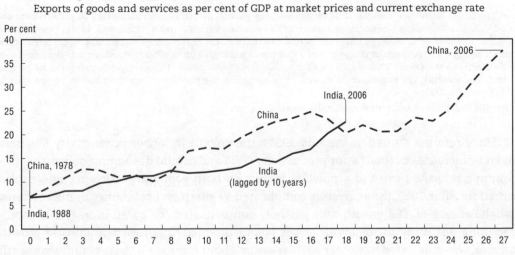

Source: CEIC and CMIE.

Figure 1.5. **Factors contributing to the catch-up process in the period 1990 to 2005**

% per year

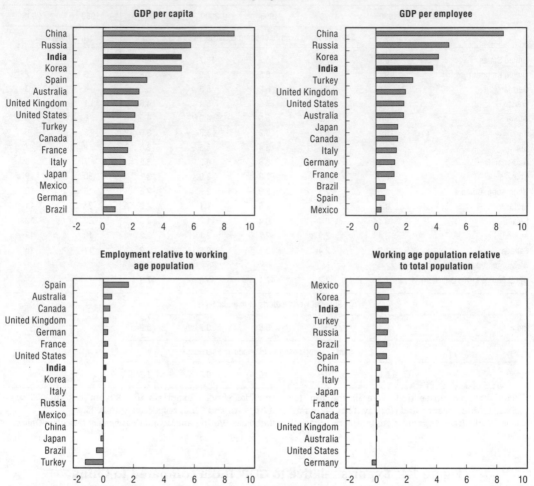

Note: For OECD countries, the charts show the average growth in variables contributing to growth over the period 1990 to 2005, using a semi-log regression of the relevant variable and a time trend. In the case of OECD countries, this average is measured over the period 1990 to 2005. For non-member countries, if there is statistical evidence of significant change in the growth of a GDP per capita then a more recent period is used. Thus, for India, the data refer to the period 2000 to 2005 and for Russia, from 1996 to 2005. Labour input is measured by persons worked. The working age population is measured by weighting the population age distribution by age-specific activity rates for 2000.

Source: OECD databases and various national sources.

Since reforms started in the mid-1980s, the growth in labour productivity has been driven by increases in total factor productivity (TFP) and capital deepening, suggesting that economic reforms have had a positive impact on both economic efficiency and capital formation. After 2000, the analysis is complicated by sharp cyclical swings in the economy. A slight easing of TFP growth was partially compensated for by an increase in capital deepening, resulting in somewhat lower labour productivity growth. Total GDP growth, however, was supported by a marked increase in labour inputs. All these estimates are still tentative as there is considerable uncertainty about recent factor inputs due to the time lag in the availability of investment and employment data.

Total factor productivity growth can be further decomposed into the effect of human capital formation and a residual which reflects all other impacts.[1] Overall, improvements

Table 1.3. **Factors behind Indian growth**

Period average compound growth rates[1]

	1950-1979	1980-89	1990-99	2000-05
GDP[2]	3.54	4.94	6.00	6.47
Employment	2.26	2.11	1.56	2.61
Labour productivity	1.25	2.78	4.36	3.76
Capital deepening	0.76	0.94	1.90	1.98
Total factor productivity	0.49	1.83	2.44	1.76
Human capital	0.29	0.38	0.38	0.16
Residual	0.20	1.45	2.06	1.60
Memorandum item				
Capital stock	3.81	4.02	5.42	6.68
GDP per capita	1.30	2.68	3.86	4.80
Labour productivity	1.25	2.78	4.36	3.76
Participation	0.11	−0.65	−0.6	0.17
Demographics	−0.05	0.56	0.12	0.83

1. Period estimates are based on a semi-log regression of a given variable and on a set of time trends covering the periods in question. The contribution of capital intensity to growth is based on a Cobb-Douglas production function in which the capital share is 0.5 – in line with the long-run average income share in India.
2. GDP is measured on a rainfall corrected basis.
Source: OECD estimates.

in human capital formation added about 0.4% per year to productivity and output growth in the 1980s and the 1990s. This contribution eased to around 0.2% after 2000 as the share of people in the workforce with at least primary education is now rising less sharply than previously as more workers have now completed primary education.

Estimating potential output growth by eliminating cyclical effects allows a more nuanced view of the impact of liberalisation on economic growth, as reforms should have boosted supply factors and thus trend growth. The estimate of potential output made by the OECD is based on a Cobb-Douglas production function estimated for the whole economy, using capital stock data from the 2007 National Accounts and employment data generated from both the annual and quinquennial National Sample Surveys. Total factor productivity has been modelled with a time-varying trend. Given the importance of fluctuations in agricultural output stemming from fluctuations in rainfall during the monsoon season, rainfall has been treated as an input into the production process by estimating the impact of weather conditions on agricultural output and then deducting their impact from overall GDP. These fluctuations can be particularly important in certain years (Figure 1.6, Panel C). The statistical results suggest a relatively large contribution of capital formation to economic growth compared to OECD countries, reflecting a low labour share in value added. The growth of total factor productivity is estimated to have improved in the mid-1980s, but there is no evidence of any further improvement since then. Potential output has been estimated from this production function by replacing actual employment input by a trend labour input calculated by smoothing the year to year movements in the ratio of employment to working age population. The labour input used in the production function was then taken as the product of the smoothed employment ratio and the working age population.

The strong performance of potential growth since 2000 has its origins mainly in an investment boom of a scale similar to that seen at the beginning of the 1990s. By 2005, the last year for which official data is available, the capital stock was growing by 7½ per cent. Since then, available data on production and imports of capital goods suggests that net fixed capital formation has continued to rise at over 20%, as in 2005, with the result that the growth of the capital stock has risen by a further percentage point and is now growing some three percentage points faster than its average growth rate over the previous two decades. In contrast to developments in the early 1990s, the increase appears to be firmly based on strong profitability and an acceleration of exports in key sectors. On the other hand, there is no statistical evidence of an improvement in the growth of total factor productivity in this decade. Nonetheless, these favourable supply side factors appear to have boosted the growth rate of the potential output to 8½ per cent by 2006 (Figure 1.6).

While estimated potential growth has picked-up significantly, actual output growth has surged at an even faster pace. Growth has now averaged over 9% for two years running and, given the continuing rapid growth in credit, seems likely to maintain a high pace in 2007. So far this expansion has been possible because of the availability of spare capacity in the economy. A broad measure of inflation, such as the non-agricultural GDP deflator, has not accelerated and increased by less than 5% in the fourth quarter of the calendar year 2006. On the other hand, a number of other inflation indicators, such as the CPI, have moved well above the government's objective of keeping inflation in the 5-5½ per cent range. This increase has mainly been due to the high weight of food and commodities in these indices. The Reserve Bank has been progressively raising interest rates and this is likely to slow growth to 8% in 2008. Such an easing should be sufficient to ensure that the non-agricultural GDP deflator does not accelerate. The Reserve Bank has lowered its desired medium-term inflation rate to 4-4½ per cent, as measured by the wholesale price index, and this should help contain inflation expectations.

The role of services and the IT sector in India's growth

The performance of individual sectors of the economy also supports the view that changes in government policies have boosted growth. In the five years between 1999 and 2004, the growth of the service sector has risen markedly above that of the overall non-agricultural business sector. Within the service sector, a number of sectors have performed significantly better than others. In particular, in areas where government regulation has been eased, output has grown more rapidly. Three sectors stand out: communications, insurance and information technology (IT) services. All of these sectors have been significantly liberalised: telecommunications saw the transformation of the historic state monopoly operator into a corporation and the introduction of private competitors (notably for wireless telephony); insurance saw the end of the domination of the state-owned companies with the opening of the sector and the creation of a new regulator; and computer services also benefited from an improved business environment in the special zones, established for the software industry, which benefited from better infrastructure and tax advantages (see below). On the other hand, the sectors that remained dominated by state-owned companies performed well below average (Table 1.4).

The most noticeable increase in service sector output has come from the development of the information technology enabled services (ITES) sector. This sector started poorly in India with the exit of multinational firms and the creation of a government monopoly to manufacture and service computers in the 1970s. This move did, however, provide the initial market for two of what are now the largest ITES service companies. This policy ended in the mid-1980s when 100% investment by foreign companies was allowed in this area prompting a number of US companies to enter the market. This new computer-oriented investment policy reduced tariffs on hardware to 60% in 1984 and exempted all

Figure 1.6. **Estimated potential output growth, output gap and impact of rainfall fluctuations**

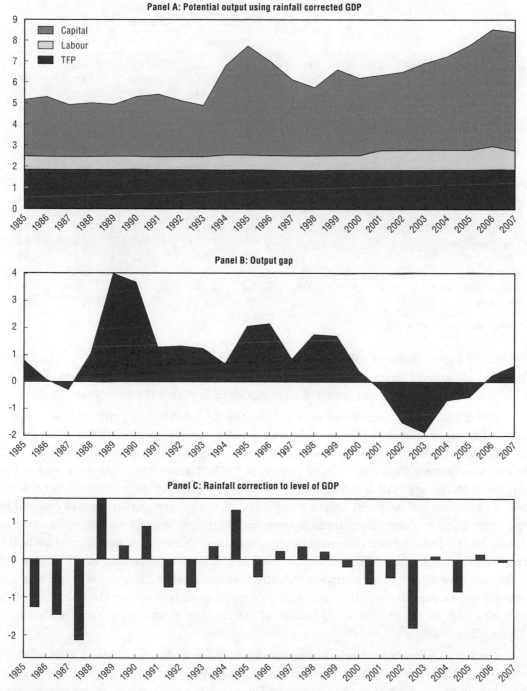

Panel A: Potential output using rainfall corrected GDP

Panel B: Output gap

Panel C: Rainfall correction to level of GDP

Source: OECD estimates.

Table 1.4. **Growth of value added by sector**
Constant prices

	2000	2002	2004	2000-04 average	1999	2004
	% per year				Share in value-added	
Services (excl. railways, post and banks)	7.3	8.5	13.0	9.3	36.5	42.2
Communications	26.9	25.7	26.5	24.9	1.7	3.9
Insurance	−0.7	51.1	13.8	14.2	0.7	1.0
Computer services	51.1	17.1	23.6	26.9	1.0	2.5
Other services	5.0	5.9	10.9	7.3	33.0	34.7
Construction	6.1	7.7	12.5	8.2	6.4	7.1
Manufacturing	7.7	6.8	8.1	6.4	16.2	16.3
Manufacturing (more than ten employees)	7.8	7.6	9.0	7.3	10.6	11.1
Manufacturing (less than ten employees)	7.6	5.3	6.2	4.8	5.6	5.2
Largely state owned sectors	2.2	9.6	1.1	4.9	9.7	9.1
Utilities	2.0	4.8	4.3	3.5	2.7	2.4
Mining	2.5	8.7	5.8	4.8	2.5	2.4
Railways and post	3.7	6.9	5.1	5.3	1.3	1.2
Banks	1.4	14.8	−5.8	6.0	3.1	3.1
Agriculture	−0.3	−7.8	0.7	1.8	25.4	20.5
Dwellings and real estate	2.6	2.3	2.7	2.5	5.7	4.8
Total of above	4.6	4.0	7.8	6.2	100.0	100.0

Source: National Accounts of India.

profits on export sales of software from corporate taxation (Dossani, 2005). The initial location chosen by these multinationals was Bangalore, perhaps as the result of the concentration of government research laboratories in that area (Balakrishnan, 2006).[2]

The growth of ITES firms was at first driven by the provision of contract labour at the sites of foreign clients – a process that was aided by the ready availability of H1B non-immigrant visas in the United States – with almost 60% of the revenues of the major ITES companies coming from this form of activity in 1999 (Kumar, 2001). One spill-over of the supply of temporary staff to the US market was to create strong longer-term links between the US software industry and Indian companies, as temporary workers initially stayed in the country, with a significant minority creating their own businesses. More than half of these Indian-born American entrepreneurs went on to establish companies in India, mainly in the areas of software development and production (Saxenian, 2002). The extent of foreign investment in the software industry is substantial and has come either through established foreign firms or through venture capital, mainly from the US, though mostly established in Mauritius as a result of its double taxation treaty with India (Upadhyaya, 2004).[3]

The initial advantage of Indian companies was the availability of trained staff who had mainly graduated from public universities and colleges. The supply was subsequently boosted by the growth of private sector colleges, helped by changes in the government licensing criteria. Having established credibility through repeated contracts, the Indian companies were able to diversify into domestic production of software and the lower value added area of business process outsourcing (Banerjee and Dufflo, 2000).

Poor infrastructure was seen as a major constraint to software companies, and government policy became oriented to overcoming this problem through the establishment of software parks. These parks were developed by the Software Technology

Parks of India and provide basic infrastructure, such as broadband satellite communication facilities and back-up generation facilities for electricity. Since 1998, private sector companies have been able to develop these parks. For firms within these zones, imports are duty free and can also be financed through foreign leases or rental agreements. In addition, the zone administration processes all necessary government forms, acting as a "one-stop shop" window for the entrepreneur. Decision-making is also devolved: zone directors can authorise smaller projects and take decisions in one day, with larger projects taking a week for approval (Bajpai, *et al.* 1998).

Two other government policies have also favoured the software industry: labour and tax laws. The restrictive labour laws that constrain large manufacturing companies do not apply to the service sector and, indeed, a number of state governments have eased regulations that restrict the employment of women and the use of round-the-clock shift working (see Chapter 4). Companies established within software parks are eligible for a complete tax holiday for five of their first eight years of operation. In addition, when this period is over, profits on export sales can be tax free within certain limits. According to INFOSYS, about one-quarter of industry sales are tax free. Views on the role of tax concessions vary. Larger companies take the view that "government support in the form of tax incentives and other benefits has been instrumental in the growth of software exports" (NASSCOM, 1999). Moreover, the industry is concerned that these concessions, which cost 0.2% of GDP, will expire in 2009. On the other hand, surveys of Indian entrepreneurs in the US, considering investing in India, put the availability of a skilled workforce well ahead of fiscal incentives as a reason for starting a business there, in contrast to the views of US-based Chinese entrepreneurs who considered low taxation and market access prime reasons for investing in China (Figure 1.7). International experience suggests that tax concessions have little impact on the destination of FDI if other general framework conditions for doing business are not also favourable (Nicoletti *et al.*, 2006).

Figure 1.7. **Reasons for investment in country of origin by US-based Indian and Chinese entrepreneurs**

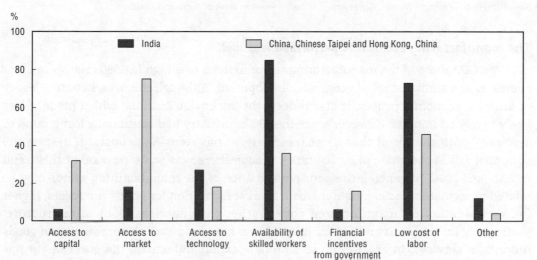

Source: Saxenian (2002).

Whatever the respective roles of human capital, infrastructure provision and tax concessions are, nearly all exports of IT-enabled services come from software parks. By 2005, about 85% of IT-enabled sales took place from the 60 software parks (25 government-owned). Although parks are now widely spread out across the country, the most successful are in Karnataka, the National Capital Region (Delhi, Haryana), Andhra Pradesh and Tamil Nadu. In the first mentioned state, IT-related sales now represent almost one-quarter of state GDP. Employment in the IT sector has risen sharply and now amounts to 1.2 million, or 0.3% of total employment. Exports of IT-related services have risen markedly, especially since the new private sector park development policy was established in 1998. In the five years to 1998, exports expanded from 0.3% to 1.3% of GDP, only to soar to 3.7% of GDP by 2005 (Figure 1.8).

Figure 1.8. **Exports of software and related services by physical location of exporter and state**

Per cent of state GDP, 2005

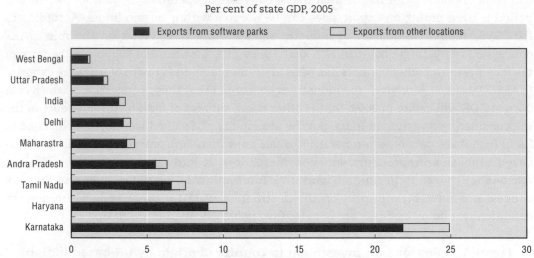

Note: State GDP has been extrapolated from the last available data point to 2005.

Source: Press Information Bureau, Government of India, Reserve Bank of India and CMIE.

The manufacturing sector has performed less well

The GDP share of the manufacturing sector in India was high in 1980 relative to other countries at a similar stage of economic development. Although this was, in part, a legacy of autarkic economic polices, it also reflects the sheer size of India, which made it less likely to rely on imports. However, since the 1980s, industry had continually lost ground to services – with the result that its share in output has remained constant, despite the continual fall in the share of agriculture – though there was some reversal of this trend in 2005 and 2006. In general, the poor performance of the manufacturing sector may be related to regulatory factors; tighter labour market legislation for goods-producers; higher indirect taxation on manufactured goods rather than services. Poor infrastructure, particularly for transport and electricity, may also have held back the production of goods more than services. In an attempt to stimulate export industries, the government has announced a policy of creating special economic zones that have many of the features of the successful software technology parks (Box 1.1).

Box 1.1. **Special Economic Zones**

The success of software parks in stimulating the development of the information technology service industry has led the government to progressively introduce legislation to enable the development of Special Economic Zones (SEZs), oriented to the manufacturing sector. The development of SEZs has, until recently, been slow. Even though India created the first such zone in Asia in 1965, only eight existed by 2004 and they provided only 5% of goods' exports, though the shares for jewellery was 55%.

The slow development of existing SEZs led the government to introduce a new policy at the beginning of 2006. The previous policy, while giving considerable tax advantages, had not overcome the administrative barriers to business that typify India (see Chapter 3) nor did it overcome infrastructure barriers, notably for road and electricity. The new policy relies on private developers to create the zone and provide all infrastructure, with the objective of generating additional economic activity and creating employment.

The new policy focuses on changes to the laws and regulations that govern SEZs and allows:

- Single window clearance for development in the zone; simplified administrative procedures and exemptions from many restrictive policies; exemption from selected central laws.
- Application of all municipal and many state laws by the SEZ Authority.
- Separate court system with internal security provided by the SEZ Authority.
- Labour laws have also been modified at the state level, with 14 states abolishing previous constraints, freely allowing contract labour, and a significant number deeming all enterprises in a SEZ to be public utilities and hence making wildcat strikes (i.e. those without due notice) illegal.

Significant tax concessions have also been granted:

- Total corporate tax exemption for five years, 50% for a further five years and a further exemption for reinvested earnings derived form exports, with developers allowed a ten-year window of tax exemption. Zone developers are exempt from the minimum alternate corporate tax and the dividend distribution tax.
- Imports into the SEZ are tax and tariff free, but sales to the domestic market are regarded as imports into India.

By February 2007, while 234 SEZ projects had been approved, 162 projects have been given "in-principle" approvals. Of the 234 approvals, 91 have full legal approval. The fully approved projects cover 67 square kilometres. The total area for proposed SEZs is 1 750 square kilometres, at most 0.11% of total agricultural land. Two major projects of a much larger size (greater than 100 square kilometres) had been approved under previous legislation in Maharashtra and Haryana. These zones will be on par with the size of two (Zhuhai and Xiamen) of the three largest SEZs in China, though only one-third the size of the Shenzen development.

At end-January 2007, the government had announced a temporary freeze on granting permission for new SEZs, but this freeze has been lifted in April 2007 with the condition that there would be no compulsory land acquisition by the state governments. This policy change followed demonstrations against a proposed car plant in West Bengal despite favourable land acquisition terms.[1] Once a new policy on compensation for land acquired from farmers has been announced, state governments may be allowed to purchase land. As a general rule, state intervention may be necessary to ensure that the totality of land in an SEZ is owned by the developer, so avoiding a few land owners blocking the development, as the SEZ area must be completely contiguous.

Box 1.1. **Special economic zones** (cont.)

The economic benefits of SEZ depend on the opportunity cost of the resources that are deployed in these areas. Where the capital comes mainly from abroad and if there is significant surplus labour in the economy, then SEZs have produced significant welfare gains to the domestic economy, notably in Asian economies at early stages of development (Jayanthakumaran, 2003). As the level of development increases the gains become less, mainly because of the much lower wage differentials in the zones. If, however, capital is drawn from the domestic economy, as has mainly been the case in existing SEZs (CII, 2006), then tax concessions may negate other benefits.

In the case of India, the SEZs are designed to overcome many of the barriers to growth identified in this *Survey* (poor infrastructure, restrictive labour laws and excessive regulation). While an optimal policy might be to remove these restrictions countrywide, the current SEZ policy, if successful, could act as a catalyst for change in the whole economy. By the end of 2007, the government expects that foreign companies will have invested up to USD 6 billion in SEZs and created half a million jobs.

1. 96% of the land had been acquired voluntarily by the state government (Sau, 2007) at a 40% premia to market prices and with a promise that one family member would be employed in the zone.

Chapter 2 examines the performance of the manufacturing sector and the overall economy in more detail. It considers a number of questions such as:

● Why has manufacturing's contribution to growth not been greater?

● What structural features have influenced the evolution of India's pattern of growth?

● How has the distribution of growth shifted over time, and what role has factor reallocation played in India's productivity performance?

● To what extent are weaknesses in framework conditions at fault?

Richer states are growing faster and reducing poverty more quickly

The acceleration of economic growth has helped reduce poverty, both nationally and at the state level. The poverty rate has now dropped to 21.8% when a short recall period is used for measuring consumption, down markedly from 26.1% in 1991. Comparisons over a longer time period are only possible using a long recall period, which tends to lower estimated consumptions and so raise estimates of poverty. These estimates show that the poverty rate has fallen markedly from 45% in 1983 to 27.5% in 2004. Thus, in the two decades since reform began in 1984 (and the period in which the growth of total factor productivity has increased), the poverty rate has fallen 15 percentage points, after having remained constant in the previous three decades. In addition, the speed of decline of poverty was markedly greater in the period from 1999 to 2004 (Himanshu, 2007 and Dev and Ravi, 2007). Using the short recall period measure, the poverty rate fell by 17% in this period, sufficient to generate an 8% fall in the absolute number of people living below the poverty line, which is the first drop in the absolute number of people below the poverty line in a five-year period since Independence.

The reasons for the more rapid fall in the poverty rate since 1999 cannot yet be decomposed with certainty but appear to be linked to a better employment performance and a reduction in the relative price of food. Employment growth has outstripped population growth since 1999, in contrast to the previous six-year period. In addition, relative food prices fell by over 4% annually between 1999 and 2004 against a very slight fall in the period 1993 to 1999. Food prices are a major factor in determining the number of people living in poverty since the weight of food in the expenditure of households below the poverty line is particularly large (see Box 1.2). While such falls in food prices reduce the

Box 1.2. **Measuring poverty**

In India, the most commonly used measure of poverty is the proportion of the population with expenditure below an absolute poverty line that is invariant over time in real terms. The level of consumption below which people are living in poverty is set by determining the overall expenditure level at which consumers could purchase a food intake of 2 400 calories in rural areas or 2 100 calories in urban areas, which was estimated as the minimum necessary food intake. This overall expenditure sum was evaluated for a base period in 1979 and has then been updated using price indices. In 2004/5, the poverty level was INR 356 and INR 538 per person per month in rural and urban areas respectively, equivalent to USD 1.28 and USD 1.89 per day respectively, when converted at purchasing power parities. The national measure represents a much lower level of spending than the internationally used criteria of USD 1.08 per day in 1993 prices at purchasing power parities. Using the international measure, the poverty rate was 34% in 2004, higher than the estimated national measure of 28%. There are two measures of poverty in India depending on the time period that is used in the survey for the recall of consumption. The shorter time period for recall generally gives a lower estimate of poverty.

real income of farmers, they improve the position of net food buyers, who are more numerous amongst the poor than food suppliers.

General well-being is affected by more than just the measured poverty rate, and a number of other indicators also point to a more rapid improvement in well-being this decade, though the picture is mixed. There has been quite rapid growth in housing quality and the ownership of some consumer durables. Health indicators also suggest a more rapid improvement in recent years. Infant mortality and maternal mortality have improved significantly, and there has been a marked decline in the overall death rate, increasing life expectancy (Table 1.5). Nonetheless, infant mortality remains high and

Table 1.5. **Alternative measures of well-being**

	1992	1998	2005	1992-98	1998-2005
	%			% change per year	
Infant mortality[1]	77.3	67.3	55.5	−2.3	−2.7
Underweight children below age three	51.1	46.7	43.3	−1.5	−1.1
Fully immunised children	38.3	44.2	46.0	2.4	0.6
Maternal death rate[2]	43.7	39.8	30.1	−1.9	−5.4
Overall death rate[1]	15.8	14.6	8.0	−1.6	−7.2
Electricity in house	50.9	60.1	67.9	2.8	1.8
Piped drinking water in house	31.3	38.7	42.0	3.6	1.2
Access to toilet facility	30.2	35.9	44.5	2.9	3.1
Live in "pucca" house[3]	23.7	32.0	41.4	5.1	3.7
Posses motorised vehicle	9.2	12.8	18.6	5.7	5.5
Have TV	20.7	34.7	44.2	9.0	3.5
Ownership of agricultural land	51.6	49.9	45.6	−0.6	−1.3

1. Per 1 000 births or people.
2. Per 10 000 births.
3. A pucca house is one built of solid materials: burnt bricks, cement, etc.
Source: USAID (1995, 2000), International Institute for Population Sciences (2007), Kumar (2005), Registrar General (2006).

maternal mortality is of particular concern. The latter is three times higher than in China and even within India there are marked variations in maternal mortality, with a much lower rate in Kerala. The government is increasing health spending; but it will be difficult to reach current targets for reducing maternal mortality without changes in health care delivery, especially in poorer states since 40% of staff at publicly funded medical centres are absent at any point in time with even higher absences for doctors (Chaudhury, et al. 2006).

There appears to have been a reasonably close relationship between economic prosperity and reductions in poverty. Growth in average per capita consumption is linked to the proportionate decline in the poverty rate across states (Figure 1.9). In urban areas there is a close linage between state GDP growth and consumption, but there is less of a relation in rural areas, weakening the overall relationship between state GDP growth and poverty reduction. Indeed, there were a number of states (Haryana, Tamil Nadu and Rajasthan) where poverty rates increased between 1999 and 2004 despite significant economic growth, suggesting that other factors also influence the evolution of poverty. There has been some increase in income inequality, both in urban and rural areas. This slight increase in inequality reduced the extent to which the poverty rate would have fallen, given economic growth, offsetting about one-third of the fall in poverty that might have occurred with unchanged overall growth and a constant distribution of income. However, such calculations are questionable in that the increase in inequality may be linked to the process that generated the increase in income growth. Overall, the evolution of poverty headcount at the national level suggests that faster economic growth is a powerful means of reducing poverty, and this effect becomes even bigger if steps are taken to make growth more inclusive.

Figure 1.9. **Statewide poverty reduction and average per capita consumption growth, 1993-2004**[1]

Annual average change, 1993-2004

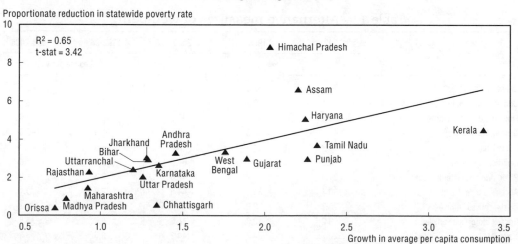

1. In this and all subsequent scatter plots in this *Survey*, the R^2 and t-statistic are derived from a regression of the variable on the vertical axis on the variable on the horizontal axis plus a constant.

Source: Himanshu (2007).

The wide disparities in economic growth that have occurred over the past 15 years have increased the dispersion of incomes across the country. There has been considerable variation in the extent of income growth across the country, with lower growth concentrated in the north (from east to some parts of west), where the reduction in poverty has been markedly less than in southern, western and north-western states which have grown more rapidly. The spread in economic performance across states is of all the more concern as there is evidence that states that were initially poor have grown less than the states that were initially better-off (Figure 1.10). Despite the rapid improvement at the national level, there are six states (accounting for 40% of the population) where the growth of per capita GDP was less than 2½ per cent annually in the period 1993 to 2004 and where there has been little improvement in the proportion of the population living under the poverty line. If a more uniform distribution of economic activity could have been achieved, then the speed of reduction in poverty could have been doubled (Datt and Ravallion, 2002). Reducing the spread in economic performance across states is a theme that runs through most of the remaining chapters.

Figure 1.10. **Growth tends to be more rapid in richer states**

Annual average change GDP per capita, 1993-2004, constant prices[1]

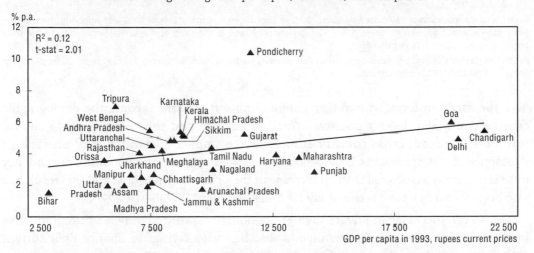

1. Except 2005: Andhra Pradesh, Bihar, Assam, Himachal Pradesh, Madhya Pradesh, Orissa, Rajasthan, Sikkim; 2003: Chhattisgarh, Goa, Tripura; 2002: Nagaland.

Source: Central Statistical Organisation National Accounts Statistics.

Looking into the future

While India has significantly improved its economic performance, by raising its potential output growth from 3½ per cent in 1980 to 8½ per cent currently, the potential for further catch-up remains large. The average level of productivity is only 9% of that in the United States and 75% of that in China, so with appropriate framework conditions in place, India should be able to reap large productivity gains. Such gains could be achieved through enlarging and modernising its fixed capital stock including infrastructure, improving the skill level of the workforce, and through shifting resources towards higher productivity sectors, in particular from agriculture to manufacturing.

Unlike many OECD and a number of non-OECD countries, India's demographic profile continues to favour the catching up of average incomes. There are two channels for this positive outcome: first, following the decline in birth rates, population growth declines faster than growth of the working age population, resulting in a decline in the dependency ratio (Figure 1.11). The higher share of workers in total population tends to boost GDP per capita growth. On the other hand, the rate of increase of the labour force is declining

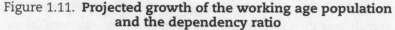

Figure 1.11. **Projected growth of the working age population and the dependency ratio**

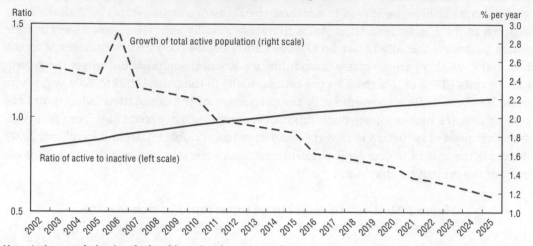

Note: Active population is calculated by using the age specific employment rate of 2000 and applying them to the Registrar-General's population projections. The dependency ratio is the ratio of the active population to the total population less the active population.

Source: Registrar General of India, Population Projections; National Sample Survey Employment-Unemployment Survey 1999/2000; OECD calculations.

over the medium term, so lowering potential output growth. Second, the demographic change could also have a positive effect on savings and thus contribute to capital formation. Indeed, cross-country studies of the impact of demography on savings (Masson *et al.*, 2005; Edwards, 2002; Modigliani, 1990) suggest that a fall in the dependency ratio is generally associated with an increase in the private savings rate, and this result has also been found in a time series study for India (Herd and Dougherty, 2007).

However, increases in private savings are not necessarily channelled into productive investment, in particular, if governments absorb private savings to finance their current spending, as has been the case in India during the past decades. Channelling savings to the most productive use also requires efficient financial intermediation. At the same time, attracting FDI inflows can add directly to domestic capital formation and contribute to TFP growth. Sound public finances, efficient financial markets and openness to FDI inflows are therefore of great importance for building up a productive capital stock.

Longer term projections of economic growth are subject to a large degree of uncertainty, but it would seem that there is scope for a further acceleration in the growth of per capita incomes in India over the medium to long term. A wide range of scenarios can be imagined. Here just two are presented: one that maintains the *status quo*, the other which introduces a series of reforms designed to achieve the government's target of 10% growth.

In the first scenario, domestic investment rises in line with the increase in private household saving that may follow from the likely fall in the dependency ratio and the acceleration in per capita incomes that has already occurred. Government saving remains negative and the current account deficit remains at the relatively low level of 1½ per cent of GDP. In such a scenario, the domestic capital stock would accelerate, but only sufficiently to offset the likely slowdown in the growth of the labour force, with the result that output might continue to grow at 8½ per cent annually. However, given the demographic transition that is occurring, the growth of per capita income would accelerate somewhat to over 7% which is almost five times higher than experienced in three decades 1950 to 1980 (Figure 1.12).

Figure 1.12. **Growth of potential GDP per capita over the longer term**

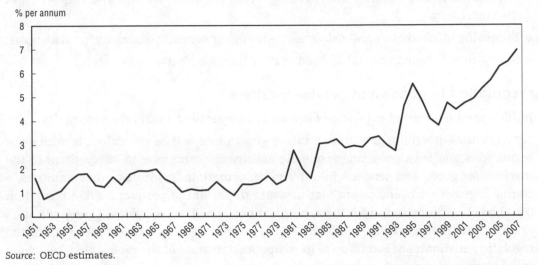

% per annum

Source: OECD estimates.

A more optimistic scenario can be imagined. In this scenario, the business environment is improved significantly by further fiscal consolidation, a marked reduction in the extent of control, and by policies that allow greater private sector involvement in both infrastructure and the financial sector (see Chapters 3, 4, 5 and 7). Such polices could result in a continued strong inflow of FDI and portfolio investment. These inflows have averaged 2½ per cent of GDP in the five years to 2006 and were even close to 3% of GDP in 2006. At the average level of the past five years, capital inflows were 12 times greater than total net flows of foreign aid in the same period. FDI inflows have the scope to expand considerably given a favourable environment. If inflows of foreign direct investment were to rise, it would be possible to sustainably finance a current account deficit of 3% of GDP. At the same time, if the government embarks on a major restructuring of public expenditure that substantially reduces government dissaving at both the central and state level, a further 3½ per cent of GDP could be invested. If these reforms were introduced over a five-year period, then the growth of the capital stock might rise to close to 11% annually, and the sustainable growth rate of the economy could rise to over 9½ per cent. Further efficiency gains could flow from improvements in the tax system and a more neutral tax tariff structure (see Chapter 6) and more rapid human capital formation (see Chapter 8).

Key challenges

Reaching the government's target for medium-term output growth of 10% will require additional structural reforms. The following sections identify a number of key challenges that policy makers should address to foster the catching-up of the Indian economy. These are:

● Increasing competition by lowering the extent of regulatory intervention.

- Raising growth in more labour intensive sectors of the economy via reform of the labour market.

- Reducing the extent of public sector domination of the financial sector and broadening capital markets.

- Achieving sound fiscal policies at all levels of government, reorienting public expenditure, and making the taxes on domestic transactions and imports less discriminatory.

- Improving infrastructure and delivering better public services, especially in urban areas;

- Strengthening human capital by making the education system work better.

Easing regulation in goods and service markets

India's product market regulations are strict compared to most other countries...

A central determinant of India's future growth rate will be the extent to which the regulations and laws governing economic activity are conducive to competition in the markets for goods and services. In order to benchmark India against other countries, a comprehensive set of indicators that measure the extent of product market regulation (PMR) has been constructed for India, both nationally and across states. These indicators draw on the framework developed for OECD countries to assess the extent to which the regulatory environment is conducive to competition in areas of the product market where technology and market conditions make competition viable (Nicoletti et al., 1999 and Conway et al., 2005). These indicators summarise data covering 139 formal rules and regulations that have a bearing on competition. The indicators cover most of the important aspects of general regulatory practice as well as some aspects of industry-specific regulatory policy.

At the economy-wide level, India has made good progress in improving some aspects of product market regulation and a few low-level PMR indicators are on a par with best practice in the OECD area. Overall, however, despite considerable deregulation during the past 20 years, product market regulation remains much more restrictive than in typical OECD countries (Figure 1.13). In particular, the degree of public sector involvement in product markets remains high. For example, despite gaining in importance, the private sector still only accounts for slightly more than half of economic activity in the formal non-farm business sector. Compared with OECD countries, India has a higher level of public sector presence in product markets. Barriers to entrepreneurship are also higher, reflecting high administrative burdens on business start-ups which could also be indicative of more widespread transaction costs in government administration.

Experience in other countries suggests that reducing regulation and increasing competition enhances productivity growth by improving the efficiency of resource use and encouraging a stronger effort on the part of managers to improve efficiency (Nicoletti and Scarpetta, 2003), but efficiency does not come at the expense of lower employment. Greater product market competition has also been found to improve employment (Nicoletti and Scarpetta, 2005) and fixed investment (Alesina et al., 2003). The link between increased competition and productive performance is related to the stimulus that a competitive market gives to innovation and technological diffusion (Aghion et al., 2001 and Conway et al., 2006). These are potentially key sources of productivity growth in India and are likely to be improved by more liberal product market regulation.

Figure 1.13. **Product market regulations: An international comparison**

The indicator score runs from 0-6, representing the least to most restrictive

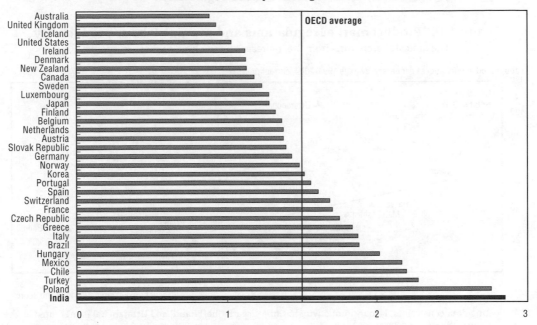

Source: OECD calculations.

... and are lower in some of the more successful states

As seen above, raising economic growth in poorer states in India is the key to reducing poverty, and so benchmarking the extent to which individual states have created an environment conducive to competition may throw light on how poorer states can improve their performance. States in India have direct responsibility for a number of areas of economic policy as well as shared responsibility with central government in other areas. Moreover, the implementation and administration of all laws is the responsibility of state governments. State government attitudes toward the role of the public sector in the economy and the efficiency with which they administer basic laws can therefore differ considerably. For example, delays in processing applications for establishing new businesses vary quite a lot across states and can impose large barriers to market entry. Cross-state differences in the regulatory environment may also be representative of the state governments' attitude towards economic efficiency that can also be seen in the way in which state-owned enterprises are operated, notably in the electricity sector, where economic performance also differs a lot between states.

On the basis of a detailed study of the policies of 21 states, it appears that there are significant differences in product market regulation across states that impact on economic performance. To assess the extent of these differences, the PMR indicators have been estimated for 21 Indian states, which cover 98 per cent of India's population and GDP. While these state-level indicators are not entirely directly comparable with the national indicators, they are comparable across states in areas where the influence of state policy on the regulatory environment may be important. Furthermore, these differences in the regulatory environment are found to have an important bearing on various aspects of economic performance at the state level. For example, states in which the regulatory environment is more conducive to competition have a higher level of labour productivity in comparison to the relatively more restrictive states (Figure 1.14).

Figure 1.14. **Product market regulations and average labour productivity**

The indicator score runs from 0-6, representing the least to most restrictive

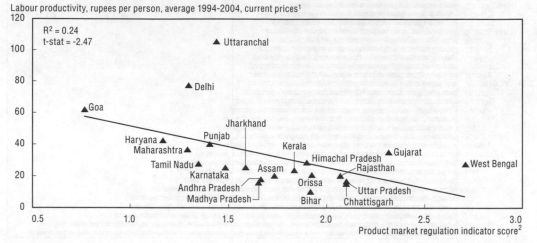

1. Reflecting data constraints, labour productivity in Chhattisgarh, Jharkhand, and Uttaranchal is measured as the average over the period 2002 to 2003.
2. The high-level PMR indicators for Indian states have been modified to better reflect the ways in which state governments influence the regulatory environment and are not directly comparable with the national indicators. (See Chapter 3 for details).

Source: OECD and Indian National Account Statistics.

Key challenges

Chapter 3 takes a close look at policy-induced restrictions on product market competition by comparing India's regulations with those in other countries and also across Indian states. It examines policies for improving the environment for business activity by focusing on the following questions:

● How can the extent of product market regulation be measured in India?

● What are the consequences of product market regulation for economic performance?

● What policy changes should be made in order to lower the degree of product market regulation?

● How can barriers to entrepreneurship and market entry be reduced?

● How can the reallocation of resources be improved by lowering barriers to closing enterprises?

● How can the performance of the public enterprises be improved?

Removing barriers to employment in the formal sector

Employment growth has mainly been in the informal sector

The acceleration of output growth since the introduction of reforms eventually increased employment growth. After stagnating in the mid-1990s, employment growth picked up in the six years to 2004 (Table 1.6). The ratio of employment to the total population has increased – both for men and women – with particularly high ratios for

Table 1.6. **Evolution of employment by type of job and employer**

	1990	1993	1995	1998	2000	2003	2004
	Millions, years beginning 1st April						
Total employment	340.5	371.9	377.7	378.4	410.1	442.3	454.3
	% of total employment						
Whole economy							
Self-employment	54.1	54.6	54.5	51.0	54.4	55.2	56.3
Casual employment	29.9	32.1	32.0	35.6	30.6	29.6	28.6
Regular employment	16.0	13.3	13.6	13.4	15.0	15.2	15.1
Organised sector	7.9	7.3	7.4	7.4	6.8	6.0	n.a.
Public sector[1]	2.7	2.5	2.5	2.6	2.4	2.1	n.a.
Public enterprises	2.9	2.7	2.6	2.5	2.3	2.0	n.a.
Private companies[2]	2.3	2.1	2.3	2.3	2.1	1.9	n.a.
Other private enterprises	8.1	6.0	6.2	6.0	8.2	9.2	n.a.

1. One administration, community service sectors.
2. Employing more than ten people.
Source: NSS, Ministry of Labour and Employment and OECD estimates.

men (around 97% between age 30 and 59) but much lower rates for women, especially in urban areas.

The Indian labour market is, however, characterised by a high degree of informality. People with regular employment contracts account for only 15% of total employment and most of these are concentrated in urban areas. Total regular employment fell during most of the 1990s but started to grow after 1998. Since then there has been a marked increase in regular employment outside the "organised" sector of the economy. This sector broadly includes all companies except in the manufacturing sector, where only firms employing more than 10 people, or 20 people if no electrical machinery is used, are counted. Based on the National Sample Survey data, regular employment outside the organised sector almost doubled between 1998 and 2004, rising from 6% to over 9% of total employment.

The increasing supply of people looking for regular employment has resulted in the real wages of such employees falling between 1999 and 2004, with the exception of graduates in urban areas. In larger enterprises, real wages have risen slightly in the same period, but by much less than the growth in productivity. As a result, there has been a considerable increase in the share of profits in total national income. Self-employment is the predominant employment status in both urban and rural areas, with casual labour by far outweighing regular employment in rural areas.

According to one measure, which only counts people as unemployed if they have not worked for a week, the rate of unemployment was low in the period July 2004 to June 2005, averaging 4.7% for the country as whole for people aged between 15 and 59. Information for the two years to 2007 is not available as there is no timely national labour force survey.[4] Moreover, much of this unemployment is a consequence of initial job search on entering the labour force: The unemployment rate is only 2.3% for those who have had at least one job. There are, however, other definitions of unemployment used in India that give a wide range of unemployment rates, especially when the extent of casual work is considered. The broadest definition of unemployment counts the shortfall in hours worked relative to the desired work week as unemployment, and shows an unemployment rate of nearly 8%.

The bulk of the growth in employment has been created in very small enterprises. There is much evidence that the main reason for the lack of job creation in larger firms in the "organised" or formal part of the private sector is the restrictive legislation governing regular employment in larger firms. Larger firms in this sector have markedly increased the capital intensity of their production techniques. Rigid labour legislation makes it extremely difficult for firms to lay-off workers, and even changing job descriptions can be problematic.

The extent of the regulatory intervention can be judged by estimating the standard OECD indicator of employment protection legislation, which shows that employment protection legislation is more restrictive in India than in all but two OECD countries and is also markedly more restrictive than in Brazil, Chile and China (Figure 1.15). There are variations in employment protection legislation across Indian states and – as shown in Chapter 4 – this affects job creation and destruction. The empirical evidence on whether employment legislation affects the total level of employment is mixed in the OECD area, but there is much evidence that restrictive labour market regulations lead to dual labour markets and prevent the upgrading of workers from irregular to regular jobs (OECD, 2006a).

Figure 1.15. **An international comparison of employment protection legislation**

Regular employment (restrictions on indefinite contracts)

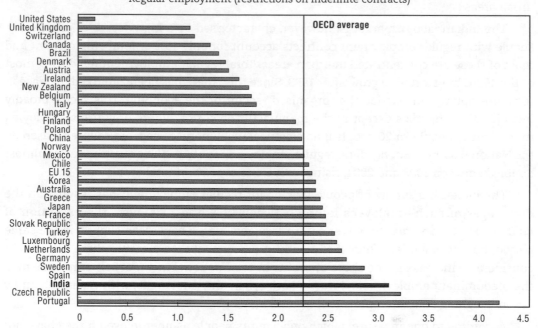

Source: India: OECD computation; OECD (2007), *Going for Growth*; OECD (2006b), *Economic Survey of Brazil*; China: OECD estimate.

Key challenges

The lack of formal sector employment reduces productivity growth as most new jobs are created in the informal sector, where productivity is much lower. The second part of Chapter 4 examines labour market policies in India and compares India's employment protection legislation with those in OECD countries and also across Indian states, focusing on the following questions:

● What has been the impact of labour legislation on the job market?

- How do labour laws and their implementing regulations differ across states?
- What has been the impact of differences across states in government regulation of labour markets on employment?
- What strategies could be implemented to rebalance labour laws while considering social objectives?

Improving the efficiency of the financial system

An efficient financial system is a key requirement for allocating capital to its most efficient use. In India, there are five major constituents of the money and capital markets: banks, insurance companies, pension funds, mutual funds and stock exchanges. These institutions have in the past been largely government-owned (with the exception of the stock markets). While private and foreign institutions have been allowed into the market, and minority stakes in some public sector banks have also been allowed, three of these four groups remain dominated by government-owned institutions, with only the mutual fund industry dominated by private sector companies.

In contrast to the goods sector of the economy, the government continues to exert considerable control over banking sector operations as well as holding majority shareholdings in most banks. The banks are obliged to provide 40% of their loans to priority areas defined by the government and must lend 25% of their assets to the government to comply with the statutory liquidity ratio requirement. New banks are required to have one-quarter of their branches in rural areas, and all banks are required to obtain central bank approval for the opening of new branches and off-site cash dispensers. Publicly owned banks have been allowed to sell minority shareholding to the public, subject to the overall shareholding of the government not falling below 51%, but the voting rights of private shareholders in banks are limited. The private shareholding in state-owned banks currently averages 36%, when weighted by operating profits, so that the government's role in the banking sector remains large in international comparison (Figure 1.16). Moreover,

Figure 1.16. The share of public sector banks in the assets of all banks

Per cent, 2002

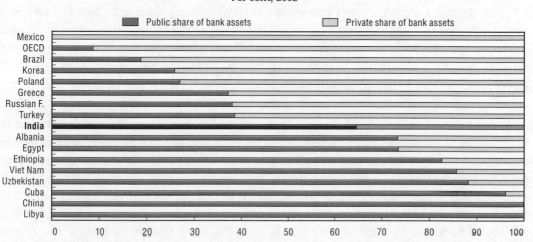

Note: The chart shows all countries with a larger share of public banks than India and selected countries with a lower share. The data only covers banks in the Bankscope database, Bureau van Dijk Electronic Publishing.

Source: Micco, Panizza and Yanez (2004).

until 2007, a majority of the shares in the largest publicly owned bank were owned by the central bank, though this shareholding will be sold to the Ministry of Finance in 2007. Overall, the expansion of the private sector has been quite limited: privately owned banks accounted for only 25% of banking assets by 2006, in part because regulations restrict the ability of foreign banks to invest in India.

International evidence has been that high state-ownership of banks tends to depress financial development, the more so if the initial level of financial development is low (de Serres *et al.*, 2006). Moreover, there is evidence that economic growth is lowered by a higher share of publicly owned banks (la Porta *et al.*, 2002) with evidence that the negative impact on economic growth is stronger for countries with relatively low financial depth such as India (Yeyati *et al.*, 2004). On the basis of one cross-country study (*op. cit.*), a reduction in the share of public bank assets in total assets to the same share as in Brazil might raise economic growth by 0.7 percentage points annually.

Key challenges

Chapter 5 looks at the financial sector and considers the evidence for the performance of the banking sector and the extent of regulation in the remainder of the financial system, notably for the insurance and pension fund sectors. Key questions addressed in the chapter are:

- How could the performance of the financial sector be improved?
- How can the governance of public sector banks be improved?
- How can capital markets be broadened?
- Could increased foreign ownership of financial institutions improve performance?

Orienting public finances to achieve more rapid growth

Lowering the use of national savings for government consumption

As mentioned above, in India government saving (net of depreciation) has been persistently negative since the early 1980s implying a significant use of private savings to finance current government spending. Net dissavings of general government peaked in FY 2001 (Figure 1.17). The government was then absorbing almost half of the nation's saving in order to finance its own consumption outlays. In addition, the government was borrowing to finance its investment, capital transfers and loans to state-owned enterprises. As a result, the borrowing requirement (fiscal deficit) of state and local governments had reached nearly 10% of GDP by 2001 and public debt was rising significantly.

To end this unsustainable situation, the central government enacted legislation to improve fiscal discipline. After close to three years of discussion, the Fiscal Responsibility and Budget Management Act (FRBM) was adopted in August 2003. This Act sets a medium-term target of achieving a balance between current revenue and current spending (*i.e.* a zero-revenue deficit) and limits the overall fiscal deficit for central government to 3% of GDP. By 2006, the revenue deficit had only been reduced to 2% of GDP, but the fiscal deficit had been reduced to 3.7% of GDP (Table 1.7). The 2007 budget confirms the faster adjustment of the fiscal deficit, which is only slightly greater than the target for 2008 incorporated in the FRBM Act. However, the current deficit is expected to be 1.5% of GDP, indicating that a very sharp reduction would be necessary to meet the target of the FRBM for this balance. In effect, the central government has not been able to stem the increase in

Figure 1.17. **India's national net savings rate and its components**

Per cent of GDP at market prices

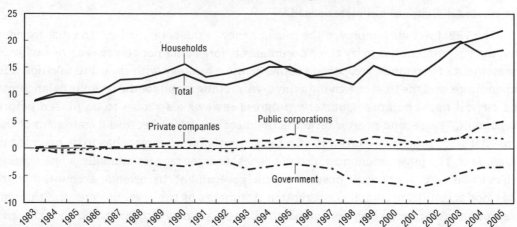

Source: Central Statistical Organisation, National Account Statistics.

Table 1.7. **Government budget balances**

Per cent of GDP at market prices, fiscal years starting 1st April

	2001	2002	2003	2004	2005	2006	2007
General government accounts							
Revenue	16.3	17.0	18.1	18.4	19.0	..	..
Expenditure	23.5	23.2	22.8	21.9	22.5	..	..
Net saving	−7.2	−6.3	−4.6	−3.6	−3.5	..	..
Net capital formation							
Administrative units	1.8	1.8	1.6	1.7	2.4	..	..
Departmental enterprises	0.1	0	0	0	0.2	..	..
Net capital transfers and other	0.7	0.8	0.7	0.5	0.5	..	..
Total above	2.6	2.6	2.3	2.3	3.1	..	..
General government balance	−9.7	−8.9	−6.9	−5.7	−6.6	..	..
Budgetary accounts							
Current balance							
Central	−4.4	−4.4	−3.6	−2.5	−2.6	−2.0	−1.5
State	−2.6	−2.2	−2.2	−1.2	−0.5	0.0	..
Central + State	−7.0	−6.7	−5.8	−3.9	−3.1	−2.1	..
Financial balance (excludes net lending)							
Central	−5.7	−5.8	−4.8	−4.2	−4.1	−3.6	−3.1
State	−4.0	−3.7	−4.1	−3.1	−2.9	−2.5	..
Central + State	−9.7	−9.5	−9.0	−7.7	−7.0	−6.1	..
Fiscal deficit							
Central	−6.2	−5.9	−4.5	−4.0	−4.1	−3.7	−3.3
State	−4.2	−4.2	−4.5	−3.5	−3.2	−2.6	..
Central + State[1]	−9.9	−9.6	−8.5	−7.5	−7.4	−6.3	..

1. The combined fiscal deficit of state and central governments is not the sum of their respective deficits as the two levels of government follow different accounting principles. Central government counts repayment of loans by state governments as part of capital income. On the other hand, state governments do not count as capital expenditure, repayments of loans from central government. The discrepancy has to be allowed for when consolidating the two deficits. In addition, state governments express their deficits relative to state GDP. The sum of the estimates of state GDP exceeds national GDP which is another reason why the aggregate deficits when expressed as a share of GDP is not the sum of the two individual deficits for central and state governments expressed as shares of national and state GDP, respectively.

Source: Reserve Bank of India, State Finances, Ministry of Finance, Public Finance Statistics, Economic Survey and Budget Documents, Central Statistical Organisation, National Accounts Statistics.

current expenditure as much as had been planned and, consequently, the hoped-for increase in the extent of investment, which would have raised the fiscal deficit relative to the current deficit, has not materialised.

The FRBM Act also improved the transparency of budgetary policy. The Act provides that the government has to lay three documents before Parliament every year: one with an assessment of economic prospects, another with its strategy with regard to taxation and expenditure, and the final one giving a three-year rolling target for the revenue balance and the overall fiscal balance. Quarterly progress reviews also have to be placed before Parliament. The second quarter review is the most important because a statement of the remedial steps that will be taken to offset any shortfall from targets has to be provided to Parliament. The government now also publishes its asset register annually, so permitting the calculation of a net asset position for the government. Its revenue account, though, does not account for capital consumption. Estimates of the revenue foregone through exemptions and concessions from standard tax rates are now also published annually, and the central government has made a first step towards accrual accounting by publishing the outstanding amounts of tax and non-tax revenue.

During 2005, 23 state governments introduced similar legislation and, by the middle of 2006, only three states – West Bengal, Sikkim and Jharkhand – had not introduced such laws, mandating a fiscal deficit of 3% of state GDP. To some extent, this move reflected the incentivisation process of the Finance Commission, a body established by the Constitution to advise on the sharing of tax revenues between the centre and the states. Standardised and rapid accounting procedures are still lacking at the state level and are almost non-existent at the municipal level with most local authorities not even using a double-entry accounting system.

States have reduced their fiscal deficits at a quicker pace than the central government in reaction to the more severe financial pressures that they faced at the beginning of this decade. These pressures were the result of a failure to adjust other expenditures after large centrally determined pay and pension increases at the end of the 1990s. With increased outlays funded from borrowing that amounted to nearly 40% of income, outlays on wages, pensions and interest increased to almost 70% of current revenues on average in the period 2000-03. The process of consolidation started in 2004 and has continued since then with the states planning to almost eliminate (on average) their revenue deficit in 2006 and reduce their fiscal deficit of 2½ per cent of GDP (Table 1.7). The increases in the states' own tax revenues has been helped by a significant increase in transfers from central government which came in the form of higher shared taxes, increased grants and write-offs of interest due to the central government.

The process of consolidation is, however, far from uniform across the states. In 2005, the remaining revenue deficit of the states was concentrated in just four states (Jharkhand, Kerala, Uttaranchal and West Bengal) where the fiscal deficit still amounted to between 35% and 60% of state government revenues, with similarly large revenue deficits for three of them. Indeed, these four states accounted for the whole of the revenue deficits of states – small deficits elsewhere were offset by surpluses in a number of states. As a result, debt levels of these four states continued to increase, rising from 37 to 47% of state GDP between 2000 and 2005 – a particularly high burden given that their total revenue from taxation and transfers from central government amounted to just 14% of their GDP.

The current FRBM targets run until fiscal year 2008 and have provided a marked check to the growth of public debt. The combined fiscal deficit of state and local governments has fallen to 6.3% of national GDP and should reach 5.7% of national GDP in fiscal year 2008, if deficit targets are met, slightly less than might be thought given that the both levels of government are aiming for a 3% deficit (see footnote one of Table 1.7 for an explanation of the differences). The combined liabilities of the states and central government have fallen from a peak of 82% of GDP in 2004 to 76% in 2006 and are likely to fall a further 6 percentage points by 2008. Assuming medium-term annual growth of nominal GDP of around 13% and interest rates of no more than 8%, then current fiscal targets would result in a further gradual decline of the debt to GDP ratio (Figure 1.18). While a gradual decline in the debt to GDP ratio indicates a sustainable fiscal position, the general government's balance sheet reveals a further deterioration of the government's net asset position as government borrowing continues to exceed the level of net capital formation. Currently, net capital formation by the general government sector (including departmental enterprises such as the post office and state road transport agencies) amounts to 2½ per cent of GDP, with a further small and declining amount of capital transfers. Part of these transfers represent infusions of capital to loss-making enterprises. They should be considered as a form of subsidy rather than capital formation. Consequently, if governments wished to restrict their borrowing to a level that covered net investment, a fiscal deficit of no more than 3% (at current levels of investment) for both levels of government, rather than the current 6% deficit, would be needed. This would ensure that government debt returns to the level of the mid-1990s by 2013 (Figure 1.18).

Figure 1.18. **Government debt**

Past development and scenarios on the assumptions that the combined fiscal deficit is maintained at 6%, or alternatively, reduced to 3% of GDP by 2013

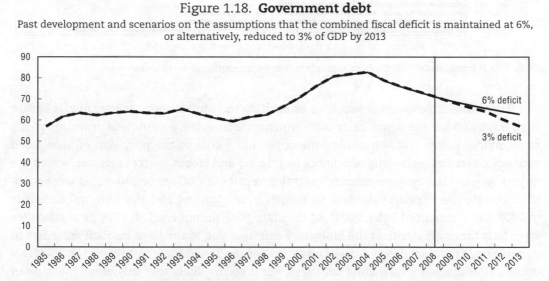

Source: Reserve Bank of India, various national sources and OECD projections.

Reorienting public expenditure to favour growth

Achieving the government's higher growth target requires greater investment. In part, that could be achieved by holding the growth of expenditure below that of revenue and thereby increasing saving and investment. However, some restructuring of public expenditure might also be possible. All levels of government have devoted a significant amount of resources to subsidising economic activities. Measuring the extent of subsidies is complicated. One approach to measuring subsidies is to use the definition of national accounts, which is similar to that used in the budget. With this definition, subsidies paid by all three levels of government amounted to 3.1% of GDP in FY 2003, markedly higher than most OECD countries and about seven times higher than in China and Brazil (Figure 1.19).

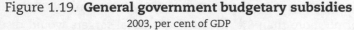

Figure 1.19. **General government budgetary subsidies**

2003, per cent of GDP

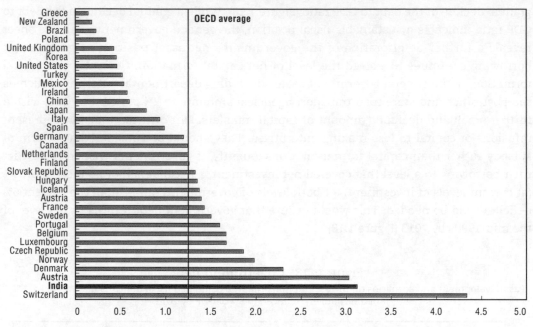

Source: OECD Economic Outlook database, Central Statistical Organisation and national sources.

These direct measures of subsidies understate their full amount as they only measure cash flows and not the opportunity costs which arise from the government providing goods and services below cost. Estimating the opportunity cost of the provision of subsidised economic services (excluding education, healthcare and labour market services, which are generally provided by government), central government outlays on subsidies were more than double the explicit subsidies measured in the budget and the national accounts in 2003 (Government of India, 2004). At the state government level, in 1998 total subsidies were four times greater than the budgetary estimate due to the large implicit subsidies to agriculture, irrigation, power, water and sanitation, and road transport (Rao, *et al.* 2003). No update is available for total state subsidies, but it seems likely that this broad measure of total subsidies for both state and central government exceeded 8% of GDP in 2003. In addition to subsidies, there are considerable cross-subsidies in India. These occur in many of the sectors where the state is a monopoly provider. Examples are electricity, railway transport, kerosene, road passenger transport and telephone calls. In total these cross-subsidies amounted to 2.3% of GDP in 1999 (Ahluwalia, 2000).

Further reducing tax distortions

India has made much progress in modernizing its tax system. First attempts to rationalize the tax system were made in the second half of the 1980s, but more fundamental tax reforms were implemented in the early 1990s as part of the market-oriented structural reforms. These reforms reduced tax distortions by cutting the very high marginal income and corporate tax rates. At the same time, and as part of trade liberalisation, import tariffs were significantly reduced and the system of excises was rationalized with the introduction of a central government value added tax for the production of goods. The latest major reform was the transformation of the state sales tax into a value added tax in April 2005. A further reform is planned for 2010 with the introduction of a nationwide Goods and Services Tax (GST).

Tax reforms over the past 15 years have made a major contribution to the improvement in India's economic performance. Nonetheless, there is still scope for further improvements. India's tax system continues to be riddled with many loopholes and exemptions, which create distortions and increase complexity. Furthermore, trade of goods within India is hampered by physical controls at state borders to prevent fraud in states' VAT.

Fiscal relations between levels of government

Within the federal structure of government, significant imbalances between the constitutional responsibilities for expenditure and the distribution of the powers of taxation are resolved by large transfers from central government to the states. These transfers result in the overall level of devolution to state, in terms of tax revenue, being at the high end of the experience of OECD federal countries. As well as dealing with the vertical imbalances, the transfers also attempt to deal with the extreme differences in income levels between states that make it difficult to provide a similar level of basic public services across the union. The transfers to states come from three sources: a constitutional body (the Finance Commission), the Planning Commission and through various central government programmes. The flows through the first two channels are largely formula driven, though it is noticeable that the first is markedly more redistributive than the second. Moreover, the second channel involves a high degree of micro-management of the uses to which the transfers are put, whereas the first essentially gives freedom to the states to use funds according to their own priorities. Increasingly, the third channel (transfers from ministries) is being used to influence state behaviour in areas that are not, constitutionally, within the sole competence of the central government.

Overall, two areas stand out from the current fiscal relations between the centre and the states: the difficulty of ensuring an adequate level of public services in the poorest states given their size and low relative income level and the difficulty of limiting the extent of state-level borrowing. To date, despite its constitutional powers, the centre has not exercised such control; rather it has encouraged borrowing through requirements to match grants with borrowing and through debt write-offs. As discussed above, central government policy has now changed and the move to market control of state borrowing is now underway.

The extent of devolution to the third tier of government is as yet underdeveloped relative to that seen in OECD countries. Although local government has existed in many urban areas for several centuries, the Constitution only recognised devolution to local bodies in 1992. Local authorities are extremely underfunded with the resultant under-provision of local services. Their total tax and grant income is only one-third that of local governments in OECD federal countries, despite the much larger average size of states in India. State governments continue to control local bodies by appointing key personnel and because of the very limited span for which elected heads of local governments remain in power. Moreover, the State Finance Commissions (that determine the extent of revenue sharing between states and their local bodies) are often not as well-staffed or competent as the Central Finance Commission. In general, states have been unwilling to share their principal revenue stream (sales tax in the past and VAT now) with local authorities, while the latter have been unwilling to develop local property taxes as a source of revenue.

Key challenges

Chapter 6 examines how public finances could be changed to durably improve economic growth and public service provision by focusing on the following issues:

- How should public expenditure be reformed to improve growth?
- How can the tax system be reformed to make the system more neutral for indirect taxes, tariffs, income tax and corporate tax?
- What are the challenges related to the fiscal relationships between the central, state and local governments?

Improving infrastructure

Macro-consequences of infrastructure

As a result of rapid economic growth, there is a high and rapidly growing demand for infrastructure services across a range of sectors. On the supply side, although capital formation by the private sector has been growing relatively strongly, the public sector capital stock has been growing at half the pace of the capital stock in the private sector (Figure 1.20). Moreover, its growth has been less than half the growth rate of GDP growth. As a result, access to infrastructure is extremely low by world standards, and bottlenecks in public infrastructure could become a major obstacle for future growth. At the state level,

Figure 1.20. **Growth of capital stock by institutional sector**

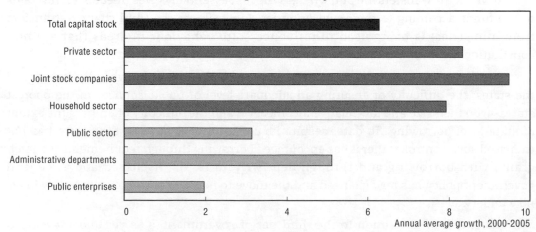

Source: Central Statistical Organisation, National Accounts Statistics.

an unequal distribution of infrastructure is an important reason why state performance has been diverging since the 1990s (Majumder, 2005 and Purfield, 2006).

If growth in the capital stock in public utilities is to match that seen in other fast growing Asian countries, additional annual investment of 1.7% of GDP would be required. Roads are the other major bottleneck area. In China, road investment rose from 0.3% of GDP in 1991 to 3.1% of GDP by 2002 (Harral, 2006). Currently, investment in roads in India is of the order of 0.4% of GDP, so an increase in outlays of the order of 2.7% of GDP would be necessary to match the growth of the Chinese road network. Just in these two areas, increased investment of 4½ per cent of GDP (USD 40 billion annually) would be needed to match the effort of fast growing Asian countries. With such an investment rate, the public sector capital stock would be growing slightly faster than that of the private sector and could add just over 1% to growth, if returns matched those in the private sector.

As well as being in short supply, India's infrastructure is often not very productive except when provided by the private sector. Private sector operators in the wireless phone market have transformed the availability of telephone communications in a few years. Relatively productive private sector operators are also making rapid inroads into the civil aviation market, and the productivity at some of India's ports has improved over recent years (albeit from a low base) as private contractors have been permitted to run port facilities. The government-run international airports at Delhi and Mumbai typically handle only 25 to 28 flights per runway per hour in comparison to 40 in a number of OECD countries (Bindra, 2006), while India's rail network is also much less efficient than China's. Agreement has been reached for airport reconstruction in Delhi and Mumbai to start through a public-private partnership.

Given fiscal constraints, the government is turning increasingly to private sector participation in infrastructure provision. It has instituted a Viability Gap Fund and the India Infrastructure Finance Company to provide partial grants and funding respectively for the private-sector in infrastructure projects. It is also trying to improve the regulatory framework and improve the governance of independent regulators in infrastructure sectors. However, unless the supply of savings is raised, a greater private sector involvement in infrastructure investment may crowd out other private sector capital formation, and so it is essential that involving the private sector is not used to bypass the fiscal constraints imposed by the FRBM legislation, but rather where there is clear evidence of greater efficiency of private sector operators.

Improving specific infrastructure sectors

Electricity

Notwithstanding the launch of a major new investment programme, the rate of capital formation in India's electricity sector has been low in comparison to other emerging Asian countries and the coverage of the power network and quality of electricity supplied are poor. This imposes high costs on the economy, particularly electricity-intensive sectors such as manufacturing, through the need for high-cost backup generators and investment in self-generation facilities for larger users. The government has launched a "Power for All" programme that is due for completion by 2012. This programme is aimed at increasing capacity by just under 6% annually, for a total addition to capacity of 47 GW with total investment commitment of about USD 44 billion (slightly less than 1% of GDP per year) against a capacity expansion of just over 3% annually in the previous five years. Moreover, plants representing a further 40 GW (a further 22% expansion) are in the pipeline for placement of orders. This represents the second largest planned capacity addition world wide.

The weakness of public sector investment in electricity reflects the inability of the state electricity companies and boards to operate profitably given the governance structure of the industry. However, new regulatory agencies, with the necessary policy framework, are starting to ensure that tariffs are set on commercial principles, independent of political interference. The objective of the state companies has, in most cases, been to extend the coverage of the electricity network to rural villages, even though they have been in most cases unable to provide a regular power supply to the resulting network. Basic low-level investment in distribution systems has been neglected and electricity theft has been widespread. Aggregate technical and commercial losses of electricity from the system have been extremely high and have only fallen from 39% to 35% in the past five years. In its "Power for All" programme, the government has set a target of reducing these losses to 20% by 2012. For consumers, prices have typically been held below cost or electricity is provided without a meter. Three states, namely, Punjab, Andhra Pradesh and Tamil Nadu, are giving free power to the farmers. In other states, farmers are being charged subsidised tariffs. Overall, gross subsidies to agricultural and domestic consumers have been falling slightly this decade, from 1½ per cent of GDP to just under 1¼ per cent by 2005 (Table 1.8). Direct subsidies from the state government budgets amount to 0.4% of GDP, with the remainder coming from excess payments by industrial and commercial customers and enterprise losses. In addition, even if the electricity industry did not make losses, there would still be an opportunity cost stemming from its poor rate of return on assets, which is almost 6 percentage points below the cost of capital in the private sector.

Table 1.8. **Subsidies in the electricity industry**

Per cent of GDP, fiscal years

	1991	2000	2001	2002	2003	2004	2005
Subsidies received							
Subsidy to agricultural consumers	1.21	1.14	1.05	0.89	0.85	0.81	0.70
Subsidy to domestic consumers	0.27	0.47	0.45	0.35	0.32	0.33	0.29
Subsidy on interstate sales	0.04	0.02	0.01	0.01	0.03	0.02	0.01
Gross subsidy	1.51	1.63	1.52	1.25	1.20	1.16	1.00
Finance of subsidies							
Subventions received from state	0.42	0.42	0.38	0.53	0.40	0.34	0.37
Excess payments by other sectors	0.44	0.16	0.16	0.20	0.22	0.20	0.23
Enterprise losses	0.66	1.05	0.97	0.52	0.58	0.62	0.60
Total	1.51	1.63	1.52	1.25	1.20	1.16	1.20
Memorandum							
Opportunity cost of capital	n.a.	1.18	1.27	1.29	1.32	1.30	n.a.

1. The opportunity cost of capital is defined as the difference between the cost of capital in the private sector and the pre-interest operating rate of return in the public utility industries.
Source: Reserve Bank of India; State Finances; OECD calculations.

All this uncompensated subsidisation results in lower revenues for the state government electricity companies and reduces their ability to invest and increase supply. State electricity companies generally produce well below optimal levels of production, given their existing resources, with one study of Uttar Pradesh finding that better organisation alone could raise production by one-third (IIB, 2005). The combined losses of the state electricity boards are around 0.6% of GDP.

Three key policy initiatives are beginning to have a positive impact on the electricity sector. First, states were obliged to settle all debts for electricity purchased from the central government generator by issuing power bonds. The government then sold a stake in this company to the private sector. Second, the Electricity Act (2003) sets out a policy framework for addressing issues in distribution and creating a competitive electricity market that is conducive to private sector involvement. In addition, it is beginning to create a favourable environment for private sector generation and will also reduce the scope for overcharging industry for electricity supply. Finally, the Accelerated Power Development and Reform Programme uses financial incentives to encourage reform of the distribution sector at the state level. States that have been more successful in implementing the Electricity Act have had some success in reducing the extent of the aggregate technical and commercial loss of the system, which is an important and necessary step for making the sector more attractive for private sector investment. However, only the states of Orissa and Delhi have privatised distribution.

Roads

Until recently, investment in roads in India has been extremely low. In 1998, however, the government launched the National Highway Development Project (NHDP) in order to substantially upgrade the interurban road network and the connectivity of ports. The first stage of this programme was substantially completed at the end of 2006, linking four cities (Delhi, Mumbai, Kolkata and Chennai) in a dual-carriageway system nearly 6 000 km long, representing a density of 1.8 kilometres per 1 000 square kilometres. This density is still only 60% of that in Turkey and Mexico and, moreover, the Indian roads are not built to motorway standard (Table 1.9). The overall road density in India is higher than in most developing countries due to the emphasis on constructing unpaved village roads. Even including other expressways that have been opened, the overall investment level in better

Table 1.9. **An international comparison of road infrastructure**

	Year of comparison	Road density		
		Expressways	Paved roads	Total roads
		Kilometres per 1 000 square kilometres		
Germany	2003	33.7	650	650
Korea	2003	28.2	753	980
Italy	2003	22.0	1 590	1 590
France	2003	19.0	1 620	1 620
Japan	2002	18.3	2 424	3 120
United Kingdom	1999	14.2	2 550	2 550
United States	2001	9.3	388	660
Average of above high-income countries		20.7	1 425	1 596
Mexico	2003	3.5	60	180
China	2003	3.1	151	190
Turkey	2003	2.4	191	460
India	2003	negligible	732	1 170
Malaysia	2001	0	171	220
Russian Federation	2000	0	20	30

Source: International Road Federation.

quality roads has been modest (1 060 km per year), against an expansion rate of 4 800 km per year in China between 2001 and 2005. Outlays for road building amount to only 0.4% of GDP annually.

The next phases of the NHDP involve a significant increase in investment in highway completion. Public funds are unable to finance such an ambitious expansion programme, and the government plans to fund all subsequent investment in highways on a PPP basis. A number of state governments are also funding roads in this way. The early indications are that PPPs are working reasonably well in the roads sector and are a significant improvement on the previous policy of 100% government funding via construction contracts and self-provision. The early experience with toll collection has generally been positive and some recent bids from private partners for viability gap funding have been negative, implying that they are prepared to pay for the right to collect tolls on some sections of highway, reflecting expectations of high traffic flow. The right to collect toll is applicable for all "build-operate-transfer" projects.

Urbanisation as a key to growth

The development of urban areas has lagged well behind developments in comparable countries (Figure 1.21). As a result, the level of urbanisation in India is well below that in other countries with similar income levels. Such a development is significant in that productivity levels are much higher in urban areas (one-quarter of the population produces 60% of output). In addition, 90% of tax revenues are also generated in urban areas.

Figure 1.21. **Urbanisation and GDP per capita**
Urban population as per cent of total population

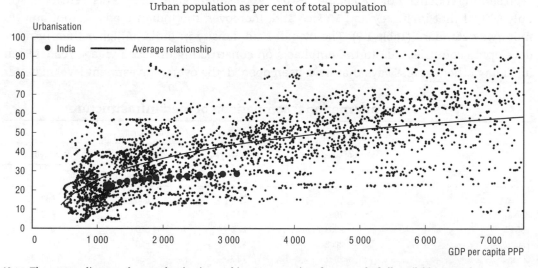

Note: The scatter diagram shows urbanisation and income over time for a panel of all available countries.
Source: World Bank World Development Indicators.

The development of urban areas has been neglected in part because of the political structure of the country. As discussed above, the Constitution did not formally recognise the existence of levels of local government below that of the state prior to the constitutional amendment of 1992. That amendment required states to establish locally elected bodies and specified the area of competencies for local authorities. However, it established no point in time by which such authorities were to be established nor did it specify the funding mechanism for the local authorities.

Key local activities have been retained in state-run boards and authorities with little or no local input. Local finances suffer from being dependent on transfers from state government rather than having independent sources of finance. Local entry tariffs at one time generated most municipal revenue but with their abolition in all but two states, cities have become even more dependent on transfers from states. Property taxes are not used as a significant source of revenue, in part because of the poor state of property registers. Strict land development and rental controls that exist in many cities restrict the most efficient use of land. Land assembly is also held back by the difficulty in establishing title.

Recognising the key role of local governments, the central government established a new initiative in 2005 to induce states to strengthen their urban local governments (although less has been done in rural areas). This should help with their capacity to provide education and other public services. The program, the Jawaharlal Nehru National Urban Renewal Mission (NURM), offers conditional transfers of resources based on a memorandum of understanding by states that requires them to implement wide-ranging reforms to strengthen local self-governance, with a particular focus on strengthening land markets, whose reform has the potential to not only stimulate urban development but also to give localities a more solid revenue base (see Chapter 6, and Mohan and Dasgupta, 2004).

The focus on land development recognises a longstanding problem, as strong restrictions on land use exist in many cities, and poor quality of land title records limits property markets. The NURM incentives focus on several areas, including reducing the land transfer tax to below 5%, repealing land ceiling laws, easing building requirements and reducing rent control acts – which is much needed as rent control acts have been exceedingly difficult to revise, with a major effort by New Delhi in 1995 never notified. A number of major reforms have already taken place, such as a reduction of stamp duty in West Bengal from 10% to 6% and a repeal of the land ceiling act in Maharashtra (including Mumbai). The Ministry of Urban Development is also providing technical assistance in targeted areas such as property records through the computerization of land title and use of geographic information systems, with a goal of doubling property tax compliance from less than 40% in the next five years.

State run boards have proved to be inadequate suppliers of local services with water and sanitation boards generally being very inefficient. Labour productivity is about five times lower than in the best-managed Asian cities such as Singapore and Bangkok (Table 1.10; Mckenzie and Ray, 2005). Water supply is intermittent and poor in quality. One

Table 1.10. **Selected indicators of efficiency in the water supply industry in Asia**

	Bangalore	Kolkata	Chennai	Delhi	Mumbai	Bangkok	Beijing	Asia Pacific average
Hours per day of water	4	9	4	4	5	24	24	19
Unaccounted water (%)	39	35	20	26	18	38	8	35
Metering	100	5	5	73	67	100	100	83
Staff per 1 000 connections	8	14	26	21	33	5	27	12
Operating cost recovery	95	15	106	68	93	112	77	95
Accounts receivable, months	n.a.	1.5	5.8	4.5	19.7	2	0.1	4

Source: McKenzie and Ray (2004).

government report found that staff in charge of disinfecting water had little knowledge of the underlying processes involved (Sukthankar, 2001), with the result that bacteriological infection of domestic water supplies was widespread. This same report indicated that 10% of urban water samples in Maharashtra were contaminated by bacteria (typically *e.coli* of faecal origin), rising to 14% in Mumbai. Even worse findings have been reported from Jaipur and Kolkata.

The water boards also have poor records in financing their activities, which necessarily holds back investment. Metering is not widespread and, in many cases, meters are not adequately maintained. Even when meters exist, billing is problematic and there is little enforcement of payment (Table 1.10). In Mumbai, outstanding water bills amounted to almost two years of revenue. Even if bills were collected, water tariffs are set in an inefficient manner. Most boards use an increasing block tariff, with the idea that a basic water supply is provided at a low price and then larger users (presumed to be well-off) are charged a higher price. The limits for the "basic block" are generally much higher than basic needs with the result that around 70% of consumers in Hyderabad and Bangalore consume in the basic block. With low metering, low productivity and poor collection of bills, few major cities even cover operating costs. Across the country, subsidies to urban water supply are estimated to cost 0.5% of GDP (Foster *et al.*, 2003).

The growth of urban areas is also held back by both inefficient land and rental markets. In the land market, most state governments charge high transfer taxes when land and buildings change ownership, so making the market illiquid. All states have rent control acts in force that strictly limit rent levels, allowing little increase in the initial nominal rental rate. As result, the private rental market has declined. A number of states have controls over the extent of ownership of land, in some cases limiting the holding of vacant land in urban areas to 500 square metres. Land title can also be difficult to establish as the land registry is poorly organised and not computerised in most states. Low rental levels also help lower property taxes as the building is generally assessed on a value basis that takes into account whether there is a rent-controlled tenant. Land development plans were developed many decades ago with little regard for the evolution of the urban economy in intervening periods. Finally, one of the few licensing restrictions that remain on new investment is location control. There is a ban on new industrial development within 25 kilometres of the outer limit of cities with over one million habitants in order to preserve the environment.

The central government is trying to give an incentive to state governments to change a large number of these policies by offering grants for urban improvement if state governments are willing to change laws. States have signed memorandums of agreement with the centre, but it remains to be seen whether the money offered by the centre will be sufficient to change state-level policies.

Air pollution

Urban development since the 1990s has not been associated with increased air pollution; rather various policies have lowered its extent, but it remains critically high. Most air pollution in large Indian cities comes from particles; other sources (sulphur dioxide and nitrogen oxides) are of lesser concern. In southern cities, concentrations of these particles have been falling and were close to the national air quality standards. In northern cities, concentrations have also fallen but are well above national standards, and these cities account for 80% of the monitored towns where concentrations are worse than air quality standard for residential areas. Small particles cause the most damage to health and, in India, come from a number of sources, including vehicles, road dust and biofuels. A wide range of policies is thus needed to combat pollution. These policies need to vary according to the climate, with northern cities being more vulnerable to winter-time pollution from residential and commercial space-heating. Policies to discourage the use of solid fuels, especially biofuels, for heating may be needed. State governments are moving to enforce legislation following Supreme Court judgements requiring them to respect their constitutional duty to protect the environment. This led Delhi to convert its public transport fleet to run on compressed natural gas.

Key challenges

Chapter 7 reviews India's infrastructure sectors, broadly focusing on the following questions:

● How can the regulation of infrastructure sectors be improved so as to encourage private sector participation and what is the role of India's independent regulators?

● What are the main benefits of PPPs in the provision of infrastructure services and how can they be used to increase infrastructure efficiency and lower the revenue risks borne by government?

Improving education

The low average level of educational achievement of the population has been a concern of the government for the past decade. Average spending per student is similar to that in other countries, once allowance is made for private spending. Nonetheless, relative to other countries, the performance of the Indian educational system has been poor and out of line with expenditure levels. Despite expenditure on primary school education that is not out of line with that of other countries, the level of literacy amongst young people was markedly lower than in other rapidly growing emerging economies in 2000. In fact, the cumulative performance of the education system over the period 1950 to 2000 left the country with a youth literacy rate some 30 percentage points below that in central and south America, 25 points below other emerging Asian countries and even 5 points below the average for Africa (Figure 1.22). Agaixnst this poor level of overall literacy, the percentage of the population with a tertiary education is relatively high.

Figure 1.22. **Youth literacy rates and primary school spending in selected countries**

Per cent of GDP, around 2000

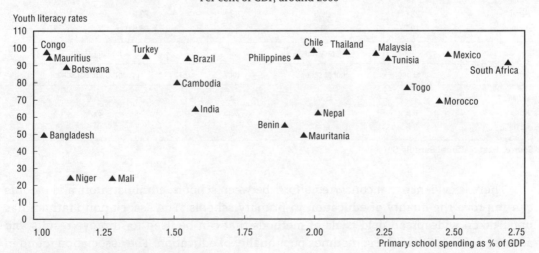

Source: UNESCO World Education Indicators.

Although primary and secondary education is a state government responsibility, the central government has embarked on a number of projects in the past decade that are beginning to turn the situation around. The first success was the programme to give a meal to all children attending school, which drew pupils from poorer backgrounds into the education system. As a result, there was a marked gain in literacy amongst children that completed their education during the 1990s (Table 1.11). It was particularly marked amongst girls, but there still remained an imbalance between boys and girls in their literacy rates. While school, attendance and completion rates did improve in the decade to 2001, still only half of all children completed primary education at that date. A second scheme is designed to transfer funds to state governments in order to achieve the goal of all children completing an eight-year education programme by 2010. This decade, there is evidence of a further improvement, with the illiteracy rate dropping 10% for the age group 10-14 for the country as a whole. Moreover, this rate has been determined on the basis of probing questions by an interviewer rather than the self-assessment basis used in the census. Such an improvement has almost halved the gap in youth literacy that was apparent at the beginning of the decade, moving India markedly ahead of Africa but still lagging behind the 90-100% youth literacy rates that are typical of many emerging economies.

The key problem in improving literacy would appear to be ensuring that school attendance remains as high as school enrolment and that children indeed learn in school. Amongst those in the 5-14 age group actually attending school, illiteracy rates are now below 10% with little difference between rural and urban areas. The major difference between rural and urban areas lies in the degree of illiteracy amongst those who do not attend school which are extremely high, especially in rural areas. Some of those shown to be absent from school in the period of the sample survey will return to school at some point, and some of the younger children in the sample will learn to read, which will no doubt result in a further fall in the illiteracy rate.

Table 1.11. **Illiteracy rates by age group**

Proportion of population age group, 2004

Age Groups	Illiteracy rate %				
	15-24	25-29	30-59	60+	15+
Urban	9.6	13.9	22.7	41.2	19.6
Rural	23.6	36.6	53.1	73.5	45.2
All India	19.7	30.2	44.7	65.5	38.2

Age groups 5 to 14	Illiteracy rate %			Schooling status %
	at school	not at school	total	proportion not at school
Urban	7.0	53.0	13.7	14.6
Rural	8.9	72.3	22.5	21.4
All India	8.5	69.1	20.5	19.9

Source: 61st National Sample Survey.

There is evidence that concerted efforts between schools, administrators and parents can improve the quality of education in primary schools. The association Pratham has undertaken widespread field trials of methods that can be used to improve results and address deficiencies in the sometimes poor quality of education. The association found in its nationwide survey that a significant proportion of the 11-year-olds actually in school were unable to undertake basic linguistic and arithmetic tasks that should be within the capabilities of such an age group. The absence of teachers from schools is also a major problem, especially in smaller schools, as is the poor infrastructure of many schools. This latter factor is a reflection of the high proportion of the education budget that is spent on salaries, which also corresponds to an internationally high level of salaries relative to GDP per capita. About half of parents decide to send their children to private schools. In this sector, teacher attendance and school facilities are better, but the evidence for better performance in standardised tests in a few core areas is weak, though the private schools generally teach a much wider range of subjects, notably including English.

At the other extreme of the education level, the emphasis should be on improving the quality of university and college education. About 9½ per cent of the 25-29 age group had a degree in 2001. The university system does appear to suffer from a number of problems. The subject mix appears to leave graduates with a major problem of entry to the labour market. While the unemployment rate of people who have held one job tends to decline with the level of education, the extent of unemployment amongst people who have never been employed rises quite sharply with the level of education. A further example of the quality of the university system is the low number of research articles published in top-quality international journals by researchers from Indian universities. The absolute number is low (relative to the population) and has been stagnating (Figure 1.23).

Figure 1.23. **Number of research articles: An international comparison**

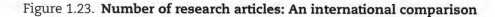
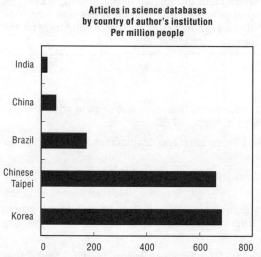

Source: United States Office of Naval Intelligence.

Key challenges

Chapter 8 will review the state of public services in education and policies to address shortcomings by discussing the following issues:

● How well does the education system perform and are there differences in performance across states?

● How can delivery of these services be improved?

Conclusions

India has made much progress in making its economy more open and more market-based. As a result – and helped by political stability and favourable international conditions – the economy has achieved a higher growth path, poverty is declining and a number of indicators of health are improving. However, average living standards remain low and there are large income gaps across states, regions and socio-economic groups. India's main challenge is to sustain, and possibly accelerate, its catch-up process and to ensure that improvements in living standards are spread as widely as possible. This requires additional reforms in a number of areas as will be discussed in the following chapters.

Notes

1. The human capital effect has been estimated by taking into account the changing educational skills of the labour force (in terms of their average number of years in education) and the extent to which their productivity (as proxied by earnings) rises with education.

2. The area hosts nine defence research laboratories, advanced computing and at least six government laboratories in the aerospace, space, mathematical modelling, and software technology (Parthasarathy, 2005), though others have queried whether the staff in these units were attracted to work in the private sector.

3. By establishing in Mauritius not only are corporate profits on export sales exempt from tax but also when the company, or shares in the company, are sold at a profit, no capital gains tax is payable in either India or Mauritius.

4. Labour market data has to be derived from the annual and quinnenial national sample surveys. They have a large sample size given their objective of providing information at the state and even district level and for developments over a period of one year. As result, the processing time for the survey is long, which reduces its utility as a macroeconomic indicator.

Bibliography

Aghion, P., C. Harris, P. Howitt and J. Vickers (2001), "Competition, Imitation and Growth with Step-by-Step Innovation", *Review of Economic Studies*, Vol. 68, No. 3, pp. 467-92.

Ahluwalia Montek, S.(2002) "Economic Reforms in India Since 1991: Has Gradualism Worked?", *Journal of Economic Perspectives*, Vol. 16, No. 3, Summer, ss. 67-88.

Alesina, A., S. Ardagna, F. Schiantarelli and G. Nicoletti (2003), "Regulation and Investment", *NBER Working Papers*, No. 9560.

Bajpai, Nirupam and Vanita Shastri (1998) "Software Industry in India: A Case Study", Development Discussion Paper No. 667, Harvard Institute for International Development, Harvard University, December.

Balakrishnan, P.B. (2006) "Benign Neglect or Strategic Intent", *Economic and Political Weekly*. 9 September, Mumbai.

Banerjee, Abhijit V. and Esther Duflo (2000), "Reputation Effects and the Limits of Contracting: A Study of the Indian Software Industry,"*Quarterly Journal of Economics*, Vol. 115, No. 3, pp. 989-1017.

Bindra, A. (2006), "Civil aviation in India: Flying higher", downloaded from *www.civilaviationweek.com/Civil%20Aviation%20in%20India%20-%20Flying%20Higher.pdf*.

Chaudhury, N., Hammer, J., Kremer M., Muralidharan, K. and F. Rogers (2006), "Missing in Action: Teacher and Health Worker Absence in Developing Countries", *Journal of Economic Perspectives*, Vol. 20, No 1.

Conway, P., V. Janod and G. Nicoletti (2005), "Product Market Regulation in OECD Countries: 1998 to 2003", *OECD Economics Department Working Papers*, No. 419, OECD Publishing.

Conway P., D. de Rosa, G. Nicoletti and F. Steiner (2006), "Regulation, competition and productivity convergence", *OECD Economics Department Working Papers* No. 502, July.

CSE (2006), *Clearing the Air in Asian Cities*, Centre for Science and Environment, New Delhi.

Datt, G. and Martin R. (2002), "Is India's Economic Growth Leaving the Poor Behind?" *Journal of Economic Perspectives*, Vol. 16, No. 3 (Summer), pp. 89 108

Deaton, A. and J. Dreze (2002), "Poverty and Inequality in India: A re-examination", *Economic and Political Weekly*, 7 September.

Deaton, A. and Kozel (2005), "Data and Dogma: the Great Indian Poverty Debate", *World Bank Research Observer*, September.

Dev, S. and C. Ravi (2007), "Poverty and Inequality: All India and States, 1983 2005" *Economic and Political Weekly*, February, pp. 509 21

Dossani, R. (2005), *Origins and Growth of the Software Industry in India*, Shorenstein APARC Working Paper, Stanford University.

Edwards, S., "Why are Saving Rates so Different Across Countries?: An International Comparative Analysis" (April 1995), NBER Working Paper No. W5097.

Foster, V., S. Pattanayak and L. Prokopy (2003), "Do current water subsidies reach the poor?", *Water Tariffs and Subsidies in South Asia Paper* 4, Water and Sanitation Programme – South Asia.

Gaurav, D. and M. Ravallion (2002), "Has India's Post-Reform Economic Growth Left the Poor Behind?"*Journal of Economic Perspectives*, Vol. 16, No. 3, pp. 89-108.

Government of India (2001), "Observations on the Customs Tariff", paper presented to the Inter-Ministerial Group on the Customs Tariff Structure, Ministry of Finance, Department of Revenue, Delhi, Herd and Dougherty, forthcoming.

Government of India (2004), *Central Government Subsidies in India*, Ministry of Finance, Department of Economic Affairs, December.

Harral, C. (2006), "Highway and Railway Development in India and China, 1992-2002", Transport Note No. TRN-32, May, World Bank.

Herd, Richard and Sean Dougherty (2007), "Growth Prospects in China and India Compared", *The European Journal of Comparative Economics*, Vol. 4, No. 1, pp. 65-89.

Himanshu (2007), "Recent Trends in Poverty and Inequality: Some Preliminary Results", *Economic and Political Weekly*, 10 February.

International Institute for Population Sciences (2007), *Key Findings from NFHS-3*, Mumbai.

Jayanthakumaran, K. (2003), "Benefit-Cost Appraisals of Export Processing Zones: A Survey of the Literature", *Development Policy Review*, Vol. 21, No. 1.

Kraay, A. (2006), "When is growth pro-poor? Evidence from a panel of countries", *Journal of development Economics*, Vol. 80, No. 1, June 2006, pp. 198-227.

Kumar, M. (2002), "Economic Reforms and their Macroeconomic Impact", in Kapila (ed.), *A Decade of Economic Reforms*, Academic Foundation, ISBN 81 7188 240 4.

Kumar, S. (2005), "Mortality Variations In India", Actuary Sahara India Life Insurance Company, Ltd, presentation to the 7th Global Conference of Actuaries, 15-16 February 2005, New Delhi.

Majumder, R. (2005), "Infrastructure and Regional Development: Interlinkages In India", *Indian Economic Review*, Vol. 40, No. 2, pp. 167-184.

Masson, P. R., T. Bayoumi, H. Samiei (1998), "International Evidence on the Determinants of Private Saving", *World Bank Economic Review*, Oxford University Press, Vol. 12, No. 3, pp. 483-501, September.

McKenzie, D. and I. Ray (2004), "Household Water Delivery Options in Urban and Rural India," paper prepared for the 5th Stanford Conference on Indian Economic Development, 3-5 June.

Modigliani, F. (1990), "Recent Declines in the Saving Rates: A Life Cycle Perspective", *Revista di Politica Econ.*, December, pp. 5–42.

Mohan, R. and S. Dasgupta (2004), "Urban Development in India in the 21st Century: Policies for Accelerating Urban Growth", Stanford Centre for International Development, October.

Mukerji, P. (2004), *Essays in International Trade Liberalization and the Extensive Margin*, Ph.D. Dissertation, University of Maryland.

Nicoletti, G. and S. Scarpetta (2005), "Product market reforms and employment in OECD countries", *OECD Economics Department Working Papers*, No. 472, December.

Nicoletti, G., D. Hajkova, L. Vartia and Kwang-Yeol Yoo. (2006), "Taxation, business environment and FDI location in OECD countries", *OECD Economics Department Working Papers*, No. 502, July.

Nicoletti, G. and S. Scarpetta (2003), "Regulation, Productivity and Growth: OECD Evidence", *Economic Policy*, No. 36, pp. 9-72, April.

Nicoletti, G., S. Scarpetta and O. Boylaud (1999), "Summary Indicators of Product Market Regulation with an Extension to Employment Protection Legislation", *OECD Economics Department Working Papers*, No. 226.

OECD (2006a), *Going for Growth*, OECD, Paris.

OECD (2006b), *OECD Economic Surveys: Brazil*, OECD, Paris.

OECD (2007), *Going for Growth*, OECD, Paris.

Panagariya, A. (2004), "India's Trade Reform", *India Policy Forum*, Vol. 1, 2004, Brookings-NCAER Washington, D.C.

Porta La, R., F. Lopez-De-Silanes A. Shleifer (2002), "Government Ownership of Banks", *The Journal of Finance*, Vol. 57, No. 1, pp. 265–301.

Purfield, C. (2006), "Is Economic Growth Leaving Some States Behind?", *India goes global: Its expanding role in the world economy*, IMF, Washington, D.C.

Pursell, G. (2002), "Trade Policies in India", in D. Salvatore (ed.), *National Trade Policies*, Greenwood Press, New York, ISBN: 0313264899.

Rao, C. Bhujanga, D.K. Srivastava, P. Chakraborty and T.S. Rangamannar (2003), *Budgetary Subsidies in India: Subsidising Social and Economic Services*, National Institute of Public Finance and Policy, March.

Registrar General (2006), *Maternal Mortality in India: 1997-2003, Trends, Causes and Risk Factors*, New Delhi.

Sau, R. (2007), "Second Industrialisation in India: Land and the State", *Economic and Political Weekly*, 17 February, Mumbai.

Saxenian, A. (2002), *Local and Global Networks of Immigrant Professionals in Silicon Valley*, Public Policy Institute of California, San Francisco.

Serres, de A., S. Kobayakawa, T. Sløk and L. Vartia (2006), "Regulation of financial systems and economic growth", *OECD Economics Department Working Papers*, No. 506, August.

Shanmugam, K.R and P. Kulshreshtha (2005), "Efficiency analysis of coal-based thermal power generation in India during post-reform era", *International Journal. Global Energy Issues*, Vol. 23, No. 1.

Subhedar, S.P., A. Thanawala and R. Sane (2004), "Regulation and supervision of occupational pension funds and gratuity fund", Working Paper 03/04, Indian Pension Research Foundation.

Sukthankar (2001), *Committee Report on Operation, Maintenance and Management of Rural and Urban Water Supply Schemes*, 28 February, Government of India.

Upadhya, C. (2004), "A New Transnational Capitalist Class? Capital Flows, Business Networks and Entrepreneurs", *The Indian Software Industry Economic and Political Weekly Special Article*, 27 November.

USAID (1995), *India: Demographic and Health Surveys, 1992/93 – Final Report*, Washington, D.C.

USAID (2000), *India: Demographic and Health Surveys, 1998/99 – Final Report*, Washington, D.C.

Yeyati, E.L. A. Micco and U. Panizza (2004), "Should the Government be in the Banking Business? The Role of State-Owned and Development Banks" in *Unlocking Credit: The Quest for Deep and Stable Lending*, The Johns Hopkins University Press.

ISBN 978-92-64-03351-1
OECD Economic Surveys: India
© OECD 2007

Chapter 2

India's growth pattern and obstacles to higher growth

India's growth performance has improved significantly over the past 20 years, but it has been uneven across industries and states. While some service industries, notably the information and communications technology (ICT) sector, have become highly competitive in world markets – yielding considerable gains for employees and investors – manufacturing industries have lagged and improved their performance only recently. A divergence in performance has taken place, with firms in those states and sectors with the best institutions gaining, and those in the more tightly regulated states and sectors falling further behind. As a result, the competitive landscape is uneven across sectors and states and a high degree of concentration continues in different industries. While this is partly the result of the legacy of licensing, change has been politically difficult, making it harder for the manufacturing sector than for the service sector to expand. The need for further institutional reforms is urgent, focusing on product and labour market regulations at the central and state levels.

This chapter examines the growth performance of the Indian economy more closely and identifies areas where further reforms could enhance growth and make it more balanced. The first section looks at the movement of production in different sectors of the economy and finds that India has been following a unique development path with the share of manufacturing in total output not increasing as income levels increase. The next section looks at possible reasons for this development and finds that there are deeply rooted problems in the manufacturing sector that have constrained its development, although some of these have been eased with reforms. India's manufacturing firms were not able to fully exploit their comparative advantages of low labour costs and have remained extraordinarily small in scale – yet capital intensive – restraining productivity gains as well as job creation. In the past five years, there have been gains in employment, driven by some liberalisation of labour laws, but many of these jobs are of low quality (casual employment, outside the formal sector with very low wages), and few have legal protection. For large firms, there remain substantial obstacles to restructuring employment, limiting their ability to compete effectively.

Productivity gains from shifting labour out of agriculture have been modest

The literature on economic development has generally argued that catch-up is associated with shifts of production away from agriculture into manufacturing and – at a later stage of development – from manufacturing into services. This so-called Three-sector (or Fisher-Clark-Kuznets) Hypothesis appears consistent with the cross-country evidence, and has been broadly confirmed for many countries and can be explained partly by demand shifts and partly by productivity differentials. This resource shift out of low-productivity agriculture into high-productivity manufacturing should boost overall productivity in emerging countries. Figure 2.1 illustrates the phenomenon for a large number of countries.

Figure 2.1. **Share of manufacturing by per capita income**[1]

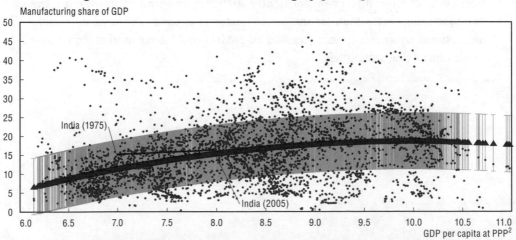

1. Shaded area represents one standard deviation around second-order polynomial trend around country observations.
2. Per capital income is in thousands of US dollars at constant year 2000 purchasing power parity.
Source: World Development Indicators (2007).

On this basis, India's development path appears to be somewhat unusual as the production shift from agriculture into manufacturing has proceeded more slowly than in most other countries at a similar stage of development while that to services has proceeded more rapidly, suggesting that India's "industrial revolution" may still be in the future. India's manufacturing share in GDP was nearly a standard deviation above the mean in 1975, yet has fallen to just above the mean in recent years, as its manufacturing industry has stagnated. Some observers have therefore questioned whether India's share of manufacturing is really so out-of-line with international experience (Kochhar *et al.*, 2006). Figure 2.1 suggests that India's share of manufacturing in GDP does not appear particularly out-of-line at present. However, such a comparison ignores the fact that India is a large continental economy, and in comparison to such economies, its manufacturing share is only a little over half that of China, Indonesia, Malaysia, Thailand, as well as Korea. Moreover, in comparison to East Asia, India has experienced weaker growth in manufacturing output and employment (Saxena and Goswami, 2007).

However, the Three-sector Hypothesis has been widely questioned as well. One problem is its reliance on local currency prices when making comparisons, which can be misleading. When international prices are used so that adjustments are made for the fact that services prices tend to rise over time as economies become more integrated with global markets – often called the Balassa-Samuelson effect – it would appear that, rather than going up with income, the real share of services in output remains nearly constant (Heston and Summers, 1992).

Even more fundamentally, in the case of India, there are different views about the effect of resource shifts on productivity. A first look at the sectoral distribution of employment and productivity suggests that India has indeed been able to increase its overall productivity through labour reallocation. Given the higher level of productivity outside the agricultural sector, the shift of employment from agriculture to manufacturing and services appears to have boosted labour productivity growth by about 0.9% per year, accounting for about one-quarter of overall labour productivity growth between 1978 and 2003 (Table 2.1, Panel 1). A more detailed analysis, using census rather than sample survey data, removing housing services from output and disaggregating the data to a greater extent, suggests even a slightly higher productivity effect from the sectoral shift in employment (De Vries and Timmer, 2007). This report also suggests that, prior to reforms in the mid-1980s, there was little gain in productivity due to sectoral reallocation. Bosworth and Collins (2007) also found that between 1993 and 2004 the reallocation of workers from agriculture to industry and services contributed 1.2 percentage points to annual productivity growth in both India and China.

There are, however, grounds for being cautious about the extent to which labour reallocation has been an important source of productivity growth in India. This caution is confirmed by an alternative breakdown of the economy into three sectors, namely: agriculture, the informal and the formal parts of the non-agricultural economy. The differences in productivity between the formal and informal sectors of the Indian economy are extremely large, with productivity in the formal sector being 19 times higher than in the agricultural sector, rising to a 27-fold difference in the formal private company sector. An analysis of the rise in productivity based on changes in the shares of labour employed in different parts of the economy thus should take into account not only flows by industry but also the shares of the different institutional sectors within each industry.

Table 2.1. **Labour productivity and employment shares by industry and institutional sector**

	Level of productivity		Share of employment		Change in productivity	Change in employment share
	Net product per person, 1999/2000 prices, rupees		Per cent of total employment		Per cent per year	
Panel 1: By industry	1993	2003	1993	2003	1993 to 2003	
Primary	15 015	17 749	64.3	58.0	1.7	−1.0
Secondary	33 039	40 036	14.9	18.1	1.9	2.0
Tertiary	71 171	113 771	20.8	23.9	4.8	1.4
Whole economy	29 399	44 706	100.0	100.0	4.3	0.0
Whole economy with 1993 industry employment weights	29 399	41 070			3.4	
Productivity growth due to change in employment composition by industry					0.9	
Panel 2: By institutional sector	1993	2003	1993	2003	1993 to 2003	
Informal	20 721	27 958	92.6	94.0	3.0	0.1
Agriculture	14 745	17 431	63.9	57.7	1.7	−1.0
Other	33 989	44 674	28.8	36.3	2.8	2.4
Formal	139 663	308 099	7.4	6.0	8.2	−2.1
Private companies	174 220	431 699	2.1	1.9	9.5	−1.3
Public enterprises	148 215	319 883	2.7	2.0	8.0	−2.8
Public services	101 756	186 891	2.5	2.1	6.3	−1.9
Whole economy	29 475	44 706	100.0	100.0	4.3	0.0
Whole economy with 1993 institutional employment weights	29 475	46 525			4.7	
Productivity growth due to change in employment composition by institutional sector					−0.4	

Source: National Account Statistics, National Sample Survey.

In practice this alternative way of looking at the changing shares of labour changes the conclusion about the impact of the movement of labour in India. Most labour has moved from agriculture to the informal non-agricultural sector and this has boosted productivity. However, at the same time, labour has moved out of the highest productivity sector – the formal sector. The proportionate fall in formal employment was greatest in the public sector and, even in the most productive formal private sector, the share of employment has fallen slightly (Table 2.1, Panel 2). As a result, the overall impact of changes in the share of employment has been to reduce the growth of labour productivity. One reason for this poor employment performance of the formal sector, notably private companies, may be restrictive labour legislation that has resulted in a growing capital intensity of the formal sector. Thus, it is possible that less restrictive labour legislation might have resulted in increased employment and greater reallocation gains. However, these gains might have been tempered by a somewhat less rapid growth in productivity if the growth of capital intensity was lowered.

Manufacturing's contribution to growth could be much greater

Labour costs in manufacturing are comparatively low

India's greatest comparative advantage is in labour costs, which on the basis of relative compensation at the industry level in registered (formal) manufacturing, appear to be extremely low – about 1/20th of the United States' and 1/30th of Germany's (which is used in the following as a reference country) at 2002 exchange rates. However, such naïve measures of costs do not take into account the considerable differences in productivity levels that exist between India and more developed countries. If productivity differences are considered by comparing effective unit labour costs (ULC), the gap between India and developed countries narrows but remains large. Currently, India's unit labour costs (in comparable terms) are only 16% of the level in Germany, an 84% gap. The labour cost gap is much larger than in the first half of the 1980s when it was only 50%. The main reason for the improved cost competitiveness of India was the depreciation of the Indian rupee in the second half of the 1980s which reduced India's wage costs in foreign currency terms, while at the same time relative productivity per hour increased by 29% (Figure 2.2), or by 71% per employee.[1]

Figure 2.2. **Relative employee compensation, productivity and unit labour costs**
Per cent of Germany

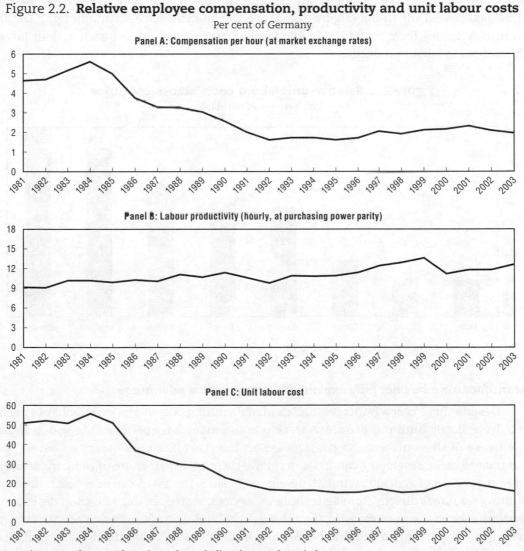

Panel A: Compensation per hour (at market exchange rates)

Panel B: Labour productivity (hourly, at purchasing power parity)

Panel C: Unit labour cost

Note: Figures are for manufacturing only, excluding the petroleum industry.
Source: Dougherty *et al.* (2007b) and Erumban (2007).

There are large differences in labour costs across industries. The unit labour costs span a range from 7% of the German level for the communications equipment sector to about 44% of German levels for the pulp and paper sector. Most of the difference in unit labour costs across industries comes from differences in labour productivity levels rather than differences in wage levels. One sector where wage levels are very different, however, is the unregistered informal sector. This sector includes a wide variety of trades such as tailoring and production of apparel, the processing of agricultural goods, and manufacture of various handicrafts. About one-third of this unregistered sector (by value added) is officially designated as "small-scale industries" (SSIs), with about half of the remainder in the informal sector, according to standardised ILO definitions (SSI Census, 2003; Kolli and Hazra, 2005). As a result of the highly dual labour market in India, there is a fivefold wage gap between the registered and unregistered sectors, in part due to the extremely low level of labour productivity in the latter (Ray, 2004).

Even in the formal sector, India's unit labour costs are low enough to place it well below other emerging markets, such as Mexico, Turkey or Poland – and certainly below the more developed OECD economies, although Indian unit labour costs are very similar to those estimated for China (Figure 2.3). Much of the difference with emerging OECD countries comes from lower levels of compensation per employee rather than large differences in labour productivity.

Figure 2.3. **Relative unit labour costs across countries**
2002, per cent of Germany

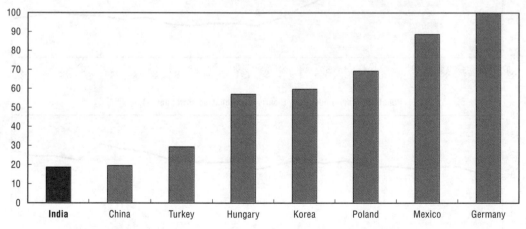

Source: van Ark *et al.* (2006) and Dougherty *et al.* (2007).

Manufacturing has not fully exploited its comparative advantage

Despite these cost advantages, India's manufacturing output and exports have grown relatively slowly until this decade. A weak overall productivity performance was seen as the cause of this outcome (Nagaraj, 2004; Kochhar *et al.*, 2006). As described earlier, in contrast to most developing countries that have increased their share of industry as they have moved out of agriculture, India's development since the 1980s can be characterized as shifting resources directly from agriculture to services. Moreover, until this decade, export performance in the manufacturing sector lagged behind that of East Asian countries that have goods exports as an important driver of growth (Table 2.2). Since the beginning of this decade, though, manufactured exports have grown faster than in most East Asian

Table 2.2. **Growth in the value of merchandise exports**

% per year, values measured in USD

	1980-85	1985-1990	1990-95	1995-2000	2000-05	1980-2005
China	8.6	17.8	19.1	10.9	25.0	16.1
Turkey	22.3	10.2	10.8	5.1	21.5	13.8
Thailand	1.8	26.5	19.6	4.1	9.8	12.0
Korea	11.6	16.5	14.0	6.6	10.5	11.8
Hong Kong, China	8.2	22.3	16.1	3.1	7.6	11.3
Mexico	8.2	8.8	14.3	15.9	5.1	10.4
India	**1.3**	**14.5**	**11.3**	**6.7**	**17.5**	**10.1**
Malaysia	3.6	13.8	20.2	5.9	7.5	10.0
Chinese Taipei	9.2	16.9	10.9	6.0	5.5	9.6
Philippines	−4.3	12.0	16.6	17.8	0.7	8.2
Pakistan	0.9	15.4	7.4	2.4	12.0	7.5
Brazil	5.0	4.1	8.2	3.4	16.5	7.3
Japan	6.3	10.2	9.0	1.6	4.4	6.3
Indonesia	−3.2	6.7	12.1	7.6	5.7	5.6

Source: World Trade Organisation Trade database.

countries except China. As a result, the gap between the growth of manufacturing output and service output has narrowed this decade, with manufacturing output even growing faster than service output in 2006.

As a result of its relatively small share in non-agricultural output, manufacturing's contribution to overall output growth has been less than a third of that for services during the past decade. Moreover, some service sectors have performed exceedingly well, with communications, for instance, contributing 3½ times its share of GDP towards growth during 2000-04 (see Table 1.4 in Chapter 1). The rapid growth of services does raise the question of whether India could follow a development path that essentially bypasses manufacturing, as it has led to an acceleration of overall growth. However, it would seem unnecessary and suboptimal for India to pursue such a unique path of development given its potential strengths and comparative advantages, and the need for more broad-based development to provide enough employment opportunities for its growing labour force. India's revealed comparative advantage (RCA) is, in fact, in many of the same labour and resource-intensive manufacturing sectors as China's, suggesting that it could better exploit its competitive export strengths by further increasing its manufacturing sector (Batra and Khan, 2005).[2]

In trying to understand why India's manufacturing is lagging behind, a number of characteristics of India's pattern of development can be cited as highly unusual and appear to be symptomatic of deeper structural distortions in the economy. These features include an extraordinarily large share of overall manufacturing employment in micro-enterprises – most of which are in the informal sector – and a relatively high capital intensity in the organised sector, despite the low labour costs, with the labour share of gross value added being only 25%. We examine each of these issues briefly below, before drawing some policy conclusions.

Manufacturing firms have remained very small in size...

Perhaps the most dominant characteristic of India's manufacturing sector is the extraordinarily small scale of establishments relative to any OECD country or other emerging countries when measured in terms of employment and output (Figure 2.4). About

Figure 2.4. **International comparison of the distribution of firm size in manufacturing**
2002 or nearby year

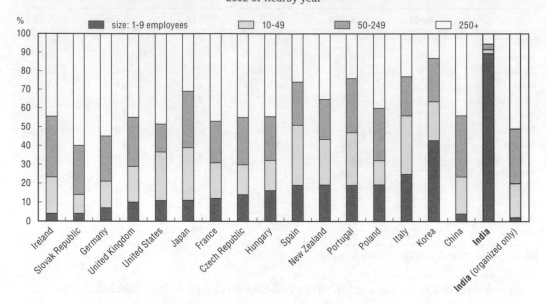

Notes: For China, India (2005) and the United States, services are included. Some countries' data does not include all micro-enterprises (Japan, Portugal and Korea).

Source: OECD Statistics on Enterprises by Size Class; India Economic Census (2005), China Economic Census (2004).

87% of manufacturing employment is in micro-enterprises of less than 10 employees, a smallness of scale that is unmatched, with the closest comparison being Korean companies, where less than half of employment is in micro-enterprises. While there is a fairly high share of very large companies – making the distribution to some extent bimodal – there are few enterprises of intermediate size.

The small scale of Indian industry arose in part by design: the pre-reform licensing system meant that, on the one hand, only one major company was allowed to operate in many industries, while on the other hand, other industries were reserved to small-scale industry (SSI). While these market entry restrictions have been largely dismantled, their legacy continues to reduce competition, scale and productivity in many sectors. In addition, some regulations persist such as those related to labour and administrative approvals, which also constrain firms' growth.

Given the relatively small size of many manufacturing firms, India is not (or much less so than other countries) reaping gains from scale economies. Larger establishments often use newer technologies[3] and thus achieve higher productivity, while smaller establishments are much less productive; although small firms' share in manufacturing employment is almost 90%, they produce only about a third of manufacturing output. An estimation of scale effects for plants, based on individual establishments that are surveyed in the Annual Survey of Industries, suggests that scale effects are indeed very large and that they have persisted for some time. Even after controlling for technology, industry, region and firms' age, total factor productivity is about twice as high in firms with more than 250 employees than in those with only 10 employees, with progressive increases in scale yielding considerable gains in productivity as well (Figure 2.5).

The extent of potential gains from larger size is perhaps not surprising considering that anecdotal information from interviews of Indian businesses and industry experts

Figure 2.5. **Gains in productivity from larger plant size in India**

Total factor productivity (TFP) in a given plant size relative to a plant with between 1 and 10 employees

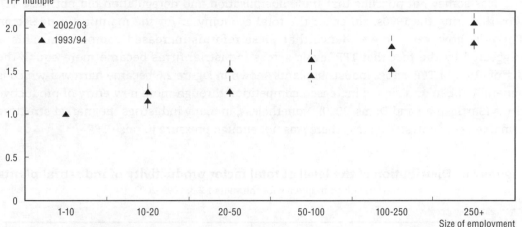

Note: The droplines in this figure represent 95% confidence intervals.

Source: OECD estimate based on production functions estimated from Annual Survey of Industries unit level data.

reveal extensive fragmentation and even progressive disintegration of business operations into small subcontracting units that further exacerbates the problem and means that comparative productivity levels in some industries are much lower for purely organisation reasons (McKinsey, 2005; Mukerji, 2006). More aggregate labour productivity data on the unorganized sector from the SSI Census and NSSO data suggest that past investment restrictions on this sector have created diseconomies of scale (SSI Census, 2004). Thus, it is not surprising that businesses operating in SSI sectors have agreed by consensus to have their protections dismantled. Moreover, it suggests that the gains to increasing scale in the SSI sectors could be even larger than those in the registered manufacturing sector.

... with a bias towards capital-intensive production...

At the same time that firms in India have remained small, a large share of India's manufacturing has been in sectors that usually require a larger scale of production.[4] Moreover, production has tended to be particularly capital-intensive, with the labour share of value added remaining very low: at about a quarter compared with nearly two-thirds in many OECD countries. Such a pattern of production appears out of line with estimates of revealed comparative advantage, that show less comparative advantages in skill-based industries relative to China (Batra and Khan, 2005). The relatively high capital intensity of the manufacturing sector also appears out of line with relative prices, given that the cost of capital has been very high relative to labour costs throughout most of the economy as, until recently, prices of investment goods have been driven up by import tariffs.[5]

... with some evidence that total factor productivity growth may have accelerated this decade

Labour productivity in manufacturing has doubled over the course of the last two decades. A number of studies suggest that most of this increase was due to capital deepening rather than to total factor productivity growth. While there were clear improvements in TFP growth during the 1980s, there is very little evidence of acceleration after 1991 (Kaur, 2006; Ministry of Finance, 2006). While a few studies have shown a slight increase during the 1990s as compared with the 1980s (*i.e.* Tata, 2003), they have been widely questioned for their methodological assumptions (see Goldar, 2004).

It is somewhat puzzling that trade liberalisation and deregulation did not raise TFP growth during the 1990s, either for the total economy or for the manufacturing sector. There is, however, some evidence that these reforms increased competition. This is suggested by the fact that TFP levels across industrial firms became more equal; the distribution of TFP across industrial plants shown in Figure 2.6 became narrower which is generally taken as a sign of increased competition through more new entry of productive firms (Bartlesman and Doms, 2000). Nonetheless, in many industries the market structure remained concentrated so that there was not enough pressure to raise TFP.

Figure 2.6. **Distribution of the level of total factor productivity of industrial plants**
Normalised frequency for the years 1993, 1999, 2003

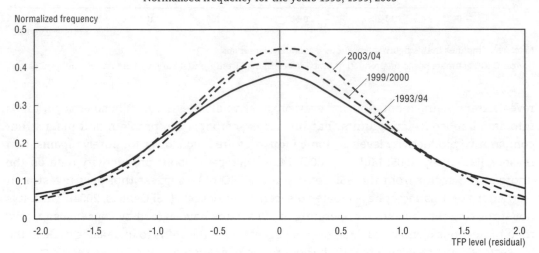

Source: OECD estimates using plant level data from the Annual Survey of Industries.

The situation may have changed after 2000. For the industrial sector as a whole it was found that TFP may have marginally increased in the past couple of years (Virmani, 2006). Our own estimates on the basis of production functions using firm-level *corporate-only* data suggest a more significant increase in annual TFP growth in the manufacturing sector from less than ½ per cent per year during the 1990s to around 2½ per cent per year during 2000–05.[6] This could suggest that the opening of the economy and higher competition is finally bearing fruit also in terms of higher TFP growth. However, the aggregate estimates shown in the first chapter suggest little acceleration in TFP at the level of total manufacturing, suggesting that such gains may have been limited to the largest firms.

Individual firms and industries benefited from reforms

There is evidence that economic reforms had a positive effect on the productivity of some firms and industries. However, as many of the firms that coped less well with increased competition and suffered relative productivity losses remained in the market, the effect of reform on overall productivity was muted. Sivadasan (2003, 2006), using plant-level ASI data through the mid-1990s and structural estimates, found an improved productivity performance in industries that liberalised (through de-licensing) in comparison to those that did not. Industries that were affected by FDI liberalisation had an 18% to 23% increase in productivity, and industries that faced tariff liberalisation experienced productivity gains of around one-third. The study also suggested that twice as much of the change occurred within plants than through reallocation. Such gains led to considerable dynamics in the rankings of the largest companies over the past decade, and a *difference-in-difference* estimation suggests that twice as much of the change was intra-firm rather than reallocative. The lack of reallocative gains appears to be a result of the difficulty of market exit and the rigidities imposed by inflexible labour market regulations.

A strong positive impact of trade liberalisation on total factor productivity was also found by Topalova (2003, 2004), using a firm-level panel dataset from 1989 to 2001. She found that a 10% decrease in tariffs resulted in a ½ per cent increase in total factor productivity. Again, the gains accrue within existing firms rather than as result of the demise of unproductive firms, as exit rates are extremely low. Bhaumik *et al.* (2006a, 2006b) found a shift in the dispersion of productivity across industries since 1991 and showed that it was associated with a substantial increase in new firm entry as pro-competitive reforms impacted firm location decisions.[7] In particular, liberalisation of entry barriers and the consequent increase in net firm entry rates had a strong positive impact on productivity, even as labour policies appear to have restrained it due to the lack of reallocation and limited exit of firms with obsolete technology. These studies all suggest that reforms led to a divergence in performance *across firms* in different industrial sectors and that overall productivity would have increased more had a greater number of the less productive firms exited the market.

Productivity-enhancing resource reallocation nevertheless remains low

The reallocation of resources to more productive uses that would be expected to occur in an increasingly open economy has occurred slowly. The most important reasons for this slow pace of change appear to be low market exits of firms, low labour migration across states and ongoing high concentration of production in some industries.

The limited impact of firm exits on productivity seen in most studies is reflected in the very low exit/hazard rates for large industrial firms which are as low as 3% per year for quoted corporations (from Prowess), many times smaller than in nearly all OECD economies and most other developing countries. This low exit rate reflects the great difficulty of closing a business in India where there is no bankruptcy code, and prior permission of the government is required before laying off workers. Firm-level analysis of the effects of liberalisation policies on productivity also suggests that most gains occur within plants rather than through reallocation (Sivadasan, 2006). Such gains led to considerable dynamics in the rankings of the largest 10 or 100 companies over the past decade (among companies in the Prowess database).

Labour is highly immobile across states in India as a whole, impeding reallocation of human resources. Almost half of the migrants across states are women moving for marriage while less than 10% move to find new employment. The bulk of internal migration in India is short-distance, with 60% of migrants changing their residence within the district of enumeration and over 20% within the state of enumeration, while the remaining 20% move across state boundaries (Srivastava and Sasikumar, 2003). Evidence from the NSS suggests that migration rates have only mildly increased over the past decade.

One often-mentioned reason for the low internal migration is the multitude of languages and dialects spoken in the country.[8] However, a comparison of migration rates across the then fifteen members of the European Union countries (EU15) with that of Indian states suggests that over a recent 10-year period, there was twice as much migration within Europe as within India, and it was heavily oriented towards employment.[9] Slow migration in India may lead to adverse impacts of trade liberalisation for states with heavily protected labour markets. And indeed, there is evidence that states with the most restrictive labour regulations experienced even less labour mobility, impeding poverty reduction (Topalova, 2004).

The extent of regional specialisation has also remained quite stable over time. A rigorous means of assessing reallocation across sectors and regions in India is to utilize regional concentration indexes. Taking advantage of Annual Survey of Industries micro-data, regional concentration indexes were computed across states and industries for 1990, 1994, and 1999–2004 (see Dougherty and Herd, 2005; 2007 for methodology). This analysis suggests almost no change in regional specialisation using employment (or firm) weights while it shows a gradual increase in regional specialisation using output weights – likely reflecting the low extent of migration across regions (Figure 2.7).

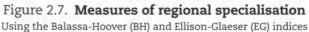

Figure 2.7. **Measures of regional specialisation**
Using the Balassa-Hoover (BH) and Ellison-Glaeser (EG) indices

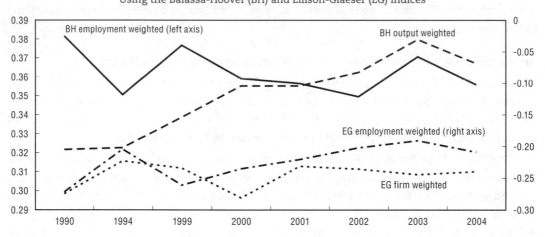

Source: OECD computation from plant level data from the Annual Survey of Industries.

On the other hand, there is evidence of growing integration of markets based on changes in retail commodity prices, likely facilitated by better telecommunications (see Chapter 7). For 24 basic commodities, price dispersion across states (as measured by the coefficient of variation) fell from 15% to 9% between 1994 and 2004, and a simple average of the price differentials for these commodities fell from 60% to 22% (Virmani and Mittal, 2006). A broader set of non-food manufactured goods commodities suggests an even lower differential (12%) when prices were expenditure weighted. In China, the mean absolute price differentials across provinces was only around 7% for manufactured products although such comparisons are inexact since they are based on wholesale rather than retail prices (Dougherty and Herd, 2007). For agricultural products, whether in their primary or processed state, differentials across states are larger and exhibit a greater

OECD ECONOMIC SURVEYS: INDIA – ISBN 978-92-64-03351-1 – © OECD 2007

degree of variability than non-food manufactured products. Thus, there still appears to be room for further gains in integrating domestic markets where taxation, lack of transport infrastructure and barriers to free sale of a number of agricultural products act as a brake on the extent of internal trade.

High concentration in industries reduces productivity gains from liberalisation

Indicators of competition suggest that stable regional concentration has been accompanied by a stable, yet high, degree of market concentration in many Indian industries. For instance, Herfindahl indexes have high values based on standard criteria and have not fallen much over time, with an approximately equal number of industries' concentration ratios rising as falling during the 1990s (Ramaswamy, 2006). Moreover, in those industries where market concentration has risen, one or two large firms typically dominate the market (a number of which are public sector undertakings). Similarly, average price-cost margins increased in the 1990s across virtually all two-digit manufacturing sectors (Balakrishnan and Suresh-Babu, 2003).

The studies cited above showed that tariff reduction helped to raise productivity but that the impacts varied across industries. The extent of competition in a given industry appears to be one factor impacting on the extent of productivity gains, as there is evidence that trade liberalisation has only improved firm and plant-level productivity in unconcentrated industries. Analysis of the impact of industry-specific tariffs on firm-level (corporate) productivity shows that liberalisation had a strong positive effect (through 2001), but only in private sector companies and for those in unconcentrated industries (Topalova, 2004). This may in part be due to the fact that regulations that raise entry barriers for foreign firms are more likely to be found in industries that are highly concentrated, diminishing the benefits of this potential foreign competition for consumers (Chari and Gupta, 2006).

The extent to which the output of industries is concentrated in a few firms is indeed remarkably high compared to other major economies. Applying a standard definition of concentration (a Herfindahl index of over 1 800) to industry census data shows India's share of highly concentrated industries to be more than three times higher than that of the United States or China, and twice as high as that for Germany (Table 2.3, first panel). It is possible that this high degree of concentration is due to the small size of the Indian market relative to optimal plant sizes. Nonetheless, the existence of market concentration and dominant firms suggests that the possibility of anti-competitive behaviour exists in many manufacturing industries.

Industries dominated by public sector firms appear not to have seen the same gains in efficiency as the result of foreign competition. The profits of public manufacturing has risen this decade, but the share of their operating surplus in net value added remains below that of private sector companies and the rate of return on capital is even lower as public sector firms tend to be more capital intensive. Efficiency may also be adversely affected in a limited number of industries due to very high concentration and the presence of dominant public sector firms. There are eight industries where the public sector accounts for more than half of output and which are highly concentrated (Table 2.3, second panel). They are shipbuilding, milling machinery, electric motors, gas turbines, basic fertiliser chemicals, paraffin wax, stainless steel and certain electronic components. Moreover, in three of these industries there is only one public sector company and each has a market share averaging 90%. This high degree of monopoly power complicates the

Table 2.3. **International comparison of industry concentration in 2002**

The concentration groupings are based Herfindahl index scores, using the US Department of Justice criteria

	India		United States		Germany (2001)		China	
	5-digit NIC sector		6-digit NAICS sectors		4-digit NACE sectors		4-digit SIC sector	
	Number	Per cent	Number	Per cent	Number	Per cent	Number	Per cent
Highly concentrated	144	36.6	46	10.2	38	17.8	63	12
Concentrated	105	26.7	88	19.4	37	17.4	83	15.8
Unconcentrated	144	36.6	319	70.4	138	64.8	380	72.2
Total	393	100	453	100	213	100	526	100

	India: Industries classified by share of public in output							
	Under 5%		More than 5% but less than 25%		More than 25% but less than 50%		Greater than 50%	
	Number	Per cent	Number	Per cent	Number	Per cent	Number	Per cent
Highly concentrated	118	38.1	13	24.1	5	35.7	8	53.3
Concentrated	84	27.1	12	22.2	7	50	2	13.3
Unconcentrated	108	34.8	29	53.7	2	14.3	5	33.3
Total	310	100	54	100	14	100	15	100

Source: OECD tabulation of Annual Survey of Industries plant level data for India; US Census Bureau data for the United States; Deutscher Bundestag data for Germany; OECD (2005), *Economic Survey of China*, OECD, Paris.

process of privatisation in these cases; especially given the lack of a competition framework until recently (see Chapter 3). In general, though, public sector companies in the manufacturing sector are not in concentrated sectors.

More fundamentally, the state or public-controlled sector in India remains relatively large, at almost just over one-fifth of total GDP and half of non-farm business sector output, even after the substantial decline seen in the 1990s. Most of this decline was in the manufacturing sector and, by 2004, the share of the public sector in manufacturing output was similar to its share in the aggregate non-farm business sector. Non-manufacturing network industries have much higher shares of public ownership, as discussed in the next chapter.

Outside of India, there is little debate about the merits of private ownership; however, until recently this has not been reflected in research on India. For example, Mohan (2005) has questioned the superior performance of private ownership despite the exhaustive survey of the international literature by Megginson and Netter (2001). And yet, while some studies of private *versus* public ownership do not fully take account of methodological issues such as selection biases, Megginson and Netter's review explicitly considers the extent to which studies take account of selection biases in their meta-analysis of over a hundred studies. Moreover, they conclude that even allowing for this selection, private ownership is more efficient than public ownership under most circumstances. This appears to be the case in India as well where profitability of public enterprises is low relative to those in the private sector (see Chapter 3).

The India-specific studies, such as Gupta (2005), find that even partial privatization has real tangible benefits on investment, productivity, profits and even employment. The few dozen privatisations that have occurred in India have been successful, but little forward movement on privatisation has occurred, perhaps on account of vested interests and the role of public firms in fostering political patronage (Dinc and Gupta, 2005). There is certainly some warranted concern that privatization of large firms with diversified shareholding structures may be more vulnerable to the transfer of assets and income to controlling shareholders, but this argues for a more pro-active stance by stock exchanges (and courts) in their enforcement of corporate governance codes rather than a reason for the government to retain control.

Estimates by the OECD of the productivity performance of private and public firms suggest that there is a clear advantage for private ownership in India. While a simplistic production function approach, without controlling for other factors, indicates that public firms have 10% higher productivity than private firms, a more rigorous analysis which controls for productivity differences across sectors shows that private firms are on average as much as 33% more productive than public enterprises. This analysis is based upon regression estimates of productivity on a panel of firms over the 1990-2006 period, including all firm observations regardless of when the firms began or ended operations.[10]

Evidence suggests that weaknesses in framework conditions are at fault

In trying to understand why India's manufacturing sector has not been more dynamic, perhaps the most persuasive explanation is that anti-competitive regulations have deterred firms' expansion and the entry of new firms. A number of national and international business surveys suggest that weaknesses in India's business environment have inhibited investment, thus reducing growth and employment creation.

Surveys by business associations of manufacturing firms, asking them to state the most important barriers to investment and expansion, typically feature labour regulation and restrictive exit policies at the top of the list (FICCI, 2004; CII, 2006). Meetings by the OECD survey team with groups of business and union representatives, as well as government officials in a considerable number of states, confirmed that these problems remain dominant, among others,[11] and indicate that considerable costs are incurred by business and labour as a result of either following or avoiding the regulations.

More perception-based evidence comes from a series of investment climate surveys undertaken by the World Bank and various collaborators (World Bank, 2004). These large-scale surveys of firms across 12 Indian states find considerable differences in investors' perceptions of the business environment. Measures of these perceptions are used in related work to examine the linkages between the perceptions and actual investment flows across states.

Drawing upon the World Bank's investment climate survey, Veeramani and Goldar (2005) examine the effect of investment climate on state-level total factor productivity in manufacturing. In their regression analysis, they find that state-level investment climate is a strong determinant of productivity performance over the 1980 to 2000 period. However, they also find evidence that states with more pro-worker labour legislation experienced lower productivity growth, a finding that is explored in greater depth in Chapter 4. The interface between business and government is a particular source of concern. Survey reports also indicate that business people in India spend more time dealing with government bureaucracy in comparison to OECD and other Asian countries, including China (World Bank-CII, 2004).

Related evidence using the detailed establishment-level survey data also suggests that the business environment has a major impact. This is troubling in some respects since the World Bank finds that India ranks 134th out of 175 countries in the overall ease of doing business. However, it has made more progress than other South Asian nations in improving its investment climate between 2003 and 2006 (World Bank, 2007). An analysis of manufacturing plant productivity across 40 Indian cities shows that gaps in productivity could to a large extent be explained by differences in regulation and city-level economic geography (Lall and Mengistae, 2005). As well, the study shows that individual plants' perception of labour restrictions had a strong impact on their productivity. This work echoes results found in comparative studies of Asian countries (Dollar *et al.*, 2005), and suggests that firms consider the specific aspects of the local investment climate in choosing locations. These include: the relative cost of business regulation; the cost of corruption; how intrusively industrial regulations are enforced; the cost and reliability of power supply; and the ease with which land rights can be secured for business premises. While these types of analysis are able to differentiate some aspects of the regulatory environment, they are more useful in highlighting areas of importance than in suggesting what specific types of regulatory reforms need to be undertaken.

Such perceptions by business of the importance of the regulatory environment and the stringency of labour laws may or may not play out in practice. Yet rigorous empirical analysis from both macrostudies of investment patterns across states as well as micro-studies of new investment projects suggests that indeed they make a difference. Micro-evidence, which looks at individual investment decisions, may be the most compelling. An important example of such evidence is Sanyal and Menon (2005), who find that the choice of where to place individual new investment projects (during 1997-2001) was significantly affected by the local business environment in each state, and especially by the extent of labour regulation and the climate of labour relations. Other factors such as infrastructure were also important, but it was the business environment that made the most difference.[12]

Given the importance of framework conditions on economic performance in India as a whole and in the individual states, more information is needed which is not only based on perceptions but on the factual regulatory settings in the various areas. For this purpose the OECD's comprehensive indicator, which measures product market regulations across countries, has been constructed for India as a whole and for most of India's states. The main results of this work are presented in the next chapter (Chapter 3), with a similar exercise for labour regulations undertaken in the following chapter (Chapter 4), using the OECD's employment protection legislation index and a state-level analogue.

Notes

1. These ULC measures rely upon an aggregation of detailed item-by-item comparisons of manufacturing census unit values between India and Germany for almost 1 000 products within 43 three-digit industrial branches. This benchmark price comparison is for the fiscal year 2002/03 and was carried out as background to this survey. It is described in detail in Erumban (2007). Such measures ensure that productivity levels are assessed in comparable prices, since many goods, especially intermediate products, may not be traded and the use of market exchange rates would be inappropriate.

2. Since actual comparative advantage is difficult to measure, RCA (or the Balassa Index) is often used in its place. It is defined as a country's share of world exports of a good divided by its share of total world exports.

3. Technology use across firms is discussed in Banerjee and Duflo (2005) and Hsieh and Klenow (2006).

4. Relative to the nine developing countires that produced more manufacturing value added than India, the average value added per establishment was more than ten times greater than that in India (Kochhar et al., 2006).

5. For instance, the price of machinery capital fell from being substantially above world levels in the early 1980s by about 1% per year during the 1980s with the initial liberalisation of capital goods imports, and declined at 2% per year in the 1990s as high tariffs and quantitative restrictions were dismantled, and finally declined at 3% per year as trade opened further during the first part of this decade (Virmani, 2006). As a consequence, machinery investment rates rose tightly in step with the decline in its price, although this uptake in investment could well have been much more rapid.

6. This estimate relies upon stochastic gross output production function estimates on corporate firm microdata from the Prowess database. The total wage bill is used to measure labour input, while an estimate of capital stock is made using available investment data. Controls for industry, region and scale are included. All data are measured in real terms using CPI for industrial workers for labour, and relevant WPIs for investment, output and weighted inputs (using the 1999 input-output table).

7. Such effects may be aggravated by the phenomenon that Burgess and Venables (2004) observe in a comparison of Indian and UK firms, where firms that were closer to the technological frontier may have benefited more from trade liberalisation than those that were further from it, feeding a divergence in productivity that may have resulted in aggregate TFP stagnating.

8. In India there are 24 major languages spoken by a million or more people. Although Hindi is spoken by half of the population, they are concentrated in less than half of the (mainly northern) states. Official estimates suggest that between 150 and 250 million people speak English out of a population of 1.1 billion.

9. This comparison is based on analysis of OECD Labour Force Survey data for the 1995-2005 period and estimates from CSO (2001) between the 1990 and 2000 population census.

10. All firm observations are included in the panel regardless of when the firms began or ended operations. Inputs and outputs are deflated with appropriate deflators: for output, these are based on WPI indexes, for labour (wage bill) it is the CPI for industrial workers; for capital (accumulated net fixed assets at official depreciation rates), it is the fixed investment deflator.

11. Other major problems cited, which are discussed in other chapters, include infrastructure deficiencies, delays in obtaining approvals, low quality public education and training programmes, and taxation of trade.

12. What is important to note, as will be elaborated upon in Chapter 4, is that regardless of the labour flexibility that may or may not exist in practice, legislative inflexibility appears to deter new investment. This point has been recognized by a number of observers but does not yet appear to have helped to build a consensus for reform (Tendulkar, 2003).

Bibliography

Aghion, Philippe, Robin Burgess, Stephen Redding, Fabrizio Zilibotti (2005), "The Unequal Effects of Liberalization: Evidence from Dismantling the License Raj in India", NBER Working Paper No. 12031, February 2006.

APO (2004), "Asia Pacific Productivity Data and Analysis", in Government of India, *Annual Report 2005*, Ministry of Labour, pp. 39-43.

Ark, Bart van and Marcel Timmer (2003), "Asia's Productivity Performance and Potential: The Contribution of Sectors and Structural Change", Paper presented at the RIETI-KEIO Conference on the Japanese Economy: Leading East Asia in the 21st Century?, Tokyo, May.

Ark, Bart van, Judith Banister, and Catherine Guillemineau (2006), "Competitive Advantage of 'Low-Wage' Countries Often Exaggerated", The Conference Board, *Executive Action*, Series No. 212, October.

Balakrishnan, Pulapre and M. Suresh Babu (2003), "Growth and Distribution in Indian Industry in the Nineties", *Economic and Political Weekly*, November 20, pp. 3997-4005.

Banerjee, Abhijit and Esther Duflo (2005), "Growth Theory Through the Lens of Development Economics", in P. Aghion and S. Durlauf (eds.), *Handbook of Economic Growth*, Elsevier Science, North Holland, Amsterdam.

Banerjee, A. (2006), "The Paradox of Indian Growth: A comment on Kochhar *et al.*", *Journal of Monetary Economics*, Vol. 53, No. 5, July.

Bartelsman, Eric J. and Mark Doms (2000), "Understanding Productivity: Lessons from Longitudinal Microdata", *Journal of Economic Literature*, Vol. 38, No. 3, pp. 569-594.

Batra, Amita and Zeba Khan (2005), "Revealed Comparative Advantage: An Analysis for India and China", ICRIER Working Paper No. 168, August.

Bhaumik, Sumon Kumar, Shubhashis Gangopadhyay, Shagun Krishnan (2006a), "Reforms, Entry and Productivity: Some Evidence from the Indian Manufacturing Sector", Indian Development Foundation Working Paper No. 0602 and IZA Discussion Paper No. 2086, April.

___ (2006b), "Policy, Economic Federalism, and Product Market Entry: The Indian Experience", William Davidson Institute Working Paper No. 843, November.

Burgess, Robin and Anthony J. Venables (2004), "Toward a Microeconomics of Growth", World Bank Policy Research Working Paper No. 3257, April.

Bosworth, Barry and Susan M. Collins (2007), "Accounting for Growth: Comparing China and India", NBER Working Paper No. 12943, February

Chari, Anusha and Nandini Gupta (2006), "Incumbents and Protectionism: The Political Economy of Foreign Entry Liberalization", Paper presented at the Darden-World Bank Conference on Financing of Corporations in Emerging Countries, April.

CII (2006), "15 Years of Economic Reforms in India: Success and Progress", *Communiqué*, Survey Series No. 1, Confederation of Indian Industry, New Delhi.

Dinc, I. Serdar and Nandini Gupta (2005), "The Decision to Privatize: The Role of Political Competition and Patronage", SSRN Working Paper, http://ssrn.com/abstract=735763.

Dollar, David Mary Hallward-Driemeier, and Taye Mengistae (2005), "Investment Climate and Firm Performance in Developing Economies", *Economic Development and Cultural Change*, Vol. 54, No. 1, pp. 1–31.

Dougherty, Sean M. and Richard Herd (2005), "Fast-falling barriers and growing concentration: the emergence of a private economy in China", OECD Economics Department Working Paper No. 471, December, OECD, Paris.

Dougherty, Sean M., Richard Herd and Ping He (2007), "Has a Private Sector Emerged in China's Industry? Evidence from a Quarter of a Million Chinese Firms", *China Economic Review*, Vol. 18, No. 3.

Dougherty, Sean M., Richard Herd, Thomas Chalaux, and Abdul Erumban (2007b), "India's growth pattern and obstacles to higher growth", OECD Economics Department Working Paper, forthcoming.

Dougherty, Sean M. (2007), "Job Flows and Labour Regulation at the State Level in India", OECD Economics Department Working Paper, forthcoming.

Epifani, Paolo (2003), "Trade Liberalization, Firm Performance, and Labor Market Outcomes in the Developing World: What Can We Learn from Micro-Level Data?", World Bank Policy Research Working Paper No. 3063, May.

Erumban, Abdul (2007), "Productivity and Unit Labor Cost in Indian Manufacturing: A Comparative Perspective", University of Groningen, GGDC Working Paper, forthcoming.

FICCI (2004), "FICCI Survey on Priority Issues for National Manufacturing Competitiveness Council", Federation of Indian Chambers of Commerce and Industry, August.

GOI (2006), *Economic Survey 2004 – 2005*, Ministry of Finance, Government of India, http://indiabudget.nic.in/es2004-05/esmain.htm.

Goldar, Bishwanath (2004), "Indian Manufacturing: Productivity Trends in Pre- and Post-Reform Periods", *Economic and Political Weekly*, 20 November, pp. 5033-43.

Goldar, Bishwanath and Anita Kumari (2003), "Import Liberalisation and Productivity Growth in Indian Manufacturing Industries in the 1990s", *The Developing Economies*, Vol. 41, No. 4, pp. 436-60.

Gupta, Nandini (2005), "Partial Privatization and Firm Performance", *The Journal of Finance*, Vol. 60, No. 2, pp. 987-1015.

Heston, Alan and Robert Summers (1992), "Measuring Final Product Services for International Comparisons", in Zvi Griliches (ed.), *Output Measurement in the Service Sectors*, University of Chicago Press, Chicago and London.

Hsieh, Chang-Tai and Peter J. Klenow (2006), "Misallocation and Manufacturing TFP in China and India", Stanford University, manuscript.

Kaur, Simrit (2006), "Productivity Growth in Indian Manufacturing: Review of Studies and New Evidence", University of Delhi, Background Report for GOI (2006).

Kochhar, Kalpana, Utsav Kumar, Raghuram Rajan, Arvind Subramanian, and Ioannis Tokatlidis (2006), "India's Pattern of Development: What Happened, What Follows?", *Journal of Monetary Economics*, Vol. 53, No. 5, pp. 981-1019.

Kolli, Ramesh and Suvendu Hazra (2005), "Estimation of Informal Sector Contribution in Net Domestic Product", Expert Group on Informal Sector Statistics (Delhi Group), Paper No. 04, March.

Lall, Somik V. and Taye Mengistae (2005), "The impact of business environment and economic geography on plant-level productivity: an analysis of Indian industry", World Bank, Development Research Group Working Paper No. WPS3664, June.

McKinsey (2005), "Fulfilling India's promise", *The McKinsey Quarterly – Special Edition*, McKinsey and Company, Washington, D.C.

Megginson, W.L. and J.M. Netter (2001), "From State to Market: A Survey of Empirical Studies on Privatization", *Journal of Economic Literature*, Vol. 39, No. 2, pp. 321-89.

Ministry of Finance (2006), *Economic Survey 2005-2006*, Ministry of Finance, New Delhi, *http://indiabudget.nic.in/es2005 06/esmain.htm*.

Mohan, T.T. Ram (2005), *Privatisation in India: Challenging the Economic Orthodoxy*, RoutledgeCurzon, Delhi, London, and New York.

Mukerji, Joydeep (2006), "Economic Growth and India's Future", University of Pennsylvania, Center for the Advance Study of India, Occasional Paper No. 26, March.

Nagaraj, R. (2004), "Fall in Organised Manufacturing Employment: A Brief Note", *Economic and Political Weekly*, 24 July.

____ (2006), "Public Sector Performance Since 1950: A Fresh Look", *Economic and Political Weekly*, Vol. 41, No. 25, 24 June.

NBS (2004), *China Industrial Census Yearbook*, National Bureau of Statistics, Beijing.

NSSO (2001), *Migration in India 1999-2000*, National Sample Survey Organisation Report No. 470 (55/10/8), September.

Ramaswamy, K.V. (2006), "State of Competition in the Indian Manufacturing Industry", in Pradeep S. Mehta (ed.), *A Functional Competition Policy for India*, CUTS International, Jaipur and Academic Foundation, Delhi, pp. 155-64.

Ray, Shri Nilachal (2004), "Unorganized *vis-à-vis* Organized Manufacturing Sector in India," Paper presented at the Seminar Series of the Ministry of Statistics and Programme Implementation, November, http://mospi.nic.in/mospi_seminarseries_nov04_3_6_final.pdf.

Sanyal, Paroma and Nidhiya Menon (2005), "Labor Disputes and the Economics of Firm Geography: A Study of Domestic Investment in India", *Economic Development and Cultural Change*, Vol. 53, No. 4, pp. 825-854.

Saxena, Himanshu and Omkar Goswami (2007), "Governance, Investment, and Economic Development: India 1991-2005", OECD Development Centre Working Paper, forthcoming.

Sivadasan, Jagadeesh (2003), "Barriers to Entry and Productivity: Micro-Evidence from Indian Manufacturing Sector Reforms", Dissertation, University of Michigan, Graduate School of Business.

____ (2006), "Productivity Consequences of Product Market Liberalization: Micro-evidence from Indian Manufacturing Sector Reforms", Ross School of Business Paper No. 1062, October.

Srivastava, Ravi and Sasikumar, S.K. (2003), "An Overview of Migration in India, Its Impacts and Key Issues", Paper presented in at the Regional Conference on Migration, Development and Pro-Poor Policy Choices in Asia, Dhaka, June.

SSI Census (2003), *Third All-India Census of Small Scale Industries 2001-02 (Quick Results)*, Ministry of Small-Scale Industries, New Delhi, *www.smallindustryindia.com/sslindia/census/sumryres.htm*.

Tata (2003), *Reforms and Productivity Trends in the Indian Manufacturing Sector*, Department of Economics and Statistics, Tata Services Limited, Mumbai.

Tendulkar, Suresh D. (2003), "Organised Labour Market in India Pre and Post-Reform", Paper presented at the MacArthur Research Network Conference on Anti-Poverty and Social Policy, Rajasthan.

Topalova, Petia (2004), "Factor Immobility and Regional Impacts of Trade Liberalization: Evidence on Poverty and Inequality from India", *Three Empirical Essays on Trade and Development in India*, Dissertation, Massachusetts Institute of Technology, June.

Topalova, Petia (2003), "Trade Liberalization and Firm Productivity: The Case of India", International Monetary Fund Working Paper No. WP/04/28, February.

Veeramani, C. and Bishwanath Goldar (2005), "Manufacturing Productivity in Indian States: Does Investment Climate Matter?", *Economic and Political Weekly*, 11 June, pp. 2413-20.

Virmani, Arvind (2006), "The Dynamics of Competition: Phasing of Domestic and External Liberalisation in India", Planning Commission Working Paper No. 4/2006-PC, April.

Virmani, Arvind and Surabhi Mittal (2006), "Domestic Market Integration", Indian Council for Research on International Economic Relations, Working Paper No. 183, July.

Vries, Gaaitzen De and M.P. Timmer (2007), "A Cross-Country Database for Sectoral Employment and Productivity", 1950-2005, University of Groningen, Groningen Growth and Development Centre.

World Bank (2004), *India: Investment Climate and Manufacturing Industry*, Investment Climate Assessment, World Bank and IFC, Washington, http://tinyurl.com/2td6m8.

World Bank (2006), *Doing Business 2007*, World Bank, Washington, D.C., www.doingbusiness.org.

World Bank (2007), *Doing Business in South Asia 2007*, World Bank, Washington, D.C.

World Bank CII (2004), *Improving the Investment Climate in India,* The World Bank, Washington DC.

ISBN 978-92-64-03351-1
OECD Economic Surveys: India
© OECD 2007

Chapter 3

Reforming India's product and service markets

The degree of competition in product markets has been found to be an important determinant of economic growth in both developed and developing countries. This chapter uses the OECD's indicators of product market regulation to assess the extent to which the regulatory environment in India is supportive of competition in markets for goods and services. The results indicate that although liberalisation has improved the regulatory environment to international best practices in some areas, the overall level of product market regulation is still relatively restrictive. In addition, estimating the product market regulation indicators for 21 Indian states shows that the relatively more liberal states have higher labour productivity, attract more foreign direct investment, and have a larger share of employment in the private formal sector in comparison to the relatively more restrictive states. The chapter goes on to review various aspects of India's product market regulation and suggests a number of policy initiatives that would improve the degree to which competitive market forces are able to operate.

T his chapter uses the OECD's indicators of Product Market Regulation (PMR) to assess the degree to which government regulation in markets for goods and services promote or inhibit competition. These indicators are based on a standardised procedure used to evaluate product market regulation in three key areas: state control, barriers to entrepreneurship, and barriers to international trade and investment.[1] The results of estimating these indicators for India suggest that there is considerable scope for improving economic performance and reducing income disparities across states by bringing government regulation in product markets into line with best practices. The chapter begins by presenting the overall PMR indicators that are used to measure the extent to which government regulations are conducive to competition in product markets at the national and state levels.[2] The chapter then goes on to evaluate policies in the three key areas covered by the indicators and propose a number of reforms that would promote product market competition and improve economic performance.

Despite extensive liberalisation in some areas regulations are on average rather restrictive

Although there a number of areas where the regulatory framework in India is now comparable with best practices in the OECD area, the *overall level of product market regulation* is still quite high and restricts competition to a greater extent than in all OECD member countries, including the emerging market economies within the OECD area (Table 3.1). The regulation of Indian product markets is also more restrictive than in Chile and Brazil, whose regulatory environments have also been assessed using the PMR indicators (OECD, 2003a and OECD, 2005a). All three of the high-level sub-components of the overall PMR index – that is, state control, barriers to entrepreneurship, and barriers to international trade and investment – are high in India relative to comparator countries. Some of the low-level indicators, however, are close to international best practices and show that India has significantly improved the business environment in selected areas.

Three factors explain the high level of *state control* in India in comparison to other countries. First, the extent of public ownership of firms is high. Second, these enterprises operate across a range of sectors, many of which are inherently competitive. Third, there is also a relatively high level of command and control regulation for private firms reflecting, for example, the imposition of universal service obligations. On the positive side, the sub-indicators imply minimal direct government interference in the conduct of private sector firms. Price formation, for example, is free of government interference in most segments of the Indian retail market and the level of direct government control over private firms is broadly comparable with that in emerging OECD economies. This reflects the absence of state-owned shares with enhanced voting rights in private sector companies, notwithstanding restrictions on the voting rights of private shareholders in government-owned banks.

Table 3.1. **Product market regulations: An international comparison**
The indicator score runs from 0-6, representing the least to most restrictive regulatory regime

	India	Latin America	OECD emerging markets	Euro area	United States
Overall indicator	2.85	2.08	1.98	1.49	1.03
State control	3.47	2.16	2.46	2.40	1.19
Public ownership	3.82	2.16	2.88	2.72	1.20
Scope of public enterprise sector	4.91	3.06	3.48	3.34	2.5
Size of public enterprise sector	4.58	2.13	3.09	3.03	0.59
Direct control over business enterprises	2.45	1.95	2.33	2.06	0.75
Involvement in business operations	3.03	1.79	1.92	2.00	1.18
Use of command and control regulation	5.00	3.13	2.17	2.78	1.50
Price controls	0.75	1.08	1.27	0.92	0.80
Barriers to entrepreneurship	2.57	1.94	1.89	1.43	1.20
Regulatory and administrative opacity	1.55	1.92	1.41	1.31	1.28
Licenses and permit system	1.81	2.00	2.00	1.83	2.00
Communication and simplification of rules and procedures	0.92	1.27	0.55	0.62	0.39
Administrative burdens on start-ups	3.82	2.14	2.61	1.89	1.02
Administrative burdens for corporations	4.25	1.85	2.82	2.06	0.75
Administrative burdens for sole proprietor firms	4.75	3.17	2.73	2.10	1.25
Sector-specific administrative burdens	3.25	1.67	2.64	1.69	1.03
Barriers to competition	1.18	1.87	0.93	0.56	1.50
Legal barriers	0.86	2.06	1.34	1.33	1.36
Antitrust exemptions	1.25	1.16	0.71	0.18	1.63
Barriers to trade and foreign investment	2.56	2.31	1.66	0.75	0.73
Explicit barriers	3.02	1.92	2.26	1.04	1.14
Ownership barriers	2.89	1.57	2.55	1.36	1.83
Discriminatory procedures	2.00	1.45	0.75	0.49	0.00
Tariffs	4.00	3.67	3.00	1.00	1.00
Other barriers	1.98	2.17	0.88	0.37	0.21
Regulatory barriers	1.60	2.21	0.46	0.17	0.00
Indicators by functional areas					
Administrative regulation	3.02	1.99	2.17	1.68	1.09
Economic regulation	2.70	2.10	2.04	1.91	1.30
Inward and outward oriented indicators					
Inward-oriented policies	3.02	2.04	2.17	1.91	1.20
Outward-oriented policies	2.62	2.36	1.72	0.88	0.78

Source: Conway (2007) and Conway et. al (2005).

Low *barriers to entrepreneurship* are an important condition for creating competitive markets. India performs very well in some of the regulatory areas covered by this indicator. In particular, reforms over the past two decades have successfully removed formal legal barriers to market entry – such as licenses to enter a particular sector – which in prior decades had reduced competition and protected incumbents. These formal legal barriers are now on a par with those in the most liberal OECD countries. Moreover, the indicator of regulatory and administrative opacity is broadly comparable with those in the emerging OECD countries, reflecting programmes in some Indian states to improve the workings of the licenses and permits system and the communication and simplification of the rules and procedures that enterprises must comply with. However, despite these efforts, the administrative burden that the government places on entrepreneurs starting a new business, whether they are corporations or sole traders, is still very high and an obstacle to new entry. These high indicator values could also be indicative of more widespread inefficiencies in government administration.

Finally, although the Indian economy has become much more open over the period of economic reform, the indicator of *barriers to trade and investment* still signals a relatively high degree of restrictiveness. Tariff revenues as a proportion of the value of imports – a broad measure of tariff barriers – has fallen substantially and a renewed programme of tariff reduction, which aims to lower tariffs to the average level of ASEAN countries, began in 2002. Restrictions on foreign direct investment have also been lowered in the past decade and a system of automatic clearances for FDI inflows into wholly owned subsidiaries in the manufacturing sector has been created. However, notwithstanding these improvements, the policy framework for international trade and investment is still relatively restrictive in comparison to OECD countries.

Some states have liberalised much more than others...

The constitutional arrangements governing India's federal structure designate control over certain aspects of regulatory policy to the state governments.[3] States may implement their own laws in certain areas, or amend central legislation prior to implementation, and usually formulate the administrative rules and procedures through which central government laws are enforced. On the other hand, the regulation of international trade and foreign investment inflows are set by the central government and are the same across states. The PMR indicators at the state level have been adapted to account for the various ways in which state governments are able to influence the regulatory environment. Most substantively, the indicators that reflect regulatory provisions set by the central government have been excluded from the indicator system constructed at the state level. As a result of these modifications, which are discussed in more detail in the annex to this chapter, the high-level PMR indicators at the state level are not directly comparable with the economy-wide indicators. In any case, the overall indicator values suggest that there is considerable variation in product market regulations across states in those areas for which states are responsible (Figure 3.1).

Figure 3.1. **Indicators of product market regulation by state**[1]

The indicator score runs from 0-6, representing the least to most restrictive regulatory regime

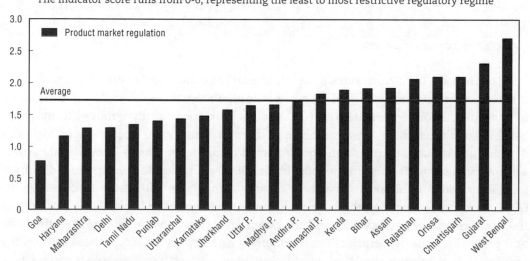

1. The high-level PMR indicators for Indian States have been modified to better reflect the ways in which state governments influence the regulatory environment they are not directly comparable with the national indicators. (See the annex to this chapter for more details.)

Source: Conway (2007).

... and are reaping the benefits in terms of better economic performance

The variation in economic performance across states does appear to be related to differences in product market regulation. As shown in Chapter 1, there is a clear negative relationship between the level of average labour productivity of states and the restrictiveness of product market regulations (Figure 1.14). There are a number of reasons for this. First, the location of foreign direct investment is negatively related to product market restrictions, with the relatively more liberal states receiving virtually all of India's FDI inflows (Figure 3.2). Second, excessive administrative burdens are associated with a lower share of private sector employment in the formal sector, suggesting that firms in relatively restrictive states prefer to remain small and informal so as to avoid government administrative requirements (Figure 3.3). As discussed in Chapter 2, firms in the informal sector have lower capital intensity and are generally much less productive than formal

Figure 3.2. **Product market regulation and foreign direct investment by state**[1]

The indicator score runs from 0-6, representing the least to most restrictive regulatory regime

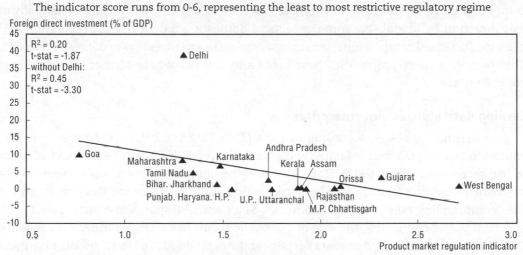

1. Foreign direct investment is measured as cumulative inflows over the period 2000 to 2006 as a share of annual average state GDP.

Figure 3.3. **Administrative regulation and average organised employment share by state**

The indicator score runs from 0-6, representing the least to most restrictive regulatory regime

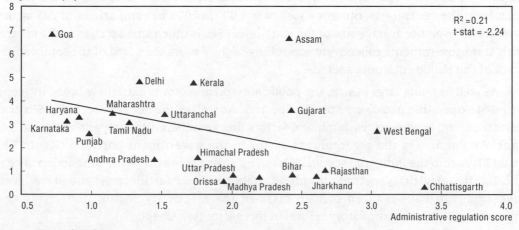

Source: Conway (2007).

sector enterprises implying that states with excessive administrative burdens suffer from relatively low fixed capital formation and small average firm size.

To begin the process of closing the gaps in economic performance across states, the relatively restrictive states need to improve their regulatory environment so as to become more competitive and productive. Econometric work on the relationship between product market regulation and labour productivity in OECD countries suggests that new and more efficient technologies would diffuse to the more restrictive states more quickly if they were to adopt the regulatory stance of the least restrictive states (Conway *et al.*, 2006). For the relatively more liberal states, the challenge is to further improve their business framework conditions towards those in the OECD area.

Policies to improve product market regulations

The key to improving product market performance in India is to focus on changing those policies that result in high levels of government interference in markets and restrict competition. Relative to recent history, the government has already moved substantially in this direction by liberalising some aspects of domestic product market regulation and allowing increased competition from foreign producers and investors in domestic markets. This section reviews progress in these areas and outlines where further improvements could be made.

Dealing with state-owned enterprises

As mentioned above, according to the OECD's PMR indicators, the extent of state control in product markets is relatively high in India reflecting the large size and scope of public sector enterprises (PSEs). Until the 1990s the public sector was widely seen as the mechanism to bring about India's industrialisation and modernisation through control of the "commanding heights of the economy". Since then, despite some initiatives to sell stakes in public companies, the size of the public sector has changed little. PSEs produce 21% of net value added and account for 38% of the capital stock of the non-farm business sector. Their dominance in the formal business sector is even larger, accounting for over half of value added. This is high in comparison to OECD countries (OECD, 2005b).

At the state level the PMR indicators suggest that there is wide variation in the degree of state control, predominantly as a result of differences in the size and scope of the public enterprise sector, reflecting different starting points and commitments to privatisation (Figures 3.4 and 3.5). The state governments collectively control a much larger number of PSEs than the central government – just over 1 000 in 2003 in comparison to 245 at the centre. However, the average size of the state-level PSEs is much smaller than at the centre, with state governments collectively controlling slightly more than 50% of the total capital stock of the public enterprise sector.

As well as being large in size, the public enterprise sector is extremely broad in scope with PSEs operating in a diverse range of sectors. As well as the network sectors, PSEs also operate in, and in some cases dominate, sectors that are inherently competitive (Figure 3.6, Panel A). Finance is the predominant sector in the government portfolio (Figure 3.6, Panel B). Within the industrial sector, PSEs have a strong presence in the production of coal and lignite, electricity, petroleum, metal industries and fertiliser. At the state level, investment in PSEs is often concentrated in the electricity sector, underlying the importance of ongoing regulatory reform in this sector (see Chapter 7).

Figure 3.4. **The PMR indicators of state control by state**

The indicator score runs from 0-6, representing the least to most restrictive regulatory regime

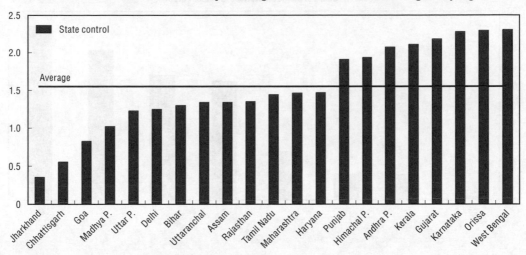

Source: Conway (2007).

Figure 3.5. **Assets of state-level public sector enterprises by state**

Per cent of state GDP, 2002

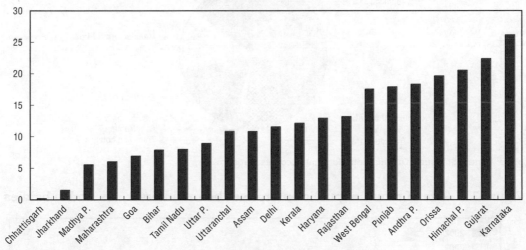

Source: OECD analysis of data from the Comptroller and Auditor General of India.

As discussed in Chapter 2, the productivity of state-owned enterprises is, on average, on third less than that of private companies. This relatively low level of productivity is reflected in low rates of return. In 2003, the return before interest, tax and subsidies on capital invested in PSEs owned by the central government was only one-third that of private companies (Figure 3.7). There has recently been some improvement in profitability, with the proportion of loss-making non-financial central PSEs falling from 43% to 33% between 1991/92 and 2004/05. This improvement brought only a modest increase in the return earned by the median public company to 3% in 2005 (after subsidies). In comparison, the rate of return for the median private sector company was almost 10% (Figure 3.8). The total losses of the loss-making PSEs controlled by the central government amounted to 0.3% of GDP in 2005.

Figure 3.6. **Involvement of government enterprises in the economy**

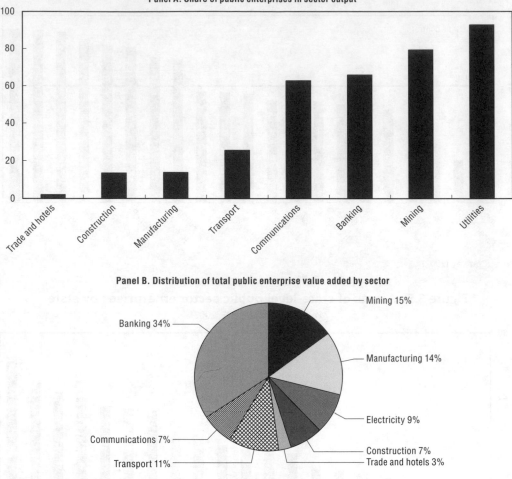

Panel A: Share of public enterprises in sector output

Panel B. Distribution of total public enterprise value added by sector

Source: Central Statistical Organisation, National Accounts Statistics.

Figure 3.7. **Rate of return of public enterprises before interest, tax and subsidies**

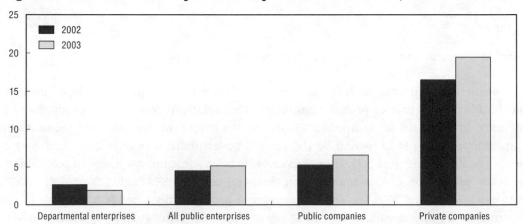

Source: Central Statistical Organisation, National Accounts Statistics.

OECD ECONOMIC SURVEYS: INDIA – ISBN 978-92-64-03351-1 – © OECD 2007

Figure 3.8. **Distribution of rates of return of central public sector enterprises**

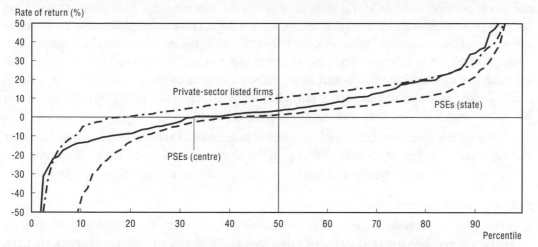

Source: OECD analysis of data from the Comptroller and Auditor General and Prowess database.

Although there is significant variation across states, the financial health of the state-owned PSEs is, on average, poor and worse than that of the central enterprises. The proportion of loss-making PSEs ranges from 15% in Andhra Pradesh to 77% in Assam (Table 3.2). The total losses of loss-making PSEs at the state-level amount to a further 0.6%

Table 3.2. **Performance of state-level public sector enterprises**

2004

	Number of PSEs	Proportion of loss making PSEs	Losses of loss making PSEs	Proportion of capital in 'non-working' PSEs	Proportion of PSEs with negative net worth	Rate of Return on Capital	
		%	% SGDP	%	%	Medium	Average
Andhra Pradesh	54	15	−0.06	2.3	14.8	5.6	10.0
Assam	43	77	−3.47	1.6	20.9	−3.3	−16.4
Bihar	54	70	−1.38	13.0	11.1	−2.5	−7.7
Chhattisgarh	11	36	−0.02	0.0	9.1	5.1	4.6
Delhi	11	45	−4.21	0.0	9.1	3.6	−27.8
Goa	16	63	−0.57	0.0	0.0	−0.1	−11.0
Gujarat	51	39	−0.38	50.5	17.6	2.2	−8.9
Haryana	29	59	−0.05	1.4	13.8	5.5	5.0
Himachal Pradesh	21	62	−0.50	27.8	23.8	3.3	5.7
Jharkhand	6	17	−0.15	0.0	0.0	33.6	43.1
Karnataka	82	41	−0.28	1.5	7.3	3.6	31.2
Kerala	114	61	−0.39	1.1	14.0	1.7	−15.3
Madhya Pradesh	42	33	−0.13	3.8	14.3	1.3	2.2
Maharashtra	82	68	−0.38	3.2	20.7	−0.3	−4.6
Orissa	69	70	−0.28	1.1	21.7	−1.3	−35.0
Punjab	57	44	−0.23	0.3	15.8	−1.2	−12.0
Rajasthan	24	38	−0.06	0.1	20.8	7.4	20.6
Tamil Nadu	68	53	−0.14	0.6	29.4	2.4	−1.6
Uttar Pradesh	94	62	−0.94	51.1	17.0	−1.0	−29.9
Uttaranchal	25	60	−0.32	47.7	12.0	−2.3	−16.4
West Bengal	86	72	−0.50	0.8	44.2	1.4	−45.2

Source: OECD analysis of data from the Comptroller and Auditor General.

of GDP and there is a large tail of highly unprofitable public-sector firms (Figure 3.8). Some of the worst performing PSEs at the state level are in the power sector, indicative of enormous (implicit) electricity subsidies. In addition to "working" PSEs most state governments also have a number of "non-working" PSEs on their books. These firms no longer produce output but, given the difficulties of retrenching staff and closing down, still exist as corporate entities. The ever increasing liabilities that result from these non-working PSEs can have severe fiscal implications. Restructuring may be a partial solution for some of these firms, but many are non-viable and will need to go through an insolvency process.

Overall, the poor profitability of the PSEs is indicative of serious inefficiencies in their management. This is especially the case given that some of these firms dominate the markets in which they operate and are often in a position to extract monopoly rents.

Privatisation has been slow

Since the late 1980s, the privatisation experiences of many developed and developing countries have shown that privatisation typically leads to improvements in firm profitability, real output, and efficiency (*e.g.* Megginson and Netter, 2001 and Kikeri and Nellis, 2004). Partial privatisation, which has been the predominant method used in India, can also lead to improvements in firm performance. However, cross-country studies of privatisations in OECD countries indicate that the gains in profitability and productivity are typically larger in firms that are fully privatised (OECD, 2003b). The disadvantage of partial privatisation is that it does not usually result in management control being passed to private owners or an infusion of new technology necessary to improve firm performance to that of the private sector.[4] In addition to a suboptimal method of privatisation, the proceeds from privatising PSEs controlled by the centre have been more than 60% below target between 1991/92 and 2004/05 (when privatisation targets were abandoned) and relatively low in comparison to some other developing countries. Indeed, in contrast to India, privatisation programmes in a number of developing countries have gone as far as selling state-owned enterprises in the network/infrastructure sectors.

At the state level there has been considerable variation in the extent of privatisation with states such as Haryana and West Bengal being particularly successful in their privatisation programmes. Successful privatisation episodes have typically involved political commitment at the highest levels and consensus building among stakeholders. Given the limited social safety net, considerable support for workers displaced by privatisation has also been an important consideration in successful privatisation programmes at the centre and state level, with workers being retrained or re-absorbed into other parts of the public sector. Although the welfare of displaced workers should be an important consideration, the latter approach risks merely shifting the burden of over-employment from one area of the state sector to another.

Minimising the anti-competitive impact of the public enterprise sector

Some attempts have been made to commercialise the activities of the PSEs. The introduction of the Navratna and Mini-Ratna concepts in the late 1990s conferred a greater degree of operational freedom on relatively successful PSEs at the centre level. In addition, there have recently been some further improvements in the independence of PSEs controlled by the centre government with the introduction of higher limits for investments that do not need to be cleared by parliament, one of the few recommendations of a recent report of the governance of state-owned enterprises that were implemented (GoI, 2005).

Despite these efforts, PSEs at the centre and state levels still have a negative impact on competition in the sectors in which they operate. First and foremost, because government often plays the dual role of major market player and policy maker (as well as regulatory agent in some of the infrastructure sectors discussed in Chapter 7), there is often no clear separation between the ownership function and other functions that influence market conditions. For example, PSEs are also often required to fulfil obligations for social and public policy purposes, with their governance adversely affected by political interference and the use of civil servants as directors. Moreover, in many states the strategic commercial choices of PSEs often have to be cleared by the state assembly. The procurement policies of the central and state governments – which typically include a price or quantity preference for PSEs – are also biased against the private sector. Because they dominate some markets, political interference in the operation of PSEs not only threatens their profitability but also adversely influences overall market conditions.

There are a number of ways in which the corporate governance of PSEs could be improved to ensure a level playing field and government neutrality in its dealings with the private sector (Box 3.1). The centre and state governments need to transparently unbundle the commercial and promotional/policy roles of the PSEs. Moving towards a more centralised model of PSE management would be a large step in this direction. Currently, at the centre, responsibility for the PSEs rests primarily with the line ministry while the Department of Public Enterprises plays a coordinating role and elaborates the overall ownership policy as well as specific guidelines. This decentralised model was predominant in OECD countries before the first wave of public sector reforms during the 1970s. With the shift from industry-specific policies to more framework-oriented and market liberalisation policies, the main advantage of this approach of allowing a more activist industrial policy has now vanished.

A more centralised approach, where PSEs are put under the responsibility of an investment agency, would achieve a clear separation between policy and commercial functions. This, together with the tendency to locate regulatory duties in specialised institutions, has been the main driving force towards a more centralised model of state-owned enterprises in OECD countries. In the Indian context, centralisation of the ownership function would facilitate a more unified and consistent ownership policy, distance PSEs from political control, simplify the often elaborate committee structures that currently supervise and control PSEs, and ensure equitable treatment of non-state shareholders by preventing government from pursuing objectives that are outside the commercial interests of the PSE. It may also facilitate the consolidation of the commercial operations of the PSEs in some of the states, where there is sometimes a number of PSEs engaged in essentially the same commercial activity. It might also help management of PSEs to focus on efficiency and profit. By improving governance, centralising the ownership function within government would ensure a more level playing field between public and private sector companies and increase competition.

Centralising the ownership function of the PSEs should not entail the creation of additional layers of control or bureaucratic function within government. Instead, as the administrative capacity for overseeing the PSEs develops within the investment agency, the functionality of the relevant departments in the line ministries would need to be reduced. One of the objectives in centralising the ownership function is to simplify the elaborate systems of control that are currently in place and the net impact on the efficiency of the public bureaucracy should be positive. Ultimately, the structure of the public

Box 3.1. **Corporate governance of state-owned enterprises in OECD countries**

The characteristics of state-owned enterprises (SOEs) raise specific challenges for their governance. Firstly, SOEs are often protected from two major threats that are essential in policing management behaviour: the threat of takeover and bankruptcy. Secondly, accounting and disclosure may be oriented towards public expenditure control and not up to private sector standards. Without appropriate governance arrangements to counter these characteristics the management of SOEs may have more discretion than in the case of private firms and demands on the government's budget for investment and expansion programmes may become excessive.

Governments of OECD countries have faced complex issues and trade-offs in reforming the corporate governance of state-owned enterprises (SOEs). Achieving a sound organisation and effective exercise of the ownership function within the state administration requires an ownership policy that is active while at the same time avoids undue interference in day-to-day management. In addition, the chain of accountability needs to ensure that the boards and management of SOEs make responsible decisions with appropriate information disclosure to the public. It is also necessary to clearly separate state ownership from the regulatory and policy-making roles and ensure that efficient decision making processes are in place.

The report *Corporate Governance of State-Owned Enterprises: A Survey of OECD Countries* (OECD, 2005b) provides a comprehensive inventory of current practices and recent experiences in reforming governance arrangements for SOEs in OECD countries. Reform has focused on a number of areas including the way in which the boards of SOEs are nominated, their composition, functions, and the way they perform their main tasks. Disclosure rules, for the SOEs themselves and the ownership entity within government, have also been reformed in a number of countries as have provisions to protect minority shareholders, where they exist, and the way in which SOEs relate to stakeholders. Incentive structures and the ways in which senior executives in SOEs are nominated and remunerated has also been the target of reform.

Provided they are soundly structured and effectively implemented, governance reform can improve SOE efficiency and access to capital, while contributing to fair competition by ensuring a level-playing field between companies in the private and public sectors. Better corporate governance of SOEs can also strengthen overall public governance through better transparency and improve fiscal discipline. OECD experience has also shown that good corporate governance of SOEs is an important prerequisite for effective privatisation, since it makes the enterprises more attractive to prospective buyers and enhances their commercial value.

To help governments meet the challenges of public sector governance the OECD has published guidelines on the corporate governance of SOEs (*OECD Guidelines on Corporate Governance of State-owned Enterprises*, OECD 2005c). In broad terms, these guidelines cover the following areas: i) Ensuring an Effective Legal and Regulatory Framework for SOEs; ii) The State Acting as an Owner; iii) Equitable Treatment of Shareholders; iv) Relations with Stakeholders; v) Transparency and Disclosure; vi) The Responsibilities of Boards of State-Owned Enterprises. These guidelines complement the OECD's Corporate Governance Principles (Revised 2004) and have been widely endorsed and welcomed by OECD and non-OECD governments.

administration needs to be reorganised to be more consistent with a modern-day focus on general framework conditions instead of the current "command and control" approach. This will entail a significant consolidation and reduction in the number of ministries and departments in both the central and state governments.

In addition to a more centralised approach, the way in which any remaining obligations and responsibilities that PSEs are required to undertake in terms of public services should be clearly mandated by laws or regulations. These obligations and responsibilities should also be disclosed to the general public and the related costs should be covered by government in a transparent manner. This will make the PSEs more attractive to potential buyers and is an important prerequisite for economically effective privatisation. Finally, in the interests of a level playing field with the private sector, PSEs should be exposed to competitive conditions in access to finance and preferential procurement policies should be ended at the state level, following plans by central government to do so in 2008.

Once these steps have been taken, the privatisation programme needs to be revitalised, especially in the competitive sectors of the economy. The improved performance of a number of PSEs and the buoyant stock market provide a good opportunity to privatise with the aim of maximizing value and improving productivity further. Although the method of privatisation will need to be assessed on a case-by-case basis, mixed sales, which combine strategic sales with public share offerings, have the potential advantages of developing strong corporate governance structures and introducing new management and technology into the company.

For PSEs operating in network sectors in which there are monopoly elements, the regulatory environment needs to be consistent with private ownership and competition prior to privatisation (see Chapter 7). For other sectors, given the high level of concentration outlined in Chapter 2, the basic elements of a competition framework need to be in place (discussed below). The worst performing and the non-working PSEs need to be restructured to the point where they can be wound up. Allowing negative bids for the equity in these firms may be a transparent alternative approach for disposing of these firms. For some of the less developed states, conditional grants from the centre may also be required to help state governments dispose of these firms.

Excessive administrative burden acts as a barrier to entry

As noted above, according to the PMR indicators, barriers to entrepreneurship in India, which deter firm entry into established markets and thus discourage competition and innovation, are high relative to other countries. With formal legal barrier to entry having been removed in most sectors, these barriers largely reflect excessive administrative burdens on firms. Many cross-country studies find that removing administrative bottlenecks and improving the transparency of regulation facilitates market entry and can have a pronounced positive impact on the overall competitiveness of the economy through a variety of channels, including enhanced foreign direct investment (Kurtzman *et al.*, 2004). Overly complex administrative procedures also increase discretion within government bureaucracy, thereby facilitating corruption. In a study of 194 countries, Bellver and Kaufmann (2005) find that institutional and political transparency are strongly correlated with competitiveness and strongly *negatively* correlated with corruption. In Transparency International's Corruption Perceptions Index, India ranks 70 out of 163 countries in 2006.

Tools for simplifying government administration

With an interventionist tradition and administrative structures that have in many cases not kept pace with economic liberalisation, a significant reengineering of administrative processes is needed to improve service delivery and simplify the interaction between government and firms. A crucial aspect of re-engineering administrative processes, especially within some of the state governments, is improving the coordination of administrative functions across government departments. In many states, departments within government operate in "silos" with minimal information flows between them. Given a lack of coordination, administrative procedures often duplicate the same function across a number of departments. Firms and citizens interacting with government find themselves in a complex maze of regulations and administrative requirements that are repetitive with different departments collecting essentially the same information, non-transparent, and sometimes contradictory. This increases compliance costs, especially for small firms, and discourages firm expansion into the formal sector, thus restraining competition and productivity.[5]

A number of initiatives have been introduced by state governments to simplify red tape, with varying degrees of success (Figure 3.9). For example, some of the state governments have improved their interface with the private sector by simplifying and consolidating various application forms and registers. However, simply combining all existing application forms into a single document, as has been done in a few states, is not enough. Instead, a composite application form should be the final outcome of a process to coordinate and improve the administrative function of government departments. There is also potential for reducing administrative burdens by better integrating the administrative functions of the central and state governments, which both process applications and collect information for areas in which they have concurrent responsibility.

Figure 3.9. **The PMR indicators of barriers to entrepreneurship by state**

The indicator score runs from 0-6, representing the least to most restrictive

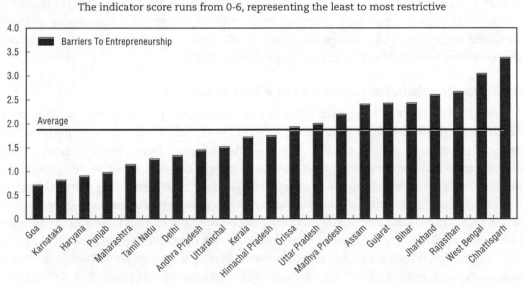

Source: Conway (2007).

Another common initiative for reducing red tape, which has been introduced in 19 of the 21 states for which the PMR indicators have been calculated, is the "one-stop shop" (OSS) for providing information and, in some cases, applying for the necessary licenses and notifications.[6] The essential idea of the OSS is that potential investors only need to be in contact with a single entity to complete all the necessary paperwork and applications in a streamlined and co-ordinated process, rather than having to go through a labyrinth of different government bodies. In practice, given the impracticalities of assuming full control of the approval process, OSSs tend to act as a co-ordination mechanism between relevant government authorities.

To be effective in reducing administrative burdens, OSSs should be implemented along with other reforms geared towards cutting red tape (Sader, 2000). In the absence of such measures, OSSs run the risk of simply adding another layer of bureaucracy to the approvals process. Indeed, because OSSs provide a focal point for investment clearance, they can act as important catalysts for process re-engineering and better co-operation across government departments.

Closely related to the OSS concept is the idea of "deemed clearance" under which licenses are issued automatically if the licensing office does not act by the end of the statutory response period. Deemed clearance regimes have been implemented in ten of the 21 states surveyed. When set and implemented judiciously, deemed clearances can be an effective method of giving teeth to the single window concept. However, the administrative system must also be reformed to the point where it is capable of meeting these statutory response periods. The objective is not to circumvent regulation but to implement and enforce it in the most efficient way possible.

Information and communications technology (ICT) offers enormous potential for reducing administrative burdens in India and has been successfully integrated into the administrative procedures of some of the state governments. At the central level, government is using Indian ICT firms to introduce electronic data interchange systems for customs clearance and providing interfaces so that the progress of documents can be checked. The tax administrations are also implementing ICT in a similar capacity. A technology infrastructure of open information on shared networks with standardised data and applications would go a long way towards improving integration across government departments and state and central government. It would also reduce opportunities for corruption by reducing subjectivity and discretion in government administrative processes. However, the introduction of ICT must be linked to re-engineering processes. Automating existing inefficient processes or using ICT to simply disseminate information will only produce a limited payoff.

Another useful ICT-related technique for improving administrative process is to make all the forms and procedural requirements of various government departments available on the Internet. Although most state governments publish their policies on line, there is very little information available on the steps and forms that must be completed to, for example, register a business. This results in opaque regulations that are not known or understood by the public. Publication would increase transparency, elicit suggestions for refinement, and reduce the scope for government arbitrariness.

An important consideration with all efforts to simplify and improve government administration is that they filter down department hierarchies and are effectively implemented at the lower levels. Otherwise, administrative processes will remain uncertain and the extent of subjective decision making and corruption opportunities will remain unchanged. Training seminars, performance based pay scales, and promotions based on merit would all help in this regard.

There is currently momentum in central and state governments to improve the public bureaucracy and reforms in some areas are lowering administrative burdens. Many of the industrial policies and other laws setting up "one-stop shops" and administrative reform committees are only a few years old and it is too early to say whether they are having a positive impact. If these efforts are successful, they will help reduce the duality between the formal and informal sectors, increase the growth potential of the whole economy, broaden the tax base, and level the playing field for doing business in India. However, there is still a long way to go and efforts to reduce administrative burdens need to be strengthened further.

Administrative reform requires a regulatory oversight body

Transparency, accountability, and efficiency are the hallmarks of a high-quality administrative system. Establishing a co-ordinated programme of administrative reform to imbue public bureaucracies with these characteristics requires institutional change and is complex and time consuming. Recognising the scope of this challenge, most OECD governments have established regulatory oversight bodies with "whole of government" responsibility for regulatory policy (OECD, 2002). One advantage of this approach is that it promotes a consistent and systematic method of reform across the entire administration. In addition, the OECD experience has been that regulatory reform will often fail if left entirely to ministries, implying that a degree of centralisation can improve the chances of successful reform.

The Indian government is also well aware of the importance of improving the quality of public administration and has moved a long way towards becoming a more service-oriented facilitator of private-sector entrepreneurship. From the centre, the Department of Administrative Reforms and Public Grievances works with central ministries and state administrations on a number of projects aimed at improving government functioning. One of the most far-reaching recent initiatives enacted at the central level is the Right to Information Act (2005), which gives citizens access to information under the control of public authorities and should greatly improve the transparency of the public administration. Ten of the 21 state governments surveyed have also established centralised institutions for managing and coordinating regulation and its reform.

At present, however, there is no centralised oversight body charged with reviewing regulatory proposals to ensure they do not impose unnecessary or unreasonable administrative burdens on firms and citizens. This important task would involve the use of Regulatory Impact Analysis (RIA) to assess the benefits and costs of significant proposed new regulation. A regulatory oversight body would also develop guidelines on the standards of good regulation and the use of alternatives to traditional command and control regulation. New ways of measuring the impact of administrative regulation would also need to be developed to identify areas of high administrative burden (OECD, 2006). Given the existing expertise within the Department of Administrative Reforms and Public Grievances and some of the state-level departments, these institutions are best placed to perform this important role.

A centralised and fully-functional regulatory oversight body would go against a tradition of ministerial independence in regulatory matters and could meet with strong resistance. This implies the need for a careful balancing act between cooperation and confrontational relationships with ministries. The need for political support means that the relevance of regulatory reform to larger social and economic goals must be clarified and clearly communicated to all concerned. Ideally, the objectives of the regulatory oversight body should be outlined as part of an explicit regulatory policy that sets out reform priorities and the tools and institutions used by government to shape their regulatory power. The OECD experience has been that countries consistently make greater progress when they have an explicit regulatory policy. Malyshev (2006) notes that "the more complete the principles, and the more concrete and accountable the action programme, the wider and more effective the reform".

Internal markets have been substantially liberalised but more work needs to be done

Although formal legal barrier to entry have been removed in most sectors there are still a number of areas in which the regulatory environment could be improved to be more supportive of competition.

Barriers to competition still exist in some sectors

The agricultural sector continues to be governed by regulations that were implemented during times of scarcity and remains subject to a wide range of price and other controls that limit the flow of goods between states and sometimes even within states. Regulatory oversight in the sector is shared between the central government and state governments. At the central level the Essential Commodities Act, introduced more than 50 years ago, is the basis for restrictions that can affect trade in food grains, edible oils, pulses, kerosene and sugar.

While some flexibility was allowed in 2002, additional legal instruments in many states mean that agriculture has only been affected indirectly by reforms initiated at the level of the central government. A number of states still restrict trade in agricultural goods, thereby limiting free internal movement and creating the possibility of price differentials at a time when food security is no longer an issue, even at the local level. The marketing of agricultural products is also restricted at the state level by the Agricultural Produce Market Regulation Act, which does not allow co-operatives and private parties to set up modern markets. This contributes to an extremely high level of post-harvest losses for grains, fruits, and vegetables of around 25 to 30% (OECD, 2007).

Encouraging private markets and allowing food-processing firms and retailers to buy directly from farmers would encourage diversification in agriculture. It would also improve the storage and post-harvest handling of agricultural products, which, combined with an increase in value added processing, could significantly increase incomes in rural areas. The public distribution system, which aims to supply low-income families with certain staples at subsidised prices, also distorts agricultural markets and hampers efforts to diversify output. Subsidised inputs, such as fertiliser, irrigation, and electricity can also distort input use with negative implication for productivity and the environment. A zero marginal cost of power, for example, promotes inefficient use and over exploitation of ground water in a number of states.

In the manufactured goods sector, producers are obliged to print a maximum retail price (MRP) on every packaged good. This requirement was introduced in 1976 under The

Standards of Weights and Measures Act. This price is determined by the manufacturer and restrains the retailer from selling the good at a higher price. The objective of the MRP is to reduce tax evasion and protect consumers from profiteering by retailers. However, because India has one of the highest densities of retail outlets in the world, the possibilities for anti-competitive practices are limited. By providing a focal point for retailers, the MRP could also become a *de facto* uniform price and thereby support retail price collusion. Similarly, maximum retail prices may also tend to limit competition in wholesale distribution and manufacturing. Thus, in other countries recommended prices are often discouraged, or even prohibited, as anti-competitive.

Road passenger transport is subject to significant entry barriers. As well as issuing operator licenses, state governments also determine the routes and times that operators are permitted to run. Even the fares that operators can charge on a particular route are determined by government. These licensing arrangements are susceptible to corruption and insulate the state transport corporations, which typically make large losses, from competition. The associated licence fees, however, are a major source of revenue for state governments, implying that reform in this sector needs to be coupled with efforts to increase the tax base (discussed in Chapter 6).

In road freight transport, the Motor Vehicles Act only mandates vehicle registration and a permit for operation and there is generally ease of entry and exit. However, Mehta (2006) reports that inefficiencies in this sector, which have been a constraint on the development of an integrated national market in India, are predominantly the result of cartels and price fixing by industry participants. This example underlies the importance of making the Competition Commission of India fully operational as soon as possible (discussed below).

A preference for small firms has held back productivity growth

A range of polices are in place to favour small companies whose investment in plant and machinery is less than INR 10 million.[7] The policies are designed to promote small industry, which contributes almost 40% of industrial value added, and compensate for the disadvantages of producing below efficiency. The principal policy, which reserves certain manufacturing products to small firms, will be phased out by 2009. By 2006, reservation was down to 336 products from a peak of over 800 at the beginning of the decade. Small firms also get fiscal benefits, as they pay a lower rate of excise tax on the goods they produce. Government procurement also favours small firms, with 338 products reserved for small suppliers who also win tenders for other products if their price is less than 15% above the lowest quote. Finally, banks are obliged to make 10% of their advances to small firms.

These policies skew the production structure towards small firms and further changes would be productivity enhancing. A number of government committees and research studies have argued that preferences for small firms have led to the fragmentation of production chains and inefficient scale.[8] It has also been noted that some entrepreneurs will split the production process between several small firms so as to retain the associated fiscal benefits. The policy of reducing reservation has so far been done by consensus with industrial groups and should be further pursued and widened to include reducing the other advantages accorded to small firms.

Barriers to exit are still formidable and hold back productivity

In OECD countries the process of "creative destruction" – whereby new firms displace unsuccessful and/or obsolescent firms – is an important mechanism for increasing productivity. Previous work at the OECD has shown that the entry and exit of firms accounted for 20% to 40% of total productivity growth over the 1980s and 1990s in OECD countries (OECD, 2003c). For countries such as India that operate behind the world's technological frontier, the positive impact of firm turnover on productivity may be larger than in the OECD given that it facilitates the introduction of new technologies from more advanced countries.

Barriers to firm exit in India are still formidable across all sectors. Under the Sick Industrial Companies Act 1985 (SICA), the Board of Industrial and Financial Reconstruction (BIFR) is responsible for either restructuring or closing companies with more than 50 employees and negative net worth (or for public companies having suffered a 50% reduction in their net worth). Directors have to report to the Board once negative net worth occurs. The Board then determines whether the company has negative net worth and institutes procedures to try and rehabilitate the company. This process can take many years during which time the company receives a moratorium on debt payments, is eligible for credit from the government, and may continue to operate. In practice, measured by the share of companies entering this procedure that are restored to financial health, the process fails in nine out of ten cases.

The BIFR does not have power to liquidate a company but will instead refer it to the State High Court for liquidation, which is a further lengthy procedure. The average time for liquidation is ten years, one of the longest delays anywhere (World Bank, 2006). The average recovery rate for creditors (including tax authorities and employees) is 13%. For OECD countries on average, the corresponding figures are 1.4 years and 74% respectively.

New laws were passed in 2002 and 2003 to simplify this procedure and repeal the legislation, but are yet to take effect. The Companies Act was modified to take over from the provisions of the SICA and the BIFR was to be replaced by National Company Law Tribunals. The composition of these tribunals was struck down in the courts and so the old system continues to function. If it had entered into force, the primary difference would have been that liquidation would be determined by the tribunal, rather than via the administrative function of the BIFR. The criteria were also changed with a precise definition of net worth and the threshold for establishing a case was changed to a 50% fall in net worth. In contrast to the SICA Act, filing a case before a tribunal would not have stopped all other legal proceedings. Given the performance of Debt Recovery Tribunals, it is not clear that the new tribunals, had they ever functioned, would have produced a markedly speedier outcome.

The failure to implement the repeal of the SICA offers a significant opportunity to introduce a separate bankruptcy law following accepted international practices. This law would aim to move all operational activities concerning a bankruptcy out of the court system and put them in the hands of an administrator who would negotiate an agreement between creditors subject to a vote and then the plan would be approved by the court and put into action. Given the delays that have plagued previous liquidation, it is important that the procedure should be time bound. It is important that the legislation should recognise that a bankrupt company can be solvent and that the appropriate test for bankruptcy is a cash test (inability to pay a debt) rather than simply insolvency (excess of liabilities over assets). A bankruptcy code is essential if enterprises are to be restructured – waiting until a company is insolvent is often too late to save any employment or goodwill of the company. It will also be important to create special bankruptcy courts with specially trained judges, given that it may be constitutionally impossible to staff a tribunal with anybody but retired High Court judges. And it will be important that the Bankruptcy Code takes precedence over all other legislation.

Improving the competition policy framework

A good competition policy framework is a vital ingredient in ensuring a dynamic and competitive business environment. With this objective in mind, the government of India passed a new Competition Act in 2002 and the Competition Commission of India (CCI), which is the principal enforcement institution of the Act, was established in October 2003. However, after judicial review, the Act was determined to need amendment in order to establish a Competition Appellate Tribunal, headed by a member of the judiciary, to hear appeals against CCI decisions. Consequently, the CCI has not begun its enforcement work and has only one board member and a small number of staff.

Once it is fully implemented, India's competition law will include many of the same principles found in competition frameworks in OECD countries. The Act prohibits agreements between firms that result in an appreciably adverse effect on competition, and it presumes such an adverse effect in the case of horizontal price fixing agreements and bid rigging. Secondly, the Act prohibits dominant firms from abusing their market power through, for example, predatory pricing, price discrimination, and denial of market access. The Act also regulates company mergers and acquisitions (M&A) if the aggregate assets of the combining parties have a value in excess of INR 10 billion (USD 220 million) or turnover in excess of INR 30 billion (USD 660 million). A merger of that magnitude that is likely to cause an appreciable adverse effect on competition is void, but notification of the proposed merger for prior review by the CCI is voluntary, not compulsory.[9] These thresholds are high relative to the average firm size and carry the risk that the merger control rules might not prevent some M&A activity that may have an appreciable adverse impact on competition. These arrangements may need to be revisited once the CCI is fully operational and has gained some experience in merger control.

The CCI is statutorily independent and does not receive any instructions from government. However, the CCI has to seek money from the government, who can overrule its budget requests. In addition, the central government can issue directions on questions of policy which are binding on the CCI. The CCI can report on sectors, policy issues (for example, privatisation), and laws or regulations issued by the legislature or administrative bodies only in response to requests; it cannot engage in such studies on its own initiative. The law authorises the CCI to impose substantial fines on firms and individuals but does not provide for imprisonment. In most cases, the top fine is 10% of average annual turnover; however, that limit does not apply in cases of price fixing, where the fine could be up to twice the profit from the violation. The CCI can grant leniency to firms that confess and co-operate. Public sector enterprises are covered by this law, which is essential given the extent to which they dominate certain industries.

One problem with the Act is that it contains no provisions relating to unfair marketing practices affecting consumers. These are covered by the Monopolies and Restrictive Practices Commission (the institution preceding the Competition Commission) and cases will be transferred to the National Consumer Commission when the former is finally wound up. Experience in OECD countries suggests that combining competition policy and law enforcement and consumer protection within the same agency can create significant synergies. Consideration could therefore be given to installing the consumer protection agency under the same roof as the CCI.

Notwithstanding these issues, India's competition law is close to "state-of-the-art". The most pressing requirement for competition law is to quickly clear the remaining parliamentary hurdles and make the policy operational. To fulfil its mandate the CCI will need to be capable of a high quality of economic analysis in competition law enforcement and need adequate staffing and funding.

Competition policy involves more than dealing with monopolies, mergers and anti-competitive practices in the business sector. In particular, the framework needs to be able to ensure that policy proposals issued by the government are compatible with competitive markets. In 2004, the government announced it was considering a policy to ensure that all levels of government and economic regulatory agencies take the competition dimension into account when formulating policy. Subsequently, a high-level committee has prepared a report. The introduction of such a policy would be a key event. A properly designed policy to support free and fair market competition should emphasise the removal of entry barriers, ensure competitive neutrality between public and private sector enterprises, establish access regimes for network facilities, provide for justification and notification when there is need to deviate from established principles of competition, and require all government bodies to undertake a competition audit of all existing and proposed policies.

External liberalisation has progressed substantially

To a significant extent, India's economic development depends on innovating through adapting production techniques and know-how developed abroad. Both international trade and foreign direct investment encourage domestic firms to incorporate foreign technologies into the production process, thereby facilitating technological diffusion. Equally, foreign affiliates tend to be more capital and skill intensive and invest more in research and development than domestic firms in the same industry (Keller, 2004; Keller and Yeaple, 2003). As a result, foreign affiliates tend to grow more quickly and make a larger direct contribution to productivity growth in comparison to domestic firms (Criscuolo, 2005) and more outward-oriented countries consistently grow more quickly than relatively closed countries (Srinivasan and Bhagwati, 1999).

Tariff barriers have come down but need to go further

As discussed in Chapter 1, the Indian economy has become much more open over the period of economic reform. Tariff revenue as a proportion of import value has fallen by a factor of six in just under two decades and the government has progressively reduced the highest standard tariff rate for non-agricultural products from 35% in 2001 to 10% in 2007. The objective of the current programme of tariff reductions, which began in 2002, is to lower the peak tariff rate to the average peak rate in ASEAN countries, which is currently around 7%. However, despite these significant improvements, tariff revenues and the average most favoured nation (MFN) tariff rate are still much higher than in OECD and a number of emerging countries (Figures 3.10 and 3.11).

There are also substantial derogations from the standard tariff rates, which mean that the yield from tariffs is considerably lower (at 5%) than the simple average of the MFN tariff (at 13% in 2007). In other countries, such as Mexico and Turkey, these derogations arise as

Figure 3.10. **Tariff revenue relative to import value in selected countries**

2005, tariff revenue (excluding domestic taxes) as percentage of import value

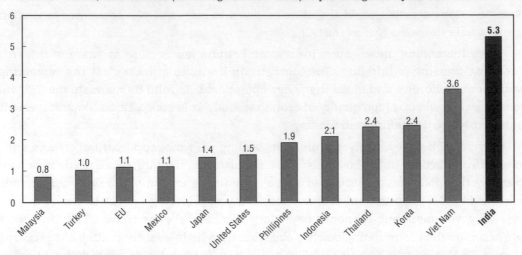

1. This figure excludes the so-called countervailing duty (CVD). This tax is levied on imported goods that are produced domestically at the same rate as the central value added (excise) tax on domestic goods. The CVD can be offset against payment of the value added tax. Given that the CVD can be offset, it should not be regarded as part of the tariff in much the same that the levy of a normal value added tax on an imported product is not regarded as a tariff. The CVD accounted for almost half of total receipts of taxes on imported goods in FY 2005/06.

Source: OECD Revenue Statistics, European Court of Auditors, Public Finance Statistics of India, various national publications.

Figure 3.11. **A cross-country comparison of simple-average tariffs**

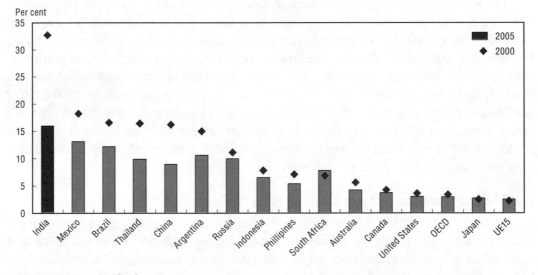

Source: UNCTAD, Trains database.

the result of regional trade agreements. In India, however, these derogations are domestic in nature. India also has one of the highest dispersions of actual tariff rates in WTO member countries (Dihel *et al.*, 2007). There are currently 134 duty exemption Acts in place which cover a wide range of activities including restaurants, agriculture, handlooms, leather and footwear, and gems and jewelry. In sectors reserved for small firms, instruments are in place to channel duty-free imports through trade associations. Other schemes mandate a 5% import duty on capital goods subject to an export obligation equivalent to eight times the duty saved over a period of eight years. Agri-export zones also grant duty-free imports of capital goods. These exemptions are partially offset by the use of anti-dumping levies, of which India is one of the largest users.

Widespread exemptions and the variability of the tariff structure result in an inefficient allocation of resources. In addition to the gains from lower average tariffs, substantial efficiency gains would result from having just one tariff rate. The priority should now be to ensure a greater degree of uniformity across the tariff structure, both reducing the numerous exemptions and the variability of actual tariffs across products.

Productivity could be raised by further reductions in FDI barriers

As with its tariff policy, India adopted a highly restrictive FDI policy after Independence, which was then liberalised somewhat during the reforms in the early 1990s. Over more recent years, the policy framework has improved further with the creation of a system of automatic clearances for FDI inflows and increases in caps on foreign ownership across a range of sectors. Currently, foreign ownership of up to 100% is permitted in many sectors (Table 3.3) with only the need to notify the authorities. In areas reserved for small scale industries, FDI is limited to 24%. In a number of sectors – alcoholic drinks, cigarettes and tobacco products; electronic, aerospace and defence equipment – government permission for FDI is required on a case-by-case basis.

Table 3.3. **Foreign direct investment: Ceiling on investment in a given company by sector**

	Permitted percentage of equity held by a foreign company
Agriculture	0
Coal mining (own use)	100
Coal mining (other)	0
Manufacturing	100
Newspaper publication	26
Electricity generation	100
Airports[1]	100
Distribution of petroleum products	100
Pipelines	100
Roads, highways, ports	100
Civil aviation[2]	49
Internet service providers (without gateways)[3]	100
Internet service providers (with gateways)	74
Telecommunication services	74
Banking	74
Insurance	26
Retail distribution	0
Retail distribution (single brand)	51
Wholesale cash and carry distribution	100

1. FDI of more than 74% in existing airports requires government approval.
2. Provided there is no direct or indirect participation by foreign airlines.
3. Subject to divestment of 26% of equity after five years if the investing company is listed in another part of the world.
Source: Department of Economic Affairs, GoI.

In addition to FDI caps in selected sectors, an industrial location licence is also required if the proposed site for an industrial undertaking is within 25 km from the standard urban area limit of the 23 cities that had a population greater than 1 million in the 1991 census. This requirement is waived if the site is a pre-existing industrial area or the plant is in a non-polluting industry such as electronics, computer software, printing and other specified industries.

At least partly as a result of recent reforms, FDI inflows have been growing rapidly since 2004, including a threefold increase in the year to March 2007. Investor sentiment has also improved significantly with a recent survey of executives of multinational corporations ranking India second behind China in an index of FDI confidence (A.T. Kearney, 2005). However, inflows are still relatively modest in comparison to some Asia and Eastern European countries (Figure 3.12).

Figure 3.12. **Inflows of Foreign Direct Investment**[1]

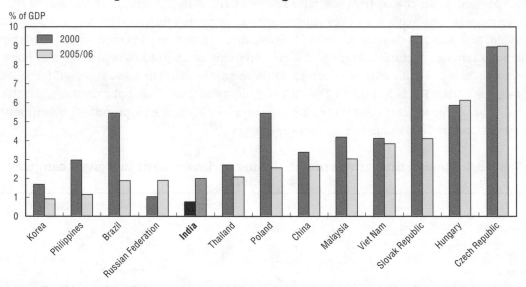

1. For India, China, and Brazil the more recent data is for 2006. For all other countries it refers to 2005.
Source: UNCTAD and OECD calculations.

Notwithstanding explicit barriers to FDI, the overall regulatory environment is the most important reason why FDI inflows into India have until recently been relatively low in comparison to other countries. A growing body of recent research has found that the regulatory environment is a key determinant of FDI. As shown in Nicoletti *et al.*, (2003), regulatory policies that restrict market access in one way or another negatively influence the share of foreign direct investment in OECD countries. Conway *et al.*, (2006) also find that the employment share of foreign affiliates in manufacturing sectors is higher in countries with relatively more liberal product market environments. These results are consistent with the fact that the relatively more liberal states in India attract virtually all of its FDI (Figure 3.2, Panel A, above).

Despite substantial recent improvements, the policy framework for FDI in India is still restrictive in comparison with OECD countries (Koyama and Golub, 2006). In addition, many of the FDI restrictions in place apply to potentially fast growing sectors with low productivity that would benefit from increased investment. Relaxing FDI restrictions in banking, insurance and retail distribution would seem likely to improve real incomes, given the poor productivity levels in these industries. In addition, allowing FDI into the retail sector would result in the modernisation of supply chains and substantially reduce the amount of food produce that rots before getting to market. In turn, this would improve incomes in the agricultural sector. Reducing barriers to entrepreneurship and state control in the central and state governments, as discussed above, would provide foreign investors with a regulatory environment that is more conducive to business development and also result in a marked increase in FDI inflows.

Box 3.2. **Policy recommendations for reforming India's product and service markets**

The public enterprise sector:

- Revitalise the privatisation programme. Address competition and regulatory issues prior to the sale of Public Sector Enterprises in infrastructure sectors (Chapter 7).

- Limit restrictions on foreign ownership and avoid post-privatisation control devices.

- Give conditional grants to poor states to restructure and close down non-working PSEs.

- "Unbundle" PSEs that currently have mixed commercial and promotional/policy objectives. Privatise the commercial operations of these companies and consolidate the promotional/policy implementation operations (potentially back into government departments).

- Improve the governance of the PSEs to improve transparency and decision making.

Administrative procedures:

- Undertake a comprehensive review of regulations at all levels of government to re-engineer processes, eliminate unnecessary steps, and optimise the process at the back-end before a service is delivered.

- Create an overarching department (in states where it doesn't already exist) to facilitate this work and coordinate between different arms of the state government. This department will also carry out Regulatory Impact Analysis to assess significant new regulatory proposals.

- Publicise permit and notification requirements and educate lower-level government bureaucrats as to the benefits of efficient administrative procedures and their role in the process.

- Use ICT to increase transparency and reduce opportunities for corruption and introduce severe penalties.

Regulation of internal markets:

- Eliminate all Small Scale Industry (SSI) reservations.

- Remove preferences for SSI and within-state firms from government procurement policies.

- Liberalise the road passenger transport sector.

- With the introduction of the VAT develop a system that will eliminate or reduce the need for "on the road" tax inspections (chapter 6).

- Amend the Companies Act 1956 to facilitate liquidation procedures for firms when necessary.

> ## Box 3.2. **Policy recommendations for reforming India's product and service markets** (*cont.*)
>
> **Competition law:**
>
> - Clear remaining parliamentary hurdles and make the Competition Commission of India (CCI) functional. Give the CCI sufficient resources to operate successfully.
>
> - Keep open the possibility of revising the thresholds for merger control once the CCI gains experience.
>
> - Implement a National Competition Policy that integrates the competition principle into policies and empowers the CCI to review regulatory proposals for their potential impact on market entry and competition.
>
> **External liberalisation:**
>
> - Continue lowering FDI and tariff barriers.
>
> - Create a uniform tariff rate for all non-agricultural products.

Notes

1. The indicators of product market regulation (PMR) summarise data covering 139 formal rules and regulations that have a bearing on competition. The indicators cover most of the important aspects of general regulatory practice as well as some aspects of industry-specific regulatory policy. For a detailed description of the PMR indicators and results for OECD countries see Nicoletti *et al.* (1999) and Conway *et al.* (2005). A full description of the PMR indictors methodology applied to India can be found in Conway (2007).

2. Extensive field trips to visit a large number government officials in a number of state capitals were undertaken to gather the underlying regulatory data used to compute the PMR indicators for India at the national and state levels. The Resident Commissioners of the state governments in Delhi were also used as a source of regulatory data. All of the state indicator values are given in the annex to this chapter.

3. As discussed in detail in Chapter 6, the Union List stipulates areas of regulatory responsibility that are the exclusive preview of the government of India (for example, exit policy and bankruptcy procedures) whereas items on the State List come under the jurisdiction of the state governments (for example, inspections and compliance with regulations). A third list – the Concurrent List – covers areas where the centre and state governments have joint responsibility (for example, entry and labour regulation).

4. For the Indian experience see, for example, Gupta (2005) and Kaur (2003).

5. There is a growing body of research that finds that poor quality government administration creates particular problems for small and medium-sized firms, which are often less able to bear the costs of bureaucratic burden than larger more established – and in some cases more influential – businesses.

6. The OSSs in Indian states typically involve three levels depending on the size of the proposed investment. For example, in Haryana, new investment proposals of a value up to IRP 50 million (USD 1 million) are dealt with by a district-level committee. Investment proposals of a value between IRP 50 million and IRP 30 million (USD 6.5 million) are dealt with by a state-level committee and investment proposals of a value of more that IRP 30 million are dealt with by a high-level committee.

7. Large firms can obtain a licence to manufacture products reserved for SSI provided 50% of their production is exported. In practice, the administrative burden of obtaining the necessary licenses has acted as a constraint on entry. See World Bank (2000).

8. See the Abid Husain Report (1997).

9. In the event either of the combining parties is outside India or both are outside, the threshold limits are USD 500 million for assets and USD 1 500 million for turnover. If one of the merging parties belongs to a group, which controls it, the threshold limits are IRP 40 billion

(USD 880 million) in terms of assets and IRP 120 billion (USD 2 640 million) in terms of turnover. The Act states that the threshold limits for assets and turnover would be revised every two years based on the Wholesale Price Index or fluctuations in the exchange rate.

Bibliography

A.T. Kearney (2005), "FDI Confidence Index", Global Business Policy Council, Vol. 8.

Bellver, A. and D. Kaufmann (2005), "Transparenting Transparency: Initial Empirics and Policy Applications", *World Bank Policy Research Working Paper*, September.

Conway, P., V. Janod and G. Nicoletti (2005) "Product Market Regulation in OECD Countries: 1998 to 2003", *OECD Economics Department Working Papers, No. 419.*

Conway, P., D. de Rosa, G. Nicoletti, and F. Steiner (2006), "Regulation, Competition, and Productivity Convergence", *OECD Economics Department Working Paper, No 509.*

Conway, P. (2007), "Product Market Regulation in India: An International and Cross-State comparison", *OECD Economics Department Working Paper*, forthcoming.

Criscuolo, C. (2005), "The Contribution of Foreign Affiliates to Productivity Growth: Evidence from OECD Countries", *OECD STI Working Paper 2005/8.*

Dihal, N., M. Martina and P. Kowalski (20007), "India's Trade Integration, Realising the Potential", *OECD Trade Policy Working Paper*, forthcoming.

Government of India (2005), *Report of Ad Hoc Group of Experts on Empowerment of Central Public Sector Enterprises*, Department of Public Enterprises, *http://dpe.nic.in/newgl/reportofage.htm.*

Gupta, N. (2005), "Partial Privatisation and Firm Performance", *Journal of Finance*, Vol. 60, No. 2.

Kaur, S. (2003), *Privatisation and Public Regulation: The Indian Experience*, Macmillan India Ltd, New Delhi.

Keller, W. (2004), "International Technology Diffusion", *Journal of Economic Literature*, Vol. XLII (September 2004), pp. 752-82.

Keller, W. and S. Yeaple (2003), "Multinational Enterprises, International Trade, and Productivity Growth: Firm Level Evidence from the United States", *IMF Working Papers 248.*

Kikeri, S. and J. Nellis (2004), "An Assessment of Privatization" *The World Bank Research Observer*, Vol 19, No. 1.

Koyama, T. and S. Golub (2006), "OECD's FDI regulatory restrictiveness index: Revision and extension to more countries", *OECD Economics Department Working Paper*, No. 525.

Kurtzman, J., G. Yago and T. Phumiwasana (2004), "Research Overview: The Global Costs of Opacity: Measuring Business and Investment Risk Worldwide", *MIT Sloan Management Review*, October.

Malyshev, N. (2006), "Regulatory Policy: OECD experience and evidence", *Oxford Review of Economic Policy*, Vol. 22, No. 2.

Megginson, W. and J. Netter (2001), "From State to Market: A Survey of Empirical Studies on Privatization", *Journal of Economic Literature*, Vol. 39, No. 2, pp. 321-89.

Mehta (2006), *A functional competition policy for India*, Academic Foundation, New Delhi.

Nicoletti, G., S. Golub, D. Hajkova, D. Mirza and K.-Y. Yoo (2003), "The Influence of Policies on Trade and Foreign Direct Investment", *OECD Economic Studies*, No. 36.

Nicoletti, G., S. Scarpetta and O. Boylaud (1999), "Summary Indicators of Product Market Regulation with an Extension to Employment Protection Legislation", *OECD Economics Department Working Papers*, No. 226.

OECD (2002), *Regulatory Policies in OECD Countries: From Interventionism to Regulatory Governance*, OECD, Paris.

OECD (2003a), *OECD Economic Surveys: Chile*, OECD, Paris.

OECD (2003b), *Privatising state-owned enterprises: an overview of policies and practices in OECD countries*, OECD, Paris.

OECD (2003c), *The Sources of Economic Growth in OECD Countries*, OECD, Paris.

OECD (2005a), *OECD Economic Surveys: Brazil*, OECD, Paris.

OECD (2005b), *Corporate governance of state-owned enterprises: a survey of OECD countries*, OECD, Paris.

OECD (2005c), *OECD Guidelines on Corporate Governance of State-Owned Enterprises*, OECD, Paris.

OECD (2006), *Cutting Red Tape: National Strategies for Administrative Simplification*, OECD, Paris.

OECD (2007), *Agricultural Policies in Non-OECD Countries: Monitoring and Evaluation 2007*, OECD, Paris.

Sader, F. (2000), "Do 'one-stop shops' work?", Foreign Investment Advisory Service, World Bank, Washington, D.C.

Srinivasan, T.N. and J. Bhagwati (1999), "Outward-orientation and Development: Are Revisionists Right?", Economic Growth Center, Yale University, Discussion Paper No. 806.

World Bank (2000), *India: Reducing poverty and accelerating development*, Oxford University Press, India.

World Bank (2006), *Doing Business 2007: Reforms Make a Difference*, World Bank, Washington, D.C., www.doingbusiness.org.

ANNEX 3.A1

OECD PMR indicators by state

This annex presents the PMR indicator values for the 21 states surveyed. The PMR indicators at the state level have been modified to reflect the ways in which state governments are able to influence the regulatory environment. In particular, the low-level indicators that measure regulations set at the central level have been excluded from the state-level PMR indicators. The resultant state-level PMR indicators are derived from the indicators of state control (excluding use of "command and control regulation" and "price controls") and barriers to entrepreneurship (excluding "legal barriers" and "antitrust exemptions"). As well as excluding regulatory provisions set by the central government, the low-level indicator of "communication of rules and procedures" has been partially modified to more accurately reflect state level reforms in this area. As a result of data availability, the indicator of "size of government" has also been calculated in a slightly different way at the state level relative to the standard PMR indicators. As a result of these modifications, the low-level PMR indicators that have been altered and the high-level PMR indicators at the state level can not be compared with the economy-wide indicators. The state-level indicators are given in Table 3.A1.1.

The collection of the regulatory data used to construct the Indian PMR indicators at the central and state levels, as well as full details on the way in which the state indicators were constructed, is given in Conway (2007).

Table 3.A1.1. **The PMR indicator values by state**

	Andhra Pradesh	Assam	Bihar	Chhattisgarh	Delhi	Goa	Gujarat	Haryana	Himachal Pradesh	Jharkhand	Karnataka
Overall indicator	1.73	1.93	1.92	2.10	1.30	0.77	2.32	1.17	1.84	1.59	1.48
State control	2.08	1.34	1.30	0.55	1.25	0.83	2.18	1.47	1.93	0.36	2.28
Public ownership	2.18	1.39	1.32	0.53	1.31	0.86	2.33	1.54	2.07	0.35	2.46
Scope of public enterprise sector	1.91	1.36	1.64	1.09	1.09	0.82	1.64	1.36	1.36	0.55	1.36
Size of public enterprise sector	4.19	2.45	1.77	0.00	2.62	1.56	5.12	2.94	4.70	0.30	6.00
Direct control over business enterprises	0.95	0.68	0.82	0.55	0.55	0.41	0.82	0.68	0.68	0.27	0.68
Barriers to entrepreneurship	1.45	2.41	2.43	3.38	1.34	0.72	2.42	0.91	1.75	2.60	0.83
Regulatory and administrative opacity	0.24	2.55	1.46	3.86	1.25	1.28	1.35	0.10	2.50	3.19	0.19
Licenses and permit system	0.00	4.00	0.00	6.00	2.00	2.00	2.00	0.00	4.00	4.00	0.00
Communication and simplification of rules and procedures	0.25	0.75	3.00	1.25	0.25	0.50	0.25	0.00	0.75	2.25	0.25
Administrative burdens on start-ups	2.24	2.34	3.06	3.10	1.41	0.36	3.15	1.45	1.29	2.23	1.24
Administrative burdens for corporations	2.83	2.94	3.60	3.55	1.37	0.60	3.78	1.72	1.48	2.30	1.40
Administrative burdens for sole proprietor firms	2.61	2.60	3.64	3.72	2.15	0.43	3.72	1.93	1.66	3.00	1.75
Sector-specific administrative burdens	1.47	1.51	2.08	2.09	0.83	0.00	2.16	0.87	0.71	1.43	0.71
Indicators by functional areas											
Administrative regulation	1.45	2.38	2.45	3.34	1.33	0.71	2.41	0.91	1.72	2.59	0.83
Inward-oriented policies	1.73	1.93	1.92	2.12	1.30	0.77	2.32	1.16	1.83	1.60	1.48

	Kerala	Madhya Pradesh	Maharashtra	Orissa	Punjab	Rajasthan	Tamil Nadu	Uttar Pradesh	Uttaranchal	West Bengal
Overall indicator	1.90	1.66	1.29	2.10	1.40	2.07	1.35	1.65	1.44	2.71
State control	2.11	1.02	1.46	2.30	1.91	1.35	1.44	1.22	1.34	2.30
Public ownership	2.14	1.03	1.46	2.40	2.02	1.43	1.46	1.26	1.39	2.39
Scope of public enterprise sector	2.73	1.36	2.18	2.18	1.64	1.09	1.91	1.36	1.36	2.45
Size of public enterprise sector	2.75	1.24	1.35	4.50	4.09	3.00	1.79	2.01	2.45	4.00
Direct control over business enterprises	1.36	0.68	1.09	1.09	0.82	0.55	0.95	0.68	0.68	1.23
Barriers to entrepreneurship	1.72	2.20	1.15	1.94	0.98	2.67	1.27	2.01	1.52	3.04
Regulatory and administrative opacity	1.47	1.53	0.41	0.39	0.31	2.18	1.24	0.50	0.45	3.73
Licenses and permit system	2.00	2.00	0.00	0.00	0.00	2.00	2.00	0.00	0.00	6.00
Communication and simplification of rules and procedures	0.75	0.75	0.75	0.50	0.50	2.25	0.25	0.75	0.75	1.00
Administrative burdens on start-ups	1.90	2.65	1.64	2.96	1.43	2.99	1.30	2.99	2.22	2.63
Administrative burdens for corporations	2.66	3.08	2.66	3.82	1.74	3.60	1.42	3.58	2.99	2.87
Administrative burdens for sole proprietor firms	1.89	3.24	1.29	3.24	1.82	3.46	1.82	3.59	2.36	3.33
Sector-specific administrative burdens	1.17	1.77	0.98	2.02	0.85	2.02	0.74	2.05	1.44	1.73
Indicators by functional areas										
Administrative regulation	1.71	2.19	1.15	1.94	0.99	2.67	1.25	2.01	1.53	3.00
Inward-oriented policies	1.90	1.67	1.29	2.10	1.40	2.08	1.35	1.66	1.44	2.71

ISBN 978-92-64-03351-1
OECD Economic Surveys: India
© OECD 2007

Chapter 4

Improving the performance
of the labour market

Over the past decade, labour market outcomes have improved in India, with net employment rising markedly for the economy as a whole. However, these gains have arisen primarily in the unorganised and informal sectors of the economy, where productivity and wages are generally much lower than in the formal organised sector. It is only India's organised sector that is subject to labour market regulation, and here employment has fallen. The role of employment protection legislation in affecting employment outcomes is controversial both in the OECD area and in India. This chapter looks at the impact of employment protection legislation and related regulation on the dynamics of employment in the organised sector of the economy, using newly constructed measures of national regulation and state labour reforms. We find that while reforms have taken some of the bite out of core labour laws, more comprehensive reforms are needed to address the distortions that have emerged.

This chapter presents new indicators that first measure the strictness of federal EPL settings in India, and second provides a quantitative indication of the extent to which states have – or have not – made changes in their implementation of labour laws and regulations. Based on these indicators, it would appear that employers have found ways to counter the rigidity of labour legislation through: switching to less protected categories of labour by using short-term contracts; substituting capital for labour to a considerable degree (using more capital intensive means of production); and by keeping plant size below the thresholds at which key laws become applicable, limiting economies of scale. The state-level indicators suggest that some states have also reacted to the perceived cost of federal laws on employment by making procedural and process-related reforms in the application of labour laws. These reforms do appear to have stabilised labour's share of income in reforming states, in contrast to the national picture of a decisively falling labour share. However, while these reforms have taken some of the bite out of core labour laws (and a range of other factors are at work), the chapter makes the case for more comprehensive labour reforms that would lower the costs of employment adjustment, better protect workers as a whole, and help address the distortions that have emerged which appear to adversely impact labour market outcomes and economy-wide efficiency.

Employment has expanded in the economy as a whole, but not in the organised sector

Contrary to widespread concerns about so-called jobless growth, employment expanded in five out of the last six years for India's economy as a whole, as well as for manufacturing, according to updated estimates based on the most recent (2004/05) round of the government of India's National Sample Survey (NSS).[1] Such estimates imply that employment growth has improved considerably, doubling the 1.3% pace of growth during the 1990s over the first five years of the 2000s. The pace of employment growth of over 2½ per cent *per annum* so far in the 2000s also exceeds the 1.9% pace of growth during the 1980s. Such an outturn is well above the previous expectations of many observers and represents a major upward shift in India's labour market performance (see Nagaraj, 2004; Anant *et al.*, 2006; Government of India, 2006).

Gains in employment from 1998 to 2005 came about nearly equally from increases in secondary and tertiary employment (representing 19% and 25% of the labour force, respectively). About 30 million net jobs were added in each of the two sectors, representing an annualised growth rate of about 6.2% for the secondary sector and 4.7% for the tertiary sector. These growth rates represent a turnaround from the anaemic pace of employment growth for much of the 1990s, and even exceed the employment growth rates of the 1980s. Net employment gains in agriculture on the other hand slowed to ½ per cent per year, as more workers moved to off-farm employment. Perhaps what is most surprising – given that industrial production has increased less than total output – is that the pattern of employment in industry (and manufacturing) has followed that of the economy as a whole, with overall net employment growth of 6½ per cent per year over the 1997 to 2004 period.

Despite strong gains in employment across the economy in recent years, a dichotomy has emerged with net increases in employment occurring almost exclusively in the least productive, unorganised, and often informal part of the economy. Meanwhile, the organised sector's employment level has actually been shrinking.[2] In industry, from 1997 to 2004, the overall 6½ per cent annual growth of employment disguises an average net loss of employment in the organised sector of about 1% per year over the period, while unorganised manufacturing employment grew at a rate of about 8% per year (Figure 4.1, Panel A). As a result of these developments, the relative share of the organised sector in industrial employment fell from 15-20% in 1981–98 to only 10% in 2004 (Figure 4.1, Panel B), a decline that was much more rapid than for the economy as a whole (shown in Chapter 1).

Figure 4.1. **Organised and unorganised sector employment in industry**

Panel A: Growth of organised and unorganised sector employment

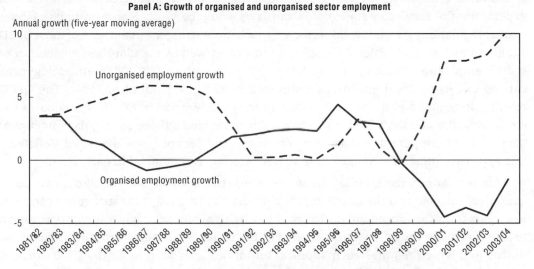

Panel B: Share of employment in the organised public and private sector

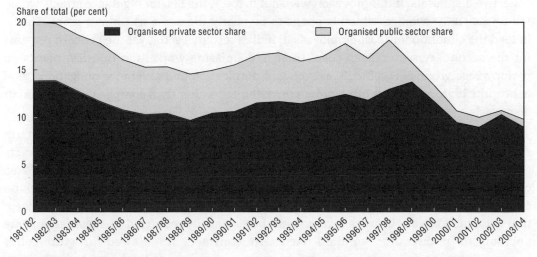

Source: OECD analysis of NSS and ASI data.

The slight contraction of organised sector employment disguises considerable underlying job dynamics

In order to better understand what has happened to the fortunes of the organised sector, this chapter examines gross flows of jobs in organised manufacturing and the potential influence of labour regulations on these dynamics. Our methodology for measurement of job flows is described in Box 4.1. The resulting job creation, destruction and turnover figures capture the annual dynamics of employment at the level of detailed industry branches from 1998 to 2004 and represents the first study of India to have compiled gross job flow statistics using unit-level microdata. These figures reveal that the slight contraction of net employment in the organised sector disguises considerable underlying job dynamics, with rates of job destruction often higher than those for creation.

The size of job flows is surprising given the strict regulatory stance of India's labour laws

Given this apparently high degree of jobs dynamics in the organised sector, one would expect that the regulatory stance of labour laws would be weak. However, India's labour market regulations for the formal sector are much more stringent than those of most OECD countries and several major developing countries as well. A standardized evaluation of India's employment protection legislation (EPL) using the OECD EPL methodology was carried out using legal information supplied by the government of India. The OECD methodology, outlined in the 1999 edition of the *OECD Employment Outlook*, evaluates the stringency of a country's labour regulations in three areas: those for regular (indefinite) contracts, for temporary or fixed-term contracts, and for collective dismissal. Following this approach, India's federal labour laws were scored, as they stood in early 2007.

For regular contracts, India's labour laws are stricter than those of all but two OECD countries, Portugal and the Czech Republic (Figure 4.2, Panel A), This stringency comes in large part from the procedural difficulty of having to obtain prior government permission to lay-off just one worker for plants covered by the Industrial Disputes Act (IDA). Chapter V-B of this Act, which requires such approval for all factories with more than 100 workers, removes much of the distinction between the EPL for regular employment and for collective dismissals. If this provision were not in force, the EPL for regular contracts would fall to the OECD average, which happens to be nearly the same as China's score. This is indeed the situation for most employees in India's tertiary sector, yet the concern remains for the secondary sector. Even then, though, dismissing workers in non-IDA plants on performance grounds is difficult, as standard notification and severance obligations tend to be quite high, and courts often order reinstatement rather than compensation for unfair dismissals.

The stance of India's EPL regime is more relaxed only for temporary and fixed-term contracts, placing it just above the mean of OECD countries' score for such contracts (Figure 4.2, Panel B). The moderate score of India for such contracts reflects the main area of labour reform that has come about in recent years, allowing employees to work on temporary work agency contracts to carry out a range of "non-core" activities, a concept that is defined in various ways across states but is usually restricted to activities that are ancillary to production.[3] Standard fixed-term contracts are allowed for white-collar workers as well as, in principle, for regular workers, following a federal notification in 2003, and about half the states have implemented analogous provisions, but public awareness of the state-level provisions is low and repeated efforts to reverse the central notification may

Figure 4.2. **International comparison of employment protection legislation in 2006**

The indicator score runs from 0-6, representing the least to most restrictive

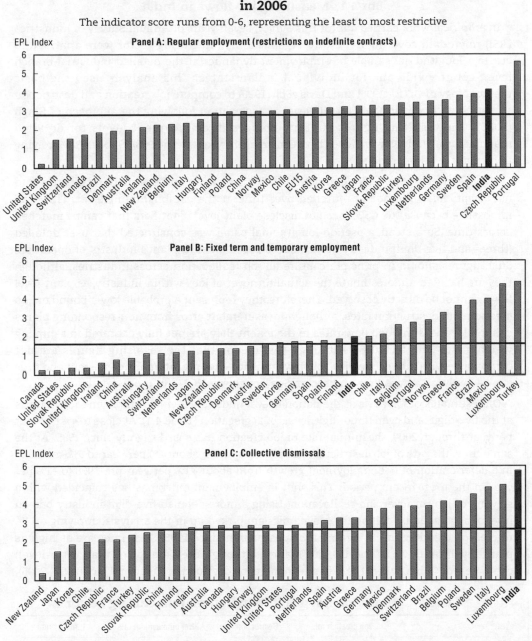

Source: OECD computation for India, estimate for China; OECD (2005), *Going for Growth*; OECD (2007), *Economic Survey of Brazil*.

be deterring its use. The most important recent shift in the temporary EPL stance was a recent Supreme Court decision (2006) that clarified the minimal restrictions on renewal of temporary contracts (although severance payments proportional to job tenure are required). This decision represented an important shift from the prior possibility of contractors being converted to indefinite contracts which could then cause the restrictions on regular contracts and collective dismissals under Chapter V-B of the IDA to come into force.

Box 4.1. **Measuring job flows in India**

In empirical work carried out for this *Survey*, seven years of Annual Survey of Industries (ASI) microdata covering the entire organised manufacturing sector were analysed to create a longitudinal sample of employment dynamics at the detailed industrial branch level, countrywide and for individual Indian states. This analysis used the basic methodology of OECD (1996) and Davis *et al.* (1998) to compute job creation and destruction statistics, with adjustments for the level of aggregation following the approach of Singh (2006). The resulting figures capture changes in employment levels for detailed manufacturing industry branches between adjacent years from 1998/99 to 2003/04, relying upon plant-level microdata.

The preferred approach for computing such job creation and destruction statistics is to use *longitudinal* microdata, matched over time at the establishment level. This was impossible because the CSO does not disclose plant-level identifiers that can be matched across time. So instead, a pseudo-longitudinal panel was constructed that uses detailed (three- and five-digit) industry branch codes based on each plant's industry of operation. Such figures should in principle capture all job reallocation across industries, although they are likely to underestimate the actual turnover of jobs within-industry, as plant-level flows cannot be directly observed. Therefore, they represent a probable lower bound on job creation and destruction rates, although measurement error from non-responding plants could raise measured job flow rates to the extent they are not fully captured in sampling weights (see Ahmad, 2006). Although this means that the resulting figures are not comparable with other countries' job flow statistics, they *are* internally consistent and thus can be analysed across time and sector. See Dougherty (2007) for more details.

Our estimates of job flows at the national level finds considerable employment dynamics at the five-digit, and even three-digit, levels of aggregation (Table 4.1). At close to 4% per cent per year through 2004, the annual rate of job creation has eased slightly since 1985. At the same time, the rate of job destruction has picked up from about 4% per year to 5%, resulting in a deterioration of net employment growth from about +1% per year pre-1998 to –1% per year in the most recent period. This shift in employment outcomes has coincided with a slowing of job turnover and reallocation. Using a more detailed five-digit industry branch level of aggregation, additional job dynamics are picked up in the analysis, implying a 14% rate of job creation and 15% rate of job destruction since 1998. Such rates are as high as plant-level job flows in the US and France, although they are lower than (firm-level) estimates for China, where there has been more job destruction (Deng and McGuckin, 2005).

Table 4.1. **Gross job flows in the Indian manufacturing sector**

Year[1]	Job creation rate	Destruction rate	Net employment rate	Turnover rate
Based on three-digit industries:				
Average 1985-1998	5.3	−4.1	1.2	9.4
Average 1999-2004	3.9	−5.0	−1.1	8.9
Based on five-digit industries:				
1999-2000	18.9	−21.2	−2.3	40.1
2000-01	11.4	−13.7	−2.3	25.0
2001-02	8.0	−10.8	−2.8	18.8
2002-03	16.5	−13.1	3.3	29.6
2003-04	15.8	−16.1	−0.3	31.9
Average 1999-2004	14.1	−15.0	−0.9	29.1

1. Year pairs are based on fiscal years from April until March.
Source: OECD analysis of ASI plant level data for period 1997-2004 and EPW data for 1985-97.

The third measure of the economy-wide stance of EPL is for collective dismissals (Figure 4.2, Panel C). Here, India's stance is especially onerous, more-so than any other comparison country. Nearly every aspect of this measure rates at the top end of the scale, from the definition of collective dismissal (one worker), to notification and delays involved, given requirements for obtaining prior government consent. Most of these rules are encompassed in the IDA legislation, and come into force for any plant with more than 100 workers, encouraging many plants to stay small and restrict their scale of operation (see Figure 4.3 below).

As a whole, India's federal EPL stance is highly restrictive for the organised sector that it covers, given its interference in a number of important respects with firms' hiring and severance decisions. Nevertheless, job flow statistics suggest that considerable dynamics exist despite the regulations. This seeming mystery could be a result of enterprises altering their behaviour to reduce the impact of the rules, or it could be that in practice EPL application or enforcement is less onerous than the regulations suggest – a possibility that is likely to vary considerably across states, given that constitutional responsibility for state labour regulation is shared between the centre and the states. Both of these possibilities are explored.

Job dynamics under heavy labour regulation are uneven and come at a great cost

While the degree of job dynamics appears to be considerable, it varies widely across different segments of the organised labour force. The unbalanced coverage of employment protection legislation (EPL) in India appears to be important in explaining the variation of job flows across segments, suggesting that EPL is distorting the decisions of employers and accentuating labour market duality:

- The EPL index for staff employed with fixed-term or temporary contracts – in India typically supplied by a labour contracting agency – showed a moderate degree of restrictiveness, similar to the average for OECD countries. Correspondingly, over the period 1998 to 2004, job creation amongst contractual staff consistently dominated job destruction, allowing the net employment of contractual staff to rise by 10% annually, while it declined by 2½ per cent a year for regular workers, for whom there was much less job creation (Table 4.2).

- For small firms employing 100 or fewer workers, the EPL index is also similar to that found in OECD countries and, over the same period, job creation rates were more than double job destruction rates for this group of firms, causing employment in these smaller firms to rise by more than 20% a year. Moreover, despite the absence of restrictive dismissal laws, the job destruction rate in small plants was actually less than that in larger ones.

- In contrast, in large firms with over 100 employees (where the EPL index is high), the job creation rate for (non-supervisory and non-contractual) regular workers was low and well below the job destruction rate, with the result that the net employment of such staff fell by more than 5% per year in the period 1998 to 2004. In contrast, job creation for contract staff in large firms was twice the rate for large firms' regular workers, and despite a higher destruction rate as well, their net employment increased almost 4% per year.[4]

The tendency for large firms to restrain job creation is associated with a marked substitution of capital for labour that is not seen in small firms. Over the 1998 to 2004

Table 4.2. **Job creation and destruction by size of plant workforce and type of worker[1]**

% per year

	Large[2]	Small	Overall[3]	Large[2]	Small	Overall[3]
	Job creation rate			Destruction rate		
All employees	11.5	24.2	14.1	−17.0	−8.4	−15.0
Workers	13.3	26.7	15.4	−18.7	−10.4	−17.5
Contract	26.7	31.0	28.7	−22.9	−13.7	−19.6
Supervisors	16.8	27.8	19.6	−27.4	−14.6	−24.7
Others	15.9	31.5	19.8	−25.2	−13.7	−22.5
	Net employment			Turnover rate		
All employees	−5.5	15.8	−0.9	28.5	32.7	29.1
Workers	−5.5	16.3	−2.1	32.0	37.1	32.9
Contract	3.8	17.2	9.0	49.6	44.7	48.3
Supervisors	−10.5	13.3	−5.1	44.2	42.4	44.2
Others	−9.3	17.8	−2.6	41.1	45.2	42.3

1. Based on five-digit industry data, 1999 to 2004, manufacturing only.
2. Large plant size is more than 100 workers, small have fewer.
3. Rates are not directly comparable with Table 4.1 due to differences in the levels of aggregation.
Source: OECD analysis of plant level data from ASI.

Table 4.3. **Capital intensity of plants**

	Fixed assets per employee				
	Constant prices, thousands INR			Index 1998/99 = 100	
Year	Large plants	Small plants	Relative capital intensity	Large plants	Small plants
1998-99	468 912	366 346	128.0	100.0	100.0
1999-2000	509 428	254 418	200.2	108.3	70.5
2000-01	491 789	332 730	147.8	105.2	89.2
2001-02	531 453	334 791	158.7	112.3	91.3
2002-03	527 071	335 996	156.9	112.5	91.7
2003-04	577 171	310 413	185.9	121.2	86.0

1. Large firms are defined as those with more than 100 workers; small firms fewer.
2. Shown in 1998/99 INR, with net investment deflated using the national accounts deflator for gross fixed capital formation.
Source: OECD tabulation of ASI plant level data.

period, constant price fixed assets per employee in plants with more than 100 workers rose by 21%, while they fell by 14% in smaller firms, according to tabulations by OECD using the Annual Survey of Industries (Table 4.3). While the large plants were already 28% more capital intensive, this raised their capital intensity relative to small plants by more than half.

A separation of job turnover rates between publicly and privately owned plants may illustrate more fully what has been happening in terms of the cost of EPL (Table 4.4). Publicly owned plants (that represent slightly less than 20% of output in the ASI data) have almost *twice* the rate of job destruction as privately owned plants over the 1999 to 2004 period. While public plants also have higher rates of job creation than private plants, public plants' net contribution to employment is highly negative, on the order of a 10% drop in employment each year. This result may appear to be strange given the presumably strict

Table 4.4. **Job flow rates for publicly and privately owned plants**[1]

% per year

	Public	Private	Overall[2]
Job creation rate	20.6	14.3	14.4
Destruction rate	−25.6	−14.4	−15.2
Net employment	−5.0	0.0	−0.9
Turnover rate	46.1	28.7	29.6

1. Based on five-digit industry data, 1999 to 2004, manufacturing only.
2. Overall rates are not directly comparable with those in Table 4.1 and Table 4.2 due to differences in the level of aggregation.
3. OECD tabulation of ASI plant level data.

compliance of public firms with the IDA legislation and the usual motive of public firms to preserve employment.

How could turnover in public enterprises be so high? The main explanation for this extensive (public plant) turnover is that voluntary retirement schemes (VRS) have been accepted by workers and unions as a mutually agreeable mechanism for downsizing. VRS schemes became common after the government set up a National Renewal Fund in 1991 as part of the structural reform programme, to fund restructuring of public sector enterprises; only later did the private sector begin to make use of VRS (Nagaraj, 2004).

The VRS scheme has made employment adjustment feasible; however, it comes at a great cost. Since it requires that settlements are collectively agreed upon, high levels of compensation are made to groups of workers. Typically, the reservation payoff to the most recalcitrant marginal worker determines the outcome of the negotiations. OECD interviews with employers and local governments suggest that such payoffs can easily reach levels of two to three months of compensation for each year of work.[5] A financial analysis of public sector redundancy schemes suggests that total average payments to staff that left ranged between almost four to over six years' pay (Morrison, 2006). The redundancy compensation component (as opposed to normal leaving benefits such as accrued leave and provident fund balances) averaged between ten and 36 months, with central government enterprises tending to pay the most. Such a cost places India among the most expensive in the world in terms of cost of dismissal, and is far above the statutory compensation that was intended by the IDA act (15 days of compensation per year of service). So while employment flexibility is feasible, it comes with an increased cost of severance – and not just to the employer who would normally have to pay for the VRS, but to the worker as well, in part because some businesses avoid payment altogether, but also because the costs create behavioural distortions that have detrimental economic effects.[6]

High labour costs in the formal sector increase capital intensity and the size of the informal sector

Such high potential compensation for dismissal and the associated *uncertainty* raises the cost of employment, inducing larger employers to substitute more capital for labour than would appear justifiable given the apparently low wages that prevail in India.[7] This effect can be observed in the low – and falling – labour share in organised industry, which can be observed in all two-digit industries from the 1980s. The share of total labour costs in value added has fallen from 36% in the early 1990s to 31% in 1999/2000 and 29% in 2003/04, with the steepest fall among large enterprises.[8] The share of wages (including bonus payments) in value added has fallen similarly, from 25.7% in 1998/99 to 23.5% in 2003/04.[9]

Average wages have risen at a slower pace than labour productivity, so that labour compensation relative to Germany has been stagnant since the early 1990s (see Figure 2.2). Moreover, wage inequality has grown considerably, with most gains going to the top two deciles, while median wages have remained stagnant (see Narain, 2006).[10]

In addition to causing business to substitute capital for labour, high implicit costs of employment for large-scale firms have induced many entrepreneurs to start small and stay small. Businesses in the unorganised (and often informal) sector with fewer than 10 or 20 workers (depending on the law) are subject to very few labour regulations and can employ casual or contract labour freely (as can most information technology [IT] and business process outsourcing [BPO] companies). Even businesses in the organised sector with fewer than 50 workers face no legal restraints on collective dismissals, while those having 100 or fewer workers are not subject to the IDA requirement to obtain prior permission before dismissing workers (or shutting down). As a consequence, the size distribution of businesses in India is highly skewed toward small units (see Figure 4.3), with visible peaks in the distribution of plant sizes at 10 and 20 workers. Considerable anecdotal evidence illustrates the extent to which entrepreneurs deliberately disintegrate their business activities into numerous small-scale units (Mukerji, 2006).[11] As discussed in Chapter 2, such small scale production reduces the efficiency of the economy and limits the productivity and incomes of businesses and workers.

Figure 4.3. **Plant size distribution in the organised manufacturing sector by size of employment**

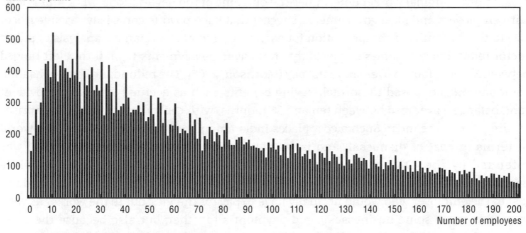

1. Sizes rounded to the nearest even number.
Source: OECD calculation from ASI plant level data.

The direct impact of India's labour regulations are subject to considerable debate

The suggestion was made earlier in this *Survey* that the local business environment, and stringent labour regulations in particular, may have a deterrent effect on firm entry and investment, and thus could reduce potential output growth and possibly job creation as well. However, the empirical evidence on the role of labour regulations in India has been subject to a vigorous debate.

A series of economy-wide studies have examined the role of two key amendments to the Industrial Disputes Act (IDA) affecting collective dismissals (see Anant *et al.*, 2006;

Bhattacharjea, 2006). The 1976 amendment mandated prior government permission for layoffs, and the 1982 amendment lowered the size threshold from establishments with more than 300 workers to those with more than 100. Roy (2002) examined accessions and separations of individuals from firms from the 1960s through 1992, and she found that the two amendments had a strong and adverse effect on labour market flexibility, a result consistent with the cross-country evidence. However, flexibility may have increased for other reasons, given the growing use of contract labour from the early 1980s. The amendments did not appear to have an impact on the slow speed of employment adjustment to shocks in India (5-6 years), a finding that may reflect the broader range of rigidities that exist in India: especially weaknesses in the insolvency framework and urban land laws (Anant and Goswami, 1995; Roy, 2004).

The variation that exists in India's labour laws across its states has offered fertile ground for empirical exploration by labour economists from around the world. Several well-known studies have been carried out, the best-known being the study by Besley and Burgess (BB) (2002, 2004), who compiled an index of state-level amendments to the IDA from 1949 through 1992, and classified them as to whether they were pro-worker or pro-employer. Their analysis of the indicator suggests that pro-worker amendments resulted in lower output, investment, employment and productivity in formal manufacturing although output in the informal sector increased. Their results also suggest that the more restrictive labour amendments had a perverse effect on the poor as they tended to increase urban poverty rates.

The BB index and its interpretation have turned out to be highly controversial and have been utilized as well as critiqued in multiple papers. Studies such as Hasan *et al.* (2003), Topalova (2004), and Sanyal and Menon (2005) use modified versions of the index (through 1992) to classify states as pro-worker or pro-employer, and find several things: states with more pro-worker labour legislation have lower elasticity of demand for labour, higher rates of poverty, and less investment, in part through interactions with trade liberalisation and state-level institutions. Further work by Aghion *et al.* (2005) updated the index (through 1997) and, using the time series of the index, found higher rates of growth following industrial de-licensing in states with more pro-employer labour institutions. Ashan and Pagés (2006) carried out a full re-scoring of the index to measure transaction costs and found at least as detrimental an impact on output and employment as the original BB study. Ashan and Pagés also separated the index into several sub-components and found that regulations that increase the cost of settling disputes appeared to be more costly for employment than the IDA's restrictions on firing and closure. On the other hand, a separate study by Purfield (2006) that further updated the BB index (through 2002) did not find significant detrimental effects of more pro-employer labour institutions on state-level growth.

Despite the robustness of the link between the BB index and poor labour market outcomes across different states in most of these studies, there are reasons to think that the index could be improved due to the sparseness of underlying amendments and its focus on just one law. Anant *et al.* (2006) and Bhattacharjea (2006) point out that many of the formal state-level amendments to the IDA used in the index would appear to be of minimal significance since they are infrequent, sometimes pertain to obscure procedural matters, and are likely to be overshadowed by court decisions and informal changes in the application of the laws. An update of the BB index carried out as background to this *Survey* (through 2005), using the most recent edition of the original data source for the index

(Malik, 2006), shows that there have been only eight amendments to the IDA in any Indian state since 1990, and they relate to only three states, of which only the 2004 amendments in Gujarat would appear to be of any consequence to labour market outcomes.[12]

Several prominent observers of India's labour markets now argue that regulations other than the IDA are likely to be more important and that the IDA may be something of a distraction in the debate over labour reforms, given the four dozen central laws and hundreds of state laws that govern labour issues (Nagaraj, 2004; Debroy, 2005; TeamLease, 2006). There have been far fewer studies that look more broadly at India's labour laws in systematic empirical analysis, perhaps due to their complexity and overlapping coverage. Moreover, some of the most important changes appear to have occurred in interpretation of the laws by the Supreme Court and through changes in the way the laws are enforced, particularly obvious in the case of the use of contract labour, which has become increasingly widespread in many states (Anant *et al.*, 2006). Such state-level reforms have been the subject of speculation, but there has been little systematic regulatory information collected beyond the IDA amendments in the BB index.[13]

State-level labour reforms

A new OECD index of state-level labour reforms in India may illuminate the way forward

In order to better understand how state-level reforms may have affected labour markets, the OECD has developed a customized survey instrument to identify the areas in which Indian states have made specific discrete changes to the implementation and administration of labour laws (Dougherty, 2007). This state-level survey covered eight major labour legal areas, identifying 50 specific subjects of possible reform, many of which could be implemented by administrative procedure rather than through formal amendments to the laws. Since few of these changes have been systematically documented, the assistance of the All-India Association of Employers (AIOE) was used to survey 21 states, about half of which were visited in person by members of the survey team. Preliminary answers to the questionnaires were drafted in most states by a labour expert designated by the AIOE or the Federation of Indian Chambers of Commerce and Industry (FICCI) affiliate in the state capital. The answers to this draft questionnaire were then corrected through discussions with local union leaders, independent labour experts, employers and state labour commissioners. Finally, the completed questionnaires were submitted to each states' labour secretary for their final review.[14]

The verified responses to the survey were complied by the OECD into an index that reflects the extent to which procedural changes have reduced transaction costs, through limiting the scope of regulations, providing greater clarity in their application, or simplifying compliance procedures. Answers were then scored as "1" if they reduced transaction costs, "0" if they did not, and (for two questions) "2" for a further reduction, with a maximum score of 50. A list of the subjects and summary scores are shown in Annex 4.A1. The reforms covered in the index concern eight specific areas: the Industrial Disputes Act (IDA), Factories Act, State Shops and Commercial Establishments Acts, Contract Labour Act, the role of inspectors, the maintenance of registers, the filing of returns and union representation.

A breakdown of the average index score across all states is shown in Figure 4.4 (Panel A), which illustrates that the largest number of reforms that were identified concern

Figure 4.4. **Areas of state-level labour law reform**

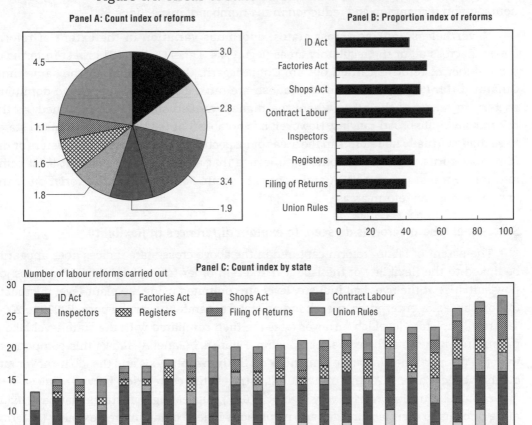

Source: OECD-FICCI-AIOE Survey of 21 states.

contract labour, an area where many reforms have been carried out (especially for IT/BPO sectors and for export processing and Special Economic Zones), but also an area for which there were more questions on the survey than for other areas. In order to adjust for the number of questions in each area, the number of cases where reform had occurred was taken as a proportion of the number of possible subjects for reform in a given reform area (Panel B, out of 100). This proportional index shows that, with the exception of reforming the role of inspectors and the rules concerning the role of unions, there was a fairly similar share of the reforms carried out across the different areas surveyed.

What is perhaps most notable about the indexes, though, is the very modest degree of reform that has actually been carried out since, even in the area of contract labour, there have been reforms in only about half of the subject areas. Moreover, no state has a raw score of more than 28 out of 50 of the possible reform subjects, and for seven of these, no more than two states made any reforms. The principal areas where there was little change were: key sections of the IDA (that concern collective layoffs); rules governing working hours; union recognition and reduction in the number of inspections.[15]

Nevertheless, looking across states, enormous variation in the extent of reform appears across all of the regulatory areas (Figure 4.4, Panel C). Ranked lowest in terms of the number of reforms carried out are Chhattisgarh, Goa and Bihar; at the same time, Gujarat, Uttar Pradesh and Andhra Pradesh are ranked highest. There is no dominant pattern in terms of the areas where the highest-ranked states have reformed, as the reforms are quite broad-ranging. However, it is notable that the three lowest-ranked states have made virtually no reforms in the areas of inspections, simplification of registers or the filing of returns. It is also of some significance that all states have made at least some reforms in the areas of the IDA and Contract Labour Act, for which the variation is the lowest among the reform areas.

State-level labour reforms do seem to explain differences in flexibility

The extent of labour reform captured in the above cross-state indices does appear to be linked to the flexibility of the labour market. In order to measure flexibility, gross job flow statistics at the five-digit industry level are computed using the plant-level microdata for formal sector enterprises in each Indian state, separately, over the period 2000 to 2004. The resulting state-level job turnover rates are then compared with the state-level labour reform index to see if there is a relationship. Figure 4.5 (Panel A) shows this comparison, with the (proportional) labour reform index on the horizontal axis and the job turnover rate on the vertical axis.[16] As the trend-line illustrates, the correlation between the reform index and job turnover rates is very high ($R^2 = 0.37$), suggesting that states that have made more reforms to their labour rules and regulations indeed obtain more flexibility (in terms of job dynamics) in their labour markets and *vice-versa*: fewer reforms significantly limit flexibility.[17] The increased job dynamics come from higher rates of both job creation and destruction, which tend to offset each other almost entirely in terms of net employment (Figure 4.5, Panel B).

There is broad cross-country evidence to suggest that job security regulations raise the cost of employment and have a detrimental effect on the creative-destruction process that is vital to economic growth and technological progress (OECD, 2004 and 2006). Job security regulations limit job turnover in sectors that for technological or market structure reasons *need* more frequent adjustment of employment to be competitive. In the case of India, the results show that state-level labour reforms appear to increase job turnover (or flexibility), and a lack of such reforms limits turnover. Across Indian states in the 2000 to 2004 period, an increase in turnover rates can be shown to *limit the fall* in the labour share of value added that has been observed nationwide (Figure 4.6). Yet no state is able to do better than to stabilise their labour share. More broadly, increases in job turnover can help productivity and output growth, and therefore increase the pace at which incomes converge to those of more developed countries (see Caballero *et al.*, 2004; Micco and Pagés, 2004; Haltiwanger *et al.*, 2006).[18]

The OECD job strategy re-assessment also found that a lack of employment flexibility accentuates labour market inequalities, as it makes it more difficult for vulnerable workers such as women, minorities and the youth to enter the workforce, and the formal sector in particular. In the case of India, the effects of the overall EPL stance are rigid enough that the marginal state-level reforms may only have moderating effects on the labour market as a

Figure 4.5. **State labour reforms and gross job flows, 2001-04**

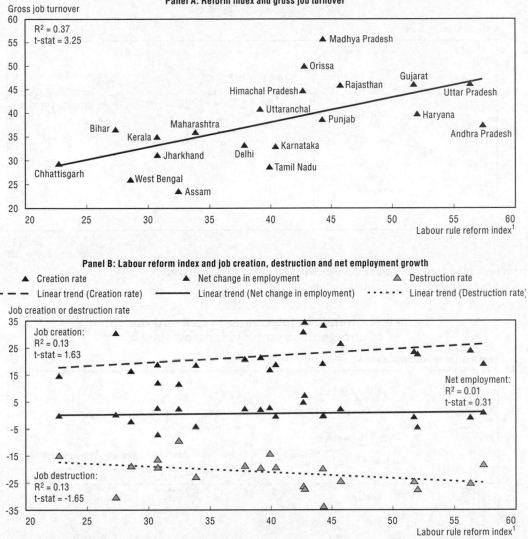

Panel A: Reform index and gross job turnover

Panel B: Labour reform index and job creation, destruction and net employment growth

1. Uses proportional index of labour law changes by state.
2. Goa not shown, as it is an outlier, having the least-restrictive product market regulation (see Chapter 3).
3. State flow rates are not directly comparable with national rates due to different levels of industry-wise aggregation.

Source: Dougherty (2007).

whole. Thus, while we cannot identify a direct relationship between the labour reform index and the size of the informal sector in given states, we do observe that higher rates of organised sector job creation *stem the rise* in the size of the unorganised sector (Figure 4.7). Again (analogous to the previous figure), no state is able to do better than to stabilise the size of its formal sector. Of course, many other factors also affect the incidence of informal employment, from competitive conditions (Chapter 2) and product market regulations (Chapter 3) to the extent of illiteracy (Chapter 8).

Figure 4.6. **The change in labour turnover and the change in the labour share of value added**

Percentage point change 2000-04

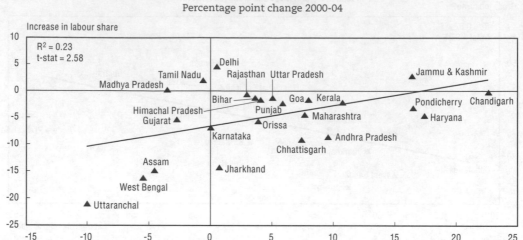

Note: Job turnover rates are per year based on five-digit national data over 2001-04.

Source: OECD tabulation of plant level data from the ASI.

Figure 4.7. **Change in job creation rates and the share of unorganised employment, by state**

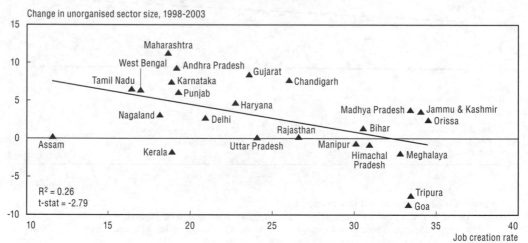

Note: Job creation rates using five-digit ASI microdata for the organised manufacturing sector.

Source: OECD calculation from ASI plant level data and NSS employment data.

What can feasibly be done to improve India's labour markets?

The priority should be to reduce the cost of formal employment

Labour reforms are urgently needed in India to reduce the relatively high cost of formal employment. Reforms could serve to limit the detrimental effects that high costs have on the dynamism of the labour market, as well as improve the wage share and enhance economy-wide productivity. The above analysis indicates that India's labour laws create a degree of employment protection (EPL) that is highly uneven, and among large firms and for collective dismissals it is higher than that of any OECD member or major emerging market. The negative consequences of this high level of protection are in line with the experiences of many OECD member countries. Considerable benefits for all workers could be had from a redesign and moderation of the current stance of India's EPL. This would allow business to become more competitive though greater economies of scale, which would not only improve the welfare of workers through higher productivity and wages thereby better benefiting even those segments of the workforce that the laws were designed to protect, as well as the vast (low productivity) workforce in the unorganised and informal sectors that they virtually ignore.[19]

... through broad-based labour reforms

Our analysis of state-level labour reforms suggests that it is not the IDA alone that is harming labour market outcomes – it is the wider range of labour legislation.[20] This result is consistent with the views of labour experts in India that cite the enormous complexity and uncertainty caused by the manifold overlapping laws and antiquated (often colonial-era) provisions, that are in dire need of simplification (Debroy, 2005; ADB, 2005; Sharma, 2006; Anant *et al.*, 2006; TeamLease, 2006; World Bank, 2006).

As a general principle, a country like India with a large informal economy should have less, not more, labour regulation than a typical OECD country. Stringent labour regulations exacerbate labour segmentation, and the negative consequences are very clear in the case of India. While a long-term goal should be to formalise all jobs, labour laws should not seek to impose conditions too different from what employers and workers would agree upon voluntarily.

Major efforts have been made over the years in an attempt to simplify the laws, but, they have met with little success. Most notable is the Second National Labour Commission's (SNLC) report in 2002, whose recommendations were widely vetted, highly detailed and for the most part quite moderate and well-regarded; yet few of its recommendations have been implemented in the past five years. While this is not entirely surprising as labour reform is perhaps the most intractable area to reform in any country, it raises the question of whether there are reform strategies which could be more effective.

Strategies to make EPL more well-balanced should focus on improving fairness

A critical challenge for Indian labour markets is to ensure that there is *greater fairness* for all types of workers – whether in the organised or the unorganised sector, and regardless of what types of establishments they work in or what type of contract they are employed under. At the same time it is critical that labour policies support the healthy functioning of markets so that overall welfare is not hurt.

Current policies work against large classes of workers, from females, whose unemployment rates of 9% (for urban females) are double the more moderate rates for males, to scheduled castes and tribes (Borooah, 2005) and even out-of-state migrant workers.[21] The bulk of these under-represented groups earn below the minimum wage,[22] and many of them are faced with the unattractive prospect of casual employment at a low wage, with neither social protections nor stability.[23] In part these limited options are a result of low levels of education and skills, but they are accentuated by the strength of employment protection, a problem that is observed for women and youth in many OECD countries.

A broader and more even-handed approach for India's labour laws and regulations is needed, in keeping with the recommendations of the recent re-assessment of the OECD's Jobs Strategy (OECD, 2006). This could address not only the cost of employment, but the unbalanced regulatory impact of current law. One promising approach would be to introduce a comprehensive new labour law (or set of only a few laws) that offers basic (moderate) protections to all types of workers and would not discriminate by size of enterprise. This law could improve statutory compensation for redundancy, provide for retraining and assistance in job search, thereby providing a balance between flexibility and security. If this law were to supersede the patchwork of existing laws and offer greater certainty and reasonable levels of compensation for dismissals, the cost of employment could perhaps be brought down enough to reverse the fall of the wage share and stem the ongoing expansion of the size of the informal sector. Efforts have been underway by the government in consultation with unions and employers to draft legislation that would offer some types of basic protections for the informal sector, including social insurance. If such vital consensus-based efforts are combined with a broad-based rationalisation of the EPL framework, considerable gains could be achieved for all workers.

Practical strategies are already being pursued and may be expanded, even if they are second-best

Given the slow progress in implementing the SNLC's reasonable recommendations since 2002, second-best strategies for carrying forward labour reform must and are being considered. These reforms are necessarily incremental, but may offer ways of demonstrating the benefits of better-crafted regulations, and thus pave the way for more comprehensive consensus-based reforms in the future:

● *Further reforms at the state level:* Reforms at the level of individual states are already occurring, as is documented in the state-level reform index. Given that the average value of the (count) index is only 20.2 out of 50, and the most reform-minded state only has a 28, there are many areas in which procedural or rule changes could be made at the state level to ease the burden of these labour regulations that raise the effective cost of labour. For contract labour, this is the route that has already been followed, with a considerable expansion of these arrangements in many states, although there remains ambiguity about when it can be utilised. In several other areas of labour regulation, there is even more that could be done, such as in rationalising inspections and streamlining union rules, which, for instance, still allow for a multitude of unions in an enterprise without clear guidelines for worker representation. While many of these reforms can be done without substantial central government involvement, states may feel restrained in what they are willing to carry out by the centre's policies. Moreover, Figures 4.6 and 4.7 suggest that the potential benefits of state-level reforms under the current framework may not be enough to actually reverse the ongoing decline in the labour share (or the shrinking of the formal sector), even if they may be able to stabilize it. Greater autonomy for individual states to make more significant legal changes to labour laws may be necessary, although this could require a constitutional amendment making labour a state issue rather than a concurrent one (see TeamLease, 2006). In the meantime, though, there would seem to be considerable scope for reform under the present governance arrangements.

● *Expansion of contract labour and fixed-term contracts:* The ongoing expansion of contract labour (and potentially fixed-term contracts) is having a major impact on India's effective EPL stance, and contract labour's growth in popularity may serve to encourage its even more widespread use (see Anant *et al.*, 2006). With last year's clarification by the Supreme Court of the legal status of contract labour as distinct from regular employment, it is likely to be used even more widely, further reducing the share of the workforce facing the highest level of EPL. While this direction of reform is generally a move in a useful direction, the widening of the extent of differences in the degree of flexibility between different types of employees (workers and contractors especially) creates distortions that segment the labour force. A broader range of reforms would seem to be needed, initially giving firms clear authority to determine what types of work are suitable for contract labour. Even less distortionary would be greater use of fixed-term contracts for workers, which are allowed under revisions to central standing orders from 2003. Although half of states have issued similar enabling provisions, interviews suggest that businesses have only made limited use of these types of fixed-term contracts.

- *Provide labour reforms in demonstration areas*: The development of Export Processing Zones (EPZs) and Special Economic Zones (SEZs) has created an enabling environment for local experimentation and reform of labour laws in many states. In fact, three-quarters of states have granted general procedural exemptions for use of contract labour in EPZs and SEZs, although only four have made formal amendments to their legislation for such purposes, according to information provided by the Ministry of Law and Justice. To the extent that SEZs provide a demonstration effect on employment illustrating the benefits of less costly regulation, they may be useful in promoting more general reforms, despite the second-best nature of such partial reforms in relatively small jurisdictions. Already, the information technology and business processing outsourcing sectors (IT/BPO) have enjoyed such exemptions in virtually all states, and the benefits to this broad sector have been visible in its tremendous growth, discussed in Chapter 1, although they remain a very small share of the labour force.

- *Enhance competition in product markets*: Recent examinations of OECD countries' experience with the political economy of structural reforms demonstrates a strong link between the extent of product market deregulation and the progress of trade liberalisation and labour market reforms (Høj et al., 2006). Such experience suggests that besides reducing tariffs and easing FDI restrictions, facilitating business entry and exit, lowering administrative burdens, and further progress on privatisation (all described in Chapter 3) would be useful in creating a more competitive operating environment that could make labour market reforms more politically feasible. In part, this feasibility reflects the fact that uncompetitive markets with high margin businesses make it easier for workers and unions to appropriate and sustain high economic "rents", which are present to a significant degree in India (see Table 2.4). More competitive product markets and associated improvements in labour market conditions, on the other hand, can make reforms easier to undertake (Bassanini and Duval, 2006). In fact, the recent upswing in Indian growth, as well as the strong employment growth highlighted earlier, would suggest that now may be as propitious a time as any to make some serious attempts at labour reforms.

Box 4.2. **Policy recommendations for labour market reform**

- *Reduce barriers to formal employment:* redesign and moderate the framework for employment protection, making it neutral across different types of firms and employees. This would at least include substantial revisions to the Industrial Disputes Act, removing the most restrictive provisions that require prior government permission for employment termination and exit decisions. As an interim step, the threshold for government permission could be raised to 300 employees and then phased out over a several year period. At the same time, compensation for retrenchment could be raised from 15 days per year of service to closer to 45 days, coming closer to actual negotiated levels, as well as norms in the OECD.

- *Revamp, consolidate and simplify all labour laws:* reduce the number of labour laws to just a few simplified laws that provide *basic* legal coverage and protections for all employees, increasing fairness. Beyond this, decisions about how labour is utilised within the enterprise should be left to the managers of the firm. Provisions that interfere with such decisions should be removed (*i.e.* Section 9A of the IDA).

- *Improve labour market data:* move toward a quarterly small-sample labour force survey so that employment outcomes can be better assessed between large-scale National Sample Survey rounds.

- *Further state-level reforms:* states should accelerate their own labour reforms in all areas, including offering special treatment for Special Economic Zones, which will not only attract investment but also provide a laboratory for demonstrating the benefits of reform. Broadening the allowances for the use of contract labour and fixed-term contracts could also effectively reduce the overall level of EPL. While some central flexibility exists at present for states to make labour reforms, they would be aided through a constitutional amendment to shift the jurisdiction of labour regulation from a concurrent central-state to just a state issue. In the absence of such a provision, greater clarity from the centre for states to make amendments in specific areas should be granted (*i.e.,* for union recognition in a multi-union situation).

- *Lay the groundwork for future reform:* Further deepening of product, service and financial market reforms could improve competition and facilitate future labour reforms (see Chapters 3 and 6).

Notes

1. OECD estimates use the quinquennial NSS household surveys (including the most recent 61st round for 2004/05) in conjunction with census data and intermediate small scale surveys (CSO, 2006). Labour force participation is (under *usual status*) 42% of the population, having risen by about 3 percentage points in the past five years. The new NSS figures also show that the unemployment rate (in terms of *usual status*) remained almost the same for rural males, and decreased by one percentage point for urban males, but increased by about one percentage point for females in both rural and urban areas.

2. The organised sector in manufacturing is composed of factories (or plants) that have ten workers or more and use power, or 20 workers or more and do not use power. For the remainder of the economy, the organised sector essentially refers to all companies and government administrations. The size of the overall organised sector has fallen, from about 28 to 27 million persons, or from about 7½ to 6½ per cent of total employment, over the period 1995 to 2004, while the number of persons in regular wage employment outside of the organised sector has more than doubled. See Table 1.6 for a breakdown of this employment data, which relies on administrative records.

3. There are blanket allowances for contract labour in the BPO/IT sector and for SEZs in some states. See Box 4.1 and Annex 4.A1.

4. Nagaraj (2004) previously found some signs of possible shifting between supervisors and workers during the late 1990s, and there would appear to be a quantitatively similar adjustment in 1999-2000 for supervisors and workers, and between contractors and workers in 2001-00, but little circumstantial evidence in other recent years.

5. Other reports suggest that compensation levels are frequently on the order of 45 days per year of service (World Bank, 2006).

6. Many OECD counties that have only partially reformed their labour markets (such as Spain) have experienced similar rapid increases in segmentation and consequential loss of efficiency (Haltiwanger, Scarpetta and Schweiger, 2006).

7. This effect can also be observed in the relatively capital and skill-intensive development pattern that India has developed, compared with countries at similar stages of development (see Chapter 2).

8. Among plants with 100 or more workers, the labour share in value added fell almost three times more rapidly than among smaller plants, during the period 1998 to 2004.

9. Official ASI wage data in value added have fallen from about 25% in the 1980s to only 12% in 2003/04, but these include neither bonuses nor the wages of supervisors and "other" (non-worker) employees.

10. There is some evidence from the newest NSS that real wages for regular salaried workers outside of the organised sector may have even fallen in the most recent five-year period (Unni and Raveendran, 2007).

11. The small scale is a consequence not only of labour laws, but also of product market regulations – especially administrative burdens – as well as tax avoidance (see Chapters 3 and 5).

12. These post-1992 IDA amendments are comprised of: an additional method for qualifying to serve on a labour court in Tamil Nadu (1998); a reduction in the prerequisites for serving on an Industrial Tribunal in Madhya Pradesh (1999, 2003); removal of state-level provisions inserted in 1982 that pertained to criminal cases in Madhya Pradesh (2003); and the introduction of a range of exemptions from the IDA's Chapter V-B for Special Economic Zones in Gujarat (2004).

13. Some surveys to examine state-level changes in the application of labour laws through notifications and changes in the application of various regulations have been undertaken (CII, 2004a and 2004b). However, these previous efforts did not include all major states and questions were limited to a relatively small set of procedural changes.

14. Detailed answers to the questionnaire, as well as a list of persons consulted, are contained in the annex to Dougherty (2007). The 21 designated states cover 98% of population and GDP.

15. A number of states have introduced self-certification schemes that allow for infrequent pre-planned inspections (for instance, Gujerat and Uttar Pradesh), but these plans have so far have attracted minimal interest, apparently because of enhanced civil and even criminal liability under the law for violations.

16. Note that the state of Goa is not included in this comparison as a result of its extreme outlier position, a position that likely results from its unique history with little industry, but perhaps most importantly from its position as the least restrictive state in India in terms of product market regulation (see Chapter 3). If Goa is included, the correlations shown are still significant with the same signs, but the R^2 statistics are halved.

17. What is also striking (although not shown here), is that there is no clear relationship between the main subcomponents of the labour reform index (i.e. IDA and contract labour) and job turnover. It appears that what is important for flexibility is the overall labour regulatory stance, rather than rules in specific areas.

18. While we will not delve deeply into this question here, it is also the case that the higher rates of turnover are associated with higher TFP at the firm level using production function estimates on ASI microdata. Recent evidence of the TFP–turnover link has also been found across US states (Autor et al., 2007).

19. In historical perspective, it is useful to note that much of the current set of labour laws were introduced during British rule and were intended to protect only a relatively privileged minority; to a significant degree, this remains the case today (World Bank, 2006).

20. This is not to say that the IDA is not in need of reform. Its ineffectiveness may be in part linked to its unrealistic interference with production decisions that must be made by firms in a market economy. These include not just Chapter V-B that requires prior government approval for layoffs and closure, but also Chapter 9A that requires 21 days' notice for change of job description, and the letter of the law that involves compensation for termination of only 15 days per year, a level so far below negotiated outcomes under VRS that it may perpetuate a bad equilibrium of the *status quo*. A level such as 30-45 days would be more in keeping with OECD countries' practices.

21. Low rates of participation among urban females (18% *versus* 57% for males) reflect high rates of discouragement in finding good jobs, a fact that is illustrated in the 2004/05 NSS results. Job activation programmes that involve training and incentives to re-enter the labour force have been found to be useful in many OECD countries. Few such programmes exist in India, and the ones that do, such as the Rural Employment Guarantee Act, offer little prospect of human capital development, and may not be as attractive to females as to males. More useful perhaps would be a programme that provides monetary incentives for educational development and training, along the lines of the *Progressa/Oportunidades* programme in Mexico (OECD, 2003). The issue is further discussed in the chapter on human capital (Chapter 8).

22. There is some indication that minimum wages in India may offer a signaling effect that could be beneficial to workers without affecting overall employment rates (World Bank, 2006). However, while this may be true for the bulk of organised workers – dominated by males – for females and minority workers, the situation is likely to be different given that the majority of these groups earn below the minimum wage and strong enforcement of minimum wage laws would likely suppress labour demand (Kantor *et al.*, 2006).

23. Wages in the unorganised sector are on average about one-sixth that of the organised sector. However, it is important to note that the distribution is highly uneven, and that 30% of self-employed workers (in the unorganised sector) earn more than the average of those in the organised sector (World Bank, 2006). But the bulk of unorganised workers engage in the informal economy, essentially perpetuating a low-productivity/low-income trap, with insufficient skill development (Anant *et al.*, 2006). In the informal economy, other abuses exist as well, including the use of child labour and even bonded labour (ILO, 2006). Restrictions on the Child Labour were strengthened in October 2006, when employment of children under the age of 14 as domestic servants or to work in hotels, restaurants and shops was banned.

Bibliography

ADB (2005), *Labor Markets in Asia: Promoting Full, Productive, and Decent Employment – Key Indicators*, Asian Development Bank, *www.adb.org/documents/books/key_indicators/2005/*.

Ahmad, Nadim (2006), "A proposed framework for business demography statistics", OECD Statistics Directorate Working Paper 2006/3, November, OECD, Paris.

Aghion, Philippe, Robin Burgess, Stephen Redding, Fabrizio Zilibotti (2005), "The Unequal Effects of Liberalization: Evidence from Dismantling the License Raj in India", NBER Working Paper No. 12031, February 2006.

Anant, T.C.A. and O. Goswami (1995), "Getting Everything Wrong: India's Policy Regarding Sick Firms", in Dilip Mukherjee (ed.), *Essays in Industrial Policy*, New Delhi: Oxford University Press.

Anant, T.C.A., R. Hasan, P. Mohapatra, R. Nagraj, and S.K. Sasikumar (2006), "Labor Markets in India: Issues and Perspectives", in Jesus Felipe and Rana Hasan (eds.), *Labor Markets in Asia: Issues and Perspectives*, Asian Development Bank and Palgrave Macmillan, London.

Ashan, A. and Carmen Pagés (2006), "Helping or Hurting Workers?: Assessing the Effects of *de jure* and *de facto* Labor Regulation in India", Background paper for World Bank (2006).

Autor, David H., William R. Kerr, Adriana D. Kugler (2007), "Do Employment Protections Reduce Productivity? Evidence from US States", NBER Working Paper No. 12860, January.

Bassanini, Andrea and Romain Duval (2006), "Employment patterns in OECD countries: reassessing the role of policies and institutions", OECD Economics Department Working Paper No. 486, June, OECD, Paris.

Basu, Kaushik, Gary S. Fields and Shub Debgupta (2007), "Labor Retrenchment Laws and their Effect on Wages and Employment: A Theoretical Investigation", IZA Discussion Paper No. 2742, April.

Besley, Timothy and Robin Burgess (2002), "Can Labour Regulation Hinder Economic Performance? Evidence from India", CEPR Discussion Papers No. 3260, March.

____ (2004), "Can Labor Regulation Hinder Economic Performance? Evidence from India", *Quarterly Journal of Economics*, Vol. 119, No. 1, pp. 91-134.

Bhattacharjea, A. (2006), "Labour Market Regulation and Industrial Performance in India: A Critical Review of the Empirical Evidence", *Indian Journal of Labour Economics*, Vol. 49, No. 2, pp. 211-232.

Borooah, Vani K. (2005), "Caste, Inequality and Poverty in India", *Review of Development Economics*, Vol. 9, No. 3, pp. 399-414.

Caballero, Ricardo, Kevin N. Cowan, Eduardo M.R.A. Engel and Alejandro Micco (2004), "Effective Labor Regulation and Microeconomic Flexibility", Federal Reserve Bank of Boston, Working Paper No. 04-6.

CII (2004a), *Labour Reforms in Southern Region States – Issues and Concerns*, Confederation of Indian Industry, Policy Primer No. 3, April 2004

___ (2004b), *Driving Growth Through Reform: A Comparative Analysis of Labour Practices in Select Northern Region States*, Confederation of Indian Industry, Northern Region, July.

CSO (2006), *Employment and Unemployment Situation in India 2004-05*, NSS 61st Round (July 2004-June 2005), Report No. 515.

Davis, Steven, John C. Haltiwanger and Scott Schuh (1998), *Job Creation and Destruction*, MIT Press, Cambridge.

Debroy, Bibek and P.D. Kaushik (2005), *Reforming The Labour Market*, Academic Foundation with Friedrich Naumann Stiftung and Rajiv Gandhi Institute for Contemporary Studies, New Delhi.

Debroy, Bibek (2005), "Issues in Labour Law Reform", in Debroy and Kaushik (eds.), pp. 37-76.

Deng, Haiyan and Robert H. McGuckin (2005), "The Dynamics of China's Labor Market: Job Creation and Destruction in the Industrial Sector", ICSEAD Working Paper Series Vol. 2005-18, November, *www.icsead.or.jp/7publication/workingpp/wp2005/2005-18.pdf*.

Dougherty, Sean (2007), "Labour Regulation and Employment Dynamics at the State Level in India", OECD Economics Department Working Paper, forthcoming.

FICCI–AIOE (2005), "Report of the Core Group on Restructuring Labour Policy", in Debroy and Kaushik (eds.), pp. 265-84.

GOI (2006), *Economic Survey 2004-2005*, Ministry of Finance, Government of India, *http://indiabudget.nic.in/es2004-05/esmain.htm*.

Haltiwanger, John, Stefano Scarpetta, and Helena Schweiger (2006), "Assessing job flows across countries: The role of industry, firm size, and regulations", World Bank, Policy Research Working Paper No. 4070.

Hasan, Rana, Devashish Mitra, K.V. Ramaswamy (2003), "Trade Reforms, Labor Regulations and Labor-Demand Elasticities: Empirical Evidence from India", NBER Working Paper No. 9879, August.

Høj, Jens, Vincenzo Galasso, Giuseppe Nicoletti and Thai-Thanh Dang (2006), "The political economy of structural reform: Empirical evidence from OECD countries", OECD Economics Department Working Paper No. 501, July, OECD, Paris.

ILO (2006), *The end of child labour: Within reach*, International Labour Organisation, Geneva, *www.un.org/aroundworld/unics/english/ilo_childlabor_2006.pdf*.

Kantor, Paula, Uma Rani, and Jeemol Unni (2006), "Decent Work Deficits in the Informal Economy: the Case of Surat", *Economic and Political Weekly*, 27 May, pp. 2089-97.

Malik, P.L. (2006), *Industrial Law: A Manual of Central Labour and Industrial Laws incorporating State Amendments with Rules, Regulations and Select Notifications*, Eastern Book Company, Lucknow.

Micco, Alejandro and Carmen Pagés (2004), "Employment Protection and Gross Job Flows: A Differences-in-Differences Approach", Inter-American Development Bank, Working Paper No. 508, *www.iadb.org/res/publications/pubfiles/pubWP-508.pdf*.

Morrison, William (2006), "Case Study: Voluntary Redundancy Programs in India", Paper prepared for the Workshop on Labor Issues in Enterprise Restructuring, Asian Development Bank, Manila.

Mukherji, Joydeep (2006), "Economic Growth and India's Future", University of Pennsylvania Center for the Advanced Study of India, Occasional Paper No. 26, March.

Nagaraj, R (2004), "Fall in Organised Manufacturing Employment: A Brief Note", *Economic and Political Weekly*, 24 July.

Narain, A. (2006), "Wage Trends and Determinants", Paper written for the India Labor Conference and World Bank Report, *India's Employment Challenge: Creating Jobs, Helping Workers*, World Bank, Washington, forthcoming.

OECD (1996), *Job Creation and Loss: Analysis, Policy and Data Development*, OECD, Paris.

____ (1999), "Employment Protection Legislation", in *Employment Outlook – Giving Youth a Better Start*, OECD, Paris.

____ (2003), *Economic Survey of Mexico*, Economic Surveys No. 2003/1, OECD, Paris.

____ (2004), "Employment Protection Regulation and Labour Market Performance", in *OECD Employment Outlook*, OECD, Paris.

____ (2005), *Economic Survey of Brazil*, OECD Economic Surveys Vol. 2005/2, February, OECD, Paris.

____ (2006), *Employment Outlook – Boosting Jobs and Incomes*, OECD, Paris.

____ (2007), *Economic Policy Reforms: Going for Growth*, OECD, Paris.

Purfield, Catriona (2006), "Mind the Gap – Is Economic Growth in India Leaving Some States Behind?", IMF Working Paper No. 06/103, April.

Roy, S. Dutta (2002), "Job Security Regulations and Worker Turnover: A Study of the Indian Manufacturing Sector", *Indian Economic Review*, Vol. 37, No. 2, pp. 141-162.

____ (2004), "Employment dynamics in Indian industry: Adjustment lags and the impact of job security regulations", *Journal of Development Economics*, Vol. 73, No. 1, pp. 233-56.

Sanyal, Paroma and Nidhiya Menon (2005), "Labor Disputes and the Economics of Firm Geography: A Study of Domestic Investment in India", *Economic Development and Cultural Change*, Vol. 53, No. 4, pp. 825-54.

Sharma, Alakh (2006), "Flexibility, Employment and Labour Market Reforms in India", *Economic and Political Weekly*, 27 May, pp. 2274-85.

Singh, Manisha G. (2006), "Labor Adjustment in an Evolving Marketplace: An Empirical Investigation", India Development Foundation Working Paper No. 0603, May.

SNLC (2002), "Report of the Second National Labour Commission", in Economica India Info-Services (eds.), *Reports of the National Commissions on Labour*, Academic Foundation, New Delhi.

Sundar, K.R. Shyam (2005), "Labour Flexibility Debate in India: A Comprehensive Review and Some Suggestions", *Economic and Political Weekly*, 28 May, pp. 2078-85.

TeamLease (2006), *India Labour Report: A Ranking of Indian States*, TeamLease Services, New Delhi, *www.teamlease.com/TeamLease-LabourReport2006.pdf*.

Topalova, Petia (2004), "Factor Immobility and Regional Impacts of Trade Liberalization: Evidence on Poverty and Inequality from India", *Three Empirical Essays on Trade and Development in India*, Dissertation, Massachusetts Institute of Technology, June.

Unni, Jeemoi and G. Raveendran (2007), "Growth of Employment (1993-94 to 2004-05): Illusion of Inclusiveness?", *Economic and Political Weekly*, 20 January, pp. 196-99.

____ (2005), "Trade Liberalization, Poverty and Inequality: Evidence from Indian Districts", in Ann Harrison (ed.), *Globalization and Poverty*, NBER and University of Chicago Press, forthcoming.

World Bank (2006), *India's Employment Challenge: Creating Jobs, Helping Workers*, Poverty Reduction and Economic Management Unit, Report No. 35772-IN, forthcoming.

ANNEX 4.A1

State labour reform questionnaire summary responses

Table 4.A1.1. **State labour reform index questionnaire**

Transaction cost-reducing actions	Question	Goa	Karnataka	West Bengal	Assam	Madhya Pradesh	Orissa	Chhattisgarh	Andhra Pradesh	Tamil Nadu	Gujarat	Kerala	Uttar Pradesh	Haryana	Rajasthan	Maharashtra	Punjab	Himachal Pradesh	Delhi	Uttaranchal	Jharkhand	Bihar	Overall
A. Industrial Disputes Act																							
More than 21 days notice req'd under 9A	1.a	0	0	1	0	0	0	0	1	0	0	0	0	0	0	0	0	0	0	0	0	0	2
Exemption given for some items	1.b	0	1	0	0	0	0	0	0	0	0	0	0	0	0	0	0	0	0	0	0	0	1
Additions to public utility list	2	1	1	1	1	1	0	0	1	1	1	1	1	1	1	1	1	1	0	1	1	1	18
Amendments made to Chapter V-B (+/−1)	3	1	1	0	1	1	1	1	1	1	1	2	1	1	1	1	1	1	1	1	1	1	21
Complete cessation is excluded	4	0	0	0	0	0	0	0	0	0	0	0	0	0	0	1	1	1	1	1	0	0	5
There is a time limit for raising disputes	5	0	1	0	0	0	0	0	0	0	0	0	1	0	0	0	1	0	0	0	0	0	3
Threshold for disputes not 100 (+/−1)	6	1	1	0	1	1	1	1	1	1	1	2	1	1	1	1	1	1	1	2	1	1	22
B. Factories Act																							
Amendments to increase work hours	7	0	0	0	0	0	0	0	0	0	0	0	0	0	0	0	1	0	0	0	0	0	1
Export units have exemptions	8	0	0	0	1	0	0	0	0	0	0	0	1	1	0	1	0	1	1	0	0	0	6
Three shift working is allowed	9	1	1	1	1	1	1	1	1	1	1	1	1	1	1	1	1	1	1	1	1	1	21
Women are allowed in shift working	10	0	0	0	0	0	0	1	0	1	1	1	1	1	0	0	0	1	1	0	1	0	9
Deemed approval is allowed	11	0	1	1	1	1	0	1	1	1	1	1	1	1	0	1	0	1	1	0	0	1	15
License renewal longer than one year	12	1	1	0	0	0	1	0	0	0	1	0	1	0	1	0	1	0	0	0	0	0	7
C. Shops Act																							
Provisions for shift working (under act)	13	1	1	0	0	0	0	0	1	0	0	0	0	1	1	0	0	0	1	1	0	0	7
More than 8 con't hours per day allowed	14	0	0	1	1	0	1	1	0	0	1	0	0	0	1	0	0	0	1	0	1	1	9
More than 48 hours allowed per week	15	0	0	0	0	0	0	0	0	0	0	0	0	0	0	0	0	0	0	0	0	0	0
More than 5 hours of overtime allowed	16	0	1	0	0	1	1	1	0	0	1	0	0	0	0	1	0	0	0	0	1	1	8
Nightshift work is allowed for women	17	0	1	0	0	0	0	0	1	1	0	0	1	1	0	1	0	1	0	0	0	0	7
Number of inspectors greater than one	19	0	1	0	1	1	1	1	0	1	1	0	1	0	1	1	1	1	1	1	0	1	15
No provisions similar to 5A of IDA	21	1	1	1	1	1	1	1	1	0	1	1	1	0	0	1	1	1	1	1	1	1	18
D. Contract Labour Act																							
Moves made to faciliate contract labour	22	1	0	0	0	0	0	0	1	0	0	0	0	0	0	0	0	0	0	0	0	0	2
Licensing at local level	23	1	1	1	1	1	1	1	1	1	1	1	1	0	1	1	1	1	1	1	1	1	20
Deemed approval is allowed	24	0	0	0	0	0	0	0	0	1	0	0	0	0	0	1	0	0	0	0	0	1	3
Not req'd to amend reg if empl contractor Changes	25	0	0	0	1	1	0	0	0	0	1	0	0	0	0	0	0	0	0	0	0	0	3
Contract labour allowed in non-core activities	26	1	0	1	1	1	1	1	1	1	1	1	1	0	0	0	1	1	1	1	1	1	17
Freely allowed in EPZs and SEZs	27	1	0	1	1	1	1	0	1	0	1	1	1	1	1	1	1	1	0	0	0	0	14

Table 4.A1.1. **State labour reform index questionnaire** (cont.)

Transaction cost-reducing actions	Question	Goa	Karnataka	West Bengal	Assam	Madhya Pradesh	Orissa	Chhattisgarh	Andhra Pradesh	Tamil Nadu	Gujarat	Kerala	Uttar Pradesh	Haryana	Rajasthan	Maharashtra	Punjab	Himachal Pradesh	Delhi	Uttaranchal	Jharkhand	Bihar	Overall
Provision for fixed-term contracts	28	0	0	0	1	1	0	0	0	0	1	1	1	0	1	1	1	1	1	0	1	0	11
Core and non-core clearly defined	29	0	0	0	0	0	0	0	1	0	1	0	0	1	0	1	0	0	0	0	1	0	5
Contract employment allowed in IT/BPO	30	1	0	1	1	1	1	1	1	1	1	1	1	1	1	1	1	1	1	1	1	0	19
E. Inspectors																							
Single annual inspection	31	0	0	0	0	0	0	0	0	0	0	0	0	1	0	0	1	0	0	0	0	0	2
Authorization is required for surprise inspections	32	0	0	0	0	1	0	0	1	0	0	0	1	1	0	0	0	0	1	1	0	0	6
Authorization is required for specific Complaints	33	0	0	0	0	0	0	0	1	1	0	0	1	1	0	0	0	0	1	1	0	0	6
Other moves to lessen inspection regime	34	0	0	1	0	1	1	0	1	0	1	0	1	1	1	0	1	0	0	0	1	0	10
F. Registers																							
Common attendance register for different acts	35	0	1	0	1	1	0	0	1	1	0	0	1	1	0	0	0	1	0	0	1	0	9
Common accident register for different acts	36	0	0	0	0	1	1	0	1	0	1	0	1	1	0	0	0	1	0	1	0	0	8
Single inspection book	37	0	0	0	0	0	0	0	0	0	1	0	0	1	0	0	1	0	0	1	0	0	4
Computerized records are accepted	38	1	0	1	1	1	1	0	0	1	1	1	0	1	1	0	1	1	0	0	0	1	13
G. Filing of Returns																							
Filing on a consolidated form is allowed	40	0	1	0	0	0	1	0	1	1	1	0	1	0	1	0	0	0	0	1	0	0	8
Single format of various returns allowed	41	0	1	0	0	0	0	0	1	0	1	0	1	0	1	0	0	0	1	0	0	0	6
Self-certification provision exists	42	1	0	0	0	0	0	0	0	0	1	0	1	0	1	0	0	0	0	0	0	0	4
Measures to simply returns taken	43	0	0	0	0	0	1	0	1	1	0	1	1	1	1	0	0	1	0	0	0	0	8
Single window proceedure exists	44	0	1	0	0	1	1	0	1	1	0	0	1	1	1	0	0	1	1	1	0	1	12
H. Union Representation																							
Minimum number of workers greater than 7	45	1	1	1	0	0	0	0	0	0	0	1	0	0	1	0	0	0	0	0	1	0	6
Provision to restrict unions in enterprise	46	0	0	0	0	0	0	0	0	0	0	0	0	0	0	1	0	0	0	0	0	0	1
Provision to recognize union as bargaining agent	47	0	1	1	0	1	0	1	0	0	1	0	0	1	0	1	0	0	0	0	1	0	8
Minimum number of workers to support strike	48	0	0	0	0	0	0	0	1	0	0	0	0	0	0	1	0	0	0	1	0	0	3
Additional restrictions beyond IDA to declare strike	49	0	0	0	0	1	0	1	1	0	0	0	0	0	0	1	0	0	1	1	0	0	6
Code of conduct between unions and employer	50	0	1	1	1	1	1	1	1	1	1	0	1	1	0	1	1	1	1	0	0	1	16
Count index	*maxi- mum*																						
A. Industrial Disputes Act	9	3	5	2	3	3	2	2	4	3	4	3	5	3	3	4	5	4	4	4	3	3	3.4
B. Factories Act	6	2	3	2	3	1	4	2	3	3	4	4	5	2	3	2	5	4	2	2	1	2	2.8
C. Shops Act	7	2	5	2	3	3	4	3	3	2	3	2	1	3	5	3	3	3	4	2	4	4	3.0
D. Contract Labour Act	9	5	1	4	6	6	4	3	6	5	6	5	5	3	4	6	5	5	4	3	5	3	4.5
E. Inspectors	4	0	0	1	0	2	1	0	3	1	1	0	3	4	1	0	2	0	2	2	1	0	1.1
F. Registers	4	1	1	1	2	3	2	0	2	2	3	1	2	4	1	0	2	3	0	2	1	1	1.6
G. Filing of Returns	5	1	3	0	0	1	3	0	4	3	3	1	5	2	5	0	0	2	2	2	0	1	1.8
H. Union Representation	*6*	1	3	3	1	3	1	3	3	1	2	1	1	2	1	5	1	1	2	2	2	1	1.9
Overall	*50*	15	21	15	18	22	21	13	28	20	26	17	27	23	23	20	23	22	20	19	17	15	20.2

ISBN 978-92-64-03351-1
OECD Economic Surveys: India
© OECD 2007

Chapter 5

Reforming the financial system

This chapter examines the performance of India's financial sector and compares its structure to that of other emerging economies. The financial sector went through a period of considerable re-organisation during the last 15 years. New regulators were introduced for all sectors of the market and this has boosted the development of highly efficient equity and commodity markets. The health of the banking sector has also improved and competition within the sector has increased. Nonetheless, costs remain high in a sector that is still dominated by public sector banks. The corporate bond market is still underdeveloped, as is the foreign exchange market. Considerable scope exists for improving efficiency in the financial sector by opening it to more foreign direct investment and removing a number of regulatory constraints that impede the development of a full set of financial markets.

India at present has a relatively low level of bank and financial intermediation both with respect to lending and deposits and one which is dominated by public sector institutions. At the end of 2006, the stock of bank deposits and corporate bonds was markedly lower than in other Asian countries, with only one other major ASEAN country having a lower ratio. This reflects a situation where, while household saving is high, individuals prefer to invest in real assets and gold rather than in financial assets. The challenge for the future is to achieve a greater extent of financial intermediation in order to improve capital allocation. Given the likely growth of the economy, the banking system itself will have considerable need for new capital. One estimate suggests that, in order to raise the bank credit ratio from 60% to 80% of GDP by 2010, the banking system will require extra capital of the order of 1¼ per cent of GDP (Lahiri, 2006). Raising such an amount of capital will require significant increases in profitability and efficiency in the sector. Other areas of the capital market are also underdeveloped and in need of an environment that will permit expansion.

The banking system

The reform path

Financial market liberalisation started after 1991. The pace of reform was slower than in product markets, in part because the introduction of stricter prudential controls on banks revealed significant problems in their asset portfolios, in part generated by greater competition in product markets. Before the reform, state-owned banks controlled 90% of bank deposits and channelled an extremely high proportion of funds to the government; interest rates were determined administratively; credit was allocated on the basis of government policy and approval of the Reserve Bank was required for individual loans above a certain threshold. Capital markets were also underdeveloped with fragmentation of stock markets across the country, with the major stock market acting mainly in the interest of its members. Derivative markets did not exist and comprehensive capital controls meant that companies were unable to circumvent domestic controls by borrowing abroad.

Reform of the banking system took a gradual sequenced path focussing on improved prudential control, recapitalisation of public sector banks and the introduction of greater competition. The control system for banks was considerably strengthened in 1994, by the introduction of a Board of Financial Supervision within the Reserve Bank to focus on supervision, and the rules governing the recognition of bad loans have been substantially tightened. Regulatory norms were progressively moved towards convergence with international best practises. In particular, procedures with respect to income recognition, asset classification and provisioning were tightened. For instance, banks were required to set aside reserves for all loans, not just non-performing loans. A system of preventive supervision was introduced under which banks are required to promptly undertake specified changes to their portfolios and management when various trigger points are reached. In addition, from the year ended 31 March 2000, banks were required to raise extra capital, bringing the minimum capital to risk assets ratio to 9%.

The task of banks in recovering bad loans was considerably eased in 2002 by the passage of new laws concerning the recovery of debts. Prior to this date, it had proved difficult for banks to recover even secured debts because of the absence of an adequate bankruptcy procedure (see Chapter 3). The new Secured Lending Law allowed banks to recover the assets that had been used to secure loans in the event of non-payment of interest or capital. This law has proved effective in aiding banks and has also lowered the incentive to default on payments.

Work to introduce the new Basel II regulatory system is underway. From 2003 onwards, a pilot project was launched to operate a risk based supervision system. The introduction of the Basel II system has been postponed to 2009 for banks with only domestic operations and to 2008 for other banks. This delay was to allow banks time to raise the necessary capital, given that a study of banks, accounting for half of total assets, indicated that the new norms would lower capital adequacy ratios by one percentage point, though no bank would breach the new limit on capital adequacy.

Competition was introduced into the banking system through two routes. First, new banks were allowed to enter the market. A dozen private Indian banks were created, some by the transformation of existing institutions, others started from scratch. Foreign banks were also allowed into the market and about 30 were operating by end 2006. Secondly, once prudential reforms were undertaken, bank interest rates were deregulated. By 2007, controls remained in four areas – saving deposit accounts, small loans in priority areas, export credits and non-resident transferable rupee deposits.

The ability to the banking system to lend freely was also enhanced by the progressive reduction of the extent to which it had to make loans to the government. At the beginning of the reform period, banks were required to lend 63.5% of their assets to the government in the form of a statutory liquidity ratio and a cash reserve ratio. In addition, the Reserve Bank acted as banker to the government. By April 2003, such pre-emptions were reduced to less than 30%. Following the provisions of the 2003 Fiscal Responsibility and Budget Management Act, the Reserve Bank ceased to participate in the primary market for government securities from April 2006 and no longer lends to the government. Following the amendment of two Acts, the legal ceiling on the statutory liquidity ratio was ended and the limits on both the floor and ceiling of cash reserve ratio were abolished. The Reserve Bank can now alter these ratios in the light of prevailing monetary and economic conditions. Given the need to neutralise the domestic consequences of the build up in foreign exchange reserves and the likely inflationary consequences of such a movement, the cash reserve ratio was raised in 2007.

The impact of reform

Government funds were used to recapitalise banks through the issue of bonds to the banks. However, in contrast to bank restructurings in many other countries, bad loans were not sold to an asset management company. Rather, the banks had to gradually use their income and capital to provision the loans. In 1994, bad loans represented one-quarter of the total advances of public banks but this has been progressively reduced (Figure 5.1). By 2001, bonds amounting to INR 225 billion (nearly 1% of GDP in fiscal year 2003) have been issued. The annual cost to the government, though, was only the interest payment to

Figure 5.1. **Development of gross and net non-performing loans for public and new private banks**

Per cent of advances

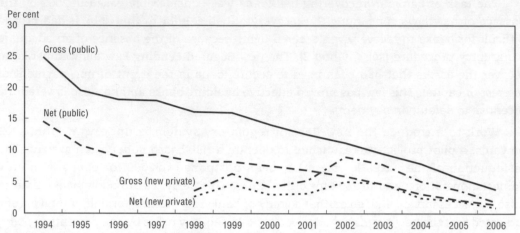

Source: 1993-2000 Muniappan (2002), 2001-06 Reserve Bank of India, *Trend and Progress of Banking in India.*

the banks, as it was expected that the banks would eventually repay the loans. In addition, public sector banks raised capital by progressively selling minority stakes to private shareholders. By 2006, about one-third of the share capital of the government banks was in the hands of the public. The older private banks also had a significant level of bad loans whereas the new private banks had a much lower level of bad loans. By 2006, the bad loan situation of Indian banks was no different to banks in major overseas markets and the difference between public banks and the new private banks had almost been eliminated.

The tighter regulatory structure has resulted in greater pressure on bank management to consider the profitability of their operations. As a result, the net revenue of banks has improved. In particular, public sector banks increased the ratio of their net profit to assets from 0.57% in the year to March 1997 to 0.82% in the year ending March 2006, with the result that their profitability is now in line with that of the new private sector banks. There is evidence that reforms also boosted productivity of the banking sector.

In addition to being largely state-owned, banks remain subject to government control over their lending portfolios. They must lend 40% of their total advances to priority sectors such as agriculture, certain small businesses and clients from scheduled castes and tribes. The objective of priority lending is to ensure adequate lending to sectors in society or the economy that have a major impact on large or weaker sections of the population and which are employment intensive. Interest rates on these loans are, however, no longer regulated, except for small loans of less than about USD 4 000 which cannot be charged at a rate higher than the benchmark prime lending rate. In the event that priority lending targets are not met, banks have had to deposit funds with the Rural Infrastructure Development Fund. However, as from April 2007, fresh deposits with this institution (and the Small Enterprises Development Fund) are no longer eligible to be counted as priority lending. Moreover, by March 2010, existing deposits will cease to have priority loan status once they mature. The new private banks appear to be able to select borrowers successfully in the priority sectors, as the extent of their non-performing loans in this area is almost the same as in non-priority areas. However, public banks still have a somewhat higher incidence of bad loans in priority areas, especially in lending to the agricultural sector (Figure 5.2).

The experience of other countries around the world has shown that directed credit programmes suffered from abuse and misuse of preferential funds for non-priority purposes, increased the cost of funds to non-preferential borrowers and involved a decline in financial discipline that resulted in low repayment rates. Moreover, where they existed, the size of directed credit programmes has not exceed 15% of the total funds mobilized by the financial system – a much smaller size of programme than that in India. Directed lending or funding result in a system wherein banks do not function as autonomous profit-maximising entities, but, to some extent, as quasi-fiscal bodies, providing virtual subsidies to selected segments of the economy which do not appear on the general government balance sheets. Only a few other countries (Nepal, Pakistan and the Philippines) continue to prescribe directed credit requirements, though a few other economies like China, the Kyrgyz Republic, and Viet-Nam, do not have directed credit requirements as such, but have similar programmes (RBI, 2005).

Indeed, in 1991, at the beginning of the reform period, the Committee on the Financial System (Narasimham Committee), while observing that the directed credit programmes had played a useful purpose in extending the reach of the banking system to cover neglected sectors, stated that the pursuit of such objectives should use the instruments of the fiscal rather than the credit system and recommended that directed credit programmes be phased out (Government of India, 1991). A latter report from the same committee observed that a sudden reduction of priority sector targets could have the danger of a disruption in the flow of credit. However, the government considers that, even after 36 years of priority lending, certain sectors of the economy continue to suffer from inadequate credit availability. Agriculture, in particular, is seen as not being likely to receive its desirable share of credit without the priority lending scheme. Similarly, in a competitive credit market, small scale industry is seen as not likely to receive the share of credit that the government thinks desirable.

Figure 5.2. **Gross non-performing loans in the priority and non-priority sectors by ownership of banks**

Per cent of loans and advances outstanding end March 2006

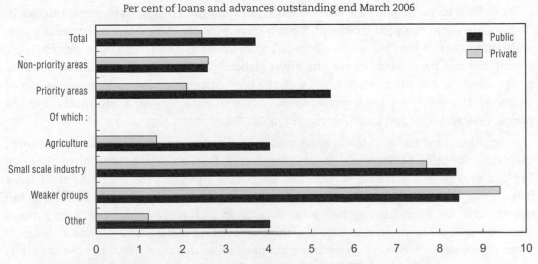

Source: Report on Trends and Progress of banking in India , Reserve Bank of India.

In addition to priority lending constraints, banks are subject both to a cash reserve ratio (6.5% of assets since May 2007) and a statutory liquidity ratio (SLR) that requires 25% of their liabilities to be kept in specified public sector securities. Overall, the sectoral allocation of 59% of bank assets is determined by regulation. In the early part of this decade, the statutory liquidity ratio was not a constraint on the lending behaviour of the banks. In particular, the public sector banks held a higher than required proportion of their assets in such investments, in contrast to the new private banks. The current upswing in bank credit to the private sector is making it more likely that this ratio will be a medium-term constraint on the management of bank portfolios. In January 2007, the President signed into law an ordinance that empowers the Reserve Bank to lower the SLR below its current level without further legislation.

The evidence on the relative efficiency of public and private banks in India appears to be mixed. In the initial period of reforms, there was little evidence of the productivity differentials between public and private banks narrowing (Mohan, 2005a). A number of studies suggested that private sector banks were more efficient than public sector banks during all of the period from 1990 to the early part of this decade. One study found that total factor productivity of private banks was double that of public banks and that rates of return on assets and equity were also markedly higher, as were lending spreads (Sanyal and Sanchar, 2005; Chakrabarti and Chawla, 2005). Such findings are similar to those found in cross-country studies of the cost structures of public and private banks (Micco *et al.*, 2004). On the other hand, recent studies give a more mixed picture and there is evidence that the performance of public banks has improved over time. Nationalised banks were less efficient at producing profits than private banks, but more efficient when value added was used as the output measure (Das and Ghosh, 2006). Another study found convergence in productivity between public and private banks over the period 1990-2000 (Mohan and Ray, 2004). However, the panel data used in that study excluded the new private sector banks, which appear to be the most productive of the banks (Das and Ghosh, 2006).

The high overall degree of inefficiency in some Indian banks during the reform period (*op cit.*) has held down the performance of Indian banks relative to international competitors. For example, a comparison of the labour productivity of the top four banks in India (which includes one new private bank) and the four major state-owned banks in China shows that the productivity of the top three publicly owned Indian banks is much lower than that of the four major Chinese banks (Mohan, 2005b). Only one private bank among the top four Indian banks has higher labour productivity than the four Chinese banks. Lending spreads are also high, with the public banks having an interest margin of nearly 3% (Table 5.1) against a typical spread of 2% in six emerging Asian markets in the period 1996 and 2003 and a similar margin in OECD countries.

Additional evidence of the lagging performance of state-owned banks comes form their slow adoption of electronic payments systems. Under the impulsion of the Reserve Bank, a real time electronic system has been developed for the settlement of large transactions. The development of a retail network, however, has lagged behind. Retail transactions are essentially settled by cash, with India having a relatively high ratio of currency to GDP. Moreover, it is relatively time-consuming to withdraw cash from publicly owned banks: they have on average one automatic teller machine (ATM) per ten branches compared to more than one ATM in each branch for new private sector banks, which also have two off-site ATMs per branch against only 0.1 off-site ATMs per public bank branch.

Table 5.1. **Interest spreads for Indian commercial banks**[1]

Per cent, years beginning in April

	1991-95	1996-2000	2001-05
Public banks	2.80	2.89	2.88
Indian private banks	3.22	2.40	2.08
New private banks	. .	2.24	1.84
Foreign banks	3.94	3.83	3.40
All commercial banks	2.91	2.90	2.71

1. The interest spread is calculated as the difference between the average interest received and paid relative total assets.

Source: Reserve Bank of India, Trend and Progress of Banking in India.

Such developments are being held back by the fact that only 10 of the 27 public banks were fully computerised by March 2006.

Productivity may also have been held back by the need for banks to consult with the Reserve Bank about the structure of their branches. For example, all specific proposals relating to opening, closing and shifting of all categories of branches, including off-site ATMs, are required to be included in their annual plan submitted to the Reserve Bank. The decision on whether or not to allow a new branch to open depends on the bank's performance in a number of areas such as how banks price their products; actual lending to priority sectors; and whether the bank is committed to providing basic banking services. In 2005, individual authorization has been replaced by aggregate approval allowing a degree of flexibility for banks to decide on opening and closing of branches and upgrading facilities, but the basic criteria for approving a plan remain in place.

The higher productivity of private banks may be linked to their management of human resources. As long as banks are controlled by the government, the Constitution gives bank employees civil service status and aligns their pay on that of the civil service, so making it difficult to adequately compensate certain skills. Employees responsible for making bad loans can be investigated by the Central Vigilance Commission which has a deterrent effect on making lending decisions (Banerjee *et al.* , 2005). Moreover, the skills of the staff of public banks are limited. In 2000, only one-fifth of their employees were computer-literate against almost total familiarity with computers in the new private and foreign banks (Reserve Bank of India, 2002).

Improvements in the corporate governance of banks would raise the efficiency of banks. The corporate governance of banks is not controlled either by the Companies Act or by the stock market regulator for listed banks. Rather, it is determined by the Bank Regulation Act that overrides any provisions made for stock market listing or by the Companies Act. In particular, shareholders owning more than 10% of the equity of a bank have their voting rights capped at 10%. The government introduced an amendment to this Act in May 2005 in order to remove this restriction but the bill had not been passed by Parliament by May 2007. For public sector banks, the limit on voting rights was set at 1% until 1994 when it was raised to 10% and this ceiling still remains. Foreign shareholders are still limited to 20% ownership of public banks. They can own up to 74% of private banks but their voting rights remain capped at 10%. Even in the case of private banks, there is still a limit on the shareholding of any one entity. Another Act passed in 2006 ended the anomaly by which the Reserve Bank was obliged to place one director on the board of every public bank. While these amendments move in the right direction, the reduction in the number of directors elected by minority shareholders – from six to three – goes in the wrong direction. As a result of this act, the government controls 9 out of 15 directors on the board of public banks, with two others being staff representatives.

The extent of government involvement in the economy has also been reflected in a very wide field of action for the Reserve Bank that has gone well beyond that of central banks of other countries. A number of possible conflicts exist. For example, the Reserve Bank lent directly to the government and is the government's investment banker, arranging sales of government debt. It is the owner of several financial institutions, including the largest commercial bank in the country, as well as the regulator of banks. These conflicts are now in part being resolved. The passage of Fiscal Responsibility Act forbade the Reserve Bank to lend to the government. Nonetheless, it continues to manage the debt of the central government by issuing new debt, as mandated by the law. As announced in the 2007-08 budget speech, a new debt management agency is proposed to be created in the Ministry of Finance. However, the Reserve Bank continues to be the banker for state governments, under the authority of the RBI Act. As to the ownership of banks, the government proposes that the RBI's majority holding in the State Bank of India be acquired by the Ministry of Finance. Its holdings in the National Agricultural Bank and the National Housing Bank may be acquired at a later date. These changes will reduce any possible conflict of interest between its ownership and regulatory functions. It is also responsible for foreign exchange controls and continues to be the owner, manager and regulator of the government securities market. It no longer appoints directors to the boards of public banks but is responsible for undertaking due diligence process prior to their nomination by the government.

Other financial markets

The introduction of a new regulatory authority for capital markets in 1992 – the Securities and Exchange Board of India (SEBI) – was a key step in the reform of capital markets. It represented a break with the previous regulatory regime which placed significant elements of regulation of different markets with the Reserve Bank of India. The regulator has helped establish corporate governance rules for listed companies that are above average for emerging markets (International Institute for Finance, 2006). However, enforcement of the rules can sometimes be held up by delays in the legal system. The capital market regulator does not, however, have full reach over major financial markets. Commodity markets are regulated by the Forward Markets Commission that is part of the Ministry of Consumer Affairs and Food while the government securities market is regulated by the Reserve Bank. Moreover, SEBI does not have complete authority over all participants in a given capital market. If the participant in a given market is owned by a company that is supervised by another regulator, then that regulator is responsible for supervising the subsidiary, and not SEBI. Regulation of securities markets was complemented by the creation of a regulator for insurance markets in 1999, while a pension regulator was created in 2004.

Equity markets

Equity markets have evolved considerably since the early 1990s and are now amongst the largest in the world in terms of transactions and have costs comparable with other major exchanges. The major determinant of this evolution was the creation of the National Stock Exchange (NSE) in 1994, a competitor to the Bombay Stock Exchange (BSE), both located in Mumbai. This exchange was created in response to the poor performance of the existing mutually owned stock exchange. Its founding shareholders were a number of public development banks (including one that founded the largest new private bank), government financial institutions and a private bank. The new exchange enabled participants from across the country to trade in one market. The new exchange was one of the first stock exchanges in the world to have a corporate structure. It rapidly became the largest market in India and, the third largest exchange in the world, measured by the number of transactions. It now has foreign shareholders (New York Stock Exchange and various banks) up to the maximum (26%) allowed by foreign direct investment regulations.

Costs were also reduced by the introduction of new clearing and settlement institutions. An integral part of the new architecture was the creation of a centralised counterparty for transactions. This was established as a subsidiary of the National Stock Exchange and resulted in the elimination of counter-party risk in the market. At the same time, a law passed in 1996 allowed the creation of a new depository institution for holding all stocks in dematerialised form. This greatly reduced the incidence of settlement risk. Overall, these reforms created a national market in shares, eliminating price differences across the country. Overall, transactions costs were reduced by a factor of thirteen between 1993 and 2004, leading to a marked rise in turnover (Table 5.2). Since 2004, the liquidity of the market has further improved with the impact cost of a trade in a major stock falling to 0.07%, comparable to that found in major OECD stock markets.

Table 5.2. **Transaction costs in India's equity market**

Per cent

	1993	1997	2004
	Before NSE	After NSE	
Trading			
Market impact cost	3.75	0.65	0.35
Brokerage	3.00	0.50	0.25
	0.75	0.15	0.10
Clearing			
Counterpart risk	Present	Some	None
Settlement	1.25	1.50	0.03
Back office	0.75	0.75	0.03
Bad paper risk	0.50	0.75	0.00
Total	5.00	2.15	0.38

Source: Thomas (2006).

In the past three years funds raised in the equity markets have been substantial, averaging slightly less than 1% of GDP annually (Figure 5.3). Domestic mutual funds have played a key role in resource mobilisation. With the creation of the capital market regulator, privately owned mutual fund management companies were allowed into the market. These funds have been preferred by investors and achieved an almost 90% market share between 2004 and 2006. The market share of the public sector fund manager (Unit Trust of India) has been progressively eroded from two-thirds prior to reforms to 6% by 2006. This public sector fund manager had to be completely restructured in 2002, for the second time, due to failure of its investment portfolio to meet the assured returns that it had promised to investors.

Table 5.3. **Funds raised in the Indian equity market**

Per cent of GDP

	2003	2004	2005	2006
Funds raised				
All new issues	0.10	1.07	0.86	0.81
Initial public offerings	0.06	0.40	0.28	0.62
Other sales	0.04	0.68	0.58	0.20
Funds supplied				
Mutual funds	1.29	0.24	0.56	2.15
Foreign investors	1.66	1.19	1.46	0.93

Source: SEBI Annual Report, Ministry of Finance Economic Survey.

Bond markets

In contrast to equity markets, the government and corporate bond markets operate within a regulatory framework that may have held back their development. The government bond market is owned by the Reserve Bank, which also regulates the market and is principle issuer in the primary market. This conflicts with the basic principles of regulation set out in Chapters 3 and 7. Experience in OECD countries suggests that there should be separation between the policy, ownership and regulation functions. Thus, progress in the telecommunication market resulted from placing ownership, regulation and policy in different institutions, so permitting change to take place without the constraints of competing interests (Chapter 7). A number of reforms were introduced to the government bond market in 1992 when the price of newly introduced bonds was set by auction. A number of other reforms have been introduced, notably to ensure a transparent reporting situation, especially for repurchase facilities. It was only in 2005, 11 years after the equity market, that the gilts market became an electronic order limit market. A number of elements could further improve the market: consolidation of illiquid issues, permitting stock lending so as to allow short-selling for longer time periods than the five-day period permitted since January 2007 and requirements for entry into the market.

The corporate bond market is regulated by SEBI and, for public issues, is subject to considerable documentation requirements that have resulted in the almost complete absence of traded corporate bonds and the domination of the market by private placements. This market is less transparent than an exchange based market and is dominated by public sector issuers (Table 5.4). Overall, total outstanding corporate bonds amounted to 1.5% of GDP in 2005, with the total funds raised abroad by Indian companies amounting to almost another 1% of GDP.

The government is attempting to address the issue of low issuance of corporate bonds. For the market to succeed there will have to be demand not just from retail investors but also from institutional investors. However, to achieve this goal, the government will need to reduce the extent to which major investors are obliged to invest in government bonds. Control of the broad sectoral allocation of credit is significant. Life insurance companies must lend 50% of their assets to the government and place a further 15% in infrastructure lending; pension funds must place 90% of their assets in government securities and postal savings deposits are invested totally in government securities. A government report recommended changing these rules to portfolio limits based on the credit rating of the instrument, irrespective of the sector of origin of the debt (Patil, 2006). The same report also made recommendations as to the architecture of the market with respect to transparency,

Table 5.4. **Gross issuance in bond markets**

Per cent of GDP, year ending 31st March

	2003	2004	2005	2006
Public sector				
Private placements				
National financial institutions	7.1	9.2	10.5	16.8
State financial institutions	1.6	1.5	0.8	0.2
National public sector undertakings	5.1	2.1	2.1	3.0
State public sector undertakings	1.8	2.4	1.1	0.3
Marketable debt				
Government	74.3	71.8	46.6	51.5
Private sector				
Private placements	4.2	2.3	3.3	2.2
Marketable debt	1.9	1.6	1.3	0.0

Source: National Stock Exchange, Indian Securities Market Review.

clearing and settlement. Both stock markets are now scheduled to start order-driven markets in corporate bonds as from July 2007 and to eventually adopt the electronic order limit structure of the gilt and equity market.

Derivative markets

Indian financial markets have shown that they can adapt quickly to trading derivatives but as yet there are a limited number of contracts available in the market place. Trading in derivatives on the National Stock Exchange started in 2000 and the Indian market is now the tenth largest market for futures contracts on single stocks and indices in the world and the largest market for futures on single stocks. This follows a 77-fold increase in the turnover of equity derivatives between the years ending March 2002 and 2006. While the market has been successful, the response of the regulator and the government to the original request of the exchange to create an index future was slow. More than five years elapsed between when the exchange first applied and when permission was finally granted in 2000. Moreover, permission came only after a rival foreign exchange announced plans to trade an Indian futures index. The options market has been less successful, accounting for only 10% of turnover. In part, this may be due to the failure of the National Stock Exchange to allow firms with direct electronic access to the market to undertake more than a very limited amount of computer-based algorithmic trading.

There is also a lack of other exchange-based derivative markets. Initial attempts to create such a market failed due to problems in contract design. Interest rate contracts are generally made over the counter with poor transparency and are small in scale by international standards. For example, the interest rate swaps market has currently only 18 dealers and 100 participants. Trading of currency futures is limited. Overall, total turnover in over-the-counter debt derivatives is estimated at USD 1 billion per day, with perhaps double that turnover in currency futures. A significant offshore market exists in the currency futures and a new exchange market is being established in Dubai. A range of foreign exchange hedging instruments has been introduced, including forwards, swaps and options, but futures contracts are not permitted. One reason for the limited turnover is that most markets are restricted to the hedging of "real" transactions, i.e. crystallised future foreign currency exposures, with speculators or arbitrageurs not being allowed due to provisions in contract law (Sarkar, 2006). Within the government bond market, short-selling is not allowed over a period of more than five days which limits the possibility of options on interest rates. Such restrictions hurt price discovery in the markets.

Legal and institutional reforms are being considered to widen the scale of derivative trading. The Reserve Bank of India has issued comprehensive guidelines in respect of derivatives, incorporating the broad regulatory framework for derivative transactions. The Clearing Corporation of India is expected to start a trade reporting system for interest rate swaps that should facilitate the development of the market. Following a recent government report (Ministry of Finance, 2007), the Reserve Bank has set up committees to consider the introduction of currency futures. In addition, it published draft guidelines for the development of a credit derivatives market in May 2007. The guidelines suggest that only a relatively narrow market should be allowed and only for credit default swaps (CDSs). The three most important restrictions on the market that it suggests are that only underlying assets that have been rated by an agency should be allowed in the market (effectively ruling out the use of CDSs based on bank loans), that the derivative can only be based on the credit risk of one issuer and that a person seeking to buy credit protection must hold the underlying asset. Thus, owning a CDS as an asset by itself would not be possible. Finally, the draft guidelines suggested that collateralised debt obligations (CDOs) would not be allowed (a CDO facilitates the hedging of a portfolio of credit instruments).

Commodity exchanges have been fundamentally overhauled this decade. Markets were fragmented and illiquid and suffered from being restricted to inessential products for a long period of time. However, starting in the mid-1990s, the commodity market regulator began to reform markets. Initial attempts were unsuccessful but three new markets were created in 2000, based on the architecture of the National Stock Exchange. These markets became viable even more quickly than the new stock exchange. Although there are 94 commodities traded, gold and silver account for half of turnover. By 2006, the gold market became the third largest derivative market for gold in the world. Turnover in agricultural commodities is held back by the system of price support for some agricultural products. Moreover, the government still occasionally considers that futures market raise prices, as when wheat futures trading was banned in March 2007, following an increase in food prices.

Institutional investors

Demand by households for financial assets has risen, both for investments in bank deposits (see above) and in institutionally managed funds, but is still low relative to other countries. Household investment in life insurance, pension and mutual funds is low, although double that in China and Mexico (Figure 5.3). Although private sector mutual funds have expanded markedly, the assets of the insurance sector are still dominated by the state-owned life Insurance Company of India, which invests 80% of its assets in public sector liabilities.

The largest pension scheme in the country (the Employees Provident Fund Organisation) has a poor record, both administratively and in terms of matching benefits to contributions (Asher and Mandy, 2006). This organisation, which is part of the government, to which about 5% of the labour force make compulsory contributions, is subject to no outside regulation. It is its own fund manager and has a cumbersome system of governance with a board of governors that has 45 members and is chaired by the Minister of Labour. It is run as a defined benefit scheme and is estimated to have an actuarial deficit

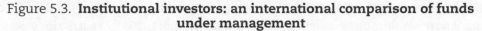

Figure 5.3. **Institutional investors: an international comparison of funds under management**

Life insurance, pension and mutual funds, as per cent of GDP 2005

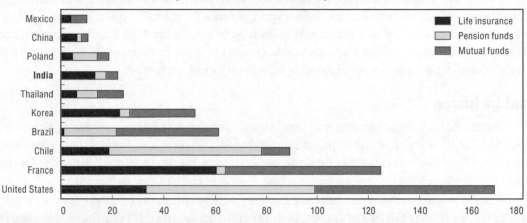

Source: McKinsey Global Institute (2006).

equivalent to seven years of contributions. Private sector pensions are often managed by the publicly owned Life Insurance Company of India which is regulated by the Insurance Regulatory Development Authority. Finally, reserve funds for employee severance payments are only regulated, to a certain extent, by the tax authorities. Even after the passage of the new Act, regulation of long-term saving schemes will remain dispersed.

For civil servants, the government has introduced a New Pension Scheme (NPS) that offers the possibility of generating a significant amount of funds for management. This defined contribution scheme is also open to people outside the government sector on a voluntary basis (see Chapter 6). Indeed, once the record keeping infrastructure for this scheme is in place, its management should be scalable and could form the base for a nationwide retirement saving system. Original plans to allow participants to choose between four different funds have faced parliamentary opposition. By March 2007, the legislation allowing investment in financial assets other than government bonds had yet to pass into law. The government is considering an executive order that would allow up to 5% of the NPS funds to be invested in the stock market, 50% in government debt and the remainder in AA corporate bonds. It has also approved four publicly owned firms to be fund managers for the scheme. Once the Act is passed, the Authority may allow a much greater mix of assets in four funds. Allowing greater investment diversity for both life insurance funds and government pension funds (including the Employees Provident Fund), along the lines of the Malaysian and Singapore Provident Funds (OECD, 2003), would help private companies diversify their sources of finance and put competitive pressures on bank lending rates.

Foreign ownership

One route for improving the efficiency of the financial system would be to allow greater foreign ownership of domestic companies in this area. At present, FDI and foreign portfolio investment in public sector banks is limited to an aggregate cap of 20%; for private banks the limit is 74% (but voting rights are capped) while for insurance companies the limit is 26%. One government report recommended raising the limit of foreign investment in public sector banks to 40%, but voting rights would remain restricted and board participation would not be allowed (Government of India, 2004). Restrictions on bank ownership are common in Asia; nonetheless, foreign ownership of banks and insurance companies would represent a way of obtaining markedly greater capital for the banking system and would bring new managerial expertise to the sector. There is also a cap on the total foreign investment in any one stock. Once this limit is reached, a dual market is created with foreign investors only being able to buy from each other.

Financial inclusion

Financial inclusion, especially in rural areas, has been a major goal of the government for the past 40 years. The role of private moneylenders in rural areas was widely perceived to be holding back development. In the period following the nationalisation of banks between 1969 and 1981, there was a major expansion of the banking sector into rural areas. In addition to the commercial banks, a number of governmental or quasi-governmental agencies were established to promote financial inclusion. Overall, there are nearly 300 000 branches of financial institutions in rural areas,[1] with the result that the density of financial institutions in India compares very favourably with that in other countries. The density of bank branches is nearly ten times that in Brazil and Chile and half that found in France.

The spread of the banking system into rural areas in the 1970s generated a significant increase in financial inclusion. The market share of institutional lending in rural areas doubled, reaching 60% in 1981 (National Sample Survey, 2005). Since then, the penetration of institutions in rural areas has barely risen while it has risen significantly in urban areas (Figure 5.4). That said, there is little difference between the penetration of financial institutions in rural and urban areas, once the asset portfolio of the household is taken into account. Nonetheless, the penetration of informal moneylenders is almost double that in urban areas due to the higher incidence of low wealth households in rural areas.

Figure 5.4. **Market share of informal lenders by asset class of households**

Per cent of total borrowing by households in a given asset class in June 2002

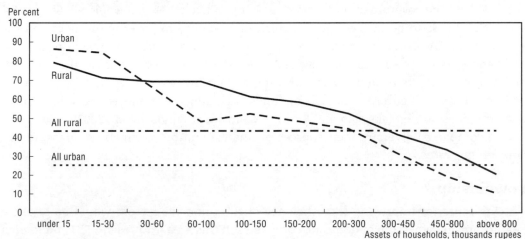

Source: National Sample Survey, Report 501.

OECD ECONOMIC SURVEYS: INDIA – ISBN 978-92-64-03351-1 – © OECD 2007

The financial performance of institutions established by the government to provide lending to rural populations has been poor. These institutions come for the most part under the control of the National Bank for Agriculture and Rural Development. This bank is owned by the Reserve Bank of India, with the government of India being a minority shareholder, and is also supervised by the Reserve Bank. This bank is sound with high capital adequacy and low bad debts. About one-fifth of its resources come from banks that have been able, until April 2007, to lend to this institution, as an alternative to make loans to priority sectors of the economy.[2] However, the lower level institutions have not performed so well. These rural institutions suffer from "poor debt recoveries, weak management information systems, lack of professionalism and huge accumulated losses", with 56% of the institutions making losses and non-performing loan ratios of between 20% and 30% (RBI, 2006). As to the state-owned commercial banks, they suffer from significant loan losses in their lending to the agricultural sector but not on the scale of the co-operative banks.

Given the apparent cost advantage of commercial banks in rural areas, the question arises as to why their market share did not continue to rise after 1981. Part of the answer appears to be poor administration. One survey of Uttar Pradesh, undertaken by the National Council for Applied Economic Research and the World Bank, showed that banks take 33 weeks, on average, to process a loan application and that one-quarter of applicants had to pay a bribe of 10% to obtain a loan from a bank, with the bribe rising to 40% if the loan came from a government scheme (Basu, 2006). On the other hand, money lenders make loans of short duration, for smaller amounts, for consumption purposes (family emergency, social purposes or regular consumption) rather than investment purposes and react quickly.

Further reducing the role of the moneylenders appears to require innovative financial instruments that are capable of reaching households with few assets. The policy of rural branch expansion as an instrument for improving inclusion appears to have reached its limit, as does the policy of direct lending. Ambitious targets for lending to agriculture have not resulted in appreciable reduction in the recourse to money lenders in the past decade. The Kissan Credit Card, whereby farmers can obtain credit on demand subject to an overall credit limit has reached 7 million farmers and has been successful, as have linkages between banks and self help groups to provide microfinance. There are some doubts, however, about whether the later can be expanded easily due to the need to form groups and the inherent constraints of groups accepting joint liability for debts.

Conclusions

India's financial markets have become considerably more efficient in the past 15 years. Banks have been restored to health. New regulatory bodies have been established in most markets and some segments of the market have developed rapidly. However, the financial market as whole remains subject to a number of constraints and these need to be eased if efficiency is to be improved. In banking, there appears to be a need to lower the extent to which credit is directed both to specific sectors and to the government. At the same time, the efficiency of public sector banks could be improved. Although most now have minority public shareholders controls remains with government. A clear time path for reducing government control, coupled with allowing more foreign ownerships of banks, is needed.

In capital markets, government ownership of intermediaries, and control over their portfolios, needs to be reduced along with allowing greater openness to foreign investment. Reducing controls over institutional portfolios would help to increase the flow of funds towards the corporate bond market. This market might also be further developed by allowing exchange-traded interest rate futures and establishing transparent markets in corporate debt, in line with recent recommendations of government committees. Finally, there is scope for reducing the range of activities undertaken by the Reserve Bank. As in product markets (Chapter 3) and in infrastructure (Chapter 7) there is also a need in the financial market to separate the ownership, regulation and policy functions. This would imply moving a number of the current activities of the Reserve Bank to other institutions. Finally, as to the regulatory bodies, there would appear to be some scope for regulating financial intermediaries according to their activity rather than according to the activity of their parent body. For instance, all asset managers would then be regulated by the Securities Regulator and not by the organisation that supervises their parent body. Finally, there have been a number of examples where regulators have been very slow in approving financial innovations. This could be avoided by moving to a more principles based regime, rather than sticking to a rule-based system.

Box 5.1. **Policy recommendations for reforming India's financial markets**

The banking sector:

- Move to a completely privately owned banking sector and allow foreign banks to fully own Indian banks.
- Reduce the extent to which the government directs credit by a phased lowering of priority lending and the statutory liquidity ratio.
- End remaining controls over interest rates.

Capital markets:

- Remove regulatory barriers to the development of exchange-traded interest rate and exchange rate derivatives.
- Ensure that plans to implement a transparent market in corporate debt are implemented.

Institutional investors

- Allow private sector fund managers for the civil service pension defined contribution scheme
- Take steps to use the new civil service scheme as the base for a wider retirement saving system.

Regulation of financial markets:

- Consider the costs and benefits of moving to a principles-based regulatory regime rather than a rules-based regime.
- Ensure that all financial intermediaries undertaking a given activity are supervised by the same regulator.
- Consider privatising the government bond trading platform run by the Reserve Bank and transferring regulation of the market to the security market regulator.

Notes

1. The institutions are as follows 32 000 commercial and rural banks; 14 000 rural co-operative banks; 98 000 primary agricultural credit societies and 154 000 post office branches (Basu, 2006).

2. However, such loans represent just 2.5% of total priority lending.

Bibliography

Asher M.G. and A. Nandy (2006), "Reforming Provident and Prension Fund Regulation in India", *Journal of Financial Regulation and Compliance*, Vol. 14, No. 3, 2006, pp. 273-84(12).

Banerjee, Abhijit V., E. Duflo and S. Cole (2005), "Bank Financing in India,"*India's and China's Recent Experience with Reform and Growth*, in Wanda Tseng and David Cowen, (eds.), Palgrave Macmillan: Hampshire, UK, 2005, pp. 138-57.

Basu P. (2006), *Improving Access to Finance for India's Rural Poor*, Directions in Development series, Improving Access to Finance for India's Rural Poor.

Chakrabarti R. and G. Chawla (2005), "Bank Efficiency in India since the Reforms: An Assessment", ICRA Bulletin Money & Finance, July-December.

Government of India (1991), *Report of the Committee on the Financial System*, (Chairman: Shri M. Narasimham), Reserve Bank of India, Mumbai.

Das, A. and S. Gosh (2006), "Financial Deregulation and efficiency: An empirical analysis of Indian banks during the post reform period", *Review of Financial Economics*, Vol 15.

Government of India (2004), *The Lahiri Committee on the Liberalisation of Foreign Institutional Investment*, June, Delhi.

Lahiri A. (2006), "Financial Sector Reforms in India: Steps and Effects on the International Financial System", presentation to the programme of seminars: *Asia in the World*, IMF/World Bank annual meeting, Singapore, September.

McKinsey Global Institute (2001), *India: The Growth Imperative*, San Francisco.

McKinsey Global Institute (2006), *Accelerating India's Growth through Financial System Reform*, San Francisco.

Micco A., U. Panizza and M. Yañez (2004), "Bank Ownership and Performance" Working Paper 1016, Inter-American Development Bank, Research Department.

Mohan, T.T. Ram (2005), *Privatisation in India: Challenging the Economic Orthodoxy*, RoutledgeCurzon, Delhi, London, and New York.

Mohan, R (2005), *Reforms, productivity and efficiency in banking: the Indian experience*, Address to the 21st Annual General Meeting and Conference of the Pakistan Society of Development Economists, Islamabad, 21 December 2005.

Muniappan, G, (2002), "The NPA Overhang, Magnitude, Solutions and Legal reforms", Reserve Bank of India.

Mohan, R. and Ray, S. (2005) "Productivity Growth and Efficiency in Indian Banking: A Comparison of Public, Private, and Foreign Banks", University of Connecticut Department of Economics Working Paper 2004-27.

National Sample Survey (2005), "Household Indebtedness in India: the All India Debt and Investment Survey", report No. 501, New Delhi, December.

OECD (2003), "Summary Record of the 2nd OECD/INPRS", Conference on Private Pensions in Asia, May, Hyderabad, India.

Patil (2006), *The RH Patil Committee on corporate bonds and securitisation*, Delhi.

Reserve Bank Of India (2005), *Draft Technical Paper By The Internal Working Group On Priority Sector Lending*; Rural Planning And Credit Department, Central Office, Mumbai.

Sanyal, P. and R. Shankar (2005), "Financial Sector Reforms and Bank Efficiency in India", unpublished paper, October, Department of Economics, Brandeis University.

Sarkar, A. (2006), "Indian derivatives markets", in *The Oxford Companion to Economics in India*, Basuk, K. (ed), Oxford University Press, New Delhi.

ISBN 978-92-64-03351-1
OECD Economic Surveys: India
© OECD 2007

Chapter 6

Improving the fiscal system

This chapter examines areas of government spending, taxation and fiscal federalism where further reforms are desirable to reduce economic distortions and improve the provision of public services. As to government spending, it finds that a large share is used to subsidise commercial undertakings, agriculture and food distribution and that there is much room to improve the quality of spending and target it better to reduce poverty. On taxes, which have undergone major reforms since the early 1990s, it points to the large number of loopholes and suggests that a broadening of the tax bases would allow further reductions in tax rates and make the system simpler and more efficient. Reforms of indirect taxes should focus on creating a common market within India so that goods can move between states without border controls. India's federal structure has led to a well-developed system of tax-sharing and transfers, both through constitutionally empowered bodies and delivered through the annual budget. Overall, this transfer system has worked well; moving resources towards the poorest states, but the system has become very complex and, in the past, weakened fiscal discipline. Furthermore, it has not been able to create an effective local government system; this would be important for improving accountability and responsiveness to citizens' needs as three-quarters of the population live in states with over 50 million inhabitants.

India's fiscal system has been reformed significantly since the early 1990s, in particular in the area of taxation. More recently, mechanisms to contain fiscal deficits have also been strengthened (see Chapter 1). This chapter examines areas of government spending, taxation and fiscal relations between the different levels of government where further reforms are desirable to reduce economic distortions and improve the provision of public services. It first looks at the structure of government spending and selected areas where reform has progressed, as in the pension system, or where additional controls are needed, as with subsidies and public-sector wages. It then describes the main elements of the tax system, which has been significantly improved since the early 1990s, and makes some suggestions for further reform. Finally, it examines India's system of fiscal federalism and recent reforms to this system.

Improving the quality of government spending

The level of general government expenditure (national accounts definition) rose only slightly from just under 23% to just over 25% of GDP in the decade to 2003. However, the quality of spending deteriorated over these ten years, though these tendencies have been checked in the subsequent four years. This level of spending is less than in all OECD countries with the exception of Mexico where spending is some five percentage points of GDP below that in India. The increase in public spending in the decade to 2003 was driven by increases in interest payments, which rose from 4 to 6% of GDP, while investment expenditure remained constant at just 1.6% of GDP. Total outlays on salaries, pensions to retired staff and interest amounted to just over half of total outlays in 2003. Since 2003, current spending by central government has expanded at a measured pace, almost 2 percentage points below the growth of GDP.

Reducing subsidies and improving their efficiency and transparency

The functional classification of spending shows that there is considerable scope for re-orienting public expenditure, particularly in the area of outlays for government enterprises and subsidies. In India, around two-thirds of total government outlays (excluding interest but including loans) is on functions other than general administration and defence. One-half of this is spent on support to commercial undertakings and subsidies for food and the agricultural sector. Three-quarters of the transfers to enterprises go to electricity, gas, water and communication enterprises, either in the form of outright subsidies or as capital transfers to cover losses and/or finance expansion. A large part of the total sum spent on the enterprises is provided as loans. However, given that most of the state-owned utilities are loss-making, such loans do not represent a source of future income for the government but rather a source of future subsidy payments (Figure 6.1). Chapter 7 lays out the steps that are necessary to ensure that government-owned units can reduce losses while at the same time improving service delivery.

Aside from subsidies and transfers to public utilities, a considerable part of the subsidies on food, fertilisers and kerosene result in the waste of public money due to faulty

Figure 6.1. **Government spending by type and function relative to GDP, 2003**

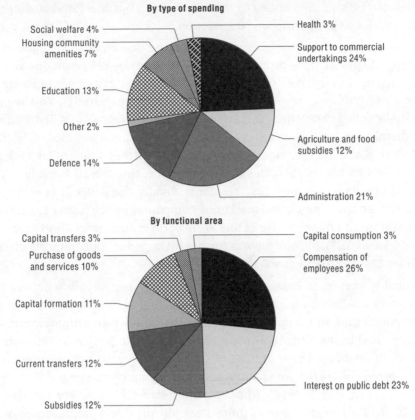

Source: National Account Statistics, 2006.

delivery. Given the proportion of families living below the poverty line, the government has put into place a programme to ensure that low income families are able to purchase a number of basic products at subsidised prices through a network of "fair price shops". Overall, expenditure on food and agricultural subsidies was equivalent to 1.6% of GDP, of which food subsides amounted to 0.8% of GDP in 2004, double their level of 1990. Analysis of the programme shows that it is bedevilled by poor administration and corruption (Planning Commission, 2005). Nationwide, over one-third of the grain distributed through the system is diverted either by the shopkeepers or through the existence of "ghost" ration cards. The beneficiaries of this diversion are officials in state governments and the Food Corporation of India and wholesale and retail dealers. In addition, one-fifth of the grain goes to people wrongly included in the programme, bringing the total loss to 58%. In two of the poorest states, Bihar and Uttar Pradesh, the loss rises to 98% and 80% respectively (op. cit.). For fertilisers, only 68% of the subsidy is estimated to accrue to farmers, with the bulk being paid to large farmers in irrigated areas (Ministry of Finance, 2004).

The wide dispersion of performance across states in the efficiency of delivering food subsidies suggests a number of possibilities for reform. In particular, the two states with the highest delivery of subsidies to the targeted population have innovative schemes in place. In Andhra Pradesh, a coupon system has been introduced that allows rationed goods to be drawn in smaller quantities which reduces the probability of undrawn rations being diverted to the market, while in Tamil Nadu, target households are allowed to trade their excess rations against other rationed commodities (sugar and kerosene). Both of these schemes point to the possibility of establishing a food stamp system, especially if the beneficiaries can be publicly verified at the village level, but the Tamil Nadu government found that even food stamps imposed transaction costs and so withdrew the scheme.

In addition to the direct on-budget subsidies, the government also grants subsidies through fixing the prices of the products of public enterprises below shadow market prices (most often there is no market price and, as a result, the prices adopted are based on international parity-import or export – mostly of the former variety). This is particularly the case with liquefied petroleum gas (LPG) and kerosene.[1] Kerosene is distributed through the public distribution system, and it is estimated that about 38% of the total deliveries are diverted to the black market, where prices are three times higher. For LPG, while the market price is 45% higher than the subsidised price, the overall subsidy is larger and largely accrues to higher income urban residents. Finally, the budget has been deprived of higher profits from the state-owned marketing companies by the failure to allow regulated prices for gasoline and diesel to rise in line with world market prices and prevalent tariffs (at a cost of 0.5% of GDP); the budget was further hit by reductions in tariffs on oil imports that may have cost the exchequer 0.3% of GDP in 2005.

The subsidy system is essentially directed at helping people who live below the national poverty line, but some people are unable to find sufficient work to purchase even subsidised goods and so the government has introduced an employment guarantee scheme. This programme aims to provide 100 days work to people in 330 districts of the country, with an estimated cost of 0.3% of GDP for this system. The programme is not restricted to people below the poverty line and some simulations suggest that a significant part of the benefit will accrue to households above the poverty line (Murgal and Ravallion, 2005). This programme is innovative but previous programmes of a similar nature have proved difficult to implement at the local level. Many analysts have suggested that the various poverty alleviations programmes are subject to considerable risk of money not being used for its prescribed purpose (Saxena and Ravi, 2006). Indeed the Planning Commission concluded that "in the absence of acceptable levels of governance, it would be preferable to eschew targeted programmes in favour of more generally applicable schemes" (Planning Commission, 2002). The government is aware of its experience with similar schemes, such as food for work and drought relief, that reveal waste, leakage and corruption caused by weak monitoring systems and lax accountability mechanisms (Rangarajan, 2005). The employment guarantee programme, though, does represent a step to providing a form of social safety net for the rural population that could be effective, though costly, in terms of reducing poverty, if efficiently administered. Indeed, the objective of the programme is to provide a safety net rather than reduce poverty.

The public pay-setting system could generate a new spending hike

One major problem for the management of public expenditure has been the method by which public sector wages are determined. Pay is set in a two-stage process. Each year, there are small pay increases. In addition, about once per decade, there is a Pay Commission established at the central level to establish the appropriate level and structure of salaries and make recommendations on personnel management. The last Commission, in 1996, recommended a 30% pay hike that boosted government pay by over 1% of GDP, relative to pay recommended by the previous Pay Commission a decade earlier. This Commission recommended compensating the pay increases by a reduction in the number of staff but this part of the recommendation was never implemented. A new Pay

Commission has just been established. The risk of major increases in pay stemming from this Commission may be lower than in previous episodes as civil service wages have been indexed on inflation, following the merging of the basic pay scale and the "dearness" allowance. In general, such a large interval between Commissions carries the risk of pay differentials moving out of line with those in the market and so the interval between Commissions should be markedly reduced. The efficiency of government administration is reduced by the relatively small number of higher skilled staff. The structure of the bureaucracy is heavily skewed in favour of lower grades reflecting the legacy of the colonial era. The structure should be oriented to recruiting more skilled staff with competitive pay scales and markedly reducing the use of paper-based transactions. At present the central government has placed severe restrictions on recruitment of lower grade staff which could yield considerable savings going forward were it fused with a reengineering of business processes (see Chapter 3).

The public pension system is presently being modernised

The government has acted to ensure that the liabilities of the public pension system are contained. Public pension payments rose from 1.1% to 2.0% of GDP between 1990 and 2005. If such an increase had continued, payments might have reached 2.3% of GDP by 2009 (Chidambaram, 2007). As from 2004, however, the government closed the existing defined benefit scheme to new entrants who, instead, will contribute to a two-tier defined contribution system. This is beginning to help ease pressure on expenditure which may grow at a slower pace over the period till 2009 when pension outlays are expected to be only 1.7% of GDP.[2] Contributors will be able to decide between three different investment strategies. The system separates management, record-keeping and fund management into separate operations. Government employees will pay 10% of their salary to the "tier one" account and this will be matched by the government. They will also be able to contribute to a "tier two" account on a voluntary basis. Withdrawals can be made from this tier but it will not attract tax concessions. Three years after its announcement, the system has not yet been fully implemented due to delays in passing the bill for a pension fund regulator. Nonetheless, contributions have been accumulating and four fund managers will be appointed, but no private sector fund managers will be allowed. State governments have also followed these reforms with 19 states, covering 82% of the population, having adopted the system by January 2007. West Bengal and Kerala are the principal states that refuse to implement the scheme at the state level.

Once the record-keeping system has been put in place, private sector employees will be eligible to join the system. They can deposit funds in the first tier of the system but there will be no matching contribution from the government as will be the case for public employees. As for civil servants, at retirement the individuals will have to use a fixed proportion of the funds in their accounts to purchase annuities with the remainder being taken as a cash sum. Once working, this system will provide the first universally available pension for private sector workers. Previously less than 3% of the private workforce was eligible for pensions.

Conclusions

Public expenditure is neither high in relation to GDP nor in relation to the needs of the economy and citizens for public services. However, there is ample evidence that spending could meet a number of the governments goals in a more efficient manner. The high proportion of expenditure that is devoted to the support of public sector enterprises is one area where considerable economies could be made through lessening the need for such transfers by making the recipient enterprises more efficient and improving governance (Chapter 3). Similarly, the use of subsidies appears to be excessive and costly in relation to the presumed goal of reducing poverty. These subsidies have other goals but these too need careful evaluation to ensure that money is being spent effectively. As yet, it is too early to evaluate the National Rural Employment Guarantee programme, but major efforts will be required to ensure that the problems seen by previous programmes do not re-occur. More broadly, there appears to be a need to improve the monitoring and control of public expenditure – as evidence not just in this chapter but also in Chapters 7 and 8 dealing with infrastructure and education, respectively. The public distribution for food and fuels, in particular, seems to need considerable reform. Reform of spending has been undertaken in some areas. The move to a defined contribution retirement saving system is to be welcomed, even if it has been slow in implementation. It could form the basis of a much wider retirement security programme to cover people working in the private sector.

India's tax system has been fundamentally reformed

Since economic reforms began in the 1980s, the Indian tax system has been markedly changed. Starting from a system with high nominal rates, tax rates have been reduced significantly. The changes have been wide-spread, affecting income taxes, tariffs and indirect taxation. Lower direct tax rates have not, however, adversely impacted on tax revenues because the tax base was widened substantially at the same time and economic growth has increased. Nonetheless, the tax system still bears the traces of past interventionism, notably in the areas of tariffs but also in indirect taxation. Thus, there remain a number of areas where the system could be further reformed in order to improve the efficiency of the economy.

India is a low tax economy…

Tax revenues in India are low compared with both OECD countries and a number of developing countries (Figure 6.2, Panel A). Two factors have resulted in this low tax ratio. First is the absence of a system of social transfers (for health, pensions and unemployment) covering the whole population, given that the current systems only cover employees of larger companies and the government. The second was the ability of central and state governments to use borrowing to cover almost one-third of total spending in the 1990s – a policy that was financially possible only because interest rates were low relative to the growth of GDP. If social security contributions are excluded from the comparison, then India's tax level is similar to that in China, Japan, Korea, Mexico and the United States (Figure 6.2, Panel B). Several forces are pushing towards an increase in the average tax burden, notably the need to reduce the deficit and the desire to introduce a basic social safety net.

… relying on indirect taxation…

As discussed in Chapter 1, since the beginning of this decade tax yields have started to rise sharply. This progression has been helped by rapid economic growth that has boosted the yield from both personal income and corporate taxation, which have been on a rising trend relative to GDP since rates were lowered in the early 1990s. By contrast, the yield of indirect taxation has been stable relative to GDP despite a further marked drop in import

Figure 6.2. **The relationship between the ratio of tax to GDP and per capita incomes: an international comparison**

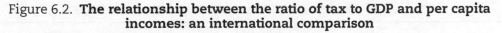

Panel A: Including social security contributions

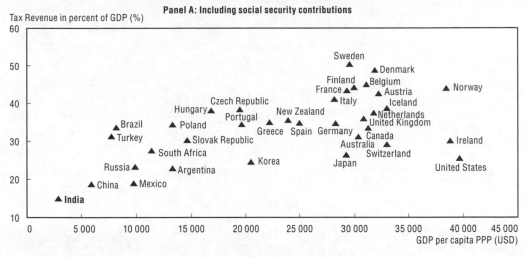

Panel B: Excluding social security contributions

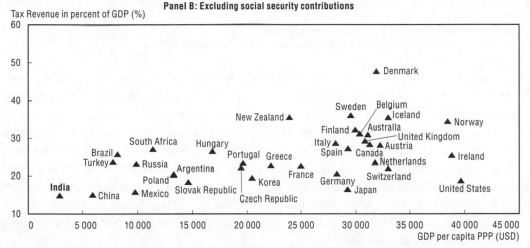

Source: OECD Revenue Statistics, Ministry of Finance, Indian Public Finance Statistics.

tariffs and a reform of central government indirect taxes. Nonetheless, indirect taxation accounts for the bulk of government revenues (Table 6.1).

Indirect taxes are levied both by the central government and the states according to demarcation lines established in the Constitution. The Constitution allows the central government to impose taxes on the production of goods and the provision of services, but not on the sale of goods at later stages, with the exception of interstate sales. State governments have the power to tax sales of goods within their state at all stages. Only the federal government is allowed to tax interstate sales of goods and this is achieved through the central sales tax. However the collection of this tax is managed by the states and the proceeds accrue to the state where the goods originate. Furthermore, only the central government is allowed to impose tariffs on international trade. It also imposes a countervailing duty on imports designed to ensure that imports pay the same central VAT as domestically produced goods.

The main indirect tax at the state level is the VAT, which was introduced in April 2005 and replaced the sales taxes. The state VAT only taxes goods, but does allow

Table 6.1. **Structure and amounts of taxation, FY 2005**

	Tax yield			Tax rates		
	% GDP		% total taxes	Number	Low–High	Commonest rate
All taxes	16.6		100	n.a.	n.a.	na
State government	6.0					
Indirect taxes		6.0	36.3			
State sales/VAT taxes[1]		3.8	22.9	3	1-12.5	12.5
Other state indirect taxes		1.4	8.7	n.a.	n.a.	n.a.
Other state taxes		0.8	4.7	n.a.	n.a.	n.a.
Central government	10.4					
Indirect taxes		5.4	32.9			
Excise taxes[2]		3.4	20.8	5	0-24	16
Tariffs		1.5	9.1	25	0-182	35
Service taxes		0.5	3.0	1	12	12
Direct taxes		5.0	30.2			
Corporation tax[3]		3.1	18.9	3	40-42	42
Income tax		1.9	11.3	3	10-33	10

1. From 2006, state sales tax became a state VAT.
2. Also known as central VAT (CENVAT).
3. Including dividend withholding tax or capital gains tax.
Source: Ministry of Finance, Indian Public Finance Statistics, various national sources.

input tax credit. The new VAT is a significant step forward in achieving tax neutrality as it avoids the cascading of taxation and reduces incentives to vertically integrate production systems. However, the state VAT does not tax services. It is destination based, so that all exports to another state are zero-rated. The central sales tax (CST) is levied on interstate sales of goods; but payments cannot be offset against the state VAT as yet and revenues accrue to the exporting state. As from April 2007, this tax was reduced from 4% to 3% and will be further reduced and finally eliminated in the coming years. The central government will compensate exporting states for this tax cut by transferring the revenue from the tax on certain services (see below) and has promised to compensate further if there is a sufficient shortfall in revenues.

The central government also taxes the production of goods through central excise taxes. This tax is known as the central VAT (or CENVAT). Within the good-producing sector, there is no cascading effect as goods' producers can offset input tax against output tax. However, distributors cannot offset the tax against their payment of state VAT and so it effectively becomes an excise tax. The central government also levies a tax, known as a countervailing duty, on imports that is set at the same rate as the excise tax on domestic production. In addition, the centre levies a service tax (of 12%) on the sale of a growing number of services.

The emphasis on the taxation of consumption has to a large extent resulted from the difficulty of taxing income when there are a large number of potential taxpayers with low incomes, with a large proportion not being literate. The collection costs are also likely to be lower for indirect taxes than for direct taxes given that, even though there a large number of small shops and manufacturers, the total number of tax points is much lower than total employment. Thus, the parameters of the income tax system have always been set to ensure that the vast bulk of the population is kept outside the income tax system. For example, after the threshold for paying personal income tax was raised to almost four times the average yearly wage in 2005, the number of taxpayers fell to 12 million from 26 million (less than 2% of the population aged 15 and over). More tellingly, the exemption limit is equal to the average salary of a male graduate working in an urban area. Perhaps surprisingly, in view of the many anecdotes on the difficulty of raising tax from the unorganised sector of the economy, the total yield of income tax from the self-employed was greater than that from wage-earners in 2004 (Kelkar, 2004). With the increasing computerisation of government records, cross-matching of data files is improving the extent of compliance and it would be less costly to include more workers in the personal income tax net.

Given the dominance of indirect taxes, the effective tax burden (as measured by tax revenues as a per cent of an estimated macroeconomic tax base) is much higher on consumption than that on labour. The effective rate on consumption has been rising in recent years with the progressive introduction of the service tax and by 2004 had reached nearly 21% when measured on a tax-exclusive base. By contrast, the tax rate on labour income is low at less than 3%, while the tax rate on capital was higher, at above 13% in 2004 (Table 6.2). It is noticeable that there are large differences in the apparent tax rates on different types of capital (see below). The corporate sector pays relatively high taxes on capital whereas the unorganised sector pays very low tax on capital – in part because of the low level of capital employed per individual tax unit so keeping much of the capital in untaxed units. While the gap between the effective tax rate on consumption and labour incomes is larger than in OECD countries, it is similar to that in China, Korea Thailand and Sri Lanka (Poirson, 2006). However, overall capital taxation appears to be similar to that in Korea and Thailand but markedly higher than in China.

Table 6.2. **Implicit tax rates on main macroeconomic aggregates**

Per cent of tax base

	1999	2000	2001	2002	2003	2004
Consumption	18.3	19.0	17.7	19.2	19.2	20.7
Capital	9.1	8.6	9.6	11.1	11.6	13.2
Labour	2.2	2.0	2.1	2.1	2.4	2.8

1. The methodology follows that of Carey and Tchilinguirian (2004). Consumption is the sum of private consumption and government consumption of goods and services. Capital income is sum of net operating surpluses for all sectors of the economy. For self-employment, capital income has been imputed and labour income computed by residual. Rates for 2004 have been estimated in the absence of data for factor incomes in that year.
Source: OECD calculations.

... with exemptions and distortions in all tax areas

Even though the tax system is – after all the reforms – not very onerous, there are numerous deductions and exemptions that result in considerable distortions to economic activity. Such tax breaks are a significant remaining element of government intervention in the economy. They are very widespread and affect nearly all central government taxes. Significant tax breaks were also offered by states but these have diminished considerably with the introduction of the value added tax.

Personal income tax

Exemptions to income tax are most noticeable in the area of saving and capital incomes. The treatment of savings is so favourable that it is often exempted from taxation at all three stages: *i.e.* at the time of the initial saving, during the period when the funds are invested and finally when the investment is liquidated. While the use of consumption as a base for taxation has a number of theoretical attractions, the Indian system goes well beyond a consumption tax base because there is no taxation of dissaving. Thus, a deposit made in an approved financial instrument (such as a one-year post office deposit) could be made out of pre-tax income and on maturity be reinvested generating a new reduction in taxation. Few of the tax-favoured saving schemes are treated on the classical system of exemption of contributions and holding income and then taxation at withdrawal that approximates a consumption tax. Moreover, there is little empirical evidence that similar, favourable, tax treatment results in increased saving in the OECD area (Antolin *et al.*, 2004).

There are a few other tax breaks that favour particular categories of taxpayers. Women and senior citizens are allowed higher exemption limits that together lowered tax revenues in 2004 by 7%. A further small tax break is extended to farmers. This source of income can only be taxed by state governments under the current constitutional arrangements but, in practice, they choose not to tax such incomes. In fact, given the current level of tax exemptions few farmers would have incomes sufficient to pay any income tax. However, this exemption does appear to result in some taxpayers deliberately misclassifying normal income as agricultural income, perhaps lowering the income tax yield by as much as 2% (Kelkar, 2004).

Corporate tax

Despite the significant rate cuts during the reform period, the statutory tax rate for corporations is at the high end in international comparison. At the same time, there are many exemptions and special treatments that substantially lower the actual tax rate paid by corporations. At 33.66%, in 2006, the corporate tax rate was exceeded in only a quarter of all countries in the world, with the unweighted worldwide average corporate tax rate (for retained earnings) being 27%. The distortion between the tax treatment of interest and dividends was markedly reduced in 1997 when dividend taxation was limited to 10% in excess of corporate taxation, through a withholding tax of 10% paid by the company. Dividends are not subsequently taxed in the hands of the shareholder. Consequently, there was only slight saving in the combined tax bill of the company and the shareholder if finance is switched from equity to debt. The 2007 budget has, however, increased the withholding tax to 15%. The total tax on dividends will thus be almost one half greater than that on interest which is only taxed under the personal income tax system.

Over the complete lifetime of an investment project, there is very little difference between the statutory rate and the effective tax rate. This effective tax rate allows for factors which affect the tax base, in particular the difference between tax depreciation and economic depreciation. In the case of India, this rate is only slightly lower (at 31.7%) than the standard rate and is relatively high in comparison to other countries (Figure 6.3).

However, these calculations refer to standard model firms and do not consider the numerous exemptions and loopholes. In particular, significant tax breaks have been given to firms located in Special Economic Zones (or similar areas) where exports are subject to a lower than standard tax rate (or no tax at all). The largest of these tax breaks has been given to firms located in Software Technology Parks or to the firms that have developed the power and telecommunication infrastructure for these parks. (see Chapter 1). In the new Special Economic Zones (SEZs), tax concessions similar to those in software parks have been introduced: a tax holiday for five years and a 50% reduction for the next ten years,

Figure 6.3. **Statutory and effective standard tax rates across countries**

2005 (India, 2006), tax rate as per cent of corporate income

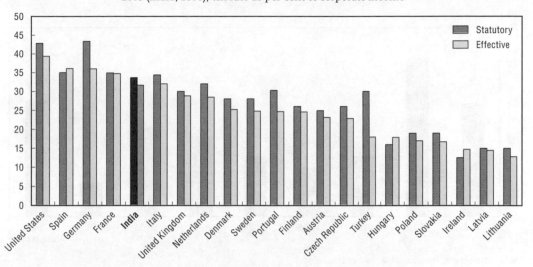

Source: Centre for European Economic Research (ZEW), Germany.

followed by halving the tax rate on export sales for the next five years. While widening the tax breaks in SEZs, the 2007 budget effectively lowered some of the concessions given to IT companies in software parks. It brought companies within the scope of the minimum alternative tax.[3] A number of IT companies have unused foreign tax credits and so the impact may be limited.

The fiscal cost of these concessions is substantial, lowering tax yields by almost one half. Based on a random sample of firms, the Ministry of Finance estimates that, on a static basis (*i.e.* ignoring the fact that behaviour is altered by the tax concessions), the concessions reduce the corporate tax yield by 47%, lowering the average corporate tax rate in 2004 to 19% against a legislated tax rate of 36.59% in that year (Ministry of Finance, 2006). However, companies are able to use these concessions to a varying extent, with the result that there is a large variation in the effective tax rate across companies, with only a small minority of companies paying the standard rate of taxation (Figure 6.4).

The cost of these concessions has been evaluated against the basic tax legislation but this may not be the appropriate base for evaluating tax expenditures. In the case of corporate taxation, depreciation allowances are not revalued to take into account inflation, so raising tax payments. There is also discrimination against groups of companies with subsidiaries. These structures are not allowed to file consolidated tax returns, so that it is possible that a group of companies can make a loss but continue to pay corporate taxes. In addition, the dividend withholding tax cannot be reclaimed on intragroup dividend payments, leading to cascading taxation.

Indirect taxation

The indirect tax system also suffers from numerous specific exemptions that reduce tax yields and favour production in certain sectors. The largest discriminatory use of taxation, though, is in the tariff regime. The low yield of tariffs relative to the weighted average tariff is noted in Chapter 3 and detailed analysis of the tariff revenues shows that

Figure 6.4. **Distribution of companies by average corporate tax rate**
Fiscal year 2004

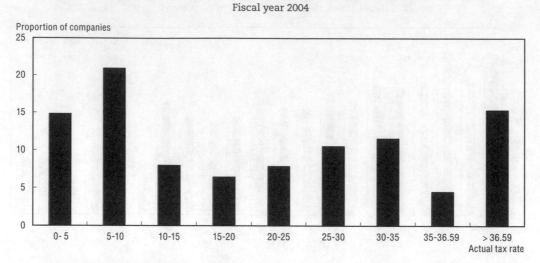

Source: Ministry of Finance, *2006 Budget Documents*.

product, industry or end-use based exemptions lowered the yield of tariffs, in a static sense, by 62% in 2004. The extent of the subsidy varies considerably across products. The revenue shortfalls from current concessions and exemptions are estimated at 18.5% of import values (Table 6.3).

Table 6.3. **Tariff revenue foregone as the result of concessions and exemptions**

	Revenue foregone	Value of imports	Foregone revenue relative to imports
	Billion INR		Per cent
Agricultural products	108.9	206.1	52.8
Ores and fuels	139.9	1 639.1	8.5
Chemicals	82.7	516.5	16.0
Organic raw materials	40.1	203.7	19.7
Filaments, clothing, textiles, footwear	49.5	54.8	90.2
Precious stones, jewellery, ceramics	153.6	956.3	16.1
Metals	89.6	268.5	33.4
Non-electrical machinery and tools	89.4	448.5	19.9
Electrical machinery	123.9	401.9	30.8
Vehicles	20.0	194.6	10.3
Other manufactured products	30.8	135.8	22.7
Total (excluding arms and munitions)	923.8	4 995.3	18.5
Simple mean (chapter level)	..	..	24.3
Standard deviation	..	..	28.4
Coefficient of variation	..	..	117%

Source: Ministry of Finance, Statement of Tax Expenditures, (2006), Ministry of Commerce and Industry, Department of Commerce, Export Import, data bank, Tradestat 6.0.

The domestic indirect tax system leads – despite recent improvements – to considerable cascading of taxes and unequal tax treatment of different firms. It is discriminatory in design because of the separation of the taxation of goods from that of services which also makes taxation complex and facilitates tax avoidance. Taxation also cascades because the central VAT on goods becomes an excise tax once the taxed item leaves the production sector, though there is a mechanism, a the central level to set-off central taxes on inputs of goods and services against taxes on outputs. The central excise taxes are subject to numerous derogations both for particular goods but also for small industries and for firms in certain geographic areas. Overall, these exemptions lower the excise tax yield by one-quarter (1% of GDP). Despite the exemptions, the indirect tax burden on goods is much larger than on services, though the extent of service taxation is being continually widened. The central sales tax on cross-border sales favours the producers within a given state at the expense of other states. Moreover, there are physical border controls between states which are costly and are barriers to the creation of a uniform internal market, but necessary to prevent tax evasion through false reporting of intrastate sales as interstate sales.

The government intends, in partnership with the states, to introduce a nationwide goods and services (value added) tax by 2010. A nation-wide GST would be a major step to creating a barrier-free common internal market. A first step in this direction has been taken with an agreement between state finance ministers and the central government to progressively phase out the central sales tax. A desirable second step would be for the central government to unify the three taxes that resemble a value added tax into one central goods and service tax. This would involve merging the countervailing duty on imports, the central VAT (CENVAT) and the services tax into one tax preferably with a unified rate. At the same time, the scope of the service tax would need to be widened. In addition, the nationwide IT system that now covers 700 000 firms and is designed to ensure that income tax can be deducted at source should be broadened so that it can also handle VAT transactions.

There are various reform options which would allow the elimination of controls at state borders so that taxation would no longer be a barrier to the development of a more dynamic internal market. Achieving this requires eliminating state entry taxes (and octroi, which still exists in some municipalities) and also further reforming the VAT system as this currently also requires physical controls at state borders.

One option for further VAT reform is to tax goods and services without allowing any tax rebates for interstate sales and collect the revenue centrally, but then redistribute the VAT yield using a formula. This system exists in most federal OECD member countries but suffers from two major drawbacks: first, agreeing on an adequate revenue distribution between the centre and states and between states is politically difficult. Second, as the VAT rate has to be set nationwide, states lose a major part of their tax autonomy – though in the case of India states have given this up by agreeing to set the same standard VAT rate of 12½ per cent (there are three other rates for certain products: 0%, 1%, 4%).

Another option would be to establish a dual VAT where both the central and the state level set their own rates on the same tax base. Individual states could then set different VAT rates (perhaps within limits). Operating a dual VAT system with a unified federal rate and different rates across states and without border controls would be facilitated by a federal VAT that did not exempt interstate exports (i.e. in line with current treatment for the central government VAT on goods and the service tax). The states' VAT would continue the current treatment of exempting interstate exports. This system ensures that the VAT chain is maintained for interstate trade (through the federal VAT) which would facilitate tax enforcement.

Among OECD countries, a dual VAT system where both the centre and the provinces levy VAT on the same tax base but with different rates exists in Canada in the province of Québec, which set its own VAT rate, on which the central VAT rate is added. However, in this system, sales between states, which only bear the federal VAT, are taxed less than sales within a state, which bear both the federal and the state VAT, there is still a risk of fraud with goods being declared as exports to other states although they are consumed within the originating state. The VAT chain is still intact, so efficient auditing is needed to limit such fraud. In the system used in Québec fraud appears to be contained, but in the European Union, which uses a destination-based system for cross-border sales, fraud is a significant problem (Nam *et al.*, 2001; IMF, 2007).

The risk of fraud could be further reduced by imposing – in addition to the ordinary federal VAT – a federal surcharge on interstate exports, as suggested by McLure (2000). This surcharge would serve to neutralize the states' VAT exemption of interstate exports while yielding no net revenues to the federal government as a corresponding tax credit would be granted to the importer (see Box 6.1 for details).

Conclusions

From the above description of the past reforms and current system, it is clear that the tax system has been modernised considerably. Nonetheless, there is still a large potential for making the system more efficient. Eliminating exemptions and loopholes for both direct and indirect taxes would level the playing field, reduce distortions and make the system simpler for both taxpayers and the administration. For example, for tariffs, the direction should be to introduce a revenue-neutral reform that markedly reduces the dispersion of tariffs ideally aiming for one tariff rate, but certainly a limited number or rates on all non-agricultural goods. For direct and indirect taxes (excluding tariffs) there are also various ways to make them more business-friendly without reducing tax revenues.

Creating room for further cuts in direct tax rates by broadening the bases

The internationally high statutory tax rates on corporations together with the existence of large tax expenditures suggest that there is scope for some further reduction in the corporate tax rate. Such a reform has started in the 2005-06 budget by the alignment of the depreciation rate for tax purposes with replacement life value. The goal could be to allow companies to unify the tax treatment of depreciation with the accounting treatment, making the tax base for corporate profits the same as profits declared in their accounts. This would remove discretion from the tax authorities and result in assets being valued at the company level. Just abolishing accelerated depreciation and various area and industry specific allowances would permit the tax rate to be lowered to just below 25%, and perhaps even lower if accounting depreciation were used for tax purposes. Reducing such special incentives and exemptions for firms, allowing group taxation (subject to single shareholding of group as well as individual units), and unifying the taxation of retained and distributed earnings would not only improve economic efficiency but also make the direct tax system fairer and simpler and thus easier to administer.

A major issue with tax exemptions is to what extent existing export-related tax allowances should be ended (covering the old type of special economic zones, export processing areas and most importantly software technology parks) and whether the generous tax holidays for companies established in the new Special Economic Zones (SEZs) should continue. Given the relatively high effective average corporate tax rates for

> ### Box 6.1. **A multi-level VAT system designed to avoid cross-border fraud**
>
> The current state-level VAT system is a destination-based tax so that exports to other states (or other countries) are zero-rated. The federal government imposes a central sales tax (at a rate of 3% from April 2007) on inter-state sales with the revenues accruing to the exporting state. This system results in goods produced and consumed in the same state being taxed less heavily than goods imported from another state. The government's objective is to move to a nation-wide goods and service tax on VAT lines.
>
> Various suggestions have been made to simplify VAT systems with respect to trade within federal countries or economic unions such as the EU. The proposal for a dual VAT seems to be particularly interesting for India as it allows states to preserve their fiscal autonomy by setting different VAT rates. With a VAT, different rates are possible across states without that being a deterrent to investment or production in that state since the VAT is essentially a tax on consumption in a given area and not a tax on the value added in the same area. As with a destination based VAT, it ensures neutrality between producers inside and outside a given state.
>
> The main change to the current system in India would be first to widen the national base of the VAT to include all goods, services and imports. Then the states' VAT base would need to be widened as well, and a federal VAT on the same tax base as the state tax would have to be introduced. The existing central VAT on goods, the service tax, the countervailing duty on imports and the central sales tax would all be rolled into the federal VAT. The federal VAT would be imposed both on intrastate sales and interstate sales, and so it would not be rebated when the goods moved from one state to another. As a result, the self-policing nature of VAT would be preserved on inter state sales.
>
> The possibility of fraudulent claims would still persist, however, because the state tax would be rebated on cross-border sales and so there is an incentive to declare sales as an export, even if they are subsequently fraudulently sold in the same state. If the system were to also include a "compensating VAT" on cross-border sales, as suggested by McLure (2000), who modified earlier proposals made by Bird and Gendron (1998) and others (as quoted by McLure), then fraud could be minimised. Such a system allows the operation of a destination-based VAT without controlling trade at state borders.
>
> Under such a system, the federal government would impose an additional surcharge (the compensating VAT) on interstate sales in order to ensure that no exporter receives a rebate. It would be set at the level of the highest state VAT. As a result of this additional tax, the tax burden on goods leaving the state is similar to that on goods sold within the state of origin, thereby eliminating the incentive for false declaration of intrastate sales as exports to another state. As the importer receives a tax credit for the compensating VAT paid by the exporter, this compensating VAT does not yield net revenues to the government. The operating of the current VAT system and of our reform proposal (with hypothetical tax rates) is illustrated in Tables 6.4 and 6.5.

domestic and foreign firms that operate outside SEZs, and which do not have access to any special concessions, such tax holidays will certainly provide a big incentive for domestic firms to establish production facilities in SEZs when they wish to expand their export operations. They will also provide a considerable incentive to foreign firms to come to the SEZs, especially as infrastructure will be better and labour regulations less onerous. The cost of these concessions will have to be balanced against the employment gains. The actual cost of the concessions is not yet known and official estimates vary considerably.

Table 6.4. **The current VAT system and cross-border trade**

| | Transactions | | Calculation of tax paid on an intrastate sale and an interstate sale | | | |
| | | | All sales entirely in State B | First sale in State A, final sale in State B | | |
	Sales entirely in State B	Sales in both State A and State B	State B VAT (8%)	State A VAT (8%), State B VAT (8%)	Federal tax on inter-state sales (3%)	Total tax
First sale						
Purchase	0	0	0	0	0	0
Sales	100	100	8	8	0	8
Value added	100	100				
Net tax			8	8	0	8
Intrastate sale or cross-border sale both with no value added						
Purchase	100	100	−8	−8	0	−8
Sales	100	100	8	0	3	3
Value added	0	0				
Net tax			0	−8	3	−5
Final sale						
Purchase	100	103	−8	0	0	0
Sales	200	203	16	16.24	0	16.24
Value added	100	100				
Net tax			8	16.24	0	16.24
Total value added	200	200				
Total tax			16	16.24	3	19.24

Table 6.5. **Illustrating the operating of VAT: Reform options with a dual VAT**

| | Transactions | Calculation of tax paid in intrastate sale and an interstate sale | | | | | | |
| | | All sales within State B where VAT is 8% | | | First sale in State A where state VAT is 6% and final sale in State B where VAT is 8% | | | |
		State tax (8%)	Federal tax (10%)	Total tax	State tax (6% and 8%)	Ordinary federal tax (10%)	Compensatory federal tax (8%)	Total tax
First Sale								
Purchases	0	0	0	0	0	0	0	0
Sales	100	8	10	16	6	10	0	16
Value added	100							
Net tax		8	10	16	6	10	0	16
Intrastate or cross-border sale with no value added								
Purchases	100	−8	−10	−16	−6	−10	0	−16
Sales	100	8	10	16	0	10	8	18
Value added	0							
Net tax		0	0	0	−6	0	8	2
Final sale								
Purchases	100	−8	−10	−16	0	−10	−8	−18
Sales	200	16	20	32	16	20	0	36
Value added	100							
Net tax		8	10	16	16	10	−8	18
Total value added	200							
Total tax		16	20	36	16	20	0	36

Source: OECD (based on McLure, 2000).

Overall, there would appear to be considerable advantages for ending all of the above-mentioned tax breaks and unifying the accounting and tax treatment of depreciation. With a far-reaching reform, the tax base would broaden significantly so that the standard corporate tax rate could probably be lowered to about 20% without creating revenue losses This would bring India's statutory and effective corporate tax rates closer to the levels which exist in a number of other emerging economies.

In line with the treatment of corporate taxation, the objective for the personal income tax should also be to make it as neutral as possible. The first priority should be to move the taxation of saving schemes to a base where only the income accumulated during saving is exempt from tax. Then, consideration should be given to reducing age and gender related allowances, or at least replacing them by a tax credit. Finally, the centre should come to an agreement with states to allow the taxation of agricultural income by the centre with the revenue raised being transferred to states. These changes would generate significant revenue which should be used to reduce the top marginal rate to, perhaps, 20% in line with the proposed corporate tax rate.

Reforming indirect taxes to create a common market for goods and services within India

The current structure of indirect taxation is complicated and still involves considerable cascading of taxation. The government has announced a target of moving to a nationwide goods and services tax by 2010. This will allow a consolidation of the whole indirect tax system, by abolishing the central VAT, the service tax and countervailing duties on imports. A path has not yet been established. One possible route would be to move to a national VAT with central revenue collection and redistribution of the tax yield according to a formula. Another option is to establish a dual VAT system, with a state and central component. This would enable states to set their own rates for taxing local consumption thereby allowing states the autonomy to adjust revenues to their expenditure needs and would also provide revenue to the centre. If the federal part of the tax was levied without a rebate on cross-border sales, then fraud could be contained, especially with an effective auditing system. If an additional federal surcharge on interstate sales was added, then the possibility of fraud would be almost eliminated. Creating a unified GST in such a way would be a major achievement and would greatly simplify of the indirect tax system. GST would also be a significant contribution to the creation of a common and efficient domestic market of goods and services, as it could be operated without physical border controls.

Improving fiscal federalism to limit borrowing and increase responsiveness to local needs

In a country as large and diverse as India, which is a union of 28 states and seven centrally administered territories, an efficient means for transferring resources from the central government to the states is needed. This is so for efficiency reasons as the centre is unlikely to be able to match local demands for public services in a country with over 1 billion inhabitants. But it is also important for equity reasons. Amongst the twenty major states, per capita income is three and half times higher in the richest three states (including the national capital territory) than in the poorest three states and the latter three contain 28% of the total population of the country. This section looks at the distribution of powers between central and state governments and at mechanism for revenue sharing as well as borrowing controls. It points to the apparent neglect of local authorities that have only been formally recognised in the Constitution since 1992, which created a three-tier system in rural areas and municipal governments in urban areas, although some decentralisation below the state level existed long before with municipal bodies in the major cities that are over three centuries old.

The powers of central and state governments

The Constitution gives the centre considerable powers over states in certain exceptional situations. The union parliament has the power (with qualified majority) to redraw the boundaries of a state (though this requires the consent of the states concerned) and to create new states. The powers have been exercised three times in the past two decades. The union also has the power to take over the administration of a state in certain circumstances and promulgate "President's Rule" (Article 356), although judicial rulings in recent years and differences in the party composition of the lower- and upper-house have made it more difficult to exercise such powers recently. Moreover, a deliberate choice was made at Independence that the recruitment and initial training of the senior civil and police employees should be undertaken by the central government which also has joint control with the states over their subsequent careers. Such personnel rotate rapidly through state and central government postings – typically at any point in time more than 50% of staff members have been in their current post for less than one year and less than 20% for more than two years (Singh and Bhandarkar, 1994 and Mishra, 1997).

The Constitution splits the powers of jurisdiction to legislate into three sectors: areas reserved to centre, areas reserved to states and areas of joint jurisdiction (the concurrent list), with any unspecified areas assigned to the centre or states. Areas with large externalities like defence, foreign affairs, international trade and macroeconomic management are the responsibility of the centre while law and order, public health, sanitation, schools, irrigation, agriculture, fisheries, industries, land rights, local government and others with statewide effects are assigned to the states. In practice, however, the centre has often intervened in areas of states' responsibility. Functions which create benefits across states and with significant effect on development (such as economic planning, energy, parts of education, health and family welfare) are undertaken concurrently with states. Supervision of a number of major economic activities (including national highways and airways) are assigned exclusively to the union. A number of activities are assigned to urban local governments, some of them concurrently with the state government (such as secondary and adult education, housing and land use, electricity distribution and industrial and commercial estates).

As well as assigning duties, and hence expenditure, to the centre and to the states, the constitution also gives the right to levy specific taxes to either the central or state governments, while any unspecified taxes can be levied by the central government. The tax assignments have been described above in the section on taxation. Furthermore, the constitutionally mandated quinquennial Finance Commission *de jure* decides on the arrangements for revenue sharing between the centre and the states (see below).

The extent of fiscal devolution to state governments

The overall pattern of finance shows that state governments receive a much higher proportion of total tax revenues than in federal countries in the OECD area (Table 6.6). The share of taxes assigned exclusively to state governments is larger than in other federal countries and this is accentuated both by the tax sharing arrangements and the extent of

Table 6.6. **Tax and revenue structure of state governments in selected federal countries**

2002, percentage of total central and second-tier government tax revenues

| | States' own tax revenue | States' shared tax revenue | States' total tax revenue | Grants from central to state governments | States' tax and grant revenue | Memorandum items | |
						Earmarked grants	Revenue excluding earmarked grants
Australia	15.9	13.4	29.3	9.5	38.8	8.5	30.3
Austria	1.7	8.1	9.7	8.8	18.5	6.9	11.6
Belgium	15.3	8.7	24	2.8	26.8	2.6	24.2
Canada	38.2	0.6	38.8	8.8	47.7	1.4	46.3
Germany	3.2	20.2	23.4	6.2	29.7	n.a.	n.a.
Mexico	2.4	0	2.4	46.1	48.5	26.4	22.1
Switzerland	29.1	3.1	32.2	18.5	50.7	14.2	36.5
United States	22.4	0	22.4	13.3	35.2	13.3	21.9
India	**39.4**	**15.8**	**55.2**	**12.1**	**67.3**	**12.1**	**55.2**

1. The data refer to provinces in Canada and *Länder* in Germany.
Source: OECD fiscal federalism network, Ministry of Finance, *Indian Public Finance Statistics*.

grants. However, this does not necessarily reflect a greater degree of autonomy of Indian states relative to states or provinces in other federations. In particular, the comparison is biased by the very low level of social insurance taxation and expenditure in India. In nearly all OECD federal countries, social insurance taxation is a significant portion of total taxation and is nearly always raised by the federal government, thereby reducing the share of the tax revenue flowing to states.

States in India are not very efficient in creating non-tax revenues with many of their commercial enterprises returning a loss, in contrast to central government enterprises. As a result, the states have a significantly lower share of spending than their share of the total tax revenue of central and state governments. Overall, the states share of spending is about 10 percentage points lower than their share in tax revenues.

The flow of funds from the centre to the states occurs through three channels. First, the Finance Commission recommends the proportion of central government taxes that should be transferred to states. These recommendations are generally followed and these transfers represent the bulk of financial flows to states. Second, the Planning Commission grants central assistance to either projects or schemes that are included in state planning documents that it has to approve. Finally, The Planning Commission also administers more than 200 schemes for selected areas of government expenditure that were originally designed by ministries. The Auditor General suggested that these schemes are often very poorly managed (Saxena, 2006). Moreover, it is often the case that funds allocated for these schemes by the Planning Commission are not fully utilised by a large number of states due to problems of the delivery system at the state level. Central government ministries administer these schemes, which are designed to ensure that state governments follow the policy directions of central government in areas outside its jurisdiction (Table 6.7).

Transfers through the Finance Commission have increased, but the share of earmarked grants has also increased, which may lower efficiency. The latest (12th) Finance Commission raised transfers to states for the period 2006 to 2010, with the states' share of central taxes being increased from 29.5% to 30.5%, while earmarked grants jumped by 143% (on average compared with the previous five-year period). It also recommended that

Table 6.7. **Central transfers to states by type of programme**

	1998	1999	2000	2001	2002
	Per cent of total assistance to states				
Tax sharing	60.0	59.3	58.0	55.7	56.5
Assistance to state plans	22.2	21.6	18.1	17.3	18.7
Other central schemes	11.9	11.0	9.2	14.2	14.8
Non-plan schemes	5.9	8.1	14.7	12.9	10.0
	Per cent of GDP				
Tax sharing	2.2	2.2	2.5	2.3	2.3
Assistance to state plans	0.8	0.8	0.8	0.7	0.8
Other central schemes	0.4	0.4	0.4	0.6	0.6
Non-plan schemes	0.2	0.3	0.6	0.5	0.4

Source: Nirmal (2004).

central government should stop lending to states. Shifting from central loans to transfers is a welcome move (see below). The growth of earmarked grants within the transfer system runs counter to the experience in a number of OECD countries where block grants were found to be more efficient than earmarked grants.

The redistributive impact

The system of grants and tax sharing essentially provides for horizontal redistribution of income between states. The amounts which are distributed to states in the form of tax sharing and grants (in both the Finance Commission and the Planning Commission routes) are determined by formulae that differ. In deciding on the distribution of shared taxes, the Finance Commission places most weight on income redistribution and less weight on the size of the state – whether measured by population or area. In the case of the Planning Commission, the weights are almost exactly reversed, with the added twist that the population structure is always based on the 1971 census, so as not to reward states that failed to implement effective family planning programmes. The Planning Commission distributes only part of its grants according to its distribution formula; the states classified as "general category" states receive less than half of their grants from the Planning Commission according to the formula while the "special category" states receive only 10% according to the formula and 90% as discretionary grants; "special category" states, with two exceptions, are physically isolated areas in either the north-eastern or north-western borders of India with strategic importance as well as poor infrastructure.

Within the general category of states, the distribution of the totality of central grants is highly redistributive. Before redistribution, poorer states have a slightly lower own tax revenue relative to state GDP than higher income states. After redistribution, there is a strong negative correlation between tax and grant revenues of states relative to state GDP and the income level of the states. (Figure 6.5). Part of this lower own tax revenue might be the result of disincentive effects with poorer states making less efforts to create own revenues as they rely heavily on central transfers. Indeed, for the special category states, such disincentives may be significant as their tax effort is markedly lower than average while their total grant income represents, on average, 40% of state GDP – though it is possible that the tax base of these states is lower than average relative to state GDP.

Figure 6.5. **State tax and grant income before and after central transfers, 2005[1]**

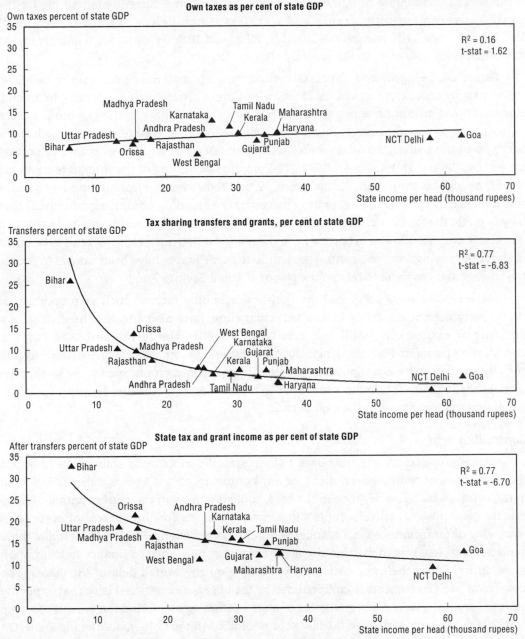

1. Correlation and t-statistics calculated using regressions on logged variables.

Source: Reserve Bank of India and OECD calculations.

Despite this high degree of redistribution of tax revenues, there remain marked differences in total current revenues across states. Although the current mechanism has reduced the coefficient of variation of tax revenues by a factor of almost two, the extent of inequality in revenues still remains more than double that in a number of OECD federal countries. However, given the scale of income differentials and the size of the poorer states, equalisation of per capita revenue would be difficult to achieve and would also create additional disincentives for creating own revenues. For example, moving to a degree of equality similar to that seen in Canada would require implausibly large transfers to a number of states (Bihar, Jharkhand, Madhya Pradesh, Rajasthan, Uttar Pradesh and West Bengal), that would be equivalent to half of the income currently remaining for the central government after grants and transfers. Nonetheless, within the group of low-income states, the transfers received by Bihar and Uttar Pradesh are relatively low as compared to the transfers to the special category states.

Part of the redistributive impact of central transfers may have been counterbalanced in the past by other elements of fiscal policy, but these offsets are now coming to an end. Horizontal redistribution was partially offset by exporting part of the tax burden from richer states to poorer states through the origin nature of interstate sales tax with taxes accruing to the (richer) exporting states while being paid by citizens in poorer importing states (Rao, Shand and Kalirajan, 1999). The progressive ending of the interstate trade tax will eliminate this tax export. Furthermore, vertical redistribution from the centre to states was lessened by the high interest rates charged by the Planning Commission for loans that largely offset the grant element of such transfers in the past. This policy was ended in 2006 and states are now allowed to borrow from the market where interest rates tend to be lower than for borrowing from the central government. Some states have been unable to access the market and continue to rely on the National Small Savings Fund.

Some studies have suggested that political economy factors, such as proportion of ruling party members coming from a particular state, have also affected the distribution not only of earmarked grants but also (with a lag) of the formulae-based Finance Commission transfers (Rao and Singh, 2004; Biswas and Marjit, 2000). Nonetheless, despite such influences, there is a significant progressive redistribution mechanism at work, even if these fiscal transfers have been unable to prevent a further widening of income inequalities across states in the past decade.

Controlling debt

Formally, the centre has the power to limit states' borrowing as states have to obtain the permission of central government for any borrowing; only if a state were not indebted to the centre, which has never been the case, could it borrow in the market without facing central government controls. India's legal arrangements for the control of state-level borrowing differ from those in a number of other federal systems (Table 6.8). In India, there is no national legal restriction on the ability of states to borrow to finance consumption expenditure, nor is their any nationally set ceiling on the overall debt of the states. The absence of such constraints is compounded by the absence of national laws that explicitly limit the central government guarantee of state borrowing and forbid the bailout of states that default on debt. Moreover, the law does not forbid states from guaranteeing loans. On the other hand, nearly all states have now introduced Fiscal Responsibility Acts that aim to eliminate revenue deficits, broadly equivalent to not using borrowing to finance consumption.

Despite its general power to limit states' debt, the central government does not appear to have used this power to a significant degree. Furthermore, in the past, numerous factors have softened states' budget constraint:

- The centre provided large loans to states to finance their deficits and sometimes these loans were later converted into grants.
- Furthermore, states were obliged to borrow most of the savings which are accumulated in the postal national savings fund (the Small Savings Scheme, see below), a regulation

Table 6.8. **Rules governing borrowing by lower level governments in selected federal systems**

	Australia	Brazil	Canada	India
Constitutional rules mandate balanced operating budgets	no	no	no	no
Statutory rules mandate balanced operating budgets	yes	no	yes	no
Penalties on state officials that violate balanced budget rules	yes	no	yes	no
States prohibited from borrowing other than for within year purposes	no	no	no	no
Ex ante registration of state borrowing with central government required	yes	yes	no	yes
National policy places ceiling on the outstanding long-tern debt of a State	yes	yes	no	no
National policy expressedly provides that state borrowing is only backed by the full faith and credit of the issuing state	yes	no	yes	no
Explicit and credible ban on bailouts of states at risk of defaulting on debt by national government	yes	no	yes	no
National policy prescribes rigorous accrual accounting standards for states	no	no	yes	no
State pension schemes required to operate on actuarially sound fully funded basis	yes	no	yes	no

Source: Reserve Bank of India (2006) and national sources.

that undermined fiscal consolidation and was particularly expensive for states.[4] They are now required to borrow only 80% of the funds raised by this scheme in their state.

- In addition, states also borrow from public enterprises and have also received overdrafts from the Reserve Bank of India.

- Past fiscal slippages by the central government also had a negative signalling effect on fiscal discipline of states and local authorities (contagion effect).

- Some features of the transfer system have weakened fiscal discipline as transfers by the Finance Commission were partly based on (initial or projected) expenditure-revenue gaps of individual states ("gap-filling" grants) rather than on normative indicators, thus rewarding states with relative poor fiscal management.

- Infrastructure projects are also often financed by newly created corporations which borrow from the market with state guarantees, thus creating contingent liabilities. Contingent liabilities also emerge through other state guarantees as well as through unfunded pension liabilities, although the recent pension reform is limiting the growth of these liabilities and will eventually eliminate them.

Given the factors that have contributed to a weakening of the budget constraint at the level of the states, their debt rose from 22% to 33% of GDP between 1990 and 2003, with the ratio of debt to total current revenue of the states rising from 1.8 to 2.9 in the same period and interest payments increasing from 13% to 26% of revenue. The main reason for this relatively modest increase was the fact that, in the 1990s, nominal GDP growth was higher than nominal interest rates, which compensated for the effect of the primary deficit on the debt ratio and resulted in a stable debt ratio between 1990 and 1998 (Rangarajan and Srivastava, 2003).[5] However, the dangers of relying on such a combination were seen between 1999 and 2003 when the interest rate-growth differential moved against the states and debt rose sharply.

The central government has now obliged the states to go to the market for new borrowing. It has stopped acting as a direct intermediary for borrowing by the states and has ended the requirements that central grants covering state investment projects should only cover 30% of total outlays with the rest covered by state borrowing. This absence of lending to states only covers expenditure through the Consolidated Fund of the government. The central government continues to lend to states through the Public Account which manages the postal savings system.

The postal savings system has played a key role in financing public sector deficits and, as designed, needs a significant reform. The states have privileged access to these funds through the National Small Savings Fund (NSSF) where all postal savings are held. Since 1999, each state government is obliged to borrow all of the cash raised in its geographic area and all pay the same interest rate which is set administratively. These postal savings attract significant tax concessions and also benefit from the administrative setting of interest rates above market rates and also from the backing by the full faith of the union government. States are charged a rate of 9.5% against their average market borrowing rate of 7.9%. Loans are unconditional and so can permit continued borrowing when access to markets might be difficult. Indeed, West Bengal – with a high debt burden – expects to finance its deficit entirely through this form of funding. States in this position are then vulnerable to any slowdown in the growth of deposit in their area. Indeed, such a slowdown is partly the cause of the recent fiscal problems in Kerala.

The obligation to borrow from the National Small Savings fund also places a burden on fiscally responsible states. In 2005, for states such as Tamil Nadu, Karnataka, Haryana, Punjab and the National Capital Territory almost one-third of the inflow of funds from the NSSF was in excess of their overall borrowing requirements. So these states were obliged to increase balances held with the central government by a similar amount. As the rate on the balances with the central government is well below that on the NSSF loans, the states make a significant loss on the transaction and are locked into a 25-year loan from the NSSF.

A reform of the NSSF mechanism is required to install greater fiscal discipline at the level of states. The increase in postal savings has amounted to 2.7% of GDP on average between 2002 and 2005 and represented one-quarter of the total acquisition of financial assets by the household sector. Even with the current FRBM targets for states, postal savings provide almost total finance for their deficits. This goes against another one of the desirable reforms of the FRBM Act, namely that the central government should cease lending to the state governments and instead oblige them to borrow on financial markets. In any case, if, over the medium term, government borrowing were to be used only to finance net capital formation, then the flow of funds from postal savings would exceed the requirements of states.

Reform should take action on a number of fronts. The interest rates on the different saving products should be aligned with market rates on an automatic basis with a sufficiently large margin to pay for the costs of collection and administration. The tax privileges accorded to this type of saving should be ended and states should be freed from the obligation to borrow from the fund. Even if all these reforms were implemented, a fundamental problem will continue with this type of intermediation by the central government. The deposits with the post office are effectively guaranteed by the central government but the assets are not central government loans, exposing the central government to a credit risk. One solution would be for the NSSF inflows to be used to fund the central government deficit, so removing the credit. An alternative would be for the fund to lend money in the commercial bond market.

The latest Finance Commission has lessened the extent of moral hazard in its grants and transfers. It recommended that states should introduce Fiscal Responsibility legislation that would involve balancing their revenue budgets and limit their overall fiscal deficit to 3% of state GDP. It further recommended that states that achieve specified targets for the reduction of revenue deficits should receive grants in the form of debt relief. Perhaps unfortunately, it tied the amount of the grant to the amount of maturing debt due to central government in a given period, thus tending to reward the highly-indebted states, i.e. the worst performers in the past more than the good performers. Nonetheless, it is unclear at this stage, if poorer states which face particularly serious fiscal strains and also have high infrastructure needs will be able to meet these fiscal targets. The Finance Commission has also reduced the extent of the grants for states deemed to be in need of assistance (where the moral hazard problem appears to be most prominent). This form of grant is now very small, accounting for less than 7½ per cent of tax sharing transfers. Moreover, from 2007 onwards no general category state will be receiving this form of grant which will be made only to the north-eastern and north-western special category states. However, the obligation of states to borrow 80% of the proceeds of the "Small Savings Fund" was not removed and continues to undermine the intended hardening of state's budget constraint as well as the flow of savings to private investment.

A further weakness in the control of state borrowing is the difficulty of obtaining consistent and timely data on the overall fiscal performance of state governments. The states do not use accrual accounting, nor is there a standardised form of accounts across states, with the result that states are able to switch expenditure between current and capital expenditure, notably for the payment of subsidies to loss-making state enterprises. Overall data for the budgets of all states are only available with a nine-month delay, with the result that nationwide data for actual spending in a given fiscal year is not available until 21 months after the end of that fiscal year when they are presented by the Reserve Bank of India.

Local bodies remain underdeveloped

While the basic principles of the vertical and horizontal distribution between the central government and states appear to work reasonably well, there is inadequate account taken of the needs of local government. This is a particularly important deficiency in a country where the median population of a general category state was 62 million in 2005. The constitution only recognised the existence of local government in 1992 and specified a number of services that should be in the domain of local authorities and also assigned taxes. More than a decade later, progress in developing an effective third tier of local government has been very limited. This is particularly the case in rural areas where there was no history of functioning institutions to build on, in contrast to urban areas where there has been a long history of municipal corporations. Even to the extent that they do function, the rural authorities have little autonomy and their own tax revenue is almost non-existent (Table 6.9). Municipal authorities scarcely do better, raising less than one-sixth of the level of own taxation seen in federal countries in the OECD area. Moreover, the autonomy of municipalities to set their own tax rates is often strictly limited while the value of the property tax base is often adversely impacted by state-level rent control laws. There is somewhat less of a difference in total local revenues from taxes and grants as a per cent of state and central taxes with some other federal OECD countries. Nonetheless, the overall tax and grant income of local bodies is only around 1½ per cent of GDP, which is about one-third that seen in the federal OECD countries shown in Table 6.9.

Table 6.9. **Tax and grant revenue of local level government in selected federal countries**

	Local taxes			Grants	Total tax and grant revenue
	Total	Tax sharing	Own taxes		
	Per cent state and central taxes				
Australia	3.1	0.0	3.1	0.7	3.8
Austria	10.6	5.9	4.7	2.1	12.7
Belgium	5.3	0.0	5.3	1.8	7.1
Canada	9.4	0.0	9.4	9.7	19.1
Germany	7.5	1.8	5.7	7.6	15.1
Switzerland	19.3	0.0	19.3	8.7	28.1
Simple average of above	9.2	1.3	7.9	5.1	14.3
India (municipalities)	2.1	0.7	1.5	4.7	6.8
India (rural)	2.2	2.0	0.3	0.9	3.1
India (total)	4.4	2.6	1.7	5.5	9.9
	Per cent of GDP[1]				
Australia	0.9	0.0	0.9	0.2	1.2
Austria	4.2	2.3	1.9	0.8	5.0
Belgium	2.3	0.0	2.3	0.8	3.1
Canada	2.9	0.0	2.9	3.0	5.9
Germany	2.5	0.6	1.9	2.5	5.0
Switzerland	4.9	0.0	4.9	2.2	7.1
Simple average of above	3.0	0.5	2.5	1.6	4.6
India (municipalities)[2]	0.6	0.2	0.4	1.2	1.8
India (rural)[1]	0.6	0.6	0.1	0.3	0.9
India (total)	0.6	0.4	0.2	0.8	1.4

1. GDP is measured at market prices.
2. It has been assumed that the distribution of GDP at market prices between rural and urban areas is the same as that of the distribution of net domestic product at factor cost.
Source: OECD Fiscal Federalism network, 12th Finance Commission, http://Indiastat.com.

The low level of municipal taxation is clearly associated with a low level of provision of basic local services. The provision of a piped water supply, a sewage disposal system and effective waste disposal are three key municipal services to which could be added an adequate road network and street lighting. Access to the first three basic services in urban areas varies enormously across different states in India (Figure 6.6). The average access across all states is 24% but the coefficient of variation is 50% with the range of individual indicators being from zero (provision of sewage disposal in urban areas in Bihar) to 79% (provision of piped water in Rajasthan). The variation of access to provision of basic services across municipalities is closely related to the average income of municipal authorities which shows considerable variation across states. In part this variation is due to the municipal income per capita being related positively to average incomes of the state in which they are located. This suggests that part of the problem of low income for municipal authorities is the failure of lower-income states, which receive large transfers, to treat local authorities in their jurisdiction in the same way as they are treated by central government.

Indeed, it would appear that the mechanism put in place to ensure revenue sharing at the state level, at the time when the Constitution was amended to formalise the role of local authorities, has never functioned in the way that was envisaged. In part this reflects poor availability of basic accounting data. Few municipalities have kept double-entry accounts and even fewer use them on an accrual basis. But the problem appears deeper.

Figure 6.6. **Access of urban population to basic services and municipal revenue per capita, by state**

Average % of population with access to piped sewage, waste collection and internal water supply, 1999

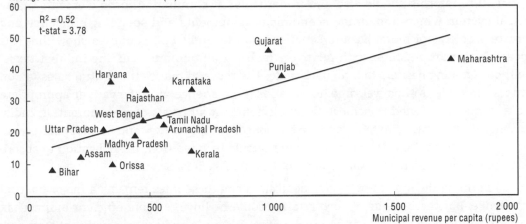

Source: Mathur and Thakur (2004), National Sample Survey (1999).

The Constitution envisages that each state should create a Finance Commission to regulate revenue sharing. They appear to be viewed as a constitutional formality, with recommendations often being ignored. According to the 12th National Finance Commission, "the delays in their constitution, frequent reconstitution, delays in reporting and reporting action taken and the qualifications of those serving on the commissions have in many cases defeated the very purpose of the institution".

Conclusions

A major achievement of India's federal system is that it has preserved the political cohesion between the states, which is a main challenge in a country of this size and with its ethnic, religious, linguistic and economic diversities. Nonetheless, there remains much room for improving the operation of India's fiscal federalism. Given the various weaknesses of the current system there is much agreement that reforms are needed and a reform path seems clear.

The first stage would be to set clear objectives for the system, which are lacking at the moment. The current tax sharing arrangements and transfer systems appear to be rather complex and not very transparent. However, designing an efficient system is notoriously difficult given the tradeoffs between the efficiency and equity objectives, and the need to make political compromises. Nonetheless, making the different functions of the transfer systems explicit, such as reducing fiscal imbalances between the different levels of government (vertical equity), supporting the financing of spending with positive externalities (efficiency) and redistributing resources in favour of poorer states and regions (horizontal equity), would increase transparency and help to improve the system. The multiplicity of channels for directing funds to states could also be simplified in order to give an overall view of the extent of redistribution.

There are large differences in state government revenues and, on this basis, it could be argued that the transfer system should be more redistributive. Here, an explicit redistribution objective might help, such as those adopted in Canada and Australia. However, relying on redistributive transfers alone will not be sufficient to achieve economic catching-up of poorer states. They will also need to implement structural reforms that improve framework conditions for the private sector, which is the main driver for growth in all OECD countries as well as in the more successful Indian states.

Future reforms should also aim in particular at eliminating those elements of the fiscal system which undermine economic developments and spending efficiency and create problems of moral hazard. Experiences in federal OECD countries show that it is possible to provide states with relatively high tax autonomy, including indirect taxes, without creating barriers to interstate trade. The move to reduce the central sales tax on interstate trade is thus welcome. International experience also shows that appropriate safeguards are needed to achieve fiscal discipline at all levels of government. In India, recent reform efforts aim to harden the budget constraint for the centre and for states, but more needs to be done. In particular, States should be freed from the obligation to absorb private savings which are accumulated in the Small Savings Scheme.

Reforming the system of fiscal federalism along these lines remains a major political challenge. But the benefits of such reforms could be huge. A more efficient indirect tax system would help to create an internal market for goods and services within the country and improve the efficiency of public spending, while more fiscal discipline would help to sustain high growth. This would – if accompanied by market-oriented structural reforms – further raise living standards in India as a whole, as well as in poorer regions and would thus help to achieve the government's objective of sustainable and inclusive economic growth.

Box 6.2. **Policy recommendations for improving the fiscal system**

Improve fiscal discipline

- Align the interest rates of the small savings fund on those of the market; end tax advantages and the obligation for states to borrow from the National Small Savings Fund (NSSF).

Improve spending efficiency

- Lower subsidies especially for fertilisers and fuel, and reduce the extent of leakages from the Public Distribution System.

- Set objectives for private sector employees joining the New Pension Scheme and allow private fund sector managers in the New Pension Scheme.

Reduce tax distortions

- Reduce the extent of exemptions for corporate taxation, agricultural incomes, excise taxes and tariffs.

- Move to a system of taxation on long-term saving that balances tax exemption on initial saving with taxation on withdrawal.

- After exemptions have been reduced, lower standard rates of taxation.

- In the context of the move to a General Sales Tax by 2010, introduce a two-tier state and central VAT, abolishing service tax and central excise taxes, and countervailing duty.

Improve fiscal federalism

- Unify formulae used for transfers to states by the Finance Commission and the Planning Commission.

- Improve the administration of central government schemes for transfers to states.

Notes

1. Three methods are used to finance the off-budget subsidies: first, the state-owned domestic oil producers are obliged to make a payment to the state-owned oil marketing companies while the latter have to bear the cost of the subsidy from their profits on gasoline and diesel sales. In addition, a small direct budgetary subsidy is paid to the oil companies. Finally, the government issued "oil" bonds to marketing companies. These bonds were granted to companies and there was no expenditure item in the budget for this grant. In total, in FY 2005 and 2006 off budget subsidies amounted to 90% of the total subsidy. Excluding the oil bonds subsidies amounted to 0.8% of GDP

2. Earlier government reports have suggest that there is considerable uncertainty surrounding pension projections due to the weakness of the underlying data on pension payments (Ministry of Finance, 2001).

3. The minimum alternative tax allows for the computation of corporate tax on the basis of the profit calculated by a company rather than the profit calculated for the tax authorities. This method of calculation is only used when the tax bill of the company is zero.

4. States are supposed to absorb 80% of accumulated savings of the savings fund of its jurisdiction. This scheme collects private households saving which is subsidized through income tax relief and also through offering returns above market rates. As the borrowing state has to bear the interest rate subsidy, its borrowing from this fund is more expensive than borrowing from the market.

5. The change of the ratio of debt to GDP is affected by two factors: the debt to GDP ratio increases if there is a primary deficit (i.e. if government non-interest spending exceeds revenues) and if the interest rate on government debt exceeds the growth rate of nominal GDP.

Bibliography

Antolin, P. de Serres, A., and C. de la Maisonneuve (2004), "Long term budgetary implications of tax favoured retirement plans", *OECD Economics Department Working Paper* No. 393, Paris.

Bagchi, A. (2003), *Fifty years of Fiscal Federalism in India, an Appraisal*, Kale Memorial lecture at Gokhale Institute of Politics and Economics, Pune, 8 December, 2001.

Bird, R.M. and P.P. Gendron (1998), *Dual VATs and Cross-Border Trade: Two Problems, One Solution?*, International Tax and Public Finance 5, pp. 429-42.

Biswas, R.and S. Marjit, (2000), *Political Lobbying and discretionary Finance in India: An Aspect of Regional Political Influence in a Representative Democracy*, Working Paper, Centre for Studies in Social Sciences, Calcutta.

Carey and Tchilinguirian (2000), *Average Effective tax rates on capital, labour and consumption*, OECD Economics Department Working Paper 207, October, Paris.

Chidambaram (2007), Statement to the Chief Ministers' Conference on Pension Reforms, Government Press Information Bureau, New Delhi, 22 January.

IMF (2007), *VAT Fraud and Evasion: What Do We Know, and What Can be Done?*, IMF Working Paper, 07/31, February

Mathur, P. and S. Thakur (2004), *India's Muncipal Sector: A study for the twelfth finance commission.* National Institute of Public Finance and Policy, New Delhi.

McLure, Ch. Jr. (2000), *Implementing Subnational Value Added Taxes on Internal Trade: The Compensating VAT (CVAT)*, International Tax and Public Finance 7, pp. 723-40.

Ministry of Finance (2001), *An Assessment of the Government of India's Pension Liability*, New Delhi, June.

Ministry of Finance (2004), *Central Government Subsidies in India*, New Deli, December.

Mishra, R.K. (1997), *The National Civil Service System In India: A Critical View*, paper presented at the Conference on Civil Service Systems in Comparative Perspective, School of Public and Environmental Affairs, Indiana University, Bloomington, 5-8 April.

Murgal and Ravallion (2005), *Employment Guarantee in Rural India: What Would It Cost and How Much Would It Reduce Poverty? Economic and Political Weekly*, 30 July.

Nam, Ch.W., R. Parsche and B. Schaden (2001), *Measurement of Value Added Tax Evasion in Selected EU Countries on the Basis of national Accounts Data*, Cesifo Working Paper No. 431, March.

Nirmal, A. (2004), *Study on transfer of resources from Centre to States*, 1st volume of the Official Statistics Seminar Series, November.

Planning Commission (2005), *Performance Evaluation of Targeted Public Distribution System*, Programme Evaluation Report 189, March, New Delhi.

Planning Commssion (2002), "10th Five-Year Plan (2002-07)", *Chapter 6: Governance and Implementation*, December, New Delhi.

Poirson, H. (2006), "Making Tax Policy Pro-Growth", in *India Goes Global*, C. Purfield and J. Schiff (eds.), International Monetary Fund.

Purfield, C. and M. Flanagan (2006), "Reining in State Deficits", in *India Goes Global*, C. Purfield and J. Schiff, (eds.), International Monetary Fund.

Rangarajan, C. (2005), "Strengthening Financial Management for Rural Employment Guarantee Scheme", paper presented to a workshop held at the National Institute of Public Finance and Policy, New Delhi.

Rangarajan, C. and D.K. Srivastava, (2003), "Dynamics of Debt Accumulation in India: Impact of Primary Deficit, Growth and Interest Rate", *Economic and Political Weekly* Vol. 38, No. 46, 4851-58.

Rao, M.G. (2000), *Fiscal Decentralization in Indian Federalism*, Institute for Social and Economic Change, Bangalore.

Rao, M.G., R. Shand and K.P. Kalirajan (1999), "Convergence of Incomes across Indian States: A Divergent View", *Economic and Political Weekly*, 27 March-2 April, pp. 769-78.

Rao, M.G. and N. Singh (2004), *The Political Economy of India's Federal System and its Reform*, Working Paper No. 566, Department of Economics University of California, Santa Cruz.

Saxena, N.C. and J.S. Ravi (2006), "Rural Poverty Reduction through Centrally Sponsored Schemes", paper prepared for the National Advisory Council, New Delhi.

Sengupta, N. (2005), *A civil servant remembers*, Samskriti, New Delhi.

Singh, N. and T.N. Srinivasan (2002), *Indian Federalism, Economic Reform and Globalization*.

Singh, P. and A. Bhandarkar (1994), *Asha, IAS Profile: Myths and Realities*, Wiley, 1994, p. 27.

ISBN 978-92-64-03351-1
OECD Economic Surveys: India
© OECD 2007

Chapter 7

Removing infrastructure bottlenecks

With high rates of economic growth and low public sector investment, India's infrastructure is in short supply and potentially a major constraint on future growth. To alleviate fiscal constraints and improve infrastructure productivity, the government is turning increasingly to the private sector to finance and run infrastructure projects. In some infrastructure sectors in which the regulatory environment is conducive to private sector involvement, performance has improved significantly. However, although infrastructure policy is moving in the right direction in some sectors, there are still a number of ways in which the regulatory environment could be improved further. This chapter outlines a range of policy initiatives that would increase private sector participation and improve infrastructure service delivery to international standards. It begins by discussing the role of public-private partnerships in the provision of infrastructure services before moving on to review the regulatory environment in a number of infrastructure sectors with a focus on regulatory settings that constrain competition.

Infrastructure is a major constraint on growth

India's infrastructure is seriously overstretched. As a result of rapid economic growth, demand for infrastructure services is at unprecedented levels and growing strongly. On the supply side, as discussed in Chapter 1, public sector investment in infrastructure is growing at less than half the rate of GDP growth and access to infrastructure is extremely low by world standards. A large body of research has found that infrastructure investment has high social rates of return, especially in low-income countries, and is a key determinant of economic growth (Estache, 2006). India's recent high rate of economic growth is at risk if infrastructure development does not increase and keep pace with demand.

Infrastructure investment can also play a role in ensuring that growth is inclusive. As well as being an effective means of spreading the benefits of growth to the poorest in society[1], infrastructure provision can have a significant impact on economic performance at the regional level. Indeed, an unequal distribution of infrastructure is one important reason why the economic performance of states has been diverging since the 1990s (Majumder, 2005 and Purfield, 2006) and cross-state differences in labour productivity appear to be closely related to differences in infrastructure provision (Figure 7.1).[2]

Figure 7.1. **Infrastructure and productivity by state**

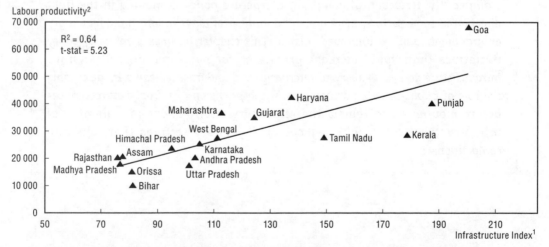

1. The infrastructure index measures access to infrastructure in eight major sectors: agriculture, banking, electricity, transport, communications, education, health, civil administration.
2. Labour productivity is measured as state GDP per worker employed over the period 1994 to 2004.
Source: Report of the 11th Finance Commission and OECD.

As well as being in short supply, India's infrastructure is in most cases also highly unproductive by world standards. For example, as discussed below, India's rail network is much less productive than China's. Indian airports also do not perform well with Delhi and

Mumbai international airports typically handling 25 to 28 flights per runway per hour in comparison to 40 in a number of OECD countries (Bindra, 2006). However, in some sectors where the regulatory environment is conducive to private sector participation, performance has been improving. For example, private sectors operators in the wireless telecoms market are relatively efficient and rapidly gaining market share. Relatively productive private sector operators are also making rapid inroads into the civil aviation market and the productivity at some of India's ports has improved over recent years (from a low base) as private contractors have been permitted to run port facilities.

The government of India is taking a number of measures to address the various infrastructure constraints that the country faces and improve the productivity of infrastructure sectors. Most notably, the Committee on Infrastructure, which is chaired by the Prime Minister, is charged with developing policy initiatives that increase private sector participation and improve infrastructure service delivery to international standards. The reminder of this chapter begins by discussing some general features of the regulatory environment that make infrastructure sectors conducive to private sector involvement. It then goes on to discuss the regulatory environment in a number of infrastructure sectors with a focus on regulatory settings that constrain competition.

The private sector has a crucial role to play in narrowing infrastructure gaps

Estimating the value of investment required to meet current excess demand for infrastructure services and expected future demands is no easy task. To give some indication, the size of the public sector capital stock in utilities and mining has been increasing by only 2¼ per cent annually over the last five years. If the growth in this infrastructure stock were to have the same relationship to income per capita seen in other rapidly growing Asian countries, it would be growing at over 9% per year. This would require an additional annual investment of 1.7% of GDP. In roads, an increase in infrastructure spending of 2.7% of GDP would be required to match Chinese investment rates in this sector. This suggests that in these two sectors combined, annual infrastructure investment of 4½ per cent of GDP (USD 40 billion annually) would be required to match the effort of fast growing Asian countries. With this additional infrastructure investment, the growth of the public sector capital stock would be slightly faster than that in the private sector and, if it obtained a normal rate of return, would boost output growth by almost 1% annually.

With public investment constrained by fiscal considerations, the role of the private sector in infrastructure provision needs to increase. With this objective in mind, the government has recently implemented two schemes to encourage private sector involvement. First, a Viability Gap Fund (VGF) has been established to partially fund projects that are not viable on a commercial basis but considered to have positive net social returns. Under this scheme interested private partners bid for the lowest level of funding required to make a project commercially feasible. Funding can cover up to 20% of the capital investment cost of approved projects and is distributed contingent on the private partner meeting pre-specified performance targets.

Second, the government has also established the India Infrastructure Finance Company (IIFC) to finance up to 20% of the capital of infrastructure projects. In effect, the IIFC fills a gap in India's financial markets for private long-term debt. The IIFC will be predominantly funded through borrowing on domestic and foreign debt markets. The borrowings of the IIFC are guaranteed by the central government within limits set by the Ministry of Finance. In effect, the IIFC will leverage the government's guarantee to offer infrastructure financing. Although this will lower funding costs, the risks around private sector provision of infrastructure services remain significant. Accordingly, the scheme has the potential to expose the government to contingent liabilities off balance sheet, notwithstanding the cap on the contingent liabilities of 0.5% of GDP under the Fiscal Responsibility and Budget Management Act. Accordingly, implementation and project monitoring are extremely important.

As well as providing an alternative source of investment funds, private sector involvement in infrastructure provision can potentially increase its operational efficiency. The experience in OECD countries, however, has been that the potential for higher efficiency can be undermined by the long-term horizon of contracts. Most efficiency gains stem from permanent exposure to competition. It is important that the process of contracting and tendering be organised in a way that reduces the government's dependence on the private partner and maintains the threat that government could contract with another private partner in the case of underperformance. More generally, as discussed in Chapter 3, the regulatory environment must allow competitive pressures to operate in as many sectors as possible. Areas of monopoly or low competition must be subject to an appropriate regulatory framework, on which more is said below.

The judicious use of PPPs also has the potential to shift risk away from taxpayers to equity owners, who are better placed to manage it. In practice, however, this transfer of risk, which is usually reflected in private sector returns, is often imperfect and government bail outs have occurred in OECD countries (Joumard et al., 2004). The distribution of risk between government and the private partner often depends to a significant extent on the regulatory and oversight mechanisms put in place for individual projects. Large public liabilities, both explicit and contingent, can result from insufficient scrutiny and transparency in approving PPPs. This highlights the importance of careful selection, structuring, and oversight of projects. It also requires sufficient capacity within government (central and state) to negotiate large and complex deals along with the administrative capacity to regulate private suppliers. A cross-sectoral unit within government that specialises in PPPs might have a useful role to play in disseminating information on PPPs to government and the private sector and working with concerned government departments or ministries to structure deals. The OECD's "Principles for Private Sector Participation in Infrastructure" provide a set of practical guidelines to help governments in working with private sector partners to finance and bring infrastructure projects to fruition (OECD, 2007).

The Indian government has already made a significant start in involving private firms in infrastructure provision, particularly in the transport sector (Figure 7.2). By end-2006, the total value of PPPs was equivalent to just under 3½ per cent of GDP, with most contracts having been awarded in the previous two years. Notwithstanding increased private sector participation in infrastructure provision, some infrastructure sectors are less well suited to private sector provision and maintenance funded by user charges and government will always have an important role to play. As discussed in Chapter 6, this highlights the need to reorient public expenditures towards enhancing growth.

Figure 7.2. **Total value of all PPP projects to date by sector**

Per cent 2006 GDP

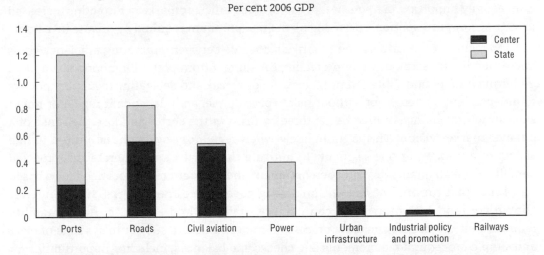

Source: Committee on Infrastructure.

A sound regulatory environment is the key to private sector involvement in the long run

In the long run, a sound regulatory environment that addresses investor concerns and promotes competition is the most effective way of increasing private sector participation in infrastructure provision and lowering the risks borne by government. Indeed, states in which the regulation of product markets is more conducive to competition have been far more successful at infrastructure provision than the relatively restrictive states (Figure 7.3).

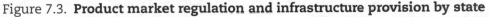

Figure 7.3. **Product market regulation and infrastructure provision by state**

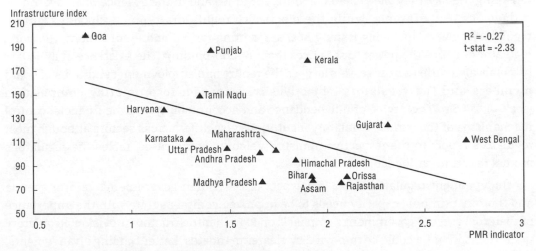

Source: Report of the 11th Finance Commission and OECD.

At the sectoral level, clearly unbundling the different roles of government is important for reducing regulatory uncertainty. As discussed in general terms in Chapter 3, separating the ownership function of Public Sector Enterprises (PSEs) from the line ministries is an important part of this separation. In infrastructure sectors that have a monopoly element, the separation of the regulatory function from the policy making and ownership functions is an equally important prerequisite for establishing efficient markets, attracting increased private sector participation, and reducing the risk premium required by private investors.

Independent regulators need to strike a balance between promoting efficiency gains and attracting investment while protecting consumers from potential monopolist abuses and firms from political interference. This is no easy task and delegating regulatory powers to independent bodies is not without risks. For example, an independent regulator might slow structural change or become captured by firms in the sector and lose the sense of a broader market vision. This is more likely when regulatory oversight is limited to one aspect of a market, or one segment. To mitigate these risks and generate the expected benefits of a high quality regulatory environment, independent regulators need to be based on proper institutional design within strong governance frameworks. Independence should go hand-in-hand with accountability, stability, and expertise. Accountability requires that the decision-making process be transparent and subject to systems of clear and simple procedural requirements and checks and balances, including opportunities for public hearings and appeal provisions.

To ensure independence, regulators should have access to their own source of funds and not be reliant on budgetary transfers decided by politicians. In OECD countries, independent regulators are often funded by a mix of fees and budgetary allocations. Levies on regulated firms, or their customers, are a type of user fee that can increase the accountability of the regulator. Independence can also be strengthened by allowing regulators to recruit their own staff outside of the civil service recruitment and salary rules. Ideally, board members should be experts in the sector without any industry or political affiliations. In practice, however, such people are difficult to come by.

In India the broad roles of the various regulatory agencies differ significantly, reflecting the fact they were created at different times and in the absence of an overriding framework. For example, while the electricity regulators typically have extensive regulatory powers, including issuing licenses, setting tariffs, and enforcement, the ports regulator only has the power to set prices that are non-binding. The existence of appellate tribunals also varies across sectors as does the tenure and employment conditions of board members and the regulators' objectives with respect to promoting competition (see GoI, 2006a). The degree of independence and accountability and the financial control mechanisms of the various regulatory institutions also differ across sectors although most regulators report to the respective ministry which, in some cases, tables the regulator's annual report in parliament.

Independent regulators are a key aspect of the Indian government's reform agenda and their institutional capacity needs to be improved commensurate with the importance of their role and the government's emphasis on PPPs in infrastructure provision. Regulatory institutions in India could be improved by clearer mandates, better funding arrangements, and less reliance on retired government officials as commissioners. In OECD countries, regulators have been most effective and credible when their independence and roles are made explicit in a distinct statute with well-defined functions and objectives. The government of India should enact a competition policy that sets out an overarching framework for the regulation of infrastructure sectors with monopoly elements. This would act as a credible signal that the objectives of regulatory policy are not going to change.

Private sector involvement is transforming certain sectors

Civil aviation

In some infrastructure sectors in which the regulatory environment is conducive to private sector participation, performance has been improving over recent years. In the civil aviation sector competition has been increasing rapidly since 1995 when permission was first given for private airlines to operate scheduled services. Since that time domestic passenger numbers have been growing at an average rate of 7% per year, with a jump of 46% in 2006. Virtually all of this growth has been driven by the expansion of private sector airlines, which now account for around 80% of the domestic aviation market.[3]

In marked contrast to the private sector, growth in the number of domestic passengers carried by the public sector airlines has been virtually flat since the mid-1990s and the market share of the domestic state-owned company has dropped to 24% in 2006-07. The central government is currently considering merging the two public sector airlines – Air India, which predominantly flies international routes, and Indian (formally Indian Airlines) which services the domestic market. As well as merging, the governance of the public sector airlines would also be improved by centralising the ownership function in a centralised investment agency (as discussed in Chapter 3). This would give management more autonomy. Recently, long delays in the granting of approvals from government departments have hampered the expansion plans of the public sector airlines and both airlines have only recently been given approval to purchase new aircraft for the first time in over ten years. Of course, there is ultimately no need for government to be involved in the airline sector and these airlines need to be privatised.[4]

The competitive framework in the civil aviation sector could also be improved further by changing the way in which universal service obligations are met. Air services to remote locations are currently ensured by requiring operators on "category 1" (profitable) routes to run 10% or their seat capacity on secondary (unprofitable) routes. This obligation can be contracted out to other airlines operating on secondary routes. The need for universal service provision has declined recently as low-cost operators have begun servicing more remote centres on a commercial basis. The provision of a direct subsidy through a process of minimum subsidy bidding would be a more appropriate method of ensuring reliable air services on remaining uneconomic routes.

Overall, rapid growth in the civil aviation sector is expected to continue and Indian airline companies are now collectively one of the largest buyers of new aircraft in the world.

Wireless telecoms

The Telecom Regulatory Authority of India (TRAI) was set up in 1997 to fix and regulate tariffs and interconnections. After an acrimonious beginning during which some of its decisions were challenged by the incumbent public sector and private telecoms operators, TRAI is now well established and proactive in recommending regulatory changes that increase competition in the telecommunications sector. TRAI is independent but reports to the Ministry of Communications and government can reject its recommendations provided they give a reason. Any disputes or appeals against TRAI decisions or orders are dealt with by the Telecom Disputes Settlement and Appellate Tribunal, which was established in 2000.

The wireless telephone sector, which includes mobile and wireless fixed subscribers, is a leading example of how the private sector can quickly deploy infrastructure when the regulatory framework is conducive to competition. This sector has been open to private sector firms since its inception in 1992. The introduction in 2004 of a unified license regime that allows licensees to provide both fixed and wireless services has also led to increased competition in this sector. In the three and a half years to January 2007, the Indian wireless network has been one of the fastest growing in the world. Over this period the total number of wireless subscribers increased more than tenfold to just under 150 million, making India's wireless network one of the three largest in the world (TRAI, 2007a). Over 10% of the population now have access to this network, up from 6% at the end of 2005 (Figure 7.4, Panel A). Most of the growth in subscriber numbers has been driven by the private sector with the historic state-owned operator having less that 20% of the market.

As well as a dramatic increase in capacity, competition in wireless telephony has also driven the price of telecom services from among the highest in the world to comparable with those in developed countries and affordable to an increasing number of people. Average revenue per user is also low in comparison to OECD countries. Judged by the criteria of operating costs per subscriber, Indian providers of wireless telecom services were slightly less productive than Chinese firms in 2005, but the gap is likely to have closed since then as the Indian operators take advantage of economies of scale (TRAI, 2006).

A more limited start has been made in other sectors

Fixed line telecommunication

The fixed line network has lagged behind the wireless networks in its development. This market is dominated by two public sector enterprises – Bharat Sanchar Nigam Ltd (BSNL), which was carved out of the Department of Telecommunications (DoT) in 2000, and Mahanagar Telephone Nigam Ltd (MTNL). The combined market share of these incumbents in fixed-line telecom is almost 95%. In contrast to wireless telephony, the number of fixed-line subscribers has actually fallen since 2003 to around 45 million or about 3.5% of the population (Figure 7.4, Panel B). In addition, despite 90% of villages being linked to the telephone network there are few subscribers in rural areas, where the fixed-line density is more than ten times less than in urban areas. In terms of operating costs per subscriber, costs for the Indian incumbents were double those of Chinese providers (TRAI, 2006).

In large part, the poor performance of India's fixed line network reflects the ready availability of the more reliable wireless option at a similar price from more efficient providers. In comparison to fixed-line connections, wireless telephony is also faster and cheaper to roll out. In addition, fixed line penetration is falling in OECD countries, but from a much higher base. Notwithstanding the technological advantages of wireless telephony, however, the regulatory environment for fixed-line telecom could be improved to enhance competition, increase productivity in the sector, and increase broadband penetration.

To begin with, the ownership function of BSNL is vested in the DoT, which plays a combined role in licensing, spectrum management, policy making, and operations. Moving the ownership function of BSNL out of the DoT to a centralised investment agency would reduce the potential for any conflict of interest. In addition, decisions on licensing and spectrum management should be moved to TRAI, who have the mandate of increasing competition in the sector. In turn, the independence of TRAI could be strengthened by

Figure 7.4. **Teledensity**

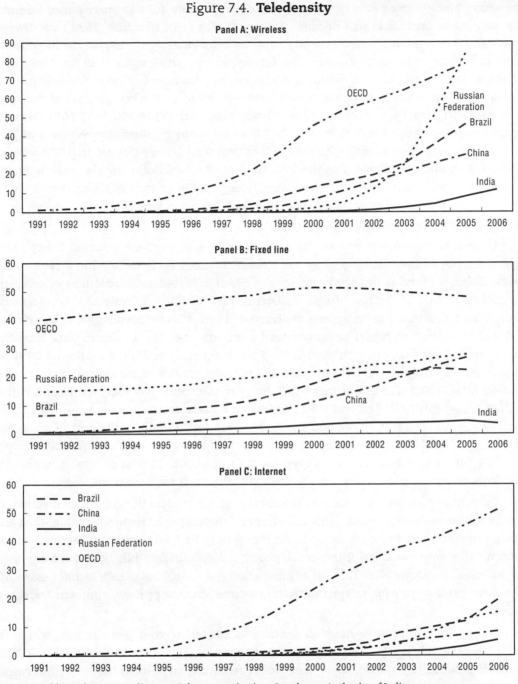

Panel A: Wireless

Panel B: Fixed line

Panel C: Internet

Source: World Development Indicators, Telecommunications Regulatory Authority of India.

shifting its funding source to an industry levy. TRAI's funding currently comes from Parliament, which can potentially reduce independence, or the perception of independence, and limits its ability to employ people from the private sector.

A contentious area of telecommunications regulation is the system of Access Deficit Charges (ADC), which was established by TRAI in 2003. Under the ADC regime private operators pay BSNL a percentage of their revenue, plus a fixed per minute charge on incoming and outgoing international calls, to compensate for the provision of telecom access in rural areas that are uneconomic given BSNL's tariff structure. TRAI have always maintained that the ADC is a temporary support measure designed to give the incumbent time to rebalance its tariff structure. Private sector operators argue that the ADC is, in effect, a tax on their business designed to sustain the incumbent at the expense of private operators. Furthermore, BSNL has not actively responded to the key purpose of the ADC and its tariff structure still has cross-subsidy elements (TRIA 2007b). TRAI currently envisages phasing out the ADC in 2008-09. There are many significant problems with the ADC and its objectives overlap with those of the Universal Service Obligation (USO) regime. The ADC should be merged into the USO fund on the basis of a simple revenue share model. It should then be wound up as quickly as possible as the USO fund continues to grow in line with increasing sector revenues and more markets become economic as a result of advances in technology.

Universal service was one of the main objectives of the New Telecom Policy 1999, which envisaged the provision of access to basic telecom services to all at a reasonable price. The USO fund is financed by a levy of 5% of adjusted gross revenues of telecom providers as part of the revenue share license fee. Providers of universal services are determined via a transparent process of reverse-bidding. This process has led to significant reductions in the benchmark subsidy rates for universal service provision. Until recently, however, USO funding was restricted to fixed line technology and thereby allowed BSNL to exploit its vertically integrated structure and win almost 75% of subsidy auctions (Malik and de Silva, 2005). The Department of Telecommunications has recently amended the Indian Telegraph Act to extend USO funding to mobile services. This is an important improvement in the framework and should result in further falls in the cost of universal service provision. Ideally, USO funding should be "technology neutral" and flexible enough to allow future new technologies. Government's role should consist of setting minimum service standards that providers must meet using the most efficient technology.

Current regulation also prohibits Internet Service Providers (ISPs) from connecting to the fixed-line network, meaning that calls from a computer to a telephone within India are not permitted. This prevents ISPs from offering fully-fledged telephony services. In an attempt to stamp out illegal Internet telephony, the government has not issued any new ISP licenses since June 2006. This stifles innovation and the rollout of new technologies and is a large price to pay for safeguarding the revenue streams of the incumbent telecoms providers.

To ensure competitive neutrality and encourage Internet penetration, which is currently relatively low in comparison to other countries (Figure 7.3, Panel C above), BSNL's local loop needs to be unbundled. This would remove a significant barrier to increased broadband penetration, which is one of the government's key policy objectives in the telecoms sector. Non-discriminatory access to the local loop has been a precondition in almost all countries with significant broadband penetration. Even if new entrants only secure a relatively small share of the market as a result of local loop unbundeling, the threat of competition can have a large and positive impact on the incumbent's efforts to provide the service at a competitive price.

Electricity: taking advantage of a new, more competitive, framework

Investment has historically been very low

As discussed in Chapter 1, the coverage of India's power network and the quality of electricity supplied are poor in comparison to other countries and continue to be a major constraint on growth. Because of poor electricity supply, a high proportion of businesses use back-up generators or self-generation, which are expensive relative to the cost of supply in a well-functioning electricity sector. Notwithstanding recent regulatory changes that allow firms to collectively set up captive power plants, small industries that are unable to afford captive generation often have to go without power. This imposes high costs on the economy, particularly electricity intensive sectors such as manufacturing. In addition, because access is more limited and power outages more common in lagging states, firms in these states are more reliant on high-cost generators. At the household level, 44% of households have no electricity at all (increasing to 66% of households in rural areas).

Despite strong economic growth and unmet demand for electricity[5], the rate of capital formation in the sector has been low. Overall, annual growth in generation capacity per person has averaged only 2.25% since 1994, which is well below the rate of GDP per capita growth (Table 7.1). In other emerging Asian countries growth in generation capacity per person has outstripped GDP per capita growth by almost 3 percentage points on average over the same period. Such rapid growth in electricity demand is typical in countries with per capita incomes between USD 2 000 and USD 8 000 in PPP terms where the income elasticity of demand for electricity appears to be around 1.25 (Planning Commission, 2006). This implies that in the absence of supply constraints, growth in electricity demand in India would currently be around 10% a year.

Table 7.1. **Electricity generating capacity: India and selected Asian countries**

Compound annual growth rate over five-year period

	1980-85	1984-89	1989-1994	1994-99	1999-2004
			% per year		
India					
Total capacity	8.8	8.8	5.6	4.2	4.2
Government sector	8.4	8.8	5.4	3	3.4
State government	7.4	6.6	3.4	2.6	2.6
Central government	14.8	17.4	10.4	4.1	4.8
Private sector	11.4	8.8	7.2	10.1	7
Utilities	9.5	1.7	6.6	22.3	8.3
Own use	12.4	11.5	7.3	5.4	6.1
Capacity per person	6.5	6.5	3.5	2.2	2.3
Income per head	3.2	4.1	2.9	4.6	4.2
Eight Asian countries					
Capacity per person	6.6	5.5	4.2	6.6	4
Income per person	2.5	3.1	4.2	1.9	2.9
Differential between capacity per person growth and average income growth (percentage points)					
India	3.2	2.4	0.6	−2.5	−1.9
Eight Asian countries	4.1	2.4	0.1	4.7	1.0

1. Eight Asian countries: Bangladesh, Indonesia, Malaysia, Pakistan, Philippines, Sri Lanka, Thailand, and VietNam.
Source: United States Energy Information Agency.

The electricity sector is on the concurrent list, so centre and state governments are both able to engage in the generation and supply of power. At the state level, growth in generating capacity fell to just 2½ per cent annually in the decade prior to 2004. At the centre level, annual growth in generation capacity also fell significantly after the mid-1990s to around 4.5%. Growth in private sector generation has generally been more buoyant than in the public sector although starting from a much lower base. However, much of the growth in private sector generation capacity has been for "own use".

Many of the industry's problem stem from the distribution sector

The poor performance of the power sector is predominantly a consequence of problems within the distribution sector. Because of sustained underinvestment in transmission and distribution lines, the network is overloaded and suffers from poor performance with large technical losses of electricity from the system. Non-technical electricity losses are also extreme with electricity theft widespread and traditionally overlooked by the authorities. Theft, which is estimated to amount to INR 200 billion (USD 4.3 billion) annually, is the most significant source of distribution loss. In addition, with a lack of metering and lax accounting procedures, only 70% of electricity generated is billed and only 66% actually paid for. More than 75% of the technical losses and almost all of the commercial losses occur in electricity distribution. A 1% reduction in these losses is estimated to generate savings of over INR 8 billion (USD 172 million) (Governmant of India, 2007).

Extensive cross-subsidisation is another major problem in the electricity distribution sector. Because of a legacy of political interference in the pricing policies of the state electricity companies, farmers who are able to invest in electrical machinery (such as pumps for irrigation) are typically supplied with free or subsidised electricity that is often unmetered. For household consumers, electricity is supplied below cost or, in some cases, without a meter. Industrial consumers, on the other hand, are charged tariffs that are much above the cost of supply and about ten times greater than agricultural tariffs.[6] As a result of cross subsidisation, the price of electricity for Indian households is amongst the lowest in the world whereas the price paid by Indian industry is amongst the highest (Figure 7.5). In conjunction with irregular and low quality power, this reduces the competitiveness of the business sector. Cross-subsidisation also renders market signals virtually inoperable, thereby extinguishing incentives for demand-side management, and can pose a risk to sustainable development. For example, the supply of low-cost or un-metered electricity to farmers is leading to excessive pumping of water for irrigation, which is lowering the ground-water table and threatening agriculture sustainability in some districts.

Large cross-state variation in the price of electricity may also be indicative of political influence in electricity pricing and physical constraints in the national transmission grid, which limit the development of a national electricity market (Figure 7.6).

Given high aggregate technical and commercial losses and cross-subsidisation, the financial performance of the electricity sector is poor with the combined losses of the State Electricity Boards amounting to 0.6% of GDP in 2005-06. Overall, gross subsidies amounted to 1.2% of GDP in 2005, with a further subsidy of perhaps 1.3% of GDP due to the low rate of return on capital in the sector (see Chapter 1).

Regulatory environment: The new act and the APDRP

The Electricity Act 2003 sets out a policy framework for addressing issues in distribution and creating a competitive electricity market that is conducive to private

Figure 7.5. **Electricity prices in selected countries, 2004**

In USD per thousand kilowatt hour

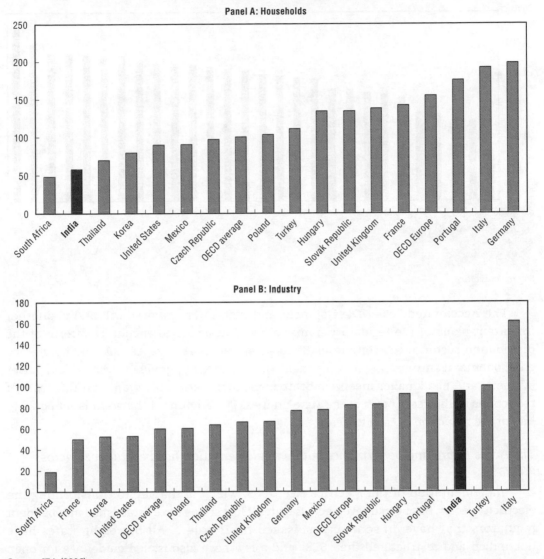

Source: IEA (2006).

sector investment. The Act is much more comprehensive than the previous regime and brings the regulatory environment significantly closer to that prevailing in a number of OECD countries. In particular, the Act mandates the unbundling of the State Electricity Boards (SEBs) via legal separation and allows private sector involvement in transmission and distribution. It also makes provisions for open access to the transmission and distribution grid for third-party generators, clears the way for electricity trading, and allows bulk electricity consumers to choose their electricity supplier from no later than January 2009. The Act also calls for state governments to pay electricity suppliers directly for any power they want delivered below cost to particular groups of consumers and allows groups of firms to set up captive power plants. It calls for cross subsidies to be progressively removed with prices moving towards the actual cost of supply. In a Tariff Policy notified by government under the Act, cross-subsidies are to be reduced to within a band of plus or minus 20% by the end of 2010-11.

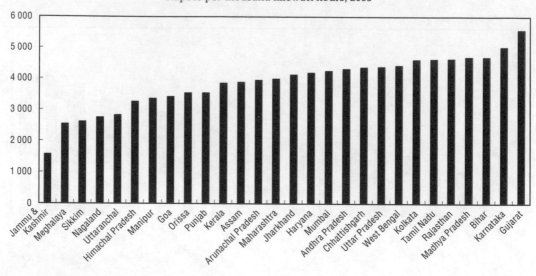

Figure 7.6. **Price of electricity for heavy industry by state**
Rupees per thousand kilowatt hours, 2005

Source: IndiaStat.

The Accelerated Power Development and Reform Programme (APDRP) is another important plank of the regulatory framework and designed to encourage reform of the distribution sector at the state level. State governments receive APDRP funding via two components: i) an investment component that finances upgrades to the states' power systems; and ii) a smaller incentive component that distributes grants on the basis of reductions in the cash losses of the state utilities. The amount of the grant is set equal to half of the reduction in cash losses.

The Act is improving performance but its implementation has been uneven across states

Implementation of the Electricity Act 2003, which is the key to transforming the electricity sector, has been uneven across states. Most states have established independent regulators that have, in some cases, issued tariff orders. All but eight states have unbundled and restructured their SEBs and a few have also issued guidelines for open access in distribution (Table 7.2).

Although the process of implementing the provisions of the Act is far from complete, there are some tentative signs of improvement overall and in some of the states. Aggregate technical and commercial (AT&C) losses of the system have fallen somewhat from 39% in FY 2001 to 34% in FY 2005. Moreover, states that are more advanced in implementing the provisions of the Act, as measured by an indicator of the extent of reforms compiled by the Ministry of Power, have achieved relatively larger reductions in AT&C losses (Figure 7.7). The government is currently targeting the reduction of these losses to below 15% in towns by 2012. Based on past performance, this is an ambitious target that will require not only financial resources but strong political commitment at all levels. Such targets are achievable, however, as evidenced by the performance of the private distribution companies in Kolkata, Mumbai, Surat and Ahmadabad. In the latter two, losses are down to 10%. The performance of a few of the state utilities in some towns also suggests that the

Table 7.2. **Status of power sector reforms in selected states**
April 2007

State	Memorandum of Understanding or Agreement signed with GoI	State Electricity Board unbundled	State Regulatory Commission	Tariff order passed	Anti-theft law passed	Privatisation
Andhra Pradesh	Yes	Yes	Yes	Yes	Yes	Strategy is being finalised
Bihar	Yes	No	Yes	..	Yes	No
Gujarat	Yes	Yes	Yes	Yes	Yes	No
Haryana	Yes	Yes	Yes	Yes	No	No
Karnataka	Yes	Yes	Yes	Yes	Yes	No
Kerala	Yes	No	Yes	Yes	Yes	No
Madhya Pradesh	Yes	Yes	Yes	Yes	Yes	No
Maharashtra	Yes	Yes	Yes	Yes	Yes	No
Orissa	Yes	Yes	Yes	Yes	No	Distribution privatised
Punjab	Yes	No	Yes	Yes	No	No
Rajasthan	Yes	Yes	Yes	Yes	No	No
Tamil Nadu	Yes	No	Yes	Yes	No	No
Uttar Pradesh	Yes	Yes	Yes	Yes	Yes	No
West Bengal	Yes	Yes	Yes	Yes	Yes	No
NCT Delhi	Yes	Yes	Yes	Yes	No	Distribution privatised

Source: Reserve Bank of India and Ministry of Power.

Figure 7.7. **Electricity reforms and the change in distribution and commercial losses, 2000/01 to 2004/05**

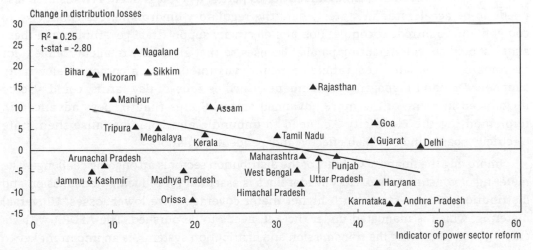

Source: Ministry of Power.

target is achievable. With firm political leadership, one state (Gujarat) has also shown that it is possible for the state-owned distribution companies to reduce their losses.

The share of capacity addition from independent power producers has not risen substantially and fell 73% short of the (revised) target in the tenth plan. The private sector is, however, increasingly establishing generation capacity for own use. Firms that construct power plants for their own use (or in partnership with other companies) have open access to the transmission grid and do not pay the cross-subsidy unless they supply other large consumers. Some state regulators appear to be reducing industrial prices and raising consumer prices. The Planning Commission expects private sector capacity generation to more than double during the 11th Plan, even without the possibility of the proposed ultra-mega power projects (of four GW each) being constructed by the private sector.

The relationship between the central government power generator and the state electricity distribution companies is also been changing for the better. Payments by state distribution companies are now guaranteed against cuts of fiscal transfers from the union to the state governments. Now, the national power company experiences no payment problems and is a quoted company with 40% of the shares traded. The change in the revenue outlook for the National Thermal Power Corporation (NTPC) has allowed this central government company to plan to more than double its rate of capacity expansion in the five years from FY 2007 to 2012 relative to the previous five years. However, in a properly functioning electricity system, investment in capacity is equally matched by investment in transmission and distribution. Here, the state distribution companies are not in a position to invest and so improvement in service levels may not automatically follow from increased capacity.

Full implementation of the Act is the way forward

The ongoing challenge is to continue implementing the Electricity Act (2003). In the states that are relatively advanced in power sector reform and at the centre level this involves building the technical capacity of regulators, clarifying their policy jurisdictions, and strengthening their independence. The regulations for third party access (TPA) to the transmission grid need to be clarified and put into practice. The absence of TPA makes private sector involvement, either directly or as part of a PPP, less likely. Privatisation also needs to be accelerated in states where the regulatory environment is conducive to competition. To introduce competition into electricity supply, state governments in these states should consider granting parallel licenses so that electricity retailers compete for customers in the same geographic area and consumers have a choice of electricity supplier.[7] Demand management techniques, such as time-of-day tariffs, could also be introduced in some of the more advanced states. States that are less advanced in implementing the Electricity Act need to unbundle and commercialise their state electricity boards and establish effective independent regulation.

Improving the financial viability of the distribution sector is an ongoing challenge. The metering of consumers and 11 kV feeder lines is essential for reducing transmission and distribution losses – states with higher meter coverage have lower losses. Universal metering, which is mandated under the Act, needs to be pursued. The APDRP, with its emphasis on improving the transmission and distribution systems, is an important key to making the electricity sector financially viable and of interest to potential investors. However, actual investment in distribution is typically much less than the funds allocated and the incentive component of the APDRP is underutilised by state governments. In addition, the poorer states with extremely low-quality electricity supply typically only use a small proportion of the funds available to them under the APDRP (Modi, 2005). The incentive effects of the APDRP will not be large if a significant amount of funds are available unconditionally.

Tariff setting needs to continue to be rationalised and cross-subsidies reduced so as to make investment outside of captive generation and supply to large consumers viable and facilitate competition in distribution. The methods used by the regulators to set tariffs could also be revisited so as to increase the incentive for productivity gains in the industry. Cross subsidies need to be eliminated. Imposing and enforcing cost of service pricing is one of the most important priorities as this would improve the investment climate, encourage demand-side management, and reduce fiscal drain. The government should encourage speedier implementation of reforms and consider fiscal penalties for states that do not advance sufficiently rapidly and reward those that find ways to reduce losses and increase private participation in the sector.

Roads

During the first phases of economic reform, the priority for road policy was to ensure that villages were connected by "all weather" roads and investment in high quality roads was extremely low. Between 1981 and 1998 the national highway network, funded by the central government, grew by only 1.2% annually (Figure 7.8).

Figure 7.8. **Highway development**

Thousand kilometres

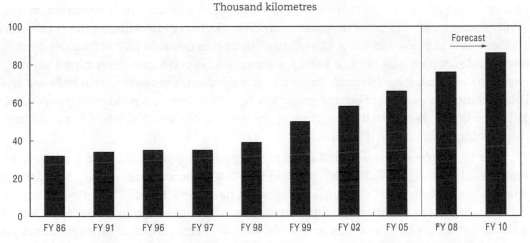

Source: National Highway Development Authority.

By 2006, only 12% of national highways were four or six lanes, 56% were two lanes, and 32% were single lane. In addition, although national highways only account for 2% of India's road network, they carry 40% of road traffic, 65% of total freight, and 85% of total passenger traffic (India Infrastructure Report, 2006). With robust economic growth over recent years, traffic is growing at 7 to 10% a year on average, with a consequent increase in journey times and accidents.

In 1998, the government launched the National Highway Development Project (NHDP) with the objective of substantially upgrading the interurban and port-road network. The first stage of this programme – the construction of a "golden quadrilateral" linking Delhi, Mumbai, Kolkata and Chennai – was substantially completed over budget and behind schedule at the end of 2006 (GOI, 2005). This dual-carriageway system is almost 6 000 km long and was mostly funded by central government. It still allows mixed traffic and does not completely separate traffic at intersections. The objective of the system is to allow average speeds of 80 km/h, as opposed to speeds of only 30 km/h on the existing network (and average speeds of over 100 km/h on motorways). Overall, however, between 2001 and 2005 investment in roads has been modest; 0.4% of GDP yielding 1 060 km of highway per year in comparison to 4 800 km per year in China over the same period.

The next phases of the NHDP involve a significant increase in investment and rate of highway completion. By December 2009, the north-south and east-west expressways and the upgrade of a significant length of two-lane national highways into four or six lanes are due for completion. If this deadline is to be met, contractors will have to complete 12 000 km in three years – a substantial increase on past performance and a rate comparable to that in China. By 2015, another 33 500 km of highway, plus a large number of flyovers, bypasses, and ring roads are due for completion. The total cost of all of these projects is currently expected to be USD 51 billion.

Public funds are unable to finance such an ambitious expansion programme and the government is turning increasingly to the private sector. In 2005, the National Highways Authority of India awarded 30 contracts for the construction of 16 000 km to private sector players on a PPP basis and almost all subsequent investment is expected to be funded in a similar way. To date, the predominant method of PPP used in the road sector is "build-operate-transfer" (BOT) under which the private-sector partner funds construction and maintenance costs and earns revenues from the collection of tolls during the concession period, which is usually 30 years. Government also plans to award BOT PPPs on an annuity basis under which the private sector partner will receive pre-determined annuity payments on project completion. Under this arrangement, the construction risks are still borne by the private partner but the risk of low traffic volumes is passed onto government. This type of PPP also gives the government the flexibility of being able to grant a separate contract for toll collection if it wishes.

The early experience with toll collection in India has generally been positive with 4 300 km of highway already tolled yielding USD 240 million annually. The entire golden quadrilateral is tolled and all four-lane highways have to be tolled. The tolling policy for two-lane highways is currently under discussion within government. Tolls are fixed by government on the basis of ability to pay and are low in comparison to other countries. As a consequence, the return on investment in highways is often less than the cost of service provision and private sector investment is eligible for subsidies from the central government's Viability Gap Fund (VGF). This funding is expected to amount to around 30% of the cost of the next phase of the highway expansion programme (CoI, 2006).[8] However, with increasing traffic volumes, a number of recent bids for viability gap funding have been negative, implying that private sector partners are prepared to pay for the right to collect tolls on some sections of highway. In general, people are prepared to pay to use a better road suggesting that tolls could be increasingly used as a source of funds by increasing tolls and/or expanding their coverage to two lane roads. In addition, there is significant scope for improving the amount of toll collection by eliminating theft and other leakages, implying that viability gap funding could be reduced in future.

Early indications are that PPPs have been working reasonably well in the roads sector and are a significant improvement on the prior policy of 100% government funding via construction contracts and self provision. Model concession agreements have been developed and the capacity for road building at the level of the state government and private sector is steadily improving with the average size of project is now 100 km plus. A number of state governments – for example, Gujarat, Maharashtra, Rajasthan and Madhya Pradesh – have also begun using PPPs to develop state roads. On the other hand, the need to obtain cabinet approval at the central level for optimally sized road contracts is a significant implementation problem and greater authority needs to be delegated to the Department of Roads and Highways to speed up the process.

Ports

Private sector involvement is leading to productivity improvements

Reflecting increased economic growth, the amount of cargo handled by India's major ports has been growing at an annual average of 11% since 2002-03 and India's port facilities have become seriously overstretched. This pressure will continue to increase along with international trade and the Ministry of Shipping expects freight volumes to almost triple from 570 million tonnes at present to reach 1.5 billion tonnes by 2012 and 2 billion tonnes by 2016.

Almost three-quarters of India's total freight traffic goes through 12 "major ports" that are administered by port authorities, which are under the jurisdiction of the central government. In some cases private-sector companies operate freight terminals and provide port services under a landlord port model where the port authorities retain ownership of the basic port infrastructure and land. In some of the major ports, private-sector and government-owned freight terminals operate side by side and compete for cargo. As well as the major ports, there are 187 "non-major" ports, 60 of which handle cargo, that are predominantly controlled by the state governments.

The central government sees private sector participation as the key for improving infrastructure in both the major and non-major ports. The National Maritime Development Plan estimates that 64% of the USD 13.5 billion investment required by the major ports to keep pace with demand over the next nine years will come from the private sector. Development of the non-major ports will require an additional USD 4.5 billion. There are no limitations on private ownership of non-major ports and some new private non-major ports are currently being developed.

India's ports are relatively inefficient in comparison to ports in other countries. Blonigen and Wilson (2006), for example, rank Mumbai Port 82 out of the 100 ports that they evaluate in terms of relative efficiency. There are, however, some encouraging signs that private-sector involvement is leading to productivity improvements. For example, since 1997-98, the average time for ship turnaround has fallen from over six to under four days and Blonigen and Wilson (2006) find that Mumbai Port has closed 20% of its efficiency gap relative to Rotterdam port over the ten years to 2003. Although private sector freight terminals are still more efficient than terminals run by port authorities[9], competition is also leading to improvements in the performance of freight terminals owned by the port authorities.

The "Tariff Authority for Major Ports" (TAMP), which was established in 1997, sets ceilings for freight rates for the major ports on a cost-plus basis. However, given the increasing number of non-major ports it is not altogether clear that a natural monopoly element exists in the sector. This calls the need for an independent regulator into question. Indeed, if ceilings on freight rate are set too low, private investment may suffer. Increasing competition to ensure that anti-competitive behaviour between ports is unlikely may prove to be a more effective way of preventing excessive pricing power.

As well as reconsidering the role of the regulator, the separation of the Government's roles could be further enhanced by converting the port authorities into corporations. Corporatisation would encourage private sector participation and facilitate unbundling into owners and service providers, which can subsequently be privatised. This issue was first raised in the mid-1990s, but currently only one of India's major ports (Ennore Port) is run by a company. Intraport competition could also be encouraged by granting multiple concessions to private operators at a single port.

Port connectivity is also a major issue, given the high growth in freight volumes. Although all major ports have both road and rail connectivity, the capacity and quality of this infrastructure needs to be improved if the sector is to benefit from efficiency gains in port terminal operations. In some of the older major ports, increased urban agglomeration around the port is a constraint in improving connectivity. In some of the newer ports, road and rail linkages are being improved with Ports in a number of instances making significant contributions to these projects.[10] Given that port connectivity is a key issue, the priorities of the ports, railways and roads need to be coordinated and synchronised.

Airport infrastructure

Strong growth in private sector airlines is putting pressure on airports

As a result of rapid economic growth and the expansion of private sector airlines civil aviation infrastructure is stretched to almost breaking point. At the major airports, congestion during peak hours is severe and there are insufficient parking bays and a shortage of landing slots. At least partly as a result of infrastructure constraints, many of the new low-cost operators are basing themselves at smaller centres. Many of the smaller airports, however, are underdeveloped and underutilised relative to their potential. Out of a total of 400 airports, scheduled airlines are currently only operating through 78 of them. With poor productivity at the major airports (discussed above) and limited development of the smaller fields, the provision of airport infrastructure services is currently falling well short of demand.

Management of India's airport infrastructure is vested with the Airports Authority of India (AAI). In addition to airport operation and management, the AAI also provides air traffic services. In 2003, the Naresh Chandra Committee on civil aviation recommended that airport management be corporatised. This would considerably enhance the transparency of airport management and help ensure equitable treatment for private and public airlines at airports. For example, despite their diminished market share, the government-owned airlines are allocated much more terminal space than private-sector airlines at Delhi and Mumbai airports and private airlines are prohibited from establishing maintenance hangers at airports. Corporatising airport management would also be an important prerequisite to future airport privatisations.

The private sector is becoming increasingly involved in the provision of airport infrastructure services. The refurbishment and upgrade of the international airports in Delhi and Mumbai – which collectively handle 44% of India's air passenger traffic – are being carried out by joint venture companies that are 74% owned by private-sector partners. The operation of ground infrastructure and passenger facilities at Delhi and Mumbai airports has recently been contracted to a joint venture between private sector operators and the AAI. New international airports in Bangalore and Hyderabad are also being constructed with private-sector participation. In all of these cases the private-sector partners were selected following a transparent and competitive bidding process.

In other sectors, the framework is not conducive to competition

Coal

India is the third largest producer of coal in the world and coal is the primary source of 50% of India's commercial energy consumption with 78% of coal mined used to generate electricity (GoI, 2006b). As a result, the coal sector has a large influence on the performance of the electricity and other downstream sectors. Liberalisation would not only improve the performance of the coal sector, but also have a large impact on the performance of sectors such as electricity that are highly dependent on coal as an intermediate input. In spite of its importance, however, regulation in the coal sector is extremely restrictive of competition.

The coal sector was nationalised in the early 1970s and virtually 100% of coal is mined by two public sector enterprises. Private sector firms – either individually or as a group of end-users – have, in principle, been able to mine coal for captive consumption since the early 1990s. In practice, however, only a few captive mines have started production. It would seem that firms in downstream sectors that use coal extensively do not necessarily want to become vertically integrated. A steel plant, for example, may not want to mine coal as it is an activity clearly outside its expertise. In addition, the output from captive mines that is not used for own consumption can only be sold to Coal India at prices set by Coal India. Coal from captive mines is also typically transported by India Rail, exposing captive miners to excessive rail freight transport charges (discussed below). Finally, significant bureaucratic hurdles also act as a barrier to establishing captive coal mines. As well as approved end-users, coal blocks have also been allocated to a number of government-owned companies for their own use. In total, captive mines accounted for just over 3% of total coal production in the three years to 2004 (Planning Commission, 2007).

The allocation of coal to downstream users such as the power, steel, and cement industries, is decided by an inter-ministerial committee on the basis of available rail capacity and other related factors. Matching the present and future requirements of coal users is a difficult coordination problem and the resultant "linkages" can quickly become obsolete with the result that coal supply falls out of step with energy demands.

Coal prices are set by long-term negotiation on the basis of a cost-plus methodology that gives no incentive for the monopoly coal firms to increase productivity. Although the world price of coal can act as an upper bound for local prices, the lack of coastal power plants, inadequate port capacity, and the expensive price of freight rail transport limits the impact of international competition on the performance of the domestic coal industry. Even so, the Ministry of Coal estimates that India will need to import around 50 million tonnes of high-quality thermal coal by the end of the 11th plan. An "e-market" for coal has recently been developed to make coal pricing more responsive to market conditions. However, with no competition in the coal sector, this is of only limited use.

A regulatory framework that encourages private sector participation in the coal sector needs to be developed. Coal blocks need to be offered to potential miners through a process of competitive and transparent bidding. Ultimately, the public sector enterprises that currently dominate the industry need to be privatised. In the shorter term, the ownership function of these companies should be separated from the regulatory and policy-making function at the Ministry of Coal. Operational norms and quality standards also need to be mandated. For example, there is currently no regular "washing" or coal benefication and Indian coal is not sold by gross heating value but by universal heating value, which is inconsistent with high-tech manufacturing processes and international practice. Sector-wide safety and environmental standards that promote "clean-coal technologies" also need to be developed. Meeting these requirements will require large-scale investment in the coal sector.

A bill to amend the Coal Mines (nationalisation) Act 1973 and open the sector to private participation without the restriction of captive mining was introduced to parliament in April 2000 but has not progressed. Coal India is one of the largest employers in India and trade unions are opposed to the amendment bill. A consensus must be actively found and progress made. Given the importance of coal and the interlinkages with other sectors, the liberalisation of the coal sector would be an important step in improving India's energy markets and enhancing economic growth.

Railways

India's rail network is the second largest in the world and a key component of the transport sector. Over recent years the financial performance of Indian Rail (IR) has improved with the return on capital and the operating ratio – working expenses divided by revenues – both moving in the right directions (Figure 7.9). To a significant extent, total revenue growth reflects improvements in IRs freight business, which generates almost 70% of total revenues. On the expenditure side, annual growth has averaged 7.3% since 2000-01, which is significantly lower than in the 1980s and 1990s (16.4 and 12.3%, respectively). This is predominantly a reflection of lower growth in the wage bill, which accounts for around 55% of total expenditure. In turn, this reflects consolidation in Indian Rail's labour force, which has fallen from 1.7 million ten years ago to 1.4 million currently as departing workers have not been replaced.[11]

Figure 7.9. **Return on capital and operating ratio for Indian Rail**

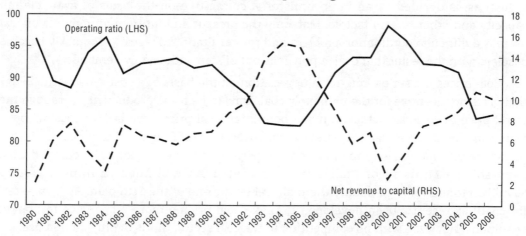

Source: Government of India, Railway budget 2006.

Notwithstanding recent improvements in financial performance, the productivity of the Indian rail network is still low. Across passenger and freight operations, the output per operational employee is less than half that in China (Table 7.3). On the freight side of the business the daily output per wagon operated is one quarter of that in China. To some extent these productivity differentials reflect very different investment profiles. In the ten

Table 7.3. **Efficiency comparison of India and China Rail**

	India			China		
	1991-92	2001-02	% change	1992	2002	% change
The network:						
Railway route (km)	62 458	63 140	1	58 100	71 879	24
Double track (km)	14 605	16 124	10	13 658	23 058	69
Electrified	10 809	16 001	48	8 434	17 409	106
Passenger and freight traffic:						
Passengers carried (millions, non-suburban)	4 049	5 093	26	997	1 056	6
Passenger km (billions)	314	493	57	315	497	58
Freight tonne km billion	257	336	31	1 157	1 551	34
Labour force:						
Operational employees (million)	1.42	1.3	–8	2 038	1 349	–34
Productivity measures:						
Output per operational employee	402	648	61	728	1 385	90
Wagon turnaround (days)	11.1	7.2	–35	4.15	5.1	23
Daily output per wagon operated (tonne km)	1 439	2 223	54	9 924	9 100	–8
Average speed (km/h)	22.7	24.4	7	29.9	32.4	8
Freight density (million tonne km/route km)	6.4	7.38	15	21.56	25.33	17

Source: Harral and Sondhi (2005).

years to 2002 China invested USD 85 billion in the rail sector, in comparison to USD 17 billion in India. As a result, additions and improvements in the Chinese rail network greatly exceeded those in India. In addition, because of its better financial performance, China rail was able to fund 57% of its investments in the five years to 2002, in comparison to 35% for IR (Harral and Sondhi, 2005).[12]

One of the major challenges facing IR is the erosion of its market share in the freight transport sector, which has been steadily declining since Independence.[13] To a large extent, the transport of non-bulk and relatively profitable freight traffic has migrated to road transport and most of IR's freight operations now involve transporting relatively low-tariff bulk commodities, with coal being the largest earner (39-42% of IR's total earnings). Competition from road transport will continue to threaten rail transport's remaining market niche in freight transport as India upgrades its road network and truck fleet. In the market for passenger transport IR also faces a serious threat – particularly in the upper-class segment – from the recent explosion of low-cost airlines.

Although rail operators in most countries face a similar challenge, this problem is exacerbated in India by heavy cross-subsidisation of passenger transport from freight transport.[14] Harral and Sondhi (2005) estimate this cross-subsidy to be INR 56.6 billion (USD 1.2 billion), which is about 46% of passenger revenue or 15% of total revenue, and increases freight tariffs by over 25%.[15] Overcharging freight movement to subsidise passenger traffic skews IR's business away from the relatively profitable freight segment towards the relatively unprofitable passenger segment. This reduces profitability and limits IRs ability to fund much needed improvements in railway infrastructure.

More broadly, cross-subsidies hamper India's industrial development. For example, because of excessively high rail freight rates, the price of delivered coal in a number of states is between two to four times the price at the mine head, which has severe implications for the geographic distribution of electricity generation. Although the current railway budget has revised the tariff structure and is reducing the cross-subsidy between freight and passenger transport, this distortion needs to be removed completely. If passenger tariffs are to continue to be capped, then the resultant subsidy needs to be directly funded by the government. Although the cross subsidy between freight and passenger services is the most damaging universal service obligation, IR is also obliged to carry "essential commodities" such as food grains, sugar, salt and edible oils for free.

Another important issue impeding the development of the railway sector in Indian is the bundling of operational, policy-making, and regulatory function within the one organisation. This reduces transparency and acts as a significant barrier to private sector participation in the sector. IR has successfully corporatised some of its activities – such as container traffic, tourism and catering, and fibre optic communication – by hiving them off into public sector enterprises that are 100% owned by IR. The bulk of its operations, however, still function from within the Ministry of Railways.

Although corporatisation has been mooted in the past, IR continues to be one of only two major railway systems in the world (China Rail being the other) that are operated from within a government ministry. This leads to confusion in the respective roles of government and enterprise in the railway sector. Corporatising IR's operations would reduce the scope for political interference and improve the organisation's commercial focus by facilitating the introduction of modern management practices, structure, and accounting methods. It would also increase transparency and provide a good opportunity for IR's to separate its freight and passenger business, at least on an accounting basis. In addition, corporatisation would allow IR to shed many of its social obligations, such as the operation of schools and hospitals, that should be administered by the relevant government departments.

Indian Rail and the government, notably the Committee of Infrastructure, have expressed a wish to increase private-sector involvement in the railway sector. The Railway Minister has proposed a number of potential areas that may be amenable to public-private partnership. Some of these activities – such as manufacturing locomotives and wagons, development of warehouses, and logistics parks, hotels, and retail outlets on vacant railways land, and the provision of telecommunication services using IR's network of fibre optic cable – are inherently competitive in nature and should simply be privatised. Privatising the many non-rail transport activities that are on the margin of IR's core operations would improve competitiveness by rationalising its business and decreasing the cost of supply.

In a significant move towards increased private sector participation in the railways sector IR announced in the railway budget 2005-06 that the Container Corporation of India would lose its monopoly on container transportation by rail. Although a number of applications from private sector players wanting to operate container trains have been approved, the policy framework under which this system would operate is yet to be made clear. In another step in the right direction the dedicated freight corridors, which are being built to separate freight from passenger traffic and ease severe capacity constraints on the existing network, will be built and run by a separate legal entity jointly owned by IR and some of the PSEs that use bulk freight services. IR and qualified private-sector operators would be given access to the track on a non-discriminatory basis and the track operator would not offer freight services. The challenge for the regulatory framework defining access rules will be to insure fair access for third party users. This may be a useful prequel to the introduction of more widespread separation of "rail from wheels", at least on an accounting basis, along with the introduction of a solid regulatory framework that mandates the terms of third party access and is enforced.[16]

Box 7.1. **Policy recommendations for improving infrastructure**

Public-private partnerships:

- Establish a cross-sectional unit within government that specialises in PPPs to disseminate information and help structure deals.
- Ensure that PPP deals are structured in such a way that maintains the threat of competition for the private partner.

Regulatory oversight:

- Enact a competition policy that sets out the overarching framework for the regulation of infrastructure sectors.
- Separate the regulatory, policy-making, and ownership functions.
- Ensure strong governance and independence for regulators.

Civil aviation:

- Centralise the ownership function of the public airlines.
- Move to a system of direct subsidy provision through minimum bidding to meet universal service obligations.

Fixed-line telecom:

- Centralise the ownership function of BSNL and improve the independence of TRAI.
- Allow ISPs to offer telephony services.
- Merge the Access Deficit Charge into the Universal Service Obligation Fund and abolish the former as soon as possible.
- Ensure USO funding is "technology neutral".
- Unbundle BSNL's fixed-line network.

Electricity:

- Continue working towards 100% metering and crack down on electricity theft.
- Eliminate cross-subsidies.
- Continue implementing the provisions of the Electricity Act 2003.

Roads:

- Reconsider the use of tolls as a source of funds by widening their coverage and eliminating theft and other leakages.

Ports:

- Reconsider the role of the Tariff Authority for Major Ports.
- Convert the port authorities into corporations.
- Grant multiple concessions at a single port.

Airports:

- Corporatise airport management with a view to privatise.

Coal:

- Open the coal sector to the private sector.
- Centralise the ownership function of the public sector coal companies.
- Develop operational, quality, environmental, and safety standards and norms.

> Box 7.1. **Policy recommendations** (*cont.*)
>
> **Rail:**
>
> ● Eliminate cross-subsidies between freight and passenger transport.
>
> ● Corporatise India Rail and unbundle regulatory, policy-making, and ownership functions.
>
> ● Privatise activities that are on the margin of India Rail's core operations.

Notes

1. In low-income countries the access to infrastructure services is substantially worse for the poor than it is for the rich (Briceno and Klytchnikova, 2006).

2. To some extent, however, the provision of infrastructure reflects demand, which is likely to be higher in the relatively productive states.

3. There are currently 13 scheduled operators, 1 cargo airline, and 53 charter (non-scheduled) operators in the market.

4. In 2001, the government attempted to sell some of its equity in Indian Airlines and Air India. However, for a number of reasons, bids were withdrawn at the last minute and privatisation has been off the table ever since.

5. On average over the period April 2006 to November 2006, the supply of electricity India-wide was 8.4% less than demand. During peak periods, the shortfall increased to 12.2% (Ministry of Power). This is notwithstanding the 44% of households that have no electricity at all.

6. For example, in 2002, the average agricultural electricity tariff across states was INR 0.42 per kwh. The average tariffs for commercial and industrial users were around INR 4.29 and INR 3.81 per kwh respectively (Sing and Wallack, 2004).

7. The issuing of parallel distribution licenses is currently under consideration in Maharashtra.

8. In turn, the VGF for PPPs in roads is partially funded by a cess levied on the sale of petrol and diesel.

9. For example, the turnaround time for the terminal operated by the Port Authority at the Jawaharlal Nehru Port Trust is 1.16 days in comparison to 0.79 days for the private container terminal at the same port (mid-term appraisal of the 10th five-year plan, Planning Commission).

10. For example, rail connectivity projects at Kandla, New Mangalore and Paradip Ports are being implemented by the Railways through Special Purpose Vehicle (SPV) in which the respective ports have also made equity contributions. Similarly, Paradip, Chennai, Visakhapatnam, New Mangalore, Tuticorin, Ennore and Mormugao Ports have contributed to the SPV set up by NHAI for road connectivity projects.

11. Approximately 3% of the workforce leaves every year whereas employment has been around 1.5% of the labour force over recent years.

12. In 2002, China Rail's operating ratio was 0.74 in comparison to 0.96 in India.

13. IR's share of the freight transport market was 89% at the time of independence verses around 30% currently. Although freight transported by IR has grown by 30.6% in last five years, freight transported by road has increased by 53.1% over the same period.

14. In 1995, the World Bank estimated that the ratio of passenger to freight rates was 32 in India in comparison to 152 in China (World Bank, 1995). Harral and Sondhi (2005) report that revenue per passenger km to ton km was 1.3 in China in comparison to 0.34 in India in 2002.

15. It is difficult to accurately calculate the size of the implicit cross-subsidy. For example, *Mehta* (2006) estimates that tariffs for rail freight transport could be brought down by as much as 40% if the social burden of under-cost pricing of passenger transport was paid by users or directly by government.

16. For a discussion of the OECD experience of this regulatory approach in the rail freight transport see ECMT (2001). For more on the regulation of rail more generally in the European context see ECMT (2005).

Bibliography

Bindra, A. (2006), "Civil aviation in India: Flying higher", downloaded from *www.civilaviationweek.com/Civil%20Aviation%20in%20India%20-%20Flying%20Higher.pdf*.

Blonigen, B. and W. Wilson (2006), "New Measures of port efficiency using international trade data", *NBER Working Paper* 12052.

Briceno, C. and I. Klytchnikova (2006), "Infrastructure and poverty: What data are available for impact evaluation", The World Bank, mimeo.

Committee of Infrastructure (2006), "Financing the National Highway development programme", New Delhi, *http://infrastructure.gov.in/pdf/NHDP.pdf*.

ECMT (2001), *Railway Reform*, OECD, Paris.

ECMT (2005), *Railway Reform and Charges for the use of Infrastructure*, OECD, Paris.

Estache, A. (2006), "Infrastructure: A survey of recent and upcoming issues", The World Bank, mimeo.

Harral, C. and J. Sondhi (2005), "*Comparative Evaluation of Highway and Railway Development in China and India, 1992-2002*", South Asia Energy and Infrastructure Unit, International Bank for Reconstruction and Development.

Government of India (2005), *National Highways Development Report – Phase 1*, Union Audit Report No. 7, New Delhi.

Government of India (2006), *Financing of the National Highway Development Programme*, Committee on Infrastructure, New Delhi.

Government of India (2006a), *Approach to Regulation: Issues and Options*, Planning Commission, New Delhi.

Government of India (2006b), *Integrated Energy Policy: report of the Expert Committee, Government of India*, Planning Commission, New Delhi.

Government of India (2007), *Report of the Working Group on Power for Eleventh Plan (2007-12): Volume II, Main Report*, Delhi.

India Infrastructure Report (2006), Urban Infrastructure, 3i Network, Indian Institute of Management.

International Energy Agency (2006), *Energy Prices and Taxes*, Paris.

Joumard, I., P. Kongsrud, Y. Nam, and R. Price (2004), "Enhancing the effectiveness of public spending: Experience in OECD countries", *OECD Economics Department Working Paper*, No. 380.

Majumder, R. (2005), "Infrastructure and Regional Development: Interlinkages In India", *Indian Economic Review*, Vol. 40, No. 2, pp. 167-84.

Mehta (2006), *A functional competition policy for India*, Academic Foundation, New Delhi.

Modi, V. (2005), "Improving Electricity Services in rural India", *Working Paper Series*, Centre on Globalisation and Sustainable Development, The Earth Institute, Columbia University, New York.

Malik, P. and H. de Silva (2005), "Diversifying Network Participation: Study of India's Universal Service Instruments", *The World Dialogue on Regulation for Network Economies discussion paper WDR0504*.

OECD (2007), *OECD Principles for Private Sector Participation in Infrastructure*, OECD, Paris, *www.oecd.org/dataoecd/41/33/38309896.pdf*

Planning Commission (2006), *Integrated Energy Policy: Report of the Expert Committee.* Government of India, New Delhi.

Planning Commission (2007), *Mid-term appraisal of the tenth five-year plan*.

Purfield, C. (2006), "Is economic growth leaving some states behind?", *India goes global: Its expanding role in the world economy*, IMF, Washington, D.C.

Singh, N. and J. Wallack (2004), "Some light at the end of the tunnel: Ingredients of power sector reforms in India", Stanford Centre for International Development, Stanford University.

TRAI (2006), *Study Paper on Financial Analysis of Telecom Industry of China and India*, June 2006.

TRAI (2007a), *The India Telecom Services Performance Indicators July-September 2006*, January, *www.trai.gov.in/trai/upload/Reports/32/Report17jan07.pdf*.

TRAI (2007b), *Consultation paper on access deficit charge*, January 2007.

TRAI (2007c), *The Telecommunication Interconnection Usage Charges (Eighth Amendment) Regulation*, *http://unpan1.un.org/intradoc/groups/public/documents/APCITY/UNPAN025615.pdf*.

World Bank (1995), India transport sector: Long term issues, March 1995.

ISBN 978-92-64-03351-1
OECD Economic Surveys: India
© OECD 2007

Chapter 8

Improving human capital formation

The provision of high-quality education and health care to all of the population is considered a core element of public policy in most countries. In India, the government is active in both education and health but the private sector also plays an important role, notably for heath, and to a lesser extent in education. At present, the quality and quantity of the outputs from education, and also form public health care, are holding back the process of economic development. Steps are being taken to draw more children into primary education and the chapter considers ways to keep children in school. The chapter also considers institutional changes that may help to improve the performance of the educational system and so boost human capital formation.

Endowments – especially of human capital – are fundamental to improving living standards and ensuring that the benefits of growth are enjoyed across all segments of society.[1] This chapter argues that a range of further measures need to be undertaken to provide a stronger institutional framework for improving educational endowments, as well as public service delivery more generally. One priority is a fuller implementation of the 73rd and 74th constitutional amendments (1992) that established local governments in both urban and rural areas. In the intervening years, little has been done to implement these amendments, especially in rural areas, and local governments often lack sufficient resources and autonomy to fully carry out the tasks that should be their responsibility. At the same time, incentives are so weak in many public institutions that the private sector has taken a large role in providing services. A more forward-looking approach by all levels of government in its regulation of public and private institutions would be appropriate and would improve India's overall development potential.

Human capital needs to be improved

Investment in education has been and remains a major priority of Indian governments. A significant effort has been made to transform the educational system over the past two generations. In the period from the creation of the Union until 1990, the number of schools increased more than threefold, outpacing the growth of the school age population (Table 8.1). The number of schools per child of school age rose by half. Most of this increase came in the provision of schools for children aged over 11. At the primary

Table 8.1. **Provision of schools by level of education**

	Elementary Education		Secondary Education			All levels	Population	Index of schools per child
	Primary schools	Upper primary schools	Secondary schools	Higher secondary schools	Total	All types of schools		Total
	Age 6-10	Age 11-13	Age 14-15	Age 16-17	Age 14-17	Age 6-17	Age 5-19	All ages
	Thousands							1990 = 100
1950	209.7	13.6	n.a.	n.a.	7.4	230.7	121.0	68.1
1990	560.9	151.5	60.6	19.2	79.8	792.2	283.0	100.0
1996	603.6	180.3	74.3	28.9	103.2	887.2	321.2	98.7
1997	619.2	186.0	76.7	30.5	107.1	912.3	328.1	99.3
1998	629.0	193.1	79.4	32.7	112.1	934.1	335.1	99.6
1999	641.7	198.0	82.3	34.5	116.8	956.5	342.2	99.8
2000	638.7	206.3	87.7	38.4	126.0	971.1	349.6	99.2
2001	664.0	219.6	91.4	42.1	133.5	1 017.2	357.0	101.8
2002	651.4	245.3	90.8	46.4	137.2	1 033.8	359.8	102.6
2003	712.2	262.3	99.1	46.8	146.0	1 120.5	359.8	111.3
2004	767.5	274.7	n.a.	n.a.	152.0	1 194.3	362.5	117.7

Source: http://Indiastat.com and Ministry of Human Development.

OECD ECONOMIC SURVEYS: INDIA – ISBN 978-92-64-03351-1 – © OECD 2007

level provision essentially kept pace with population growth but at the secondary level (upper primary, secondary and higher secondary in Indian terms) provision rose greatly, with the number of schools rising 10-fold. During this period, public spending on education rose from 0.6% of GDP to 3.8% of GDP. During the 1990s, the expansion of the education system slowed, with the number of schools only rising in line with the school-age population, but from 2001 the expansion started once again, gaining momentum in the following years. At the tertiary level, the number of universities rose 15-fold between 1950 and 2004, while the number of undergraduate colleges rose 30-fold.

The increase in education provision has been associated with a marked improved in the literacy rate, which rose from 18% in 1951 to 65% in 2001. Nonetheless, there were concerns that the performance of the educational system was not as good as might be expected given the level of expenditure. The performance of the Indian educational system has lagged that in other countries, with low levels of literacy despite a level of expenditure per pupil that is not out-of-line with that of other emerging economies and even developed OECD countries, when measured relative to GDP per capita (16%). Moreover, in 2002, total expenditure on primary and secondary education is similar to that in the OECD area and that in emerging countries when measured as a share of GDP (Table 8.2).

Table 8.2. **Expenditure on education (2002)**

	India	OECD	Emerging countries
Expenditure as a per cent of GDP			
Overall	4.8	5.8	5.6
Private only	1.4	0.7	2.0
Primary and secondary	3.8	3.8	3.9
Tertiary	0.8	1.4	1.3
Expenditure per student as a per cent of GDP per capita			
Primary	16	20	14
Secondary	29	25	20
Tertiary	100	40	54

1. Overall expenditure is greater than the sum of components due to missing data for some countries.
Source: UNESCO-OECD (2005).

There is evidence, though, that the performance of the education system has been improving this decade. The overall literacy rate is necessarily a very slowly moving indicator, as it includes people who may have left the education system more than 50 years previously. A more up-to-date indicator can be obtained by looking that the literacy rate by age group. The timeliest data can be obtained from the National Sample Survey rather than relying on census data. The survey data has the advantage of requiring the interviewer to ask questions to determine whether a person not only reads but also understands. On this basis in 2004, the literacy rate for the 10-14 age group (the most recent five year cohort to leave primary school) had risen to 90% in 2004 (Figure 8.1). Moreover, by 2004 the spatial and gender dispersion of the age-specific literacy rates has narrowed markedly, from a gap of close to 70 percentage points between that for rural females and urban males for those age 60 and over, to just 10 percentage points for those aged 10 to 14.

The gains seen at a national level are also apparent at the state level. In 2004, 13 states and union territories had literacy rates for the 10-14 age-groups that exceeded 95%, on a

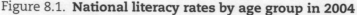

Figure 8.1. **National literacy rates by age group in 2004**

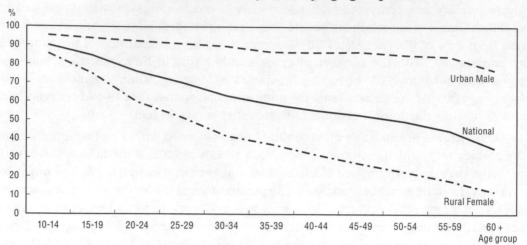

Source: National Sample Survey Organisation Report No. 517, December 2006.

state-wide basis (Annex 8.A1). Given past differences between male and female literacy rates, it is noticeable that 19 states have managed to achieve 90% or higher literacy among girls age 10-14 living in rural areas. Illiteracy amongst children that have recently left primary school is now essentially concentrated in four states (Bihar, Uttar Pradesh, Jharkhand and Rajasthan) which account for nearly 60% of total illiterates in the 10-14 age group. On average, these states have a literacy rate 10 percentage points lower than in the remainder of the country and 14 points lower for rural females.

The improvement in literacy seen in the age groups that had just left primary school in 2004 should have positive impacts on India's growth, even though the low overall literacy rate may restrict the share of India's population that benefits form economic growth for some time to come. In particular, increased literacy amongst the young will open employment opportunities in the formal sector of the economy. At the moment, the large size of the unorganised and often informal sector, a large portion of which is engaged in low-wage and low-productivity casual employment, holds back income levels (discussed in Chapter 2). It turns out that most casual labour is illiterate, while most regular employment is carried out by people with at least primary or lower secondary education. The positive correlation between literacy rates and the size of the formal (organised) sector is apparent across states, as shown in Figure 8.2.

Primary education needs attention

The improvement in performance is a result of concerted policy efforts. The major programme designed to raise educational outcomes is the Sarva Shiksha Abhiyan (SSA) "education for all" initiative, which represents an important step toward universalising education across states. This programme aims at increasing the number of schools, improving facilities, providing free textbooks to selected groups and spending more on teacher training. In addition, there are a number of other targeted programmes, notably a nutritional supplement programme called Mid-day Meals, supported in part by the central government. In total, the central government has spent INR 516 billion in fiscal years 2002 to 2006 on this programme alone (0.3% of GDP) and sanctioned the construction of 240 000 schools. At the same time, states have been gradually implementing the

Figure 8.2. **Literacy rates and the size of the organised sector**

Size of organised sector employment in manufacturing (%)

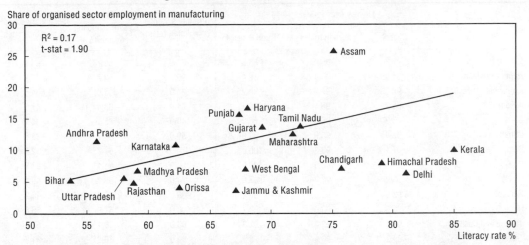

Source: NSS data and OECD tabulations of ASI microdata.

86th constitutional amendment (2002) that *mandates* free and compulsory education for children between the ages of 6 and 14 across states, going beyond the previous *desired objective* of compulsory education originally set in the Constitution. More recently (October 2006), employment of children under the age of 14 as domestic servants or to work in hotels, restaurants and shops was banned.

Improved enrolment rates are just the first step to improving outcomes, and the goal of the SSA programme is for all children to complete five years of primary schooling by 2007. This goal is unlikely to be achieved. Official figures suggest that in 2005-06, completion rates for Grade 5 had only reached 70%, with marked variations across states (Table 8.3), although this figure represents a continuing improvement over the past three years (rising from 63% in 2002-03). The next goal of the SSA programme, to achieve eight years of schooling by 2010, is even further behind schedule. Only slightly more than half of all 15-year-olds had completed eight years of schooling in 2004. In the 11-13 age group, enrolment exceeds 90% in all states except for Bihar, Chhattisgarh, Jharkhand, Orissa, Rajasthan and West Bengal (ASER, 2007), with completion rates in these states some 10 percentage points below the national average (Table 8.3).

Beyond completion rates, an even more fundamental concern about the *quality* of education has been highlighted by *Pratham*, a non-governmental organisation. Pratham and its partners annually carry out a random sample survey of rural districts in each state in order to evaluate the extent to which students at different grade levels can complete basic reading and mathematics tasks. Their most recent survey suggests that about 40% of children aged 7-14 cannot read a small paragraph with short sentences, and 66% cannot divide a three-digit number by a one-digit one (ASER, 2007). While the overall quality of education cannot be reduced to these two simple tests, such findings do raise some concerns about the quality of the education that is delivered in India's schools.

Directions for making progress at the primary level

Low educational quality can be attributed to a number of factors, among which is the relatively high level of teacher absenteeism. A representative national survey of teacher

Table 8.3. **State educational indicators 2004**

Per cent

	Literacy rates for ages 10 14			Primary school completion rates	Completion of 8 years schooling by age 15	Secondary school attendance rates
	Overall	Urban males	Rural females			
National	89.8	95.0	85.3	70.0	53.7	58.6
Andhra Pradesh	91.5	96.9	86.0	90.0	62.7	35.2
Arunachal Pradesh	92.2	96.9	88.9	35.0	59.9	34.6
Assam	95.2	98.1	95.4	64.0	63.4	47.5
Bihar	76.2	89.8	68.2	46.0	45.1	34.4
Chhattisgarh	92.0	93.9	90.6	59.0	36.7	33.8
Delhi	97.1	95.3	100.0	79.0	64.7	52.2
Goa	98.9	100.0	100.0	89.0	64.4	62.2
Gujrat	93.3	96.2	87.9	74.0	65.8	40.4
Haryana	93.9	96.0	90.2	88.0	45.2	43.2
Himachal Pradesh	98.8	100.0	98.2	100.0	67.9	66.8
Jammu and Kashmir	93.1	99.4	92.3	83.0	58.1	55.5
Jharkhand	84.2	96.9	75.8	39.0	36.8	31.3
Karnataka	93.2	98.4	88.2	99.0	67.8	49.1
Kerala	99.7	99.9	99.9	100.0	94.6	73.8
Madhya Pradesh	87.2	94.6	79.5	72.0	38.2	32.5
Maharashtra	97.1	98.4	96.2	87.0	79.1	56.7
Manipur	99.1	99.8	98.2	40.0	68.8	46.1
Meghalaya	96.0	99.5	97.7	38.0	42.9	33.0
Mizoram	99.8	99.8	99.8	71.0	82.8	63.1
Nagaland	97.4	98.8	95.6	56.0	71.2	69.1
Orissa	88.3	94.3	85.9	82.0	56.6	31.9
Punjab	93.3	90.3	93.4	94.0	54.5	44.3
Rajasthan	85.7	91.9	76.9	54.0	40.8	31.5
Sikkim	98.1	99.7	98.6	66.0	22.7	31.0
Tamil Nadu	99.3	99.5	99.1	97.0	80.1	54.8
Tripura	97.7	92.8	98.3	71.0	45.3	36.2
Uttar Pradesh	85.5	88.7	80.2	62.0	41.8	36.6
Uttaranchal	93.8	95.3	92.0	67.0	56.9	51.0
West Bengal	91.5	95.0	90.6	80.0	38.4	34.2

1. Eight years of schooling is defined as completion of at least upper primary school education. The secondary school attendance rate is for pupils aged 14-17 relative to the population of the same age-group.
Source: Tabulation of 61st National Sample Survey and DISE (2007).

attendance suggested that on a given day, only 75% of teachers are present in the school (Kremer *et al.*, 2005). An official survey of 14 states has confirmed these low attendance rates, suggesting that absence rates were 20% in primary schools and 13% in upper primary schools (Ministry of Human Development, 2007). Moreover, random surveys suggest that, of the teachers present, only half are teaching. In a comparison among eight large developing countries of teacher absence, India was second-to-last. While some of this non-attendance can be attributed to non-teaching duties (Ramachandran *et al.*, 2005), the low attendance of teachers has been a longstanding problem, and seems linked to weak performance incentives and poor teaching conditions. For instance, schools with more recent inspections and better infrastructure had lower absence rates.[2]

One solution that many state governments have used is to move toward the use of contract-based teachers and assistants referred to as *para*-teachers. Such staff are paid much less than regular teachers, yet their performance appears to be no worse.[3] Given the need to more fundamentally address teacher absence, alternative mechanisms have been tried, including the use of controlled experiments of various incentive-improving schemes. It would appear that only a few schemes work, with the most promising among them based on automatic mechanisms to facilitate monitoring (Banerjee and Duflo, 2006). One such programme used a time and date-stamp tamper-proof camera to monitor attendance, with a portion of the teacher's wages linked to such verified attendance. This programme was shown to substantially improve teacher attendance in the small number of Indian schools where the experiment was undertaken, as well as improving student achievement (Duflo and Hanna, 2005). This programme achieved an increase of 30% in the number of days for which a child was taught at a cost of $ 6 per child per year. Costs may have fallen since as this programme was not based on digital technology. As this study was based on 60 schools run by a non-governmental organisation, much larger pilot studies would be needed to determine whether this type of intervention could be operated on a larger scale. In any case, much better monitoring of teacher and school performance appears to be essential to improve educational quality.

The National Curriculum Framework, which will provide a comprehensive approach to child-centred education, is being introduced with the objective of moving away from rote learning and promoting understanding and the ability to solve problems. In addition, the SSA programme recognises that improving quality will require devoting more resources to teacher training. At present, a national system monitors inputs into schools and represents a major improvement in knowledge of what is happening in schools. It needs to be supplemented by a measure of educational outputs in terms of quality based on standardised measures of achievement. Improving quality could result in a significant improvement in economic growth: recent evidence suggests that the *quality* of education – and cognitive skills in particular[4] – is more important than sheer educational achievement in supporting economic growth and education quality is highly dependent on the performance of schools (Hanushek and Woessmann, 2007).

While official targets focus on achieving higher enrolment rates, it is as important to reduce student absence rates. These are high: in 2006 about 7 million children did not attend primary school, but this is down from 44 million prior to the introduction of the SSA programme, according to both official and independent estimates. When families are asked whether a child is attending school, however, the attendance rates are not as good. The National Sample Survey, for example, finds absence rates of 18% for primary school ages (6-11), representing a total of 37 million children. The problem appears to manifest itself especially at the end of primary education, when dropout rates peak. About two-thirds of the children who do not attend school are in five of the poorest states: Bihar, Uttar Pradesh, West Bengal, Madhya Pradesh, and Rajasthan.

Households with illiterate parents constitute one of the largest problems of attendance and these are concentrated amongst the Muslim, Scheduled Castes or Scheduled Tribes population (SRI, 2005). In this respect, the increase in literacy amongst young girls in rural areas is a welcome development as this can have a significant positive feedback effect and generate higher levels of demand. As education levels improve, there is greater awareness of the returns to education, with evidence that literate mothers are four times more likely than illiterate mothers to send their children to school and keep them there (ASER, 2006). Such a dynamic is an important motivation behind the government's adult literacy programs, such as the National Literacy Mission, that focuses on the 15-35 age group and women in particular.

Secondary education also requires action

With the improvement in literacy rates and primary school completion rates, the focus of policy will have to increasingly move towards improving education for those aged 11 and over. Although secondary school enrolment has been increasing, those students who enrol in secondary education have high dropout rates (60% in 2003/04), resulting in lower graduation rates than in most countries for which data is available. The government's objective is that all children should receive three years of lower secondary education (upper primary in Indian terms) by 2010. There is some way to go to achieve this target as in 2004, only 53% of 15-year-olds had completed this level of education, with marked variations across states (Table 8.3). Moreover, at the next level of education and especially for the highest level of secondary education, there is a major problem of equity, with better-off families more likely to educate their children to this level and much more likely to use private schools (Figure 8.3). The attendance rate at secondary schools of children aged 16 to 17 is 50 percentage points higher for households in the highest consumption bracket identified by the National Sample Survey than in lowest consumption bracket. Moreover, three quarters of this difference occurs because of higher attendance in private schools for better off families. Lower attendance by the children of poorer families can in part be attributed to physical access problems, poverty and liquidity constraints that induce teenagers to work, and a particular problem of non-participation of women due to social discrimination. Central government funded programmes, which have set up special residential schools, some specifically for girls, have met with some success; yet the scale of these programmes is overall quite limited.

Figure 8.3. **Participation rate in secondary education at ages 16 and 17**

By consumption level of households and type of school

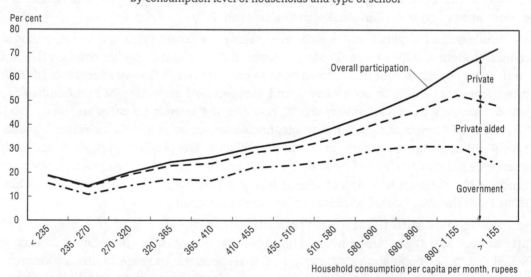

Source: Tabulation of 61st National Sample Survey.

With lower-income and less educated households being much less likely to prolong the education of their children, one possible strategy (beyond the Mid-day Meals programme mentioned earlier) would be to use an approach that has been applied successfully in a number of Latin American countries, modelled after the *Progresa* programme in Mexico. Such programmes offer cash payments to parents of poor students

– particularly girls – in exchange for their attendance, and also serve to deter child labour. Studies suggest that such payments can have significant effects on school attendance and may have their largest impact towards the end of lower secondary education (see Box 8.1). While the cost of such a large-scale programme would be considerable in India, experience with the programme suggests that if it is expanded gradually, the benefits easily justify the costs. Moreover, to the extent that its measures would be better-targeted on poor families than subsidies or other types of welfare-related programmes – like the Rural Employment Guarantee Scheme described in Chapter 6 – it could represent a much better value for achieving government poverty-reduction objectives.

Box 8.1. **The *Progresa* programme in Mexico**

The *Progresa* programme in Mexico (renamed *Opportunidades* in 2002) was developed as a poverty alleviation scheme to promote education, healthcare and nutrition. The most innovative aspect of the programme was its focus on *cash* transfers and the explicit *conditionality* of the benefits on certain behaviours, such as children attending school. The programme was developed in phases, starting on a relatively small scale. At each stage, systematic evaluation was carried out. This was possible because the programme was implemented from the start as a randomized experiment, facilitating ongoing improvements in programme design, and enabling the success of the programme to strengthen its political sustainability and funding basis (see Levy, 2006).

Studies suggest that the cash payments to parents based on their children's school attendance had significant positive effects, with their largest impact observed at the end of lower secondary education (Attanasio *et al.*, 2004; Todd and Wolpin, 2005), a period of high dropouts observed in India as well. It would seem likely that such a policy could work well in India as the only group for which high returns to education are not associated with longer stays in education are boys from poorer backgrounds. For pupils in this group, income effects outweigh substitution effects, suggesting that liquidity constraints are present in poor families. In Mexico, the programme has been expanded to the extent that its income support represents as much as a quarter of a poor rural household's income.

Source: OECD (2003) and Levy (2006).

Health care is an interrelated problem

On a related note, children's health is an important issue that can also affect learning capacity. Child health has been improving both in the 1990s and this decade. Infant mortality has declined as has the proportion of children that are not fully immunised. In addition, maternal mortality has declined and the proportion of underweight young children has also fallen (Chapter 1). All of these measures of health remain high and vary markedly across states but, in terms of international rankings, these indicators reflect the ranking of India in terms of its GDP per capita. Health care provision in general remains a serious problem in India. There does appear to be evidence that increased spending on health care can reduce the extent of infant mortality (Bhalotra, 2007), and perhaps other health outcomes as well.

The failure of the public health system is evident through the choices that individuals make: the number of babies delivered in private institutions doubled between 1998 and 2002 (World Bank, 2006a). Nevertheless, the typical quality of health care services appears to be low for both public and private providers (Das and Hammer, 2007), although some top-end high quality health service providers exist. There is also wide variation in outcomes across districts, suggesting considerable inequality in access (Amrith, 2007). Although the health system is public in principle, of the 195 countries covered by the World Health Organisation, only five have a higher *private* health provision rate compared with India, and many countries that have privatized their health systems still have much higher public contribution rates.

The prevalence of private spending appears to be a reaction to low and poor quality public health services. In particular, Health Centres appear to suffer from many of the same problems as public schools. Random survey evidence suggests that there is an average absence rate of 43% for primary health care workers across all Indian states, with a peak rate of 58% in Bihar. The National Rural Health Mission, introduced by the government for the period 2005 to 2012 may result in some changes in this area as it provides for decentralisation of management of some primary health care facilities to the local level.

Deeper institutional changes are the best hope

Private sector is expanding as the quality of public services is questioned

The failure of public providers to deliver on education as well as health has forced those who can afford private providers to turn to them. Among primary school students in rural areas, over 20% (and rising) are enrolled in private schools (Figure 8.4). The motivation to choose private providers at the primary level is apparent from a reading of the *Pratham* study findings that shows test scores that are more than 10 percentage points higher on reading and math benchmarks (although this could be a result of more motivated parents choosing these schools). In urban areas, the newest NSS estimates suggest that the private share is three times higher. At the upper secondary level (higher secondary in Indian terms), almost 60% of schools are in the private sector – almost equally split between completely private school and grant-aided schools.

One factor that makes private schools more attractive is that their students typically also learn English, a skill that is of increasing relevance in India's service sector. Learning English well may only be possible with a firm knowledge of the mother language, but the National Knowledge Commission has recommended that this gap between public and private provision should be closed by the teaching English in public schools from first grade. The Commission found that command over this language is perhaps the most important determinant of access to higher education, employment possibilities and social opportunities. It recommended that education policy should have the objective of achieving proficiency in two languages after twelve years of schooling.

With the public system's failure to deliver quality educational services, the rise of a significant private sector in education could have a beneficial effect on outcomes by increasing competition. However, since the more privileged students may be the only ones who can afford to attend private schools (although some private schools receive government aid), the current set-up aggravates inequalities. Some type of portability of public funding, such as through vouchers or scholarships for low-income students, should be considered and experimented with on a trial basis. Such a measure was successfully introduced in Colombia where low-income students were given credits (vouchers) that could be used to purchase private education. The programme for low-income students was successful in increasing their participation in secondary education and raising their

Figure 8.4. **Participation in private grade schools**
Per cent of children in grades 1 to 8 in private schools

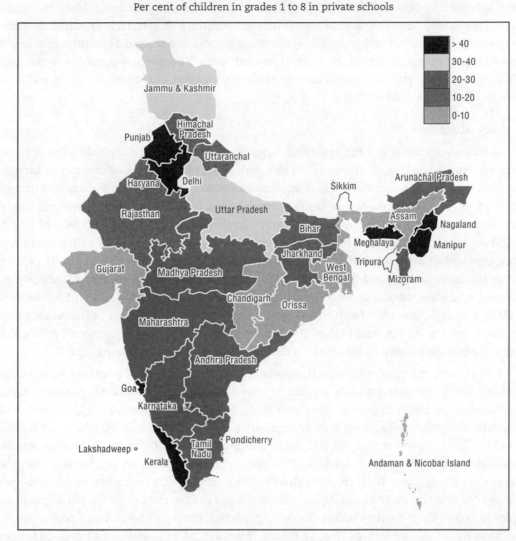

Source: Pratham's Annual Status of Education Report 2006 (ASER, 2007).

completion rates (Bettinger and Kremer, 2006). Broader voucher schemes have been introduced in only a few countries (Chile and Sweden) and a number of US states and school districts (Hoxby, 2003). They appear to improve school efficiency and disproportionately benefit the students who were performing badly in regular public schools.

An education voucher scheme could be considered in order to improve access to secondary education. Given that the private sector is already the predominate supplier of higher secondary education in India, a complete voucher system would incur considerable deadweight costs. However, a voucher scheme for low-income households would seem feasible given that the typical cost per student in Indian private schools is significantly lower than in public schools, principally a result of more market-based teacher salaries in private schools and better attendance by teachers. Such a scheme could have very positive results for equity. It might also mean that spending on government schools might have to be reduced if numbers fell markedly, though this outcome seems unlikely in the context of a rapidly growing demand for secondary education. Such a scheme could draw on the experience of the two newly introduced programmes. The first is the "National Means cum Merit Scholarship Scheme" that will provide 100 000 grants per year for children to attend secondary education. Given that secondary education has a four-year duration, this programme will fund 25 000 students, against a population of around 14 million that could potentially enter into secondary education each year. The second provides a grant of INR 3 000 for every girl that enrols into secondary education but which is only payable at the end of secondary education.

Tertiary education

Tertiary education is a fundamental requirement for an economy that aspires to be competitive in the global economy. In the public sector, tertiary education is largely provided by state governments, which accounted for 80% of current public expenditure in this area in 2003. The structure of tertiary education is based on a two-tier system. There are a limited number of universities (371) and a large number of colleges (17 265) of which 14 000 are under the purview of the University Grants Commission. The colleges are not autonomous but are affiliated to a university that grants the degree. Non-profit private sector institutions have made increasing headway, notably in "professional" education. The share of engineers educated in private colleges has risen from 15% in 1960 to 86% in 2003, for medicine it has risen to 40% and may be as high as 90% for management and business courses (Kahpu and Mehta, 2004). Overall, three-quarters of technical education is already being provided by institutions that are not aided by the government.

Investment in tertiary education has been rising. The numbers of students enrolled for undergraduate and post-graduate studies has been increasing by almost 5% per year, about twice as fast as the numbers of people in the relevant age groups. The total number of students in tertiary education was estimated to be 10.5 million (8.5% of the 18-23 age group) in 2003. However, the official figures underestimate the number of students in vocational and diploma level studies. This data is only available on the basis of sample surveys which suggest that, in 2004, the overall participation in higher education was 11½ per cent for the 18-23 age group, as almost 3½ per cent of the age group participated in diploma rather than degree studies (Table 8.4). International comparisons of participation are usually made by comparing the total number of students to the population aged 18 to 23 (a gross enrolment rate). Despite this growth in numbers, the gross enrolment rate in India, at 13%, is still below that in other developing countries where the gross enrolment rate is around 18%. In 2001, about 6½ per cent of the population over 25 had a tertiary degree. This proportion rises to 9½ per cent in the age group 25-29. Graduates are concentrated in urban areas where the proportion of the population with degrees is twice as high as in the country as a whole.

In contrast to enrolments, public spending on higher education, at 0.7% of GDP, is in line with that found in other developing countries for which data is available. However the extent of private contributions toward the costs of tertiary education is low relative to many developing countries, although it is similar to the OECD average (Figure 8.5). It has been growing rapidly, rising from less than 1% in 1995 to 22% in 2003 in the figures reported to UNESCO. This may be a considerable underestimate as national sources suggest private expenditure was already 28% of total expenditure at all levels of education in 2001 (Selected Education Statistics, 2003) and unofficial estimates suggest that the private share may have risen substantially higher since then (Agarwal, 2007).

Table 8.4. **Participation in higher education by type of study, institution and age**

	Gross enrolment rate	Net enrolment rate			Type of institution			
	All students	\u00A0	Age groups		Government	Local body	Private aided	Private unaided
			18-23	24-29				
	Per cent of population				Per cent			
Degree students	9.5	8.7	1.5		54.1	1.5	29.4	15.0
Agriculture	1.3	1.2	0.2		58.4	2.3	30.2	9.1
Engineering/technology	0.7	0.6	0.1		26.2	0.7	32.1	41.0
Medicine	0.1	0.1	0.0		38.1	4.0	27.9	30.1
Other subjects	7.4	6.8	1.2		56.1	1.4	29.1	13.4
Diploma student (below degree)	1.9	1.7	0.4		40.8	1.6	25.0	32.5
Agriculture	0.0	0.0	0.0		37.2	3.8	35.0	24.1
Engineering/technology	0.8	0.7	0.1		35.8	0.4	29.5	34.3
Medicine	0.2	0.1	0.0		13.1	0.5	36.5	49.9
Crafts	0.0	0.0	0.0		33.2	0.0	31.4	35.3
Other subjects	1.0	0.8	0.2		49.6	2.8	19.0	28.6
Diploma student (above graduate level)	1.5	1.1	0.6		43.3	1.4	28.2	27.1
Agriculture	0.0	0.0	0.0		22.1	6.6	71.3	0.0
Engineering/technology	0.2	0.2	0.1		22.1	2.4	28.3	47.2
Medicine	0.0	0.0	0.0		40.9	0.0	34.7	24.4
Crafts	0.0	0.0	0.0		58.2	0.0	5.0	36.8
Other subjects	1.2	0.9	0.5		47.7	1.1	27.8	23.4
All students	13.0	11.6	2.5		50.8	1.5	28.6	19.1

Source: Tabulation of 61st National Sample Survey.

Figure 8.5. **Private expenditure on tertiary education for selected countries**
Share of total expenditure from private sources (2003)

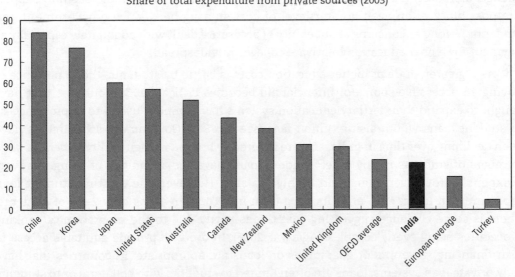

Source: OECD-UNESCO (2005) for India in 2002 and *Education at a Glance: OECD Indicators 2006* for other countries.

In order to further broaden the coverage of higher education and produce more college graduates, expansion of the sector is needed. However, expansion may be held back by a lack of supply of suitably qualified students from secondary schools. Already, 59% of students who finished the higher secondary level of education move to tertiary education

(Thorat, 2006). There is scope for this to rise further, as participation rates in rural areas are generally low. However, at present, if rural students made the transition to higher education at the same rate as urban students, the overall participation rate of rural children in tertiary education and would still be less than half that of the urban children, as a much lower proportion of rural children graduate from higher secondary schools in comparison to urban children. A major expansion of tertiary education would require increased graduation rates from higher secondary schools, notably in rural areas.

Disadvantaged social groups are also under-represented in higher education. But for these groups too the proportion of higher secondary school graduates that enter into tertiary education is only slightly lower than the national average. The government has introduced a policy that will expand the range of groups that can benefit from "reservations" (*i.e.* quotas) that is intended to ameliorate some of these imbalances (Hasan and Mehta, 2006). Given that the existing rates at which qualified students form these groups move into tertiary education are quite high, a focus on disadvantaged groups' primary and secondary education *enrolment* and *completion* rates would seem to be essential, as the underlying source of the imbalances for these groups appears to be a lack of well-prepared students. To do this, broader institutional strengthening needs to be undertaken, along similar lines as that for primary education, by improving the incentives of both students and teachers. Thus the key would appear to be improving the attendance of children, especially in rural areas, at the secondary level.

While increased public expenditure is one option, the fiscal position of the government would not appear to allow for a rapid increase in the overall scale of public outlays. At present, universities and colleges have little incentive to increase fees, as funding from fees results in a lower grant from central or state governments. If colleges were allowed to keep all grants irrespective of the fees they receive, then incentives would change. Moreover, the rate of return to higher education in India would seem to support the possibility of an even greater level of cost-sharing between the government and students, as long as concerns about equity of access are dealt with adequately especially as payment for higher education in private colleges is widespread.

As a greater share of higher education costs is borne by students, the importance of having an accessible source of financial aid becomes critical. OECD countries that have sought to expand their tertiary education systems have found it useful to improve access to student loans when raising tuition fees (see Box 8.2). Government scholarships have been declining over time in India, and are inherently limited in their ability to benefit large numbers of students in any case.[5] Student loans have the advantage of being relatively inexpensive for government and highly scalable. However, the existing student loan programme in India, even after its expansion in 2001/02, reaches only 2-3% of students. There is some evidence suggesting that this is partly due to the programme's banking procedures being overly complex (Agarwal, 2006). In order to provide equitable access to loan financing, government guarantees on loans are appropriate. In countries that have fully private loan systems, loans are often limited to students with collateral or to students in fields that offer especially high future earnings.

More subtly, the structure of a student loan programme can have strong effects on student behaviour particularly in the case of risk-averse students who are unsure of their career-earning potential. Income-contingent loans have been found to be a useful antidote to this information asymmetry, although they may have unforeseen costs if not designed

Box 8.2. **The returns to education in India and financing of higher education**

Private rates of return are an important determinant of the level of investment in education. As a result of substantial segmentation in India's labour market, rates of return to education are very low in the casual employment market (where the bulk of workers are illiterate), but in the wage-earning regular employment market, private rates of return are strongly increasing with education. Moreover, the returns for primary and secondary education increased over the 1990s, and the returns for college education are especially large, particularly in the most recent year (2004), and are now well above the typical OECD return of 10% per year (Table 8.5), this suggests that the use of private financing for higher education is an entirely feasible strategy for funding its expansion in India, presuming that liquidity constraints can be overcome.

Table 8.5. **Private rates of return to education**

% per year

Completion of:	Regular workers[1]			Casual workers		
	1983	1999	2004	1983	1999	2004
Primary school	5.8	5.3	5.4	1.9	1.9	1.5
Middle school	3.1	3.4	5.8	0.2	0.2	2.6
Secondary school	6.0	6.3	8.6	0.6	0.2	1.5
College education	9.4	12.4	15.4	1.1	0.9	3.6

1. All coefficients for regular workers are significant at the 99% level.
Source: Estimates based on OECD analysis of the 61st NSS Survey for 2004 and Dutta (2006) for 1983 and 1999.

Financing approaches in OECD countries vary substantially for higher education, but the trend in recent years has been to increase private participation, by increasing the share of private institutions, the share of costs covered by student fees or both. Some countries have created universal loan systems (*e.g.* most English-speaking countries), although others continue to provide generous grants (*e.g.* Nordic countries), while the remainder still rely heavily on family transfers. A recent review of tertiary education policies by the OECD suggests that rates of return to higher education are sufficient in most countries to make student loans the most appropriate approach to fund expansion (Oliviera Martins *et al.*, 2007). India's rate of return to higher education suggests that a well-designed student loan program could facilitate expansion of higher education, if a solid framework for new institutions is put into place.

1. The rates of return are somewhat lower if the effects of the selection of workers into either regular or casual employment are taken into account econometrically. Dutta (2006) finds that in 1999, for instance, after taking into account selection bias, the rate of return to college education is lower, at 10.3% (*vs.* 12.4%). A lower rate of return is also found for other levels of education if such effects are included, with primary school lowest.

correctly (OECD, 2007). Some screening for the quality of the institution, for instance, may be necessary.

Beyond greater personal contributions, more choice among public and private institutions could instil a degree of competition that would keep costs down and improve quality. The National Knowledge Commission has recognised that improving the quality of most higher education leaves much to be desired and recognised that better quality was a key to improved performance. This is particularly the case amongst the undergraduate colleges where quality is variable – even amongst the one-third that are assessed by the

University Grants Commission, one-quarter were found to be of low quality and most of the two-thirds that are not assessed are presumably of low quality (Thorat, 2006). The affiliation system means that colleges find it difficult to adapt and there is difficulty in adapting curricula to changing needs – indeed in many cases curricula have not changed for decades. A second and perhaps more serious problem is the affiliation process that allows unaccredited colleges to affiliate with accredited ones and issue recognized degrees, even though they themselves have not been recognized by the University Grants Commission (UGC). According to UGC data, two-thirds of higher education institutions fall into this category. Independence of new institutions is needed, so that they can establish their own reputations. In addition, independent bodies need to be set up so that more credible accreditations can be provided (Agarwal, 2006). The sector needs an institution that provides better quality control and which controls the establishment of new universities which would otherwise require Acts of Parliament.

OECD experience based both on an assessment of practice in different countries (Kis, 2005) and studies of specific countries suggests that a successful certification and assessment requires:

- Mandatory accreditation in order to grant diplomas or receive public funding;
- Renewable accreditation, *e.g.* every five years, to ensure institutions make a long-term commitment to quality, with adjustment of the period of accreditation to the perceived quality of the institution with more frequent evaluations for lower quality institutions;
- Common system-wide accreditation standards for various types of institutions, while allowing for institution-specific evaluations;
- Outcome measures should be used (such as students and graduate surveys, employers views, labour market performance of graduates) as well as input variables;
- Develop an accreditation framework in line with international standards and processes, and allow some reputed international accreditation bodies to operate at the national level, including use of foreign assessors on review teams.

The UGC is currently introducing a new accreditation procedure, but it is still voluntary and does not incorporate a significant number of output measures.

Greater competition between universities for government funding though foundations, similar to what is done in the United States using funds from the National Science Foundation and other endowments, might also help improve quality. As well, greater competition over students can also provide strong incentives to improve the value of educational services, especially if there are substantial student contributions.

Until recently, however, court decisions (and legislation) have severely restricted the set-up and operation of private universities (Kapu and Metha, 2004). While these have in part been a reaction to the mushrooming of low-quality institutions in some states, and there have been some examples of successful new entrants, on the whole, government restrictions on private universities' operation have not allowed the sector to develop very broadly (Mukerji, 2006). Nevertheless, private universities have considerable potential in India.

Greater competition and higher rates of student contribution may also help to solve a problem of relevance of fields of study that has arisen, and is manifest in the difficulty of new graduates' entry into the labour force.[6] This problem is illustrated by the positive correlation between new graduates' education levels and unemployment rates described in Chapter 1. Large numbers of students continue to study arts disciplines, even though technical and professional skills are much more in need.[7]

The potential for moving towards a more market-oriented choice of disciplines is illustrated by the recent study of vocational training in the 61st National Sample Survey, which found that almost a third of informal vocational training was in computer trades, with more traditional areas becoming increasingly unpopular. Industrial Training Institutes and polytechnics (often on private initiative) have served to fill some of the unmet needs through training especially in computer skills.

The quality of higher education also has important effects on the capacity of the economy to generate new knowledge through innovation and R&D. India's R&D intensity was similar to China's as recently as the late 1990s, at just under 1% of GDP, but China's intensity has skyrocketed since. India's R&D expenditure has continued to grow, but the number of researchers has declined, suggesting much of the growth has come from rising wages (see Figure 8.6). More fundamentally for universities, India's share of R&D performed in the higher education sector is much smaller than in other countries' – one-third of China's, for example, and one-fifth of Japan's. With its gradually improving level of intellectual property rights protection (IIPA, 2007), India's R&D performance could be much higher. The lack of strong R&D capacity likely reflects broader institutional constraints, and is reflected in low citation counts (noted in Chapter 1), and few institutions with strong international standing, making it difficult to attract and retain top scholars.

Figure 8.6. **Growth rates of R&D expenditure and personnel**

Annual rate, 1995-2004

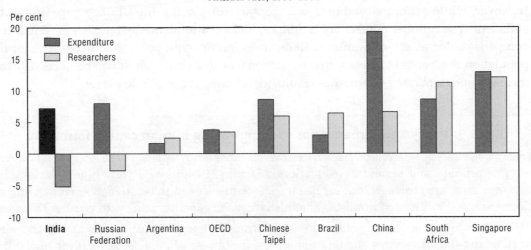

Note: Expenditure based on growth rate in domestic currency at current prices, deflated with GDP deflators.
Source: OECD (2006), Science and Technology Outlook.

Decentralisation would help with basic education and other services

Institutional weaknesses in Indian schools stem partly from the incomplete decentralisation that has taken place. Following the constitutional amendments in 1992, local governments have been set up in many states, but few of these governments have been given access to sufficient resources or granted responsibility for core functions – education included (Government of India, 2006).

Yet there are positive examples. Evaluations of education reforms in Madhya Pradesh illustrate that decentralising control to local communities can have strong positive benefits. The programme in Madhya Pradesh gave rural local governments (Panchayati Rajs) responsibility for hiring and monitoring of teachers as well as for building and maintaining schools, leading to improved attendance, accessibility and outcomes (World Bank, 2006b). While such programmes require concerted efforts and considerable political will (another trial in Rajasthan ended badly after political support was withdrawn), they can be successful if they can correctly align functions and responsibilities at a local level. Evidence from OECD countries suggests that decentralisation and increased autonomy at the local level is systematically associated with higher levels of efficiency in primary and secondary education (Sutherland *et al.*, 2007). Further moves to strengthen localities should help to improve India's education outcomes. However, experience in the OECD suggests that such decentralisation has to be done in a coordinated way so that there is adequate capacity building and a progressive transfer of budgetary responsibility.

Conclusion

The delivery of educational and health services in India needs to be improved significantly. Considerable progress has been made through such government initiatives as those designed to draw more children into schools through projects such as the "Free Mid-day Meals" and the "Education for All" programmes. Further action along the lines of cash grants in exchange for attendance, as in a number of Latin American countries, may be necessary in five of the poorest states where two-thirds of the out-of-school children are found. These grants should be, for equity purposes, financed directly by the centre. However, while school attendance is necessary for closing the literacy gap, it is not sufficient. The number of teachers is limited, making attendance *and* quality essential to compensate for a lack of numbers. Here, transparency and accountability to the local population is essential to ensure that educational outputs are high. It will be necessary to measure and publicise performance results for schools, at the primary level.

Box 8.3. **Policy Recommendations for improving human capital formation**

- *Improve the efficiency of basic educational services*: overall expenditure appears to be adequate; however, the quality of primary and secondary education is lacking. Despite relatively high salaries, teacher attendance rates are strikingly low, for instance. Incentives need to be strengthened by tying pay to performance, and further decentralising administration and experimenting with voucher schemes.

- *Further decentralise government*: greater local government budgetary and substantive control over education and health services should improve the incentives of providers to deliver higher quality services.

- *Improve participation of disadvantaged groups through providing special intervention*: efforts to target the poor and socially excluded groups should be enhanced, ideally through programmes that are self-selecting such as those that offer cash payments for participation among the worst-off groups, especially in the poorest states, so minimising the need for quotas.

- *Provide a more realistic framework for higher education*: given the potential for higher levels of private financing and development of more private institutions, a less discriminatory framework for their establishment is needed. Income-contingent student loan programmes should be expanded to ensure equity.

Notes

1. Lack of adequate investment in human capital can have serious and perverse consequences: simulations suggest that while increasing openness generally improves incomes, if inadequate investments in human capital are made, it can also lead to increasing poverty and informality (Gibson, 2005). There is some indication of such a phenomenon taking place in some of the laggard states in India (Topalova, 2005). Moreover, India's Human Development Index rating in 2002 was ten positions behind its rank in GDP per capita at purchasing power parity (UN, 2004).

2. India's expenditure per student on secondary education is practically the lowest among comparison countries, in PPP dollars, with capital expenditure the culprit (UNESCO-OECD, 2005). Expenditure appears to be focused primarily on payment of salaries, with India having by far the lowest share of expenditure on capital, explaining the lack of basic facilities in many schools.

3. An assessment of the relationship of teacher characteristics and pupil performance finds, in a sample of private schools, that pay appears to be a good motivator for performance, except in unionised schools where there is no relationship between performance and pay (Kingdon, 2006). The productivity of teachers also appears to fall markedly with the length of teaching experience in unionised schools but not in non-unionised schools.

4. Cognitive skills are the mental skills that are used in the process of acquiring knowledge including reasoning, perception and intuition.

5. A few top schools offer financial aid (IITs), but other institutions have lacked sufficient resources.

6. The McKinsey Global Institute found that only one-quarter of college graduates in India were employable by multinationals, for instance (Farrell *et al.*, 2005; NASSCOM-McKinsey, 2005).

7. Students are more generally unprepared for the labour market, according to appraisals by TeamLease.

Bibliography

Agarwal, Pawan (2006), "Higher Education in India: The Need for Change", ICRIER Working Paper No. 180, June, *www.icrier.org/publication/working_papers_180.html*.

____ (2007), "Higher Education in India: Growth, Concerns and Change Agenda", *Higher Education Quarterly*, Vol. 61, No. 2, pp. 197-207.

Amrith, Sunil (2007), "Political Culture of Health in India: A Historical Perspective", *Economic and Political Weekly*, 13 January.

ASER (2006), *Annual Status of Education Report (Rural) 2005*, Pratham, Delhi, January.

____ (2007), *Annual Status of Education Report 2006*, January, *www.pratham.org/aser2006.php*.

Attanasio, Orazio, Costas Meghir, and Ana Santiago (2004), "Education Choices in Mexico: Using a Structural Model and a Randomized Experiment to Evaluate *Progresa*", EDePo Centre for the Evaluation of Development Policies, The Institute for Fiscal Studies EWP04/04.

Banerjee, Abhijit and Esther Duflo (2006), "Addressing Absence", *Journal of Economic Perspectives*, Vol. 20, No. 1, pp. 117–32.

Bettinger E., Angrist J, , Kremer K. (2006), "Long-Term Educational Consequences of Secondary School Vouchers: Evidence from Administrative Records in Colombia", *American Economic Review* Vol. 96, No. 3, 847-62.

Bhalotra, S. (2007), "Spending to save? State health expenditure and infant mortality in India", *Health Economics*, forthcoming, September.

Das, Jishnu and Jeffrey Hammer (2007), "Money for nothing: The dire straits of medical practice in Delhi, India", *Journal of Development Economics*, Vol. 83, No. 2, pp. 1-36.

DISE (2007), "Elementary Education in India: Progress toward UEE", National University of Education Planning and Administration, *www.educationforallinindia.com/diseflashstatistics2005-06.pdf*.

Drèze, Jean and Amartya Sen (1997), *Indian Development: Selected Regional Perspectives*, Oxford University Press, Delhi.

Duflo, Esther and Rema Hanna (2005), "Monitoring Works: Getting Teachers to Come to School", NBER Working Paper No. 11880, December.

Dutta, Puja Vasudeva (2006), "Returns to Education: New Evidence for India, 1983–1999", *Education Economics*, Vol. 14, No. 4, pp. 431-51, December.

Farrell, Diana, Martha A. Laboissière, and Jaeson Rosenfeld (2005), "Sizing the emerging global labor market", *McKinsey Quarterly*, 2005, No. 3, www.mckinseyquarterly.com.

Gibson, Bill (2005), "The transition to a globalized economy: Poverty, human capital and the informal sector in a structuralist CGE model", *Journal of Development Economics*, Vol. 78, No. 1, pp. 60-94.

Government of India (2006), *Annual Report 2005-06*, Ministry of Panchayati Raj, New Delhi.

____ (2007), *Selected Educational Statistics 2004-05*, Ministry of Human Resource Development, Department of Higher Education Statistics, New Delhi.

Hanushek, Eric A. and Ludger Woessmann (2007), "The Role of School Improvement in Economic Development", NBER Working Papers No. 12832, January.

Hasan, Rana and Aashish Mehta (2006), "Under-representation of Disadvantaged Classes in Colleges: What do the data tell us?", *Economic and Political Weekly*, 2 September.

Hoxby, Caroline M. (2003), "School choice and school competition: Evidence from the United States", *Swedish Economic Policy Review*, Vol. 10, pp. 11-67.

IIPA (2007), "India: Special 301 Report", International Intellectual Property Alliance, Washington, D.C., www.iipa.com/countryreports.html.

Kapu, Devesh and Pratap Bhanu Mehta (2004), "Indian Higher Education Reform: From Half-Baked Socialism to Half-Baked Capitalism", Harvard University, CID Working Paper No. 108, September.

Kingdon, Geeta Gandhi (2006), "Teacher characteristics and student performance in India: A pupil fixed effects approach", University of Oxford, Department of Economics, September.

Kis V. (2005), *Quality Assurance in Tertiary Education: Current Practices in OECD Countries and a Literature Review on Potential Effects*, OECD Thematic Review of Tertiary Education, Paris, August.

Kremer, Michael, Nazmul Chaudhury, F. Halsey Rogers, Karthik Muralidharan, and Jeffrey Hammer (2005), "Teacher Absence in India: A Snapshot", *Journal of the European Economic Association*, Vol. 3, No. 2-3, pp. 658-67.

Levy, Santiago (2006), *Progress Against Poverty: Sustaining Mexico's Progresa-Oportunidades Program*, Brookings Press, Washington, DC.

Ministry of Human Development (2007), *Submission to the OECD*.

Mohan, Rakesh and Shubhagato Dasgupta (2004), "Urban Development in India in the 21st Century: Policies for Accelerating Urban Growth", Stanford Center for International Development, October.

Mukerji, Joydeep (2006), "Economic Growth and India's Future", University of Pennsylvania, Center for the Advanced Study of India, Occasional Paper No. 26, March.

Munshi, Kaivan and Mark Rosenzweig (2006), "Traditional Institutions Meet the Modern World: Caste, Gender and Schooling Choice in a Globalizing Economy", *American Economic Review*, Vol. 96, No. 4, pp. 1225-52.

NASSCOM-McKinsey (2005), *Extending India's leadership in the global IT and BPO industries*, NASSCOM and McKinsey & Co., Mumbai, India.

OECD (2003), *Economic Survey of Mexico*, Economic Surveys No. 2003/1, OECD, Paris.

____ (2006), *Education at a Glance: OECD Indicators*, OECD, Paris.

____ (2007), *Economic Survey of United States*, OECD, Paris.

Oliveira Martins, Joaquim, Romina Boarini, Hubert Strauss, Christine de la Maisonneuve and Clarice Saadi, (2007), "The Policy Determiniants of Investment in Higher Education", *OECD Economics Department Working Paper*, forthcoming.

Ramachandran, Vimala, Madhumita Pal and Sharada Jain (2005), "Teacher Motivation in India", Education Resource Unit, Delhi.

SRI (2005), "Survey on Assessing the Number of Out-of-School Children in the 6-13 Year Age Group", Social and Rural Research Institute, Delhi.

Sutherland, Douglas (2007), "Linkages Between Performance And Institutions In The Primary and Secondary Education Sector", OECD Document No. ECO/CPE/WP1(2007)4, Paris.

Todd, Petra and Kenneth Wolpin (2005), "*Ex-Ante* Evaluation of Social Programs", University of Pennsylvania, PIER Working Paper No. 06-022.

Thorat S. (2006), "Higher education in India: Emerging Issues Related to Access, Inclusiveness and Quality", Nehru Memorial Lecture, University of Mumbai, Mumbai, Novmber.

Topalova, Petia (2005), "Trade Liberalization, Poverty, and Inequality: Evidence from Indian Districts", NBER Working Paper No. 11614, September.

UN (2004), *Human Development Report*, United Nations, New York.

UNESCO-OECD (2005), *Education Trends in Perspective – Analysis of the World Education Indicators*, UNESCO Institute for Statistics and OECD, Paris and Montreal, www.uis.unesco.org.

World Bank (2006a), *Inclusive Growth and Service Delivery: Building on India's Success*, Development Policy Review, Report No. 34580-IN, World Bank, India, May.

World Bank (2006b), *Reforming Public Services in India: Drawing Lessons from Success*, Sage Publications and the World Bank, New Delhi and Washington, D.C.

OECD PUBLICATIONS, 2, rue André-Pascal, 75775 PARIS CEDEX 16
PRINTED IN FRANCE
(10 2007 14 1 P) ISBN 978-92-64-03351-1 – No. 55719 2007